HISTORY AND THE STATE IN
NINETEENTH-CENTURY JAPAN

Imperial Rescript on Historiography, 4 April 1869 (*Meiji Tennō shinkan gosatasho, Meiji ninen shigatsu yokka*, Historiographical Institute at the University of Tokyo, S0471–4).

History and the State in Nineteenth-Century Japan

The World, the Nation and the Search for a Modern Past

Margaret Mehl

The Sound Book Press
Copenhagen
2017

Published in 2017 by
The Sound Book Press
Copenhagen, Denmark

ISBN 978-87-997283-4-3 (paperback)
ISBN 978-87-997283-5-0 (mobipocket)

First published in Great Britain 1998 by Macmillan Press Ltd
Houndmills, Basingstoke, Hampshire RG21 6XS and London
ISBN 0-333-69088-5

First published in the United States of America 1998 by
St. Martin's Press, Inc.
Scholarly and Reference Division, 175 Fifth Avenue, New York, N. Y. 10010
ISBN 0-312-21160-0

Typeset by Taylormade Book Production

In memory of
Professor Ōkubo Toshiaki
1900 – 1995

Contents

Preface to the New Edition ix
Notes on the New Edition xliv
Acknowledgements...xlvi
Preface to the 1998 Edition xlvii
Note on Japanese Names and Terms xlix

1   Introduction 1

2   Historiography in the Service of the Meiji Government 18
2.1 The Meiji Restoration and the Revival of Historiography
     by the Government..18
2.2 Centralization of Government and the Department of History 24
2.3 The Osaka Conference and the Office of Historiography 26
2.4 The Political Crisis of 1881 and the Reorganization of the
     College of Historiography 29
2.5 On the Way to the Meiji Constitution: From Government
     Office to University Institute 32

3   The Activities of the Office of Historiography........................40
3.1 Organization and Staff up to 1881 40
3.2 Organization and Staff after 1881 50
3.3 'Applied History'...56
3.4 The Office of Historiography and Its Rivals 66

4   The Form of Official Historiography 71
4.1 Recording the Restoration 71
4.2 Collecting Materials and Writing History 74
4.3 The Language of Official Historiography 80

4.4   Studying Western Methods (1): Zerffi 83
4.5   The *Dainihon hennenshi* 94

5   History as an Academic Discipline 101
5.1   Scholarly Traditions 101
5.2   History at the Imperial University 108
5.3   Studying Western Methods (2): Rieß 113
5.4   The *akademizumu* School of History 119

6   History and Ideology in Conflict..............................132
6.1   History and the Public 132
6.2   National Learning versus Chinese Learning 138
6.3   'Dr Obliterator' 141
6.4   The 'Kume Affair' 148
6.5   The End of the Official History 156
6.6   Scholarship versus Education: The Textbook Controversy
      of 1911 163

7   Conclusion...172
7.1   The Legacy: The Historiographical Institute since 1895 172
7.2   History and the Nation in Germany and Japan 179

Notes 195
Select Bibliography..225
Index 233

Preface to the New Edition

'Historians place the highest value on monographic research, based on the archives.'[1]

'We historians, I often think, tend to stop too soon, when we might continue our interpretive work until it reaches for more general conceptions.'[2]

Why am I publishing a new edition of *History and the State in Nineteenth-Century Japan*,[3] a book with a narrow focus on a single institution over a period of less than thirty years (1869–95)? *History and the State* deals with the Historiographical Institute at the University of Tokyo (Tōkyō Daigaku Shiryō Hensanjo) and its predecessors; well might one argue that I clearly stopped 'too soon' when I could have continued to work out the wider implications of my research on history and the nation state. Why have I nevertheless decided to publish the work with little more than cosmetic changes to the original edition?

My aim in this preface is not just to explain my motives, but also to share some of my reflections upon my work as a historian, especially the dilemma faced by many historians and phrased so well in the observation by Carol Gluck quoted above. Re-reading *History and the State* I feel that back in the 1980s and 1990s I made some effort at interpretation and that, as I reached for general conceptions, I even arrived at a few tentative generalizations. Ultimately though, I timidly hinted at what I now feel I

---

[1] Bruce Mazlish, *The Uncertain Sciences* (New Brunswick, NJ: Transaction, 2007 (1998)): xv.
[2] Carol Gluck, 'The End of Elsewhere: Writing Modernity Now (AHR Roundtable)', *American Historical Review* 116.3 (2011): 676–87, 687.
[3] Margaret Mehl, *History and the State in Nineteenth-Century Japan* (Houndmills, Basingstoke: Macmillan, 1998).

might have boldly explored. I am not sure I regret this. I finished my Ph.D. thesis in what by German standards was fairly good time (around four years) and moved on to new projects. My next book, *Private Academies of Chinese Learning in Meiji Japan*, was on a subject largely, although not entirely, unrelated to historiography.[4] Meanwhile, other scholars have produced work that now enables me to approach the subject of *History and the State* in a way I could not have done back then. So rather than revise the old book, I use this preface to outline some broader implications that might be explored further by the next generation of scholars.

On a superficial level, the answer to the 'why re-publish' question is easy enough: in June 1999, while on sabbatical in Tokyo, I applied for an academic post at the University of Copenhagen. Applicants were required to send in copies of their publications, so I duly attempted to purchase extra copies of *History and the State* (published the previous year), only to find that, apart from a copy in one of the second-hand bookstores in Kanda at a price I was not prepared to pay, there were apparently none to be had, at least not before the application deadline. Believing that under the circumstances I could hardly be blamed for copyright infringement, I borrowed the book from the Waseda University Library and had it copied at the Sōbisha print shop nearby.

Next time I checked, I found that *History and the State* indeed appeared to be out of print, and some years later I found that it was available from the publisher (which had now become Palgrave Macmillan) or from Amazon through 'print on demand' or as an 'e-book' (meaning a pdf-file). Of course, authors do well to keep track of what happens to their book after it has been published.[5] Young academics, however, quickly learn not to expect too much from their publications, beyond, if they are lucky, the next step up the career ladder. Besides, in my early years in the profession, I was too busy teaching new courses and writing my next book.

---

[4] Margaret Mehl, *Private Academies of Chinese Learning in Meiji Japan: The Decline and Transformation of the Kangaku Juku* (Copenhagen: NIAS Press, 2003).

[5] As I well knew from the copious literature for aspiring authors, some of which I had studied as I worked on the book.

Meanwhile, the digital revolution was transforming book publishing.[6] A few years into the new millennium, I realized that print-on-demand and e-books had become so easy and cheap to produce that they offered new opportunities for authors as well as publishers; more precisely, they offered opportunities for the author-publisher. Following helpful advice from the Society of Authors,[7] I asked Palgrave Macmillan for the reversion of the rights to *History and the State*, which they graciously granted. *History and the State* was now mine to do with as I liked, and I decided to re-issue it myself in order to retain full control over my work.

Full control means full responsibility, and so I feel I owe the reader an explanation for the decisions I have made.

My main reason for re-issuing the book is my belief that *History and the State*, despite its narrow focus, represents an important contribution to broader discussions relating to nation-building in the nineteenth century (and beyond), to the role of the past in creating national identity, as well as to the development of history as a modern academic discipline, which is so intimately linked to the formation of the nation state that to this day historians can struggle to overcome methodological nationalism. I will return to this point later. My confidence in *History and the State* as a useful contribution to scholarship has been further strengthened by the fact that a team of Japanese historians led by Chiba Isao and Matsuzawa Yūsaku have been working on a Japanese translation of the work for the last few years. In the draft of his postscript (*kaisetsu*), Matsuzawa describes *History and the State* as unique in its comprehensive and detailed treatment of official historiography by the Meiji government. Apparently, although several books and articles relating to aspects of historiography in modern Japan have been published by Japanese scholars since I completed my research, none of them provides a similarly comprehensive treatment, much less attempted to place official historiography into a comparative perspective.

---

[6] Richard Guthrie, *Publishing: Principles & Practice* (London: Sage, 2011): 14. By the beginning of the twenty-first century the very survival of the book, at least in its printed form was in doubt, but so far predictions about its imminent extinction appear premature, and for scholars in the humanities and social sciences, publishing books remains a necessity as well as a choice.

[7] Society of Authors: www.societyofauthors.org, accessed 17 January 2017.

Writing about Historiography in Meiji Japan in the 1980s

Before I discuss developments in historical scholarship since I wrote my book, however, I will say a little about the circumstances in which I wrote it. *History and the State in Nineteenth-Century Japan* started life as a doctoral dissertation. This was submitted to the University of Bonn in 1991 and published in 1992, more or less as I had submitted it.[8] I gave it the title, *Eine Vergangenheit für die japanische Nation* (A past for the Japanese nation), because this was what I perceived to be the book's main theme: the Meiji government, as part of its nation-building project, made efforts not only to take control of the present and determine the future, but also to reshape the past. The German version also has a subtitle that describes the content of the work more precisely: *Die Entstehung des historischen Forschungsinstituts Tōkyō daigaku Shiryō hensanjo (1869–1895)* (The origins of the institute for historical research, *Tōkyō daigaku Shiryō hensanjo*). For the English version I revised the work thoroughly, having duly familiarized myself with the Anglo-American difference between a thesis and a book – in contrast to Germany, where such a sharp distinction was not generally perceived at the time.[9] I redoubled my efforts to flesh out the broader perspective, but essentially the work remained limited in its focus.

The historian in me wishes to let the work stand as a product of its time, both of my own academic biography and of the age. Never since have I been able to immerse myself in my primary sources so deeply and exclusively and for such a sustained period of time as in the two years from October 1987 to November 1989, which I spent as a research student at the University of Tokyo, thanks to a grant from the Japanese Ministry of Education and, when that expired, the German National Academic Foundation (Studienstiftung des deutschen Volkes). Never since have I had quite the same experience of regular exchanges with fellow students

---

[8] Margaret Mehl, *Eine Vergangenheit für die japanische Nation: Die Entstehung des historischen Forschungsinstituts Tōkyō daigaku Shiryō hensanjo (1869–1895)* (Frankfurt a.M.: Peter Lang, 1992).

[9] Regarding this distinction, see for example Beth Luey, *Handbook for Academic Authors (Revised Edition)* (Cambridge: Cambridge University Press, 1990 (1987)): 26–38.

and scholars, both Japanese and foreign, as in the history seminars of Professor Itō Takashi,[10] the Ph.D. Kenkyūkai research group at International House, and on various other, less formal occasions. And never since has Japan been as it seemed then, the economy 'bubbling', the atmosphere vibrant; if there was a sense of unease in the air, I was too preoccupied with my own concerns to notice.

The 1980s, the time of my extended stay in Japan, have now apparently receded sufficiently into the past to qualify as history; at the most recent conference of German-speaking Japanologists in Munich in August 2015, the modern history panel (convened by Urs Matthias Zachmann) was under the overall theme of 'new approaches', and one of the proposed innovations was that 'modern history' was now explicitly to extend to 1989. In January of that year, the Shōwa era finally came to an indisputable end with the passing of the emperor, described in the media as 'the last of the World War II leaders and Japan's longest-reigning monarch'.[11] Months later the Berlin Wall came down, another highly symbolic event, which signalled the end of an order created in the aftermath of the Second World War. I only learnt about it on the Sunday morning after that memorable Thursday night of 9 November, when my radio alarm clock woke me in time to attend the Shigakukai's hundredth anniversary conference (the Historical Society of Japan was founded in 1889, the year the Meiji Constitution was promulgated), thus fully living up to the cliché of the scholar too wrapped up in the past to take notice of the present.[12] I played a tiny part in helping some of Professor Itō's

---

[10] Although I was never able to fully participate in the activities relating to the justly acclaimed work of Itō Takashi and his students in collecting, transcribing and making available primary sources, I did experience a taste of what George Akita has described so well: see Akita, *Evaluating Evidence: A Positivist Approach to Reading Sources on Modern Japan* (Honolulu: University of Hawai'i Press, 2008): 9–19.

[11] See, for example Susan Chira, 'Hirohito, 124th Emperor of Japan, is Dead at 87', *New York Times* (7 January 1989). http://www.nytimes.com/learning/general/onthisday/bday/0429.html, accessed 7 April 2016.

[12] An anecdote about the Austrian Orientalist August Philipp Pfizmaier (1808–87) relates that he only learned about the Franco-Prussian war six months after the event, from a Japanese (or Chinese) newspaper: Josef Kreiner, *Deutsche Spaziergänge in Tōkyō* (Munich: iudicium, 1996): 61, 62.

students prepare an exhibition of relevant documents, such as a selection from the papers of several historians treated in *History and the State*.[13]

The 1980s were also a time characterised by revisionism in historical writing and a preoccupation with national culture, as well as sharp criticism of such trends. I remember that, in addition to the discussions about the emperor's responsibility for Japan's wartime aggression (*sensō sekinin*),[14] two instances in particular caught my attention that during my time in Japan. One was the responses to the textbook controversy that broke out in 1982, when the treatment (or rather non-treatment) in the ministry-approved school textbooks of Japan's war role as an aggressor caused international outrage, chiefly in the Asian countries that had suffered from it. What perhaps was less known abroad is the fact that the Ministry of Education's stance was strongly criticized by many Japanese historians as well.[15] The second was the establishment of the International Research Center for Japanese Studies, commonly known as Nichibunken, in Kyoto as an Inter-University Research Institute of the Ministry of Education in May 1987. In 1988 I spent two months in Kyoto as an intern at the German Goethe Institute and during this time (on 9 March) I had the chance to attend one of the first public events organized by Nichibunken, a public symposium where the speakers were Claude Lévi-Strauss, Donald Keene and Nichibunken's founding Director General, Umehara Takeshi. The founding of the Institute was controversial both

---

[13] It was only at this point that I had the chance to see some of the papers of Shigeno Yasutsugu, which had not yet been systematically catalogued and were not accessible to the public.

[14] Only rarely did I observe evidence of a discussion about the people's responsibility for the war. An exception was Hikohiro Takahashi, *Minshū no sensō sekinin* (Tokyo: Aoki Shoten, 1989).

[15] My personal library includes topical publications I bought at the time: Nagahara Keiji and Yamazumi Masami, *Rekishi o gakkō de dō oshieru ka*, Iwanami bukkuretto: 90 (Tokyo: Iwanami Shoten, 1987); Yamazumi Masami, *Kyōkasho mondai to wa nani ka*, Iwanami bukkuretto, 21 (Tokyo: Iwanami Shoten, 1983); Ienaga Saburō, *Kyōkasho saiban* (Tokyo: Nihon Hyōronsha, 1981); Nagahara Keiji, *Kōkoku shikan*, Iwanami bukkuretto, 20 (Tokyo: Iwanami Shoten, 1983); Amino Yoshihiko, *Nihon shakai to tennōsei*, Iwanami Bukkuretto 108 (Tokyo: Iwanami, 1988); Iwai Tadakuma and Gotō Yasushi, *Tennō-sei to jidaigawari*, Kamogawa Bukkuretto 21 (Kyoto: Kamogawa Shuppan, 1989) and, a couple of years later, Kamei Jun, *Kōshitsu hōdō no yomikata*, Iwanami bukkuretto 168 (Tokyo: Iwanami, 1990).

in Japan and abroad; it was seen as an expression of nationalism and an essentialist view of Japanese culture.[16]

Controversies of a different kind (and mostly limited to Germans) centred on the German Institute for Japanese Studies in Tokyo, founded in 1988. Although the new institute was officially represented as belonging to a tradition of German research institutes abroad, starting with the German historical institute in Rome in 1888, its research focus took a very different direction. The focus was to be on contemporary Japan in order to remedy the deficit in knowledge about Japan, of which many had become painfully aware when Japan displaced Germany as the second largest economy in the world.[17] One major controversy was between those who wanted it to be devoted to research of immediate relevance to the German business community, while others, chiefly scholars and others who considered themselves Japan experts, wanted a broader focus. There was also the question of who was or was not involved in the decision-making about the institute's aims, with old 'Japan hands', many of them resident in Tokyo, complaining that their views were ignored.[18]

While Japanese and foreigners alike were trying to make sense of Japan's history and culture, in Germany there was the 'Historikerstreit' (historians' dispute), which broke out in the summer of 1986 and continued into 1987.[19] Although in part a controversy about the uniqueness or otherwise of the annihilation of the Jews under the Nazis, it also related to broader issues about the place of National Socialism in German history and memory, including the long-standing debate about

---

[16] Examples in Gavan McCormack, 'Kokusaika: Impediments in Japan's Deep Structure', in *Multicultural Japan: Palaeolithic to Postmodern*, ed. Donald Denoon et al. (Cambridge: Cambridge University Press 1996): 278–9.

[17] According to the website of the Max Weber Foundation, of which the institute became a part in 2002: http://www.maxweberstiftung.de/institute/institute-dij-tokyo.html, accessed 19 October 2016.

[18] Discussions at the first Japanese Studies conference in Tokyo organized by the German Asiatic Society (OAG) 7–8 April 1988.

[19] I followed the debate at the time to some extent. One publication I found useful a few years after the event is the German translation of a book by the British historian Richard Evans (with a new postscript for the German edition): Evans, *Im Schatten Hitlers?*, trans. Jürgen Blasius, (Frankfurt a. M.: Edition Suhrkamp, 1991).

the German 'Sonderweg'.[20] Questions about the nature of Germany's modernization (whether belated, special or otherwise) have featured in studies of Japan's modern history, where the two 'latecomers' are compared, not least in the context of German influence on Meiji Japan. Needless to say, the 'Historikerstreit' attracted the attention of Japanese historians. One of the few Japanese works on German history that I read at the time was Mochida Yukio's book *Futatsu no kindai* (1988), where the author, a historian of Germany, discusses the 'Historikerstreit' and the 'Sonderweg' debate.[21]

Was it in part under the impression of these events that I felt it was safest to stick to 'facts' documented in primary sources and to be over-careful about interpretation, just as the scholars I treated in my dissertation are perceived to have done?[22] Probably not. I think it is more likely that I felt overwhelmed by the complexity of the many questions my research raised. My training in history at the University of Bonn, moreover, not to mention the 'positivist studies'[23] predominant at the 'Department of National History' (yes, the Department of Japanese History was still named Kokushika in those days!) did not exactly predispose me to venture too far out into the precarious territory of historical interpretation.

---

[20] For a succinct treatment of that debate published in the wake of the 'Historikerstreit', see Jürgen Kocka, 'Germany before Hitler: The Debate about the German Sonderweg', *Journal of Contemporary History* 23.1 (1988): 3–16. As Kocka points out, the word 'Sonderweg' was not necessarily used by historians who contributed to that debate.

[21] Especially the refutation of the "Sonderweg" thesis by the British historians Richard Evans, Geoff Ely and David Blackbourn; see Mochida Yukio, *Futatsu no kindai: Doitsu to Nihon wa dō chigau ka* (Tokyo: Asahi Shinbunsha, 1988). One of my few memories of conversation about the Historikerstreit in Japan is from my first Shigakukai conference in November 1987, when one professor, on hearing that I had studied at the University of Bonn, asked me (in German), whether Professor Klaus Hildebrand was 'streitbar' (pugnacious), a description that amused me because the word seemed so quaintly old-fashioned (Hildebrand was to become my examiner in the Ph.D. *viva voce* in Medieval and Modern History, but at the time I had only attended his lectures and never spoken to him).

[22] These scholars represent what is known as *kangaku akademizumu*: see *History and the State*, pp. 103–12.

[23] George Akita, 'Trends in Modern Japanese Political History: The "Positivist" Studies', *Monumenta Nipponica* 37.4 (1982): 497–521.

Reception of *History and the State*

The narrow focus of *History and the State* was pointed out by some of the reviewers of the English edition.[24] Bob Tadashi Wakabayashi suggested that the focus could have been broadened in three ways: by examining historians who worked outside the government; by providing a more detailed comparison between Japan and Germany; and by pursuing the theme of my chapter 6 ('History and Ideology in Conflict') through 1945. While I agree that all these dimensions would have merited (and still merit) further investigation, I submit that pursuing any one of them would have resulted in a different kind of book rather than an improved version of the book I actually wrote.

Interestingly, the desiderata for future research suggested by Matsuzawa in his (draft) postscript to the forthcoming Japanese edition amount to a call for more detailed studies on some of the themes treated in *History and the State*, rather than for a broader perspective. The three areas he singles out for more detailed investigation are, first, the overall shape of the government historiography project (*shūshi jigyō*). The second is the government compilation of chronicles and documents relating to the most recent history and the process by which the compilation of a history of the more distant period starting with the fourteenth century (the Nanbokuchō period) came to take precedence as well as the relationship between the history of historical scholarship and the archive. Third, Matsuzawa suggests that there is a need to examine more closely the historians themselves, not only luminaries like Shigeno Yasutsugu and Kume Kunitake, but also the lower-ranking members of the Office of Historiography. In short, Matsuzawa's call for yet more detailed studies suggests that the historiographical tradition I treated in *History and the State,* a work which itself shows many characteristics of that tradition, is still alive and well today.

---

[24] John S. Brownlee, 'Review of *History and the State in Nineteenth-Century Japan*, by Margaret Mehl', *Journal of Asian Studies* February (1999): 208–9; Bob Tadashi Wakabayashi, 'Review of *History and the State in Nineteenth-Century Japan*, by Margaret Mehl', *Monumenta Nipponica* 53.4 (1998): 560–2; Shimazu Naoko, 'Review of *History and the State in Nineteenth-Century Japan*, by Margaret Mehl', *Japan Forum* 11.1 (1999): 150–1; Stefan Tanaka, 'Review of *Japanese Historians and the National Myths, 1600–1945* by John S. Brownlee and *History and the State in Nineteenth-Century Japan* by Margaret Mehl', *Journal of Japanese Studies* 25.2 (1999): 406–12.

This impression is reinforced by the fact that most of the subsequent Japanese works on related subjects cited by Matsuzawa appear to be narrow in focus: articles on Ludwig Rieß;[25] historiography and the compilation of topographies in the context of the nation state;[26] the role of textual criticism in the *kōshōgaku* tradition and the place of the *Dainihon hennenshi* (the chronological history of Japan compiled by the Office of Historiography) in historical scholarship;[27] the collection of information by the Meiji government, and at the local level;[28] as well as the emperor-centred view of history and the controversy about the Northern and Southern courts.[29] Finally, Matsuzawa cites recent work on a subject I barely touched upon: official historiography by Japan in its colonies, namely Korea.[30] Although some of the authors cited by Matsuzawa do appear to place their research in a wider context, the titles of these works, mostly journal articles and book chapters, nevertheless suggest that no attempt at a comprehensive study of historiography and related activities by the Meiji government has been made.[31] Recently,

---

[25] Nishikawa Yōichi, 'Shiryō shōkai: Berurin Kokuritsu Toshokan Rūtowichi Riisu shokan ni tsuite', *Kokka Gakkai zasshi* 115.3/4 (2002); ———, 'Tōkyō to Berurin ni okeru Rūdowichi Riisu', in *Rekishigaku to shiryō kenkyū*, ed. Tōkyō Daigaku Shiryō Hensanjo (Tokyo: Yamakawa Shuppansha, 2003); Hayashima Akira, 'Kindai Doitsu daigakushi ni okeru Rūtowichi Riisu', *Shōgaku kenkyū* 50.1/2 (2002).

[26] Nishikawa Nagao and Matsumiya Hideharu, eds., *Bakumatsu-, Meijiki no kokumin kokka keisei to bunka hen'yō* (Tokyo: Shin'yōsha, 1995); Shimazu Toshiyuki, 'Meiji seifu no chishi hensan jigyō to kokumin kokka keisei', *Chirigaku hyōron* 75.2 (2002).

[27] Katsurajima Nobuhiro, 'Kindai kokushigaku no seiritsu: kōshō shigaku o chūshin ni' in *Shisōshi no jūkyū seiki* (Tokyo: Perikansha, 1999). Kojita Yasunao, 'Nihonshi no tanjō: "Dainihon hennenshi" no hensan ni tsuite', in *Seiki tenkanki no kokusai chitsujo to kokumin bunka no keisei*, ed. Nishikawa Nagao and Watanabe Kōzō (Tokyo: Kashiwa Shobō, 1999).

[28] Ōta Tomiyasu, *Kindai gyōseitai no kiroku to jōhō* (Tokyo: Iwata shoin, 2010); Shigeta Masao, 'Saitama ni okeru Kōkoku chishi no henshū katei', *Bunshokan kiyō* 18. (2005).

[29] Ikeda Tomofumi, 'Kindai "kokushigaku" no shisō kōzō', *Ryūkoku Daigaku Daigakuin Bungaku Kenkyūka kiyō* 25 (2003); ———, '"Nanbokuchō seijun mondai" saikō – kindai "kokushigaku" no shisōteki mondai to shite', *Nihonshi kenkyū* 528 (2006).

[30] Nagashima Hiroki, 'Nihon tōjiki no Chōsen ni okeru "shigaku" to "shiryō" no isō', *Rekishigaku kenkyū* 745 (2004); Hakoishi Hiroshi, 'Kindai Nihon shiryōgaku to Chōsen Sōtokufu no Chōsenshi hensan jigyō', in *Zen kindai no Nihon rettō to Chōsen hantō*, ed. Satō Makoto and Fujita Satoru (Tokyo: Yamakawa Shuppansha, 2007).

[31] Admittedly, I have not studied these works myself.

Matsuzawa has edited a volume about historiography in modern Japan; here too, the focus is on detailed study of selected topics.[32] As for works in English (and German), I will not pretend to have kept up with scholarship in this field while my research turned to other topics.[33] Nor is my intention here to report on subsequent research in the field of historiography in modern Japan. Indeed, I fear that an immersion in such research might draw me into yet more study of details, in spite of myself, when what I wish to do at this stage is to reflect upon some of the broader issues regarding which I believe the history of historical scholarship and writing under the auspices of the Meiji government is relevant and important.

I believe that I touched upon several important larger questions in my thesis (completed in 1991), and certainly in the 1998 edition. These questions can be grouped under two themes. The first has to do with the function of history in the context of the nation state and the relations between nation states at the time when Meiji Japan embarked on its course of modernization following Western models. Although I did not make this sufficiently explicit at the time, *History and the State* represented a contribution to a growing body of work that challenged the conventional narrative at the time, which imagined the process of fundamental reform after 1868 as far smoother than it actually was. The second has to do with historical research and writing, the nature of historical knowledge and the tensions between scientific history and the expectation that history provides societies with meaning.

---

[32] Matsuzawa Yūsaku ed. *Kindai Nihon no hisutoriogurafī* (Tokyo: Yamakawa Shuppansha, 2015).

[33] Two useful recent overviews are Sato Masayuki, 'A Social History of Japanese Historical Writing', in *The Oxford History of Historical Writing, Volume 3: 1400–1800*, ed. José Rabasa, et al. (Oxford: Oxford University Press, 2012); and Axel Schneider and Stefan Tanaka, 'The Transformation of History in China and Japan', in *The Oxford History of Historical Writing Volume 4: 1800–1945*, ed. Stuart Macintyre, Juan Maiguashca and Attila Pók (Oxford: Oxford University Press, 2012). Recent publications in German include Sebastian Conrad, Hans Martin Krämer and Tino Schölz, eds., *Geschichtswissenschaft in Japan: Themen, Ansätze und Theorien* (Göttingen: Vandenhoeck & Ruprecht, 2006). Conrad has also published an excellent study of historical scholarship in Japan and Germany after 1945: Sebastian Conrad, *Auf der Suche nach der verlorenen Nation: Geschichtsschreibung in Westdeutschland und Japan 1945–1960* (Göttingen: Vandenhoeck & Ruprecht, 1999).

Of course, it is easy to make such claims with hindsight. I can, however, cite passages from the book itself to support my claim. In my introduction, I suggest that 'the emergence of a national ideology in late nineteenth-century Japan was not unique and must be seen in the contemporary world described by Barraclough.' I add that Japan, in adopting Western models, was not merely following the West, but actually 'appears as contemporaneous with it'.[34] In the conclusion I write that my purpose with the brief summary of historiography in nineteenth-century Germany and its influence on Japan was not so much to show the extent of Japanese cultural borrowing from Germany as 'to demonstrate how similar challenges, a newly formed nation state that had to be filled with meaning and define its purpose, caused Japan to look to Germany.'[35] Concerning cultural borrowing, I point out that Japan was highly selective in what it imported from foreign countries (as well as in which countries it imported from) and that the selection was in part determined by Japan's own cultural traditions.[36] I also attempt to generalize about cultural borrowing by highlighting two points: one is that when Japan imported ideas and concepts from the West, it imported them as they manifested themselves at that particular point in time, without always recognizing how they had developed and changed over the centuries. The second point is that it was not necessarily the content of a system of ideas or practices that attracted Japanese attention, but the function it had within the Western society of the time.[37] I see this now as part of my effort at a more nuanced evaluation of 'Western influence'. Not everything that superficially looked 'Western' (such as the collection and investigation of primary sources by the members of the Office of Historiography) had exclusively Western origins; as often as not, Western models were used to justify existing indigenous practices.[38]

---

[34] Mehl, *History and the State*, 4. Here and in the following passage, page numbers refer to the 1998 edition.

[35] Ibid., 158–9.

[36] Ibid., 159.

[37] Ibid., 4.

[38] See Margaret Mehl, 'The European Model and the Archive in Japan: Inspiration or Legitimation?', *History of the Human Sciences* 26.4 (2013): 107–27. This point is also made in Akita, *Evaluating Evidence*, 120.

Regarding the second broader theme, historical research and writing, the book demonstrates an effort to address the tension between history as a modern academic discipline centred on research, on the one hand, and the representation of history, commonly in a narrative, on the other. The three most important questions I ask are, first, why the historians at the Historiographical Institute did not become 'interpreters of the nation' and failed to play a major role in shaping the Japanese empire, in contrast to Ranke and his early disciples in Germany. Second, and related to this: why did these historians fail to complete the official history they were employed to produce? And third: why did emperor-centred myth-history ultimately prevail over source-based scientific history? My answers, as I was painfully aware at the time, are tentative. I argue that 'the emergence of a "scientific" history, which neglected to address the representation of knowledge in the historical narrative and the function of historical knowledge in educating society and that left speculation about the meaning of history to non-historians, resulted in similar problems in Germany and Japan'. Not only were the official historians unable 'to formulate a new conception of history that matched the new era', but they failed to realize that even the kind of 'objective' history they envisaged involved making choices not given by the primary sources themselves.[39] They wished to distinguish clearly between fact and myth, and yet they perceived the myths as indispensable for giving meaning to the nation. Their solution to this dilemma was to distinguish between two kinds of history: scientific and educational. The position of Shigeno and his colleagues as government officials within the East Asian tradition of distinguishing sharply between officials (*kan*) and the people (*min*) encouraged the idea of knowledge as 'the privilege of an academic elite, not to be imparted to the masses'.[40]

I may have relied too much on Japanese secondary sources when I wrote my German thesis, accepting the argument of Japanese scholars that historians of the *akademizumu* school retreated into positivist studies and were unable to withstand the emergence of a dominant emperor-centred view of history based on national myths. Thinking about it now, this seems like a conventional 'science-versus-authority' narrative,

---

[39] Ibid., 161; 165.
[40] Ibid., 159–60.

familiar from the history of the natural sciences in Europe, with the *akademizumu* school's claim to objectivity accepted at face value. By the time I was preparing the English version of my original work, I could refer to Stefan Tanaka's *Japan's Orient*, in which the author reminds us that the historians representing the *akademizumu* approach to historical research with its emphasis on primary sources on facts were far from 'objective.'[41] Ultimately, I am not sure that this, or for that matter Tanaka's history of the construction of *tōyōshi*, helped me much as I grappled with the paradox that the nineteenth century saw the emergence of history as both science and national history.

I reconsidered and elaborated on my argument a few years later, when I was invited by Professor Suzuki Jun of Tokyo University to act as a commentator at the hundredth general conference of the Shigakukai (Historical Society) in November 2002.[42] I rephrased my question as follows: How was it possible that Shigeno and his colleagues, who wanted to write history impartially and whose research has often been described as 'objective', nevertheless ended up compiling historical works that were highly biased? And why did they at the same time fail to produce the intended national history? I attempted to address the question in a way that went beyond the two prevailing lines of argument, namely (1) that the critical researchers' efforts to write history objectively were suppressed by the increasingly nationalistic emperor state, and (2) that the annalistic compilations they produced were in fact far from objective and reflected a view of history centred on the imperial institution.[43] My thoughts about historical narrative were inspired by Jörn Rüsen's work

---

[41] Stefan Tanaka, *Japan's Orient: Rendering Past into History* (Berkeley: University of California Press, 1993). See also Margaret Mehl, 'Review of *Japan's Orient: Rendering Past into History* by Stefan Tanaka', *History* 80. (1995): 259.

[42] Published as Margaret Mehl, 'Ari no mama no kako – Shigeno Yasutsugu to rekishika no shigoto ni tsuite no saikentō', in *Rekishigaku no saizensen: Frontiers of Historical Studies*, ed. Shigakukai (Tokyo: Tokyo University Press, 2004).

[43] Stefan Tanaka points out that the historical school of *akademizumu* represented by Shigeno and his colleagues was not 'objective'. James Edward Ketelaar rightly remarks that the *Kokushigan*, the only overview of Japan's entire history the scholars at the Historiographical Institute did complete and publish, interpreted Japanese history as imperial and as divine history. See Tanaka, *Japan's Orient*; James Edward Ketelaar, *Of Heretics and Martyrs in Meiji Japan: Buddhism and Its Persecution* (Princeton: Princeton University Press, 1990): 92.

on historical narrative or narration.[44] According to Rüsen, historical narration is based on facts; but it is a creative process in which the facts are selected and structured to form meaning. In this process, whereby past experiences are recalled in the present and whereby intentions for the future are related to these recalled experiences, both (experiences and intentions) become part of a continuum we call history and which provides orientation for humans within the flow of time.

My attempt to answer the questions has three parts. First, the supposed 'objectivity' of Shigeno's approach to history cannot lie in recording past conditions 'as they were' (*ari no mama*), because historical research depends on its object having been identified. It is identified through a construction of meaning in narrative form. It follows that, whether or not Shigeno and his colleagues were aware of it, their research was dependent on a pre-existing construction of meaning. Second, they seem not to have been conscious of this, because they shared the positivist assumption that there is an objective history out there waiting to be discovered. They appeared to believe that the chronicles they compiled were objective, because they were no more than a collection of facts that their research had verified. Third, their preoccupation with facts appears to have precluded any reflection on meaning in Rüsen's sense of a continuum linking past experience and future intentions. The Meiji Restoration had introduced a strong element of discontinuous change into the age they lived in, including the necessity to take up a position on the international stage and the large-scale importation of an alien civilization. How could this discontinuity be integrated into a continuous narrative that would affirm Japanese identity and provide orientation? I found no evidence that the historians working on the *Dainihon hennenshi* in their professional role as historians had even asked this question. It seemed to me that the question of Japan's new position and destiny was only addressed by the next generation of historians. I will return to this point later.

---

[44] Jörn Rüsen speaks of 'historisches Erzählen'; he prefers the nominalized verb to the noun 'Erzählung'. See Rüsen, 'Geschichtsschreibung als Theorieproblem der Geschichtswissenschaft: Skizze zum historischen Hintergrund der gegenwärtigen Diskussion', in *Formen der Geschichtsschreibung*, ed. Reinhart Koselleck, Heinrich Lutz and Jörn Rüsen (Munich: dtv, 1982). Then as now I felt that Rüsen's model raises as many questions as it attempts to answer, but it does provide a useful framework for my reflections.

The Bigger Picture (1): the Nation and the Modern World

Revisiting *History and the State* today, I am much more aware of the global historical context of modernity within which Germany and Japan faced the challenges I had mentioned only briefly. For historians, modernity is in part defined by chronology: 'a condition, historically produced over three centuries around the globe in processes of change that have not ended yet'. Modernity 'possesses commonalities across time and space, however differently it is experienced in different places'.[45] The commonalities include the nation state, the call for national political participation, major social shifts, major changes in values and 'global forces of capitalism and industrialization', as well as 'incorporation into the reigning geopolitical world order' and experience of tensions between the global and the local.[46] Other commonalities, particular relevant for the developments discussed in *History and the State*, are state-building, with the nation-state as the state form widely aspired to, and the growth and worldwide dissemination of a modern system of the sciences that includes institutions such as the research university with its laboratories and seminars.[47]

The global nature of modernity means that, certainly by the nineteenth century (if not earlier), in Bayly's words, 'national histories and "area studies" need to take fuller account of changes occurring in the wider world'.[48] Both Bayly and Osterhammel, another recent author of a global history of the nineteenth century, argue that the history of this period cannot be anything less than global history. In practice, of course, most histories will be much less.

Certainly, Japan's political and intellectual leaders were well aware of the global dimension of modern times from the start. The encroaching world, in the form of Russia, the United States and several European powers, forced the Tokugawa shogunate to abandon its isolation policy, which precipitated the collapse of the regime and the establishment of the

---

[45] Gluck, 'End of Elsewhere', 676–7.
[46] Ibid.
[47] Jürgen Osterhammel, *Die Verwandlung der Welt: Eine Geschichte des 19. Jahrhunderts* (Munich: C.H. Beck, 2009): 1105, 1779.
[48] Christopher Alan Bayly, *The Birth of the Modern World 1780–1914: Global Connections and Comparisons* (Malden, MA: Blackwell, 2004): 3.

Meiji government. The new leaders, both at national and at local levels, saw from the start the need to act within a global context. The pledge in the Imperial Oath of 1868 that 'knowledge shall be sought from all the countries of the world' found its remarkable expression in 1871, when half of the new government, which had only just managed to secure control over the entire country, embarked on what is known as the Iwakura Embassy, which took the Ambassador Extraordinary and Plenipotentiary, four vice-ambassadors and an entourage of nearly one hundred men, over a period of 21 months, to 12 countries as well as to every major sea port between Marseilles and Nagasaki.[49]

Meanwhile, in the remote prefecture of Kashiwazaki (soon to be absorbed into Niigata prefecture), in the spring of 1873, the Deputy Councillor, in a public notification to all village headmen concerning the 'Control of Customs during the Spring and Autumn Festivities', condemned young people's dancing together, pointed out the government's efforts 'for our country to hold its own among the countries of the world (*bankoku to gotaiji*)'[50] and said that Japan must not be put to shame by the countries of the world (*bankoku no chijoku o ukuru*).[51] And in the Office of Historiography in September the same year, members expressed concern over the fact that a book about Japan's recent history (*Kinsei shiryaku* by Yamaguchi Ken), the sale of which had been prohibited in 1872 because of its many factual errors, had been translated into English and thus become known abroad.[52]

Situating modernity within a chronology, albeit an open-ended one, and emphasizing its global nature renders problematic the notion of

---

[49] In addition, the embassy included students who stayed abroad, among them six girls. See introduction in Kume Kunitake, *The Iwakura Embassy 1871–73: A True Account of the Ambassador Extraordinary and Plenipotentiary's Journey of Observation through the United States of America and Europe*. ed. Graham Healey and Tsuzuki Chushichi, trans. Martin Colcutt et al., 5 vols., vol. 1: The United States of America (Kamiyakiri, Matsudo, Chiba: The Japan Documents, 2002).

[50] The expression (*bankoku to gotaiji*) appears twice in the *haihan chiken* (abolition of the domains and the establishment of prefectures) order of Meiji 4 (1871).7th month.14th day.

[51] Niigata-ken, ed. *Niigata-kenshi: Shiryō hen 14 (Kindai 2: Meiji ishin hen II)* (Niigata: Niigata-ken, 1983): 931–2.

[52] Mehl, *History and the State*, 51.

'alternative' or 'multiple' modernities.[53] It does not follow, however, that the modern is unitary or universal. Certainly, modernity, often in the form of emulating the West, was widely aspired to and even regarded as inevitable. In the famous (or infamous) editorial 'Datsu-A ron' (Escape from Asia), usually attributed to Fukuzawa Yukichi, the spread of Western civilization is likened to that of measles.[54] Sanjay Subrahmanyam is probably nearer to the mark when he says that modernity is not so much a 'virus that spreads from one place to another' as 'historically a global and conjunctural phenomenon'.[55] Nevertheless, Fukuzawa, writing in the late nineteenth century, did have a point. As Osterhammel convincingly argues, the nineteenth century *was* characterized by European dominance because European powers controlled and exploited large parts of the world, because changes in Europe significantly influenced the rest of the world and because Europe was widely perceived as a role model.

Modernity nevertheless manifested itself differently in different times and places. The differences result from the 'plurality of pasts' and the 'plurality of futures'[56] or, in other words, the variations in 'preexisting conditions' and 'available modernities'.[57]

In *History and the State* I stress the significance of such 'preexisting conditions' as I draw attention to the early education and careers of Shigeno and his colleagues and to historical scholarship before the Meiji period. Such conditions were more than 'preexisting'; they were persistent. Western civilization did not replace overnight the Chinese-inspired scholarship and culture that had dominated Japan for centuries. The forms of knowing and learning predominant in the preceding Tokugawa era blended with the new Western models, a process that had its parallels in other areas, particularly in education.[58] As David

---

[53] Gluck, 'End of Elsewhere', 676.

[54] For an English version, see Fukuzawa, Yukichi, 'Good-bye Asia (Datsu-a), 1885', in *Japan: A Documentary History 2: The Late Tokugawa Period to the Present*, ed. David J. Lu, (New York: Armonk, 1997).

[55] Quoted in Gluck, 'End of Elsewhere', 677.

[56] Sudipta Kaviraj, 'An Outline of a Revisionist Theory of Modernity', *European Journal of Sociology* 46.3 (2005): 497–526, 498, 500.

[57] Gluck, 'End of Elsewhere', 679, 681.

[58] Margaret Mehl, 'Chinese Learning (*kangaku*) in Meiji Japan', *History* 85 (2000): 48–66; Mehl, *Private Academies*.

Mervart, citing recent research by Japanese scholars, argues, 'China' as a universal and a normative reference (in contrast to empirical China) continued to hold the significance it had held for centuries. The fact that Western countries became the new frame of reference from the mid-nineteenth century did not immediately change this: the West was worth emulating because it excelled in '"Chinese" normative virtues'.[59]

The history of the Meiji government's efforts to produce an official national history illustrates the continuing significance of a normative China. The chronological history *Dainihon hennenshi* owes much to similar works compiled before 1868 and next to nothing to Western examples. The collection and eventual publication of sources followed the model of the late Edo compilation *Shiryō* by Hanawa Hokiichi (1746–1821). For all his interest in Western historical writings and scholarship, and all his calls for innovation, Shigeno never abandoned the Chinese epistemological and scholarly traditions in which he had been educated. Even Kume, who pioneered the systematic study of primary documents (*komonjo*), did so largely independently of Western influences.[60] In stressing this I emphatically do not wish to imply that their scholarship lacked innovation;[61] merely that their early education and beliefs decisively influenced their willingness and capacity to incorporate Western ideas and methods into their work.[62] Innovation and

---

[59] David Mervart, 'Meiji Japan's China Solution to Tokugawa Japan's China Problem', *Japan Forum* 27.4 (2015): 544–58, 555. See also Ben-Ami Shillony, 'The Meiji Restoration: Japan's attempt to inherit China,' in *War, Revolution & Japan*, ed. Ian Neary (Sandgate, Folkestone, Kent: Japan Library, 1993).

[60] Mehl, 'The European Model and the Archive in Japan'.

[61] For works that stress the innovative aspects of Shigeno's writings, see Tao Demin, 'Shigeno Yasutsugu as an Advocate of 'Practical Sinology" in Meiji Japan', in *Nihon kangaku shisō ronkō* (Suita: Kansai Daigaku Shuppanbu, 1999); Matsuzawa Yūsaku, *Shigeno Yasutsugu to Kume Kunitake: 'Seishi' o yume mita rekishika* (Tokyo: Yamakawa Shuppansha, 2012). See also Margaret Mehl, 'Shigeno Yasutsugu: Ein Überlebender kämpft um die Vergangenheit der Nation', in *Von Bauern, Beamten und Banditen. Beiträge zur historischen Japanforschung. Festschrift für Detlev Taranczewski zu seinem sechzigsten Geburtstag von seinen Schülern und Kollegen*, ed. Marie-Luise Legeland, et al. (Bonn: Bier'sche Verlagsanstalt, 2007).

[62] The fate of Zerffi's *Science of History* illustrates among other things how much Zerffi took for granted concerning historiography which would have been alien to his Japanese readers.

modernization could – and, as both Shigeno's and Kume's work demonstrate, did – certainly take place without directly imitating Western models.

Even so, cultural borrowing from the West was such an important characteristic of Meiji Japan that it is difficult to separate modernization from Westernization: both were determined by 'preexisting conditions'. Sir Hamilton Gibb, who (in 1964, in his discussion of Islamic influence in medieval Europe) states that three general principles determine what and how one culture borrows from another, argues that cultural influences are always preceded 'by an already existing activity in the related field' of the culture doing the borrowing. As I show in *History and the State* this was obviously the case with historiography. Gibb's second and third principles are closely connected to the pre-existence of certain conditions: that which is borrowed will only develop if it adapts and blends with the 'native forces'; and, the recipient culture 'disregards or rejects all elements in other cultures which conflict with its own fundamental values, emotional attitudes or aesthetic criteria'.[63] These principles might explain, for example, why the Japanese found some interpretations of history expressed by Western writers more attractive than others, or why the enormous efforts poured into collecting and arranging sources did not lead to the establishment of a system of national and regional archives.[64] Gibb's notion of the blending of imports with the indigenous also explains why it can be difficult to distinguish between the two. And in a transnational context of intermingling and hybridization (Gluck refers to 'blended modernities'[65]) disentangling origins may have little significance except as an academic enterprise.

---

[63] Sir Hamilton Gibb, 'The Influence of Islamic Culture on Medieval Europe', in *Change in Medieval Society*, ed. Sylvia L. Thrupp (New York: Appleton-Century-Croft, 1964). See Mehl, 'The European Model and the Archive in Japan'.

[64] Kondō Shigekazu, 'Joshō: "Hisutoriogurafi" to rekishi shori', in *Rekishigaku to rekishi kenkyū*, ed. Tōkyō Daigaku Shiryō Hensanjo (Tokyo: Yamakawa Shuppankai, 2003). The National Archives of Japan were not established until 1971. Another interesting absence might be the lack of footnotes in the publications of the early Japanese historians, although this can in part be explained by the fact that many of the published articles were originally lectures. The footnote is generally regarded as one of the most significant characteristics of modern scholarship: Bruce Mazlish, *The Uncertain Sciences*.

[65] Gluck, 'End of Elsewhere'.

As for the 'available modernities' for Meiji Japan, intellectuals and political leaders at the time perceived them as 'civilization and enlightenment' (*bunmei kaika*) modelled by Western countries (*Ō-Bei shokoku* or 'the countries of Europe and America'), which they understood to be to a larger or lesser degree ahead of them on a universal ladder towards progress.[66] The report of the Iwakura Embassy compiled by a future pioneer of modern historical scholarship, Kume Kunitake, provides striking illustrations of this understanding, for example when he reflects on Britain's prosperity and the differences between East and West:

> *To speak of the error of being over-hasty to put knowledge to work* is enough to suggest that the East is far behind the West on the path of development, but *the fact is* that even Britain and France, the most advanced countries, have taken a mere fifty years to reach their present prosperity. There are still innumerable countries in the world which lag behind in development, (...) [*emphasis in the original*][67]

The message here and elsewhere is that Japan does not lag so far behind that it cannot catch up in the near future. The means to achieving the envisaged modernity was a unified nation, wealthy and with a strong army (*fukoku kyōhei*). Accordingly, Japan became a textbook case of state- and nation-building in the nineteenth century, and by 1900 was 'one of the most tightly integrated nation-states in the world'.[68]

In Japan as in other places, however, the nation was not initially a psychological reality, or, in the words of contemporaries, the Japanese

---

[66] Ibid., 681.

[67] Kume Kunitake, *The Iwakura Embassy 1871–73: A True Account of the Ambassador Extraordinary and Plenipotentiary's Journey of Observation through the United States of America and Europe*, eds. Graham Healey and Tsuzuki Chushichi, trans. Martin Colcutt et al., 5 vols. (Kamiyakiri, Matsudo, Chiba: The Japan Documents, 2002): 2: 174. The italics (by the editors) reflect Kume's markings for emphasis. The appearance of the complete English translation of the *Bei-Ō kairan jikki* enabled me to do something I had tried and dismally failed to do with the Iwanami bunko edition: to skim through the entire work and get an overall impression of it in a short time. Even Japanese readers might find this impossible with the original, written as it is in a heavily Sinicized style.

[68] Jürgen Osterhammel, *The Transformation of the World: A Global History of the Nineteenth Century*, trans. Patrick Camiller (Princeton: Princeton University Press, 2014): 414.

people lacked a sense of nation.[69] This is where national history had a role to play, by representing the nation as naturally evolved and thus as given. The connection between nationalism and national history, and – particularly in the German case – the modern academic discipline of history, has received plenty of scholarly attention and not much need be added here.[70] In *History and the State* I argued that the historians I examined did not become interpreters of the nation in a way comparable to Ranke or the historians of the Prussian School of history,[71] and attempted to answer the question why. I am no longer entirely sure to what extent this argument holds or whether the question is appropriate. But there is certainly a difference between Japan and Germany, where Ranke is remembered not only as a pioneer of the modern scientific discipline but also as a writer of grand historical narratives, and where academic historians wrote histories of the emerging and newly formed German nation. Shigeno and Kume, meanwhile, let alone their less prominent colleagues, if they are remembered at all, are associated with a school of institutional historiography that over-emphasized factual details (*kangaku akademizumu*) and the failure of national history in the *seishi* tradition of official histories by rulers. Matsuzawa's booklet on the two is subtitled, 'The historians who dreamt of a "seishi"'.[72]

Thus it is hardly surprising that these historians appear insignificant or at least uninteresting to scholars writing about conceptions of history or historical interpretations. For example, one Western scholar discussing the term *shigaku* as a concept for a series entitled 'Working Words' devotes most of the article to discussing Mori Ōgai's views rather than examining those of academic historians.[73] Even more striking, Christopher Hill in his justly acclaimed book, *National History and the*

[69] *kokkateki kannen* or *kokuminteki kannen*. See Carol Gluck, *Japan's Modern Myths: Ideology in the Late Meiji Period* (Princeton, NJ: Princeton University Press, 1985): 23, 318 n.320.
[70] The state control of memory and preoccupation with the nation were certainly not limited to Germany or Japan. Osterhammel names them among the salient features of the nineteenth century world: Osterhammel, *Die Verwandlung der Welt*.
[71] The best known representatives are Johann Gustav Droysen (1808–86), Heinrich von Sybel (1817–95) and Heinrich von Treitschke (1834–96).
[72] Matsuzawa, *Shigeno Yasutsugu to Kume Kunitake*.
[73] Thomas Keirstead, 'Shigaku/History'. EScholarship, University of California, http://escholarship.org/uc/item/32t6g8nf, accessed 12 January 2017.

World of Nations, in which he analyses and compares the representations of national history in nineteenth-century Japan, France and the United States, mentions the government's *seishi* project only in passing; the representatives of academic history are largely ignored.[74] *National History and the World of Nations* is otherwise an important book, drawing out exactly the kind of connections between narrating national history and the global context (defined by Hill as global capitalism and the system of sovereign states) which I only skirted and did not explore further. He shows how the authors he examined employed similar rhetorical and narrative strategies in response to challenges resulting from global change. His selection of Japanese writers includes the narrative histories of Fukuzawa Yukichi, Taguchi Ukichi and Tokutomi Sohō, but also prose fiction by Suehiro Tetchō and Mori Ōgai.

Of course, for those who believe that, ultimately, historians construct a past like a novelist constructs a plot, who perhaps even deny that there is anything approaching a scientific method in history (or in the humanities in general), the distinction between historians claiming to write scientific history and other writers of history is meaningless, and Shigeno might simply be regarded as an inferior storyteller compared to Ōgai.

My contention, however, is that Shigeno, Kume and others are interesting precisely because of their aim to write scientific history and their contribution to what became the modern, research-based discipline of history. In the following discussion, I will turn to the nature of historiography, here understood as historical scholarship and writing, in order to examine the foundation of history as a scientific discipline in Meiji Japan in a global context.

The Bigger Picture (2): National History and Scientific History

Before I move on to my second major theme, a word about 'science'.[75] One of my greatest dilemmas in preparing the English version of my work was the problem of translating the German word 'Wissenschaft'. I did not

---

[74] Christopher L. Hill, *National History and the World of Nations: Capital, State, and the Rhetoric of History in Japan, France, and the United States* (Durham and London: Duke University Press, 2008): 53. Neither Shigeno nor Kume appear in the index.

[75] See also Richard J. Evans, *In Defence of History* (new edition with an extensive new afterword) ed. (London: Granta Books, 2000 (1997)): 45.

fully realize the broader scope of the word, compared to 'science', until I casually referred to history as a 'science' during a conversation with a fellow historian from Canada in the Komaba dormitory for foreign students, only to be told that history was definitely not a science. To be sure, the title of the book written by the Hungarian G.G. Zerffi in 1879 for the members of the Office of Historiography was entitled, *The Science of History*. But the discipline of history is not commonly described as a 'science' in the English-speaking world (nor are the other humanities disciplines, such as literature or music). On the other hand, it is usual to speak of the 'social sciences', which are sometimes taken to include history. Then there are 'human sciences', used synonymously with 'social sciences' or else taken to include the humanities.[76] It appears that in the Anglophone world as well, the need for a term that covers the same ground as *Wissenschaft* is felt, and the adjective 'scientific' (often in quotation marks) is sometimes used in connection with the humanities, in order to describe the changes they underwent in the course of the nineteenth century. The characteristics that make history a science in the sense of *Wissenschaft* are 'an organized body of knowledge acquired through research carried out according to generally agreed methods, presented in published reports and subjected to peer review'.[77] Many, if not most, historians would agree that history is a Wissenschaft in this sense, even if they simultaneously share some of the postmodernist scepticism about truth and the possibility of researchers ever ascertaining it.[78]

---

[76] Mazlish, *The Uncertain Sciences*, 7; Rens Bod, *A New History of the Humanities: The Search for Principles and Patterns from Antiquity to the Present* (Oxford: Oxford University Press, 2015 (2013)): 4.

[77] Evans, *In Defence of History*, 73.

[78] When I first started work on the English edition as a postdoctoral fellow at Cambridge (1991–93; incidentally, the controversial award of an honorary doctorate to Jacques Derrida in 1992 was a topic of discussion at college dining tables during that time), I read numerous works about the nature of history and historical knowledge, from diehards like Sir Geoffrey Elton and Arthur Marwick to radicals like Keith Jenkins, without feeling much the wiser: G.R. Elton, *The Practice of History* (London: Fontana Press, 1989 (1967)); Arthur Marwick, *The Nature of History*, 3rd edn.(London: Macmillan, 1989); Keith Jenkins, *Rethinking History* (London: Routledge, 1991). One of the best discussions addressing both ends of the spectrum is Evans, *In Defence of History*. Newer texts that likewise adopt a balanced view and ultimately defend history as a *Wissenschaft* include Knut Kjeldstadli, *Fortiden er ikke hvad den har været: en*

The problem remains that *Wissenschaft* has long been broader in its meaning than 'science'. Still, in the English translation of Osterhammel's global history, *Wissenschaft* has been translated as 'science', and in the following discussion, 'science' should be understood in the broad sense of *Wissenschaft*.

The rise of science is one of the common characteristics of modernity. While much has been written about the natural sciences and a fair amount about the social sciences, a general history of the humanities is, in the words of Rens Bod, who published the first such work in 2010, 'conspicuous by its absence'.[79] Bod's groundbreaking work, in which he has made a commendable effort to include developments outside Europe, provides a useful basis for re-examining the history of historiography in Japan in a broader context. Bod emphasizes systematization and institutionalization as the most important innovations of the nineteenth century. He even concludes, 'If there was anything like a revolution, it was on the institutional rather than on a conceptual level'.[80] On the institutional level, moreover, developments in the nineteenth century applied equally to the natural (and the social) sciences and the humanities, namely the systematization of academic disciplines and the emergence of research institutions (particularly the research university with its science laboratories and humanities seminars), of the scientist as a new social type and of an increasingly global scientific community. In fact, the very concept of science as distinct from other kinds of knowledge acquisition was new, characterised by 'an emphasis on the conditional validity, intersubjectivity and autonomy of knowledge'.[81]

Bod questions the prevailing assumption of a major conceptual break in modern times; indeed, he emphasizes continuing trends from antiquity to modern times, such as the quest for patterns (and at the same time a parallel tradition of pattern-rejection). The contribution of Ranke to

---

indføring i historiefaget (Frederiksberg: Roskilde Universitets Forlag, 2002); John Tosh, *The Pursuit of History* (Revised Third Edition) (London: Longman, 2002); Ludmilla Jordanova, *History in Practice*, 2nd edn (London: Hodder Arnold, 2006).

[79] Bod, *New History*. The 2010 Dutch version is thus aptly named *De Vergeten Wetenschappen* (The forgotten sciences).

[80] Ibid., 348.

[81] Osterhammel, *Die Verwandlung der Welt*: 1106. ———, *Transformation of the World*: 780.

historiography, for example, lay in the systematization and proliferation of existing practices.[82] Bod does not, however, downplay the importance of the changes in the way the subjects of the humanities were investigated. The central role of textual criticism ('philologization' in Bod's words) in the new discipline of history represented a new paradigm, and the basis for historiography's claim to objectivity. At the same time, philology changed from a classical discipline into a national one, just as history increasingly became national history.[83]

Bod's outline of Rankean historiography is not in itself new; the innovation lies in the way he treats historiography in the broader context of the humanities in general and their interaction with the natural sciences, which in the nineteenth century became the model not only for the social sciences, but also to some extent for the humanities. Bod even describes source criticism, so central to scientific history, as one of the world-changing contributions of the humanities.[84] And, as he points out, the humanities in the form they took in nineteenth-century Europe (like the natural and social sciences), came to dominate the rest of the world.

The transformation of philology from a classical into a national discipline, and, we might add, the formation of the scientific discipline of history as a national discipline in the nineteenth century, characterized Meiji Japan as well. It is in part a result of Western influence, but the development of Japanese Learning (*kokugaku*) as a challenge to Chinese Learning (*kangaku*) in the Edo period represents another example of pre-existing trends. Both Japanese Learning and Chinese Learning were transformed into a series of new academic disciplines, including the history of the East (*tōyōshi*) and national literature (*kokubungaku*) among others. Chinese-style chronicles of ruling houses (whether imperial or shogunal) gave way to national history, as Chinese-derived imperial ideals gave way to the concept of a world of nations.[85] And in Japan, just as in Europe, the liberation from previous yokes achieved by embracing nationalism resulted in a new yoke

---

[82] Bod, *New History*, 347–8.
[83] Ibid., 250, 251.
[84] Ibid., 352.
[85] For a discussion of the imperial imagination at the time of the Yamato imperial court, see Torquil Duthie, *Man'yōshū and the Imperial Imagination in Early Japan* (Leiden: Brill, 2014). For Meiji Japan, see Shillony, 'The Meiji Restoration: Japan's attempt to inherit China'.

that all too soon proved equally limiting.[86] As long as nations were taken as given, however, nationalism did not necessarily appear as a yoke.

One might ask how far *kangaku* scholars of Shigeno's and Kume's generation took the nation as given at all, given that they had lived their formative years within a different frame of reference. These scholars themselves and the whole project of a government-sponsored history in the dynastic tradition might be described as representing a transition from one cognitive map to another and being engulfed in a major epistemic shift while simultaneously contributing to it. Possibly, Kume was more aware of this than Shigeno (and his other colleagues), and his experience of travel abroad with the Iwakura Embassy may well have been the main reason for this. I believe I might have underrated this when I wrote *History and the State*, although I did note the broad scope of Kume's writings.[87]

The narrative in *History and the State* effectively ends in 1895; Chapter 6.6, about the textbook controversy, is included because of its significance to the story of conflict between scientific history and national ideology and because several of the scholars I discuss were involved in the debates. The closure of the Institute in 1893 and its reopening in 1895 marked the end of the transitional phase and a new departure for the former Office of Historiography.

Equally significantly, perhaps, 1895 marked a turning point for Japan as a nation. By the time the Historiographical Institute reopened, Japan had won its victory against China, an event that was celebrated as a new beginning. Scholars who had recently been engaged in lively discussions about history and historiography during what contemporaries diagnosed as a 'history fever', such as Kume Kunitake and Tsubouchi Shōyō, were among the first to discuss the significance of the victory in the new journal *Taiyō*.[88] It may well be that Japan's new departure on the road to empire –

---

[86] Bod, *New History*, 357.

[87] In the German version, I devote an entire section to Kume as a historian: Mehl, *Vergangenheit*, 180–9.

[88] Marius B. Jansen, 'Changing Japanese Attitudes toward Modernization', in *Changing Japanese Attitudes toward Modernization*, ed. Marius Jansen (Princeton: Princeton University Press, 1964): 74–5. See Margaret Mehl, 'The mid-Meiji "history boom": professionalization of historical scholarship and growing pains of an emerging academic discipline', *Japan Forum* 10.1 (1998): 67–83.

the victory over China resulted in its first foreign colony, Taiwan – gave impetus to the next generation of academic historians, with the result that at least some of them did play a major role in 'interpreting the nation' in the context of Japan's newly won empire. One might even say that the victory changed the goalposts for writing national history, since now not only the Japanese nation itself, but also its claims to dominance in East Asia had to be legitimated. In *Japanese Historians and the National Myths, 1600–1945*, published at around the same time as *History and the State*, John S. Brownlee analyses the positions of Mikami Sanji, Kuroita Katsumi and Tsuji Zennosuke (all of whom were employed in the Historiographical Institute at some time in their careers) and shows how, to varying degrees, these historians accepted the distorted view of history propagated by the state.[89] Kuroita's work shows that historians of the *akademizumu* school did in fact contribute to interpreting the nation. This is also evident from Lisa Yoshikawa's work, which shows that Kuroita played a significant part in the public representation of national history even while insisting on scientific research.[90] His wide-ranging activities included publishing historical works for a larger audience, commemorating historical figures and participating in research and writing on Korean history, all of which helped to legitimize not only the emperor state but also Japan's dominance over Korea. Kuroita's activities suggest active complicity rather than submission in a repressive political climate: far from being passive in the shadow of a state-sanctioned national history, he was one of its architects.

A similar role of complicity in the Japanese colonization of Korea is described for Kita Sadakichi (1871–1939), the historian whose lecture sparked off the 1911 textbook controversy about the treatment of the Northern and Southern Imperial courts in medieval Japan.[91] Unlike

---

[89] John S. Brownlee, *Japanese Historians and the National Myths, 1600–1945: the Age of the Gods and Emperor Jimmu* (Vancouver: University of British Columbia Press, 1997). See also Margaret Mehl, 'Review: Brownlee, Japanese Historians and the National Myths, 1600–1945', *Monumenta Nipponica* 53.4 (1998): 554–7.

[90] Lisa Yoshikawa, 'Kuroita Katsumi and his State-sanctioned National History' (Yale University, 2007). ———, *Making History Matter: Kuroita Katsumi and the Construction of Imperial Japan* (Yale: Harvard University Asia Center, 2017).

[91] Etsuko H. Kang, 'Kita Sadakichi (1871–1939) on Korea: A Japanese Ethno-Historian and the Annexation of Korea in 1910', *Asian Studies Review* 21.1 (2007): 41–60.

Yoshikawa, however, the author, Etsuko Kang, does not discuss the quality of Kita's historiography as scholarship, raising the question of whether she regards this as irrelevant comparted to Kita's political engagement.

As Japan became a colonial power, it also exported its version of modern historical science to the colonies. In Korea, for example, Japanese historians conducted research into the origins of the local culture with the aim of proving that Korea was a natural part of the Japanese empire. While their interpretation of Korean history was roundly rejected by Korean scholars after 1945, the work of Japanese scholars in collecting and preserving primary sources (texts and artefacts) represented a lasting contribution to research into Korean history, for use by Korean historians in their efforts to demonstrate Korean distinctness. In this endeavour they are often caught up in the same framework of methodological nationalism and the 'colonial historical and anthropological paradigms of racial invasions and territorial conquests to explain cultural change' as the Japanese scholars whose versions of Korean history they reject.[92]

Lessons from the History of History?
In the introduction to *History and the State* I predict that 'for some time to come the story of history and national identity will be an ongoing one', and I conclude the book by observing, 'In the end the tensions experienced by Shigeno and his colleagues attempting to write a history for their nation – between truth and myth, fact and interpretation, disinterestedness and partisanship, science and art, research and writing – have to be confronted by historians in every time and place'.[93]

In fact, as I was working on the book, developments in Japan provided ample illustration of both statements. In 1990–91 the 'comfort women' issue, until then essentially one of historical scholarship, turned into a political problem when, in response to calls for an investigation, Prime Minister Kaifu Toshiki claimed that the government and the military had

---

[92] Hyung Il Pai, *Constructing "Korean" Origins: A Critical Review of Archaeology, Historiography, and Racial Myth in Korean State-Formation Theories* (Cambridge, Massachusetts: Harvard University Press, 2000): 56.

[93] Mehl, *History and the State*, 15, 166.

played no part in forcing the women into prostitution. Kaifu was proved wrong, not only by the testimonies of former comfort women (the first one publicly told of her experience in 1991), but also by the investigations of the historian Yoshimi Yoshiaki. Yoshimi discovered the first official document that proved the military's involvement, and subsequent research revealed the extent of state and military complicity.[94] Since then, the comfort women controversy has never been out the media for long. The agreement between the governments of Japan and South Korea in December 2015 and the joint statement of their foreign ministers that the issue had now been 'resolved once and for all' have done little to resolve the problem.[95] This became evident when, only months later, verdicts were handed down in two court cases involving historians and their scholarly work on the comfort women. Yoshimi Yoshiaki, a well-known Japanese historian on the subject, had sued a right-wing Diet member for libel, because he had denounced Yoshimi's work as 'fabrication'. On the other hand, a Korean scholar, Park Yu-ha, was sued for her interpretation of the comfort women's perception of their role at the time.[96]

The treatment of Japan's wartime aggression in history textbooks has likewise proved a hardy perennial. From the mid-1990s, right-wing politicians attacked textbooks that included references, however brief, to the comfort women. The most salient neo-nationalist initiative was the launch in 1996 of the Atarashii Rekishi Kyōkasho o Tsukurukai (The Japanese Society for History Textbook Reform, hereafter Tsukurukai) by Fujioka Nobukatsu, professor of education at the University of Tokyo, and others. Their aim was to publish a junior high school textbook that broke with the allegedly 'masochistic' view of Japanese history found in

---

[94] Mark Selden and Yoshiko Nozaki, 'Japanese Textbook Controversies, Nationalism, and Historical Memory: Intra- and Inter-national Conflicts', *The Asia Pacific Journal: Japan Focus* 7.24.5 (2009): 1–24, 10.

[95] 'Japan, South Korea reach "final" deal to settle "comfort women" issue', *The Japan Times*, 28 December 2015.

[96] Jordan Sand, 'A Year of Memory Politics in East Asia: Looking Back on the "Open Letter in Support of Historians in Japan"', *The Asia-Pacific Journal* 16.9.3 (2016). The phenomenon of history in the courtroom is not limited to Japan and Korea; for a European example relating to Holocaust denial, see John Tosh, *Why History Matters* (Houndmills: Palgrave Macmillan, 2008): 107–8.

current textbooks, a criticism which, by the way, was not unique to Japan: similar criticism of the way national history was portrayed in textbooks was voiced at around the same time in the United States and Australia.[97] *Atarashii Rekishi Kyōkasho* was duly licensed in 2001, although few schools adopted it. Meanwhile, an edition for the general public (*shihanbon*) published in 2001 became an instant bestseller.[98]

Despite my having turned my research interests to other topics, it could not, of course, escape my notice that the members of Tsukurukai included Itō Takashi, formerly my supervisor at the University of Tokyo, whom I have so much to thank for.[99] When I first met him in October 1987, he had long secured his fame as a scholar working tirelessly to unearth historical documents and ensure that they were safely archived, catalogued and made accessible to historians. Or, in the more down-to-earth words of a student in the department of Western history at Tokyo University: 'nikki no suki na hito' (the guy who likes diaries). In 2015 he published a memoir with the telling subtitle, 'Reminiscences of a historian who has deeply engaged with historical sources (*shiryō*)'.[100] Clearly, his achievements in securing primary documents for future research are what he wishes to be remembered for. And yet, asking myself why he had teamed up with such unsavoury nationalists and amateur historians as Fujioka Nobukatsu and Kobayashi Yoshinori,[101] I was uncannily reminded of the prewar scientific historians who both pursued scientific, source-based historical research and collaborated in the creation of myth-history

---

[97] Margaret MacMillan, *The Uses and Abuses of History* (London: Profile Books, 2010 (2008)).

[98] Janet Ashby, 'Controversial textbooks are big sellers for Fusosha', *The Japan Times*, 15 July 2001.

[99] He was a board member until 2006, when he resigned because of the continuous internal conflicts, but subsequently participated in other associations with similar aims. For his views on the most controversial topics in connection with Japan's role in the war (based on an interview conducted by the authors in March 2010), see Gi-Wook Shin and Daniel Sneider, *Divergent Memories: Opinion Leaders and the Asia-Pacific War* (Redwood City: Stanford University Press, 2016).

[100] Itō Takashi, *Rekishi to Watakushi: Shiryō o ayunda rekishika no kaisō* (Tokyo: Chūō Kōron Shinsha, 2015).

[101] Fujioka is a scholar of education and Kobayashi a manga artist; professional historians are, in fact, almost 'wholly absent from the ranks of historical revisionists'. Sven Saaler, 'Nationalism and History in Contemporary Japan', *The Asia Pacific Journal: Japan Focus* 14.20 (2016): 8–9.

in the service of the nation.[102] Certainly, government suppression could not serve as an explanation here.

The present Abe government, however, does appear to be curtailing freedom of expression. Its efforts to influence history education have extended to history textbooks even in the United States, where it has attempted to suppress passages about the comfort women in a world history textbook. In response to what was perceived as a massive campaign of denial of Japan's wartime aggression by right-wing politicians and media, a group of mostly North American scholars of Japan released an 'Open Letter in Support of Historians in Japan'. It was eventually signed by over 500 supporters, including many from Europe.[103] The letter received more attention from the Japanese media than the signers had anticipated and was both praised and criticized. Reflecting a year later on his and his colleagues' role and on the criticisms, the historian Jordan Sand considered the broader issue of history education and nationalism and the role of the historian in public debates. He concluded that 'the record of our influence in the public sphere appears ambiguous' and that academic historians might do better to concentrate on their role in the classroom.[104] This sounds disconcertingly like Mikami Sanji, who one hundred years ago drew the curtains of his lecture room to emphasize the separation of academic history from public history.

But should professional historians really retreat from public debates about history? Two eminent historians, Margaret MacMillan and John Tosh, who in 2008 published books about public history, have argued that professional historians should not leave the field to amateurs.[105] *The Uses and Abuses of History* and *Why History Matters* differ in their approaches and emphasis, but the most important message is the same: history matters and professional historians' contribution to public history matters because they are trained to work with causality and sequence, both crucial to history,

---

[102] However, despite the textbook's serious flaws (I myself published a short critique: Margaret Mehl, 'The Right History? Historical Scholarship and History Education in Japan', *NIAS nytt* 4 (2002): 10–11.) , claiming that it perpetrates myth-history would be overstating the case.

[103] The initiators deliberately refrained from seeking signatures in East Asian countries: see Sand, 'Year of Memory Politics'.

[104] Ibid.

[105] MacMillan, *The Uses and Abuses of History*; Tosh, *Why History Matters*.

to deal with complexities, to highlight historical context as well as the otherness of the past and to challenge assumptions and point out alternatives.[106] Both authors stress the importance of reliable historical knowledge as a basis for responsible citizenship. Tosh describes history as 'a critical resource for the active citizen in a representative democracy'.[107] This is his main thrust. The historian's task as he sees it is to disseminate reliable knowledge of the past that is relevant to issues of the day and to promote 'thinking with history' and historical awareness. While he acknowledges history's potential to give 'a sense of belonging', he sees the aim of history education not so much as fostering loyalty, but rather as developing citizens able to form a 'considered and informed view of matters of public concern'. He ends by urging historians to become more engaged in public history, concluding that '(t)he prize is a critically armed and better informed public, providing the basis for a revitalized democratic culture'.[108]

Tosh thus offers a solution to the dilemma of how history education can both be based on scientific history and serve the interests of the nation (at least, a nation that values democracy). The Tsukurukai's main criticism of existing history textbooks was that their portrayal of Japan's past was not suitable for fostering a positive attitude to Japan, a criticism that rests on the assumption that the purpose of history education is to promote patriotism. If this notion is abandoned in favour of educating critical citizens, then the question of how to represent those aspects of the past which show the nation in a less than positive light will lose much of its sting.

Both MacMillan and Tosh (and they surely speak for most professional historians) more or less directly defend history as a science. Precisely their professional scientific training, however, can cause historians to shy away from engaging in public or 'applied' history, just as it makes them reluctant to write 'big history'.[109] They find it difficult to reconcile

---

[106] MacMillan, *The Uses and Abuses of History*, 38, 39, 167–9. See also Tosh, *Why History Matters*, 22–3.

[107] MacMillan, *The Uses and Abuses of History*, 165; Tosh, *Why History Matters*, ix.

[108] Tosh, *Why History Matters*, 140, 143.

[109] While Tosh cites the nature of historical science as one of the reasons for professional historians' reluctance to engage in public history, Osterhammel states that the professionalization of historical science has made historians shy away from 'Big History'. See Ibid., 17–22; Osterhammel, *Die Verwandlung der Welt*, 14–15; ———, *Transformation of the World*, xv–xvi.

detailed examination of the primary sources with generalizations and sustained interpretative work.[110] If, however, the aim is to make the fruits of historical research relevant to the public (or even just to scholars with other specializations) then to 'stop too soon' may well result in missed opportunities for learning from history. On the other hand, if historians can convince the public that 'the merit of history lies in opening rather than in closing questions – in revealing options rather than insisting on answers',[111] then they need not fear applied history as a threat to their professional integrity.

Here, then, is perhaps the main reason why I believe my detailed study of historiography in the service of the Meiji state is important and relevant. The history of scientific history and the emergence of the historical profession matter because professional, scientific history matters. The ways in which Japan's earliest representatives of the modern historical profession attempted (and ultimately failed) to combine their new professional ethos with serving the equally new constitutional nation state matter, because the essential challenge of upholding 'the core principles of historical enquiry'[112] and at the same time contributing to public debate is still our challenge as historians today.

History and the State offers a glimpse into the thoughts and preoccupations of scholars in Japan who lived much of their life before 1868, in a world that was in many ways quite different from the world that was emerging towards the end of that century. In their lifetime they saw their country transform itself into a modern nation and then into a major imperial power. For their successors, Japan's position has presented different kinds of challenges in the search for meaning, as it in turn became a defeated nation, an economic superpower, a country in crisis. By the turn of the millennium Western countries presented neither models to emulate nor the likeliest threat to Japan's security. Global challenges necessitate global responses and thus cooperation between nations. The historians discussed in *History and the State*, while aware of being part

---

[110] Many historians do succeed in demonstrating the wider implications of their detailed studies based on close reading of the primary sources: for examples of how such studies have contributed to our understanding of modern Japan, see Akita, *Evaluating Evidence*, 65–124.
[111] Tosh, *Why History Matters*.
[112] Ibid., 22.

of a wider world of nations, were preoccupied with the history of their own nation.

Historians today do well to treat even national history, whether of their own nation or of another, as global history, not only by being aware of the global dimensions of a nation's history, but by accepting that national history is an international concern.[113] Ideally, history will contribute to the education of informed and critical world citizens rather than merely citizens of a nation. The way national history is told and taught affects the coexistence between nations and thus our global future.

---

[113] Both MacMillan and Tosh discuss history and international relations: MacMillan, *The Uses and Abuses of History*; Tosh, *Why History Matters*.

Notes on the New Edition

For reasons explained in my 'Preface to the New Edition', the text of the first edition of *History and the State* has been left largely intact apart from conservative copy-editing and the correction of obvious mistakes. An effort has been made to eliminate obvious inconsistencies in the transcription of Japanese terms, but generally they have been left as they were, even if they do not conform to the most common conventions for English-language publications.

While revisiting *History and the State* I corresponded with the Japanese scholars who have been preparing a Japanese translation for submission to Tokyo University Press. Their thoroughness has been both gratifying and embarrassing. Fortunately they do not seem to have discovered any major flaws in my work. Their comments have led me to reword a few passages (which I have not pointed out one by one) as well as to correct a number of inconsistencies and mistakes in the references. One point of terminology should probably be addressed. In *History and the State* I generally use the term 'historiography' in a broad sense of 'doing' history, including both research and writing, especially the latter. With the meaning of 'writing history', historiography also serves as a translation of the Japanese word *shūshi*. The Japanese translators rightly point out that I do not distinguish between *shūshi* and *shiron* (theoretical discussions of history, historical treatise). I see no need to do this in English, since the meaning of 'historiography' is broad enough to cover both.

'Today' in the 1998 edition obviously refers to the 1990s. Some things have changed since then, others have not, but I have left it to the reader to reflect upon. Among the most salient changes is that the rise of the internet has made many historical sources more easily accessible. Among

---

[114] https://www.hi.u-tokyo.ac.jp/index.html (English), accessed 17 January 2017.

the most important ones are the digitalized publications of the Meiji period available through the National Diet Library as well as the sources held by the Historiographical Institute, many of which are now available electronically, including the document collection *Shiryō hensan shimatsu*, one of my main sources. When I embarked on my project I had a hard time gaining access to materials relating to the Institute's history, namely the *Shiryō hensan shimatsu*, which until that time were only accessible to the Institute's own employees. Fortunately, my request to examine them came at a time when their declassification was being considered, and eventually I was given permission to consult them. Among my fondest memories of that time is virtually racing the veteran historian Ōkubo Toshiaki, then well into his eighties, to the Institute's reading room counter in order to obtain the volume of my choice before he did. Professor Ōkubo was at this time revising – and sometimes rewriting – his writings on the history of historiography for Volume 7 of his collected works.

Information about the Historiographical Institute itself is likewise available, in English as well as Japanese, on the Institute's website.[114] The short Appendix entitled 'Hints for Using the Historiographical Institute' has been therefore been omitted.

Finally, a note about the jacket illustration of the first edition of *History and the State*: it represents the Imperial Rescript on Historiography of 1869, which I introduce and translate on page 1 of the book. As two of the reviewers cited previously noted, half of it is upside down. This is actually a result of the way the rescript was written, that is, on a piece of paper which is folded in the middle with the direction of the (vertical) writing running downwards from the fold. Images of this document, including the one on the Historiographical Institute's homepage, invariably show the second part of the text upside down.

Acknowledgements

I can only reiterate my thanks expressed in the earlier editions, especially to Itō Takashi and Hōya Tōru, who have continued to help me whenever I approached them with queries. At the Historiographical Institute I am also indebted to Kondō Shigekazu (recently moved to the The Open University of Japan), whose generous help over the years has even included translating my paper (delivered in Japanese but submitted in English) for the Institute's publication, *Rekishigaku to rekishi kenkyū* (2003).

Furthermore, my thanks go to the authors of the forthcoming Japanese translation of *History and the State*, Chiba Isao and Matsuzawa Yūsaku, with whom I corresponded while preparing this edition for publication, as well as Chung Nyung, Eshita Ichiko, Katō Yūki, Kobyashi Noburu, Mitsumatsu Makato and Nakano Hiroki.

Thanks also to Tessa Carroll for the copy-editing, David Stuligross for proofreading, Ian Taylor of Taylormade Book Production for typesetting and Anthony Horton for an index that far surpasses my feeble effort in the first edition of *History and the State*.

Preface to the 1998 Edition

When I published my doctoral dissertation, *Eine Vergangenheit für die japanische Nation. Die Entstehung des historischen Forschungsinstituts Tōkyō daigaku Shiryō hensanjo (1869–1895)* (Frankfurt am Main etc.: Peter Lang, 1992), I announced in the preface that I intended to publish a revised version in English. It has taken me longer than anticipated to do so. I have revised the original work extensively. The first and last chapters have been rewritten from scratch. Other chapters have been rewritten in part; I have omitted much biographical detail on the members of the Office of Historiography, including two entire chapters, on Shigeno Yasutsugu and Kawada Takeshi and on Kume Kunitake. Detailed summaries of articles in the historical journal *Shigaku zasshi* have also been omitted. In some cases I have been able to shorten my own summaries and refer to recent publications, for example in the chapter on the Kume Affair. Other chapters that are substantially different from the original version are the chapters on the *Dainihon hennenshi* (4.5), on *akademizumu* (5.4) and on history and the public (6.1). Finally, I have made an effort to address some of the questions I raised in the original version without dealing with them. Some changes are in response to reviews of the German book, and I thank the reviewers for their constructive criticism.

This book would not have been possible without the help of more people than I can name individually. My original research was supported by grants from the Japanese Ministry of Education and the German Scholarship Foundation. In all the libraries and archives I used, I found the staff very patient and helpful. At the Historiographical Institute I am especially indebted to Mr Hōya Tōru, who assisted me not only in locating obscure sources but also in understanding their contents. Professor Josef Kreiner, my supervisor at the University of Bonn, and Professor Itō

Takashi, my adviser while I was studying at the University of Tokyo from 1987 to 1989, have continued to offer their advice and assistance generously. I am especially grateful to Professor Ōkubo Toshiaki, who was still giving me valuable hints for my research shortly before his death. That I cannot present him with a copy of this book is my main reason for regretting that I did not finish it earlier; I dedicate it to his memory.

MARGARET MEHL
Edinburgh

Note on Japanese Names and Terms

Japanese terms are transcribed according to the Hepburn system, Chinese terms according to the Pinyin system, but without indicating the tones. Diacritics signifying long vowels are essential in romanizing Japanese; they are indicated with Ō, ō and ū, except in a few well-known place names. Japanese personal names are given in the Japanese order, family names first. To avoid confusion, I refer to the 'Office of Historiography' irrespective of its Japanese name for the period from 1875 to 1888 and thereafter to the 'Historiographical Institute'.

1

Introduction

The Meiji Restoration in 1868 heralded a new era in Japanese history: the Tokugawa shoguns, who had ruled Japan for 250 years, were overthrown, and a new government was established in the name of the emperor. The profound changes that followed are often described with the words Westernization and modernization. Nevertheless the new government not only looked to the West and to the future but also to Japan itself and the past. In April 1869, the following imperial rescript was issued:

> Historiography is a forever immortal state ritual (*taiten*) and a wonderful act of our ancestors. But after the Six National Histories it was interrupted and no longer continued. Is this not a great lack! Now the evil of misrule by the warriors since the Kamakura period has been overcome and imperial government has been restored. Therefore we wish that an office of historiography (*shikyoku*) be established, that the good custom of our ancestors be resumed and that knowledge and education be spread throughout the land, and so we appoint a president. Let us set right the relations between monarch and subject, distinguish clearly between the alien and the proper (*ka'i naigai*) and implant virtue throughout our land.[1]

Why did the new government take such an interest in writing history just one year after the Restoration? The rescript itself gives us part of the answer: history is seen as an important task of a legitimate government; a clear connection is established between the restoration of imperial rule and the revival of historiography, referring to the time of the imperial bureaucratic state of ancient Japan, when historiography was the task of a legitimate ruler. Furthermore, a written history is seen to serve a purpose in government: it promotes knowledge, education and understanding of the relationship between monarch and subject and generally establishes what is appropriate behaviour and what is not – *ka'i naigai* refers both to what is morally right and wrong and to what is appropriate to Japan, as opposed to other countries. The wording of the rescript suggests the reinstatement and stabilization of a previous order which assigned everyone to their own place in the state and Japan to its place in the world. This was in fact what the Meiji Restoration was intended to achieve, an ideal that is reflected in the term first used for the events, *ōsei fukko* (restoration of imperial rule).

At the time the rescript was issued, the leaders of the Meiji Restoration, members of the court nobility and samurai from the domains of Satsuma, Tosa, Hizen and Chōshū had not yet secured fully their power to determine the fate of the country; the bakufu forces had only just been overthrown and the former feudal domains still retained much of their independence. Not until the abolition of the domains and the establishment of the prefectures in 1871 did the Meiji government consolidate its jurisdiction over the entire country and its populace and the control of the revenues and military strength of the former domains. The reforms introduced in the years following the Restoration changed Japan so profoundly that some scholars speak of a revolution rather than a restoration, and in fact the term commonly used in Japan (*ishin*) means 'renewal'.[2]

Nevertheless, to justify their actions, the leaders of the Restoration preferred the term *fukko* at the time.[3] The first new government institutions after 1868 were modelled on those of the Nara and early Heian periods, that is from the eighth century to the eleventh, when imperial power was at its height. They were gradually changed or replaced by institutions more suited to meet modern needs. Of the ancient practices revived, official historiography in the tradition of the Six National Histories, compiled between the eighth and early tenth centuries, endured for longer than most. The first office of historiography, established at the time of the rescript, was soon abolished, but a new office replaced it and was reorganized several times, until in 1888 it was transferred to the Imperial University (today the University of Tokyo). In 1895 it became what is now the Historiographical Institute at the University of Tokyo (*Tōkyō daigaku Shiryō hensanjo*), a research institute dedicated to the collection and publication of historical sources. This supposedly traditional office produced the first professional historians and played an important role in the emergence of history as a modern academic discipline in its own right.

The changes the original Office of Historiography underwent were closely linked to the political developments in the two decades following the Meiji Restoration (Chapter 2). The Restoration had been brought about partly because of the inability of the bakufu to cope with the threat from Western powers. Among the goals of the Meiji leaders, striving to stand up and become equal to Western countries by learning from them was foremost. They accepted the fact that they would have to borrow heavily from the West in order to become a 'rich country' with a 'strong army' (*fukoku kyōhei*). At the same time they were aware of the need to preserve Japanese identity while borrowing heavily from the West. It was here that history had an important role to play.

More than ten years after the rescript was issued and after several attempts to organize effectively the work on a national history, in January 1882, work was finally begun on an official history of Japan, the *Dainihon hennenshi* (*Chronological History of Great Japan*). By then Japan was well on its way to establishing a constitution and parliament along Western lines; the need to root the new political order in tradition can be seen behind a renewed interest in Japan's cultural heritage at this time, of which the history was just one expression. The year in which the constitution was finally proclaimed, 1889, also saw the establishment of a department of Japanese history at the Imperial University, where the Office of Historiography had been transferred the previous year. This was more than a coincidence. While the Meiji Constitution set Japan firmly on the route toward a constitutional monarchy according to Western models, the study of Japan's past became an academic discipline in its own right and would ensure that new developments were rooted in the country's own heritage.

At first, work on the official history *Dainihon hennenshi* continued as before, but the transfer of the Office spelled the beginning of the end of official historiography in the tradition of the Six National Histories. Already, within the former government office, the emphasis had shifted from historiography to the compilation of source materials, and from 1885 members of the Office had begun travelling all over Japan to collect primary documents. In 1893, following the so-called 'Kume Affair' the year before, the Institute was closed and, when it reopened in 1895 (Chapter 6.5), its defined aims were much the same as they are today, that is, researching, compiling and publishing historical documents.

The emergence of Japan as a modern nation state and of the study of history as an academic discipline pursued by professional historians are closely linked. History had an important function: it legitimized political change by representing it as an outgrowth of tradition and it was expected to provide answers to questions about Japan's position and future course in the world.

The link between historical scholarship and the nation state is by no means unique to Japan. In her opening chapter of *Japan's Modern Myths*, Carol Gluck points out that Japan's development around 1890, when according to the British historian Geoffrey Barraclough, the world entered the contemporary era, in many ways paralleled that of several Western nations. The decades around 1890 saw the profound changes that make the contemporary era fundamentally different from the preceding ones: industrialization, the emergence of a mass society and of new political forms and of an ideology that stressed national unity. In Japan, as in France and Germany, ideologists sought national unity and 'inner spiritual revival' and Meiji ideology's insistence on 'social conformity as the binding principle of national loyalty' was not unlike American nativism.[4]

Thus, the emergence of a national ideology in late nineteenth-century Japan was not unique and must be seen in the context of the newly contemporary world described by Barraclough. In this process Japan, rather than following the West, appears as contemporaneous with it. What Gluck says about ideology in general seems equally true in the field of historical writing and scholarship, which received major impulses from the nationalist ideology beginning to take shape. Moreover, historiography and the establishment of history as an academic discipline were directly influenced by the study of history in the West. In examining this influence, two points are important. One is that when Japan imported ideas and concepts from the West, it imported them as they manifested themselves at that particular point in time, without always recognizing how they had developed and changed over the centuries. The second point is that it was not necessarily the content of a system of ideas that attracted Japanese attention, but the function it had within the Western society of the time. It is therefore important to understand what the state of historical studies in Europe was in the late nineteenth century and what the function of history was within the nation state.

If one general experience characterized nineteenth-century Europe, it was the accelerated pace of change generated by the revolutionary upheavals at the turn of the century and the developments we associate with the emergence of contemporary society.[5] This experience profoundly changed thought and transformed the study and writing of history in Europe. The revolutions showed how much human behaviour and social institutions were subject to change. As some of the economic and social costs of change became apparent, the Enlightenment's belief in progress was questioned. The assumption of natural laws governing political order was also given up. Origins and developments became a focus of interest, and tradition and historic law came to be regarded as the basis for political order. At the same time there was a romantic yearning for the past, typified in historical novels, but also in the desire to fully understand past periods in their own right. The pragmatic view of history as a series of causes and effects was followed by an idealist philosophy of history. The increase in knowledge about past and present human societies widened the scope of historical interest. All fields in the humanities were studied in their historical dimension.

The above developments form the background for the approach to the humanities in general and history in particular known as 'historicism', which dominated nineteenth-century thought and the emergence of history as an academic discipline in this period. In the broadest sense, historicism means a way of thinking that aims at understanding the characteristics of past periods as distinct from the present and the relationship between these periods. History is seen as a succession of individual, distinct periods in one continuing development. This view of history characterized the new academic discipline as it established itself at university level.[6]

The name most commonly associated with the formation of the modern discipline of history and with its establishment at university level is that of Leopold von Ranke. In his seminars in Berlin he taught research techniques based on the analysis of historical texts. As research techniques developed in other disciplines (Ranke himself had studied theology and philology) were applied to the study of history, they came to be regarded as the only legitimate basis for serious historical writing. Ranke's seminars became the model for the teaching of history all over Europe and in North America and, by the second half of the century, history was becoming an independent discipline throughout the Western world – and, as this book will show, in Japan.

The rise of historical research based on primary texts was aided, if not made possible by the opening of archives, which provided an unprecedented wealth of sources.[7] Arranging, cataloguing and publishing these sources to make them available for research became an important task increasingly carried out by professional historians in institutions sponsored by the state, such as the Historical Commission in the Bavarian Academy of Science established by King Maximilian II, and headed by Ranke until his death (Chapter 7.2).

Historicism and the professionalization of history it promoted evolved at the same time as the modern nation state, a connection that has frequently been pointed out.[8] History served to define national identity by using the past to guide the present and the future.[9] In this function, historical scholarship was only one aspect of using tradition, whether discovered, invented, reinvented or otherwise, to legitimize the nation and to represent it to its citizens. The nation was a recent construct;[10] it was moreover too large a community to be tangible to the individual and needed symbols to represent it.[11] Tradition linked the past, the present and the future, providing continuity, and was shared by the members of the nation, providing community.[12]

In sum, the study of history in nineteenth-century Europe was dominated by historicism with its emphasis on individuality and on evolution; it was establishing itself as an autonomous discipline with a defined area of study, a canon of methods and organizational structures; it had a role to play in fostering national identity, a role that was recognized by the state and by the educated public. This was how the study of history in Europe appeared to the Japanese when they were looking to the West for models in their attempt to modernize, and what they saw seemed relevant to their own situation.

The pace of change in Japan since the Meiji Restoration was even greater than in nineteenth-century Europe; by the end of the century, only 50 years after its forced opening to the West, it in many ways resembled other Western countries more than previous ages in its own country: it was a modern nation, a centralized state with a parliamentary constitution; industrialization was well on its way, a mass society was emerging in the cities and a national ideology was being transmitted in schools, the conscript army and elsewhere. As a result, a need for orientation, similar to that of their European contemporaries, was felt by those who witnessed these rapid changes.

If Japanese society in general possessed some of the characteristics identified as crucial in the emergence of history as a modern discipline, what about the study of history in Japan? Historiography had a long tradition in Japan before it was transformed in the Meiji period.[13] The first historical writings which have been preserved are the chronicles of the eighth century, the *Kojiki* (*Records of Ancient Matters*, 712) and the *Nihongi* (*Chronicles of Ancient Japan*, 720). The latter became the first of the Six National Histories. The early chronicles were compiled at the end of a period of political reforms, through which a centralized bureaucratic state modelled on the Chinese state was established. The histories also imitated Chinese models, namely the standard, dynastic histories (*zheng shi*, Japanese *seishi*). Like these, the Japanese chronicles were compiled by government officials to legitimize imperial rule and centred on the reigns of rulers. With the decline of the imperial bureaucratic state from the eleventh century the compilation of the chronicles was abandoned, but the practice of compiling chronicles was later resumed by the shoguns to document and legitimize their own rule.[14] The *seishi*, the definitive, standard history, remained the ideal of historiography, just as the imperial bureaucratic state remained a political ideal.

Meanwhile, another form of historiography, this time indigenous, emerged from the eleventh century. This was the historical tale (*rekishi monogatari*). Influenced by works of fiction, such as the *Tale of Genji*, it aimed to capture the reader's interest and to generate a more subjective understanding of history by presenting the facts from a particular viewpoint and devoting more attention to characterizing people and describing the forces of history. These literary narratives were in part a result of dissatisfaction with traditional historical writing that merely chronicled the bare facts.[15] A special form of the historical tale was the war tale (*gunki monogatari*), which told of the exploits of participants in the numerous civil wars which raged in Japan from the twelfth to the sixteenth centuries.[16] Among the narrative histories of medieval Japan, two works stand out; they are of a kind usually described as *shiron* in Japan because of their attempts to interpret history as a whole. The first is the *Gukanshō* (*Outline of a Foolish View of History*); written in 1220 by the Buddhist monk Jien from a Buddhist viewpoint, it presents the first philosophical treatment of Japanese history. The second is the *Jinnō shōtōki* (*Report on the Right Succession of the Divine Emperors*), written in 1339 by Kitabatake Chikafusa. It provides a philosophical view inspired by Shinto and centring on the imperial house; beginning with the assertion that Japan is the unique 'land of the gods' (*shinkoku*), Kitabatake stresses Japanese superiority over all countries. The *Jinnō shōtōki* became one of the sources of Japanese nationalism and had considerable influence on historiography and political thought.

Annals and narratives form the main strands of Japanese historiography; the division is still evident in the early Meiji period. While the annals claim to present the facts as they are and leave the reader to judge, the narratives aim to engage the reader and to provide a subjective understanding of the forces that determine history.[17]

It was during the time of peace and political stability under Tokugawa rule (1600–1868) that the study and writing of history made advances in those areas most associated with modern scholarship: the collection of documents, and textual criticism.[18] The importation from Korea of the printing press with movable types at the end of the sixteenth century made it possible to print documents on a large scale when the political rulers turned their interest to scholarship. The emperor at the time, Goyōzei, and the first Tokugawa shogun, Ieyasu, were the first to have old documents collected and copied to be preserved for future generations, and later rulers, including those of several domains, followed and made their own collections.

The new rulers, like their predecessors, saw historiography as a means to legitimize the order they had established and sponsored the compilation of genealogies and chronicles. The Tokugawa distinguished themselves from the previous shoguns in that they sought to define military rule as rule over the whole of Japan and legitimize it through history. The work that became central to the legitimization of military rule in general and Tokugawa rule in particular was the *Honchō tsugan* (*The Comprehensive Mirror of this Court*, 1644–70).[19] It was begun by Hayashi Razan (1583–1657) and completed by his son Gahō (1618–80). The Hayashis' private academy later became the official institution of higher learning of the shoguns, the *Shōheizaka gakumonjo*, where most of the official compilations were placed under the responsibility of the director. This organizational reform improved the standards of scholarship, removing the compilations of the histories from direct intervention by the rulers and making it possible to plan long-term projects.[20] The resulting compilations were claimed to be objective, but, not surprisingly, they had a clear tendency to legitimize shogunal rule. Histories were compiled in the service of the shogunate right up to the time of its downfall.

Apart from compilations under the auspices of the Hayashi, two works stand out among the achievements of historical scholarship in the Tokugawa period. They influenced directly the work in the Office of Historiography and helped pave the way for modern historical scholarship; the *Dainihonshi* (*History of Great Japan*), initiated by Tokugawa Mitsukuni, feudal lord of the Mito domain, and the collection *Shiryō* (historical materials) by the blind scholar Hanawa Hokiichi.

Mitsukuni intended the *Dainihonshi* as a definitive history of Japan, which would illustrate the moral principles that should guide human behaviour, namely, loyal behaviour of subjects towards their sovereign. Above all, Mitsukuni's aim was to demonstrate clearly the legitimacy of the Imperial line and at the same time the legitimacy of the shoguns, who were invested with political power by the emperors. The *Dainihonshi* provided a revised list of the imperial line and its new version became the basis for the modern list of emperors. At the same time the *Dainihonshi* is the first and only Japanese history that imitates faithfully the format of the Chinese standard histories.[21] It was composed in *kidentai* as opposed to *hennentai*, a strictly annalistic form that presents the facts without establishing connections between them. In *kidentai* the material is arranged into sections according to subject; the main part is structured by political criteria, usually ruling houses. In the main section (*honki*) of the *Dainihonshi* each chapter is centred on the rule of a legitimate sovereign, defining the line of legitimate rulers by their treatment in the main section. The other sections are biographies (*retsuden*), essays (*shi*) and tables (*hyō*).

The most remarkable feature of the *Dainihonshi*, distinguishing it from its Chinese models, was that all the sources from which the information was obtained were cited and comments on their reliability added. Mitsukuni had established a history office (*shikyoku*), which from 1702 had a branch in both Mito and Tokyo and assembled scholars from different regions, who were sent all over Japan to collect and copy documents. The Mito scholars carefully examined the sources they collected; they aimed to record the facts as they were without adding any moral judgement, the idea being that the facts would speak for themselves. However, judgement was expressed by the choice of words and the selection of what was included in the different sections of the history. On the whole, the *Dainihonshi* can be said to be objective, but as the account focuses on Japan's line of imperial rulers it is limited in scope.

Most of the *Dainihonshi* was completed in Mitsukuni's lifetime, although the final version was not published until 1906. In 1809, it received imperial sanction; thus it could be regarded as a standard history. In the last decades of Tokugawa rule, its emphasis on imperial rule was interpreted as a challenge to the shoguns, and the ideology of the 'Late Mito School' is chiefly known for its contribution to the intellectual foundations of the Meiji Restoration.[22] The *Dainihonshi* is significant both as an achievement of scholarship and for the ideology that was derived from it, and its influence on official historiography by the Meiji government must be rated highly.[23]

The second compilation was sponsored by the shogunate, but again centred on Imperial rule.[24] In 1793 the shogunate helped the blind scholar Hanawa Hokiichi found the Institute of Japanese Studies (*Wagaku kōdansho*). The Institute was placed under the administration of the Hayashis' school, the official Confucian academy of the shogunate, and its main purpose was to collect and publish materials relating to Japanese laws and history. The collection *Shiryō* was only one of several compiled at the Institute. It was to provide a basis of materials for continuing the Six National Histories, which Hokiichi recognized as definitive history. His own compilation did not aim to be a definitive standard history. The events since Emperor Uda (887–97) were listed chronologically and relevant excerpts from the sources added. This format is known as *kōmoku*; the *kō* aimed to provide exact information and the *moku* to document it. *Kōmoku* reflected the new tendency to collect and arrange the primary documents (*shiryō* is the term used for historical sources today) with critical comments as the sources for a definitive history (*seishi*), rather than the formulation of a correct version of history. The value and significance of the 'source' was not sufficiently questioned, a problem of Japanese positivist historiography to this day.[25] Hokiichi's format is still used for compilations of sources.

Both works, although very different from each other, illustrate a characteristic of historiography which grew in importance during the Tokugawa period: the extensive and to some extent critical use of primary documents as a basis of historical writing. The critical study of texts was the foundation of a branch of scholarship known as *kōshōgaku* (Chinese *kao zheng xue*; 'school of verifications and proofs'). It originated in China at the time of the Qing Dynasty (1644–1912) when Neo-Confucian studies in China flourished. The new school of textual criticism was characterized by its close examination and interpretation of Confucian classics. In Japan, *kōshōgaku* became part of mainstream Confucianism. By the late Tokugawa period its methods were being applied to the study of Japanese texts by the scholars of National Learning (*kokugaku*), a branch of learning that challenged Confucian orthodoxy. Scholars of

National Learning turned to ancient Japanese literature in their attempt to free 'pure' Japanese thought from the influences of Confucianism and Buddhism. Their studies had a significant influence on modern Japanese scholarship; textual criticism in the *kōshō* tradition was perfected in the Meiji period.[26]

National Learning later divided into a more scholarly branch, devoted to research on ancient texts, and a political branch, which rejected all foreign influence and sought to revive Shinto as a basis of the state. Both branches of National Learning provided significant impulses for historiography; the philological studies based on ancient Japanese literature widened the scope of historical interest and its preoccupation with the 'ancient way' (*kodō*) contributed to a debate over what is specifically Japanese, challenged the existing order and prefigured modern nationalist ideas. National Learning, together with the eclectic Late Mito school, was credited with having contributed decisively to the intellectual foundations of the Meiji Restoration after 1868 and played an important role in the legitimation of the Restoration.[27]

Thus, when the Meiji government sought to employ historiography to legitimize its rule, several features of historical scholarship as it existed at the time lent themselves to the task: there was a tradition of scholarship, including historiography, sponsored by the government and organized within a government office. There was the assumption that collecting as many sources as possible formed an important part of producing a definitive history. There were established methods of examining texts to determine their reliability and their meaning. Moreover, the thought of the National school and of the late Mito school provided much of the foundation for the modern nationalistic ideology.[28]

This book aims to show how government interests, indigenous traditions of scholarship, impulses from the West and the rise of the modern nation state combined in shaping the modern academic discipline of history in Japan. The focus is the government office and the research institute that succeeded it.

Official historiography sponsored by the Meiji government became the basis of academic history as it was practised at universities, spreading from the Imperial University to the newer universities. Studying the history of the Office of Historiography and the Historiographical Institute is therefore vital for understanding how the historical discipline in Japan developed, because institutional organization at once reflects and influences the way history is pursued.

However, although historical scholarship as it evolved from the work of the Office of Historiography can thus be seen as the 'mainstream', the scholars employed by the Meiji government were not the only ones who wrote history.[29] From the last years of the Tokugawa shogunate there was a widespread popular interest in history, which continued into the Meiji period. One expression of this was the enormous popularity of earlier historical works, especially the *Nihon gaishi* (*Extra History of Japan*, 1827) by Rai San'yō, a literary narrative dealing with the fate of the military houses, from the Minamoto and Taira to the Tokugawa. Similarly popular were the *Kokushiryaku* (*Outline of Our National History*, 1826) by Iwagaki Matsunae and the *Kōchō shiryaku* (*Historical Outline of Japan*, 1826) by the Mito scholar Aoyama Nobuyuki. These and other works of the Tokugawa period went through several printings in early Meiji; commentaries on them were published and they were used as school textbooks.[30]

Translated Western works on world history also became popular, including philosophical discussions of universal history.[31] These influenced a new type of historical writing which treated Japanese history as the history of human progress (*bunmeishi*), reflecting the general trend towards Westernization and modernization. The most important works were *Bunmeiron no gairyaku* (*Outline of a Theory of Civilization*, 1875) by Fukuzawa Yukichi and *Nihon kaika shōshi* (*A Short History of Enlightenment in Japan*, 1877–82) by Taguchi Ukichi. *Bunmeishi* (enlightenment history) flourished until the end of the 1880s, when the intellectual climate became more conservative. Influenced by the former *bunmeishi* historians, the *Min'yūsha* historians, named after the publishing group founded by Tokutomi Sohō in 1887, produced several histories; they wrote histories of Japan rather than 'world' histories. Tokutomi Sohō himself published among other works *Kinsei Nihon kokumin shi* (*Modern History of the Japanese People*). Takegoshi Yosaburō published *Shin Nihonshi* (*A New History of Japan*) and *Nisen gohyaku nenshi* (*History of Two Thousand Five Hundred Years*), a history of Japan from the beginning to his own times. Yamaji Aizan published biographies of well-known personalities of the Edo period (Ogyū Sorai, Arai Hakuseki, Tokugawa Ieyasu), and from 1897 to 1899 was involved in the compilation of the official history of Chōshū (*Bōchō kaitenshi*). He also publicized his views on history and sharply criticized the historians at the Imperial University of Tokyo.[32]

These then were the two main currents of historiography in the Meiji period; the first was based on textual criticism and verification of facts and mainly practised by specialists in government offices and the Imperial University. The second produced historical narratives endeavouring to provide an interpretation of history, including the history of the economy, society, culture and ideas, and was mainly practised by private scholars and journalists. One of its foremost representatives, Yamaji Aizan, coined the term *minkan shigaku* (private historical scholarship) to describe it.[33] To some extent these two currents reflect the traditional main strands of historiography before 1868, annalistic and narrative.

The different trends in historiography gradually merged with the more orthodox mainstream, and by the Taishō period (1912–25) history had shed many of its pre-Meiji and early Meiji characteristics and become a modern academic discipline.[34]

Of course the writing of more or less scholarly histories was not the only way in which the past was invoked to define national identity and to give meaning to the present and the future. It must be seen in the wider context of what Hardtwig has called 'Geschichtskultur' (historical culture), which includes the diverse forms in which historical traditions and historical knowledge manifest themselves in society; including the use of history to provide arguments in social and political debates, material culture, monuments, ceremonies, anniversaries, state symbols. Interest in history takes different forms in answer to different needs: Nietzsche spoke of a monumental history, which answers the need to venerate; antiquarian history, which aims to preserve, and critical history, which seeks to destroy that which threatens the life force, and the classification could be applied to Japan.[35]

In discussing the development of official historiography it will become apparent that it failed not only because it proved impossible to produce a definitive history that took into account all existing sources and recorded the past exactly as it was, but also because it was unable to cater to the needs of government and public that history in its various forms is expected to fulfil. This became obvious when the scholars in the Office of Historiography began to cast doubt on the existence of certain heroes from Japanese medieval history that had fired popular imagination for centuries (Chapter 6.3); in the indignation that ensued, Shigeno Yasutsugu, the foremost representative of official historiography, was labelled 'Dr Obliterator' (*massatsu hakase*).

However, it would be wrong to look at historiography only with regard to whether or not it fulfilled the expectations brought to it from the outside. Shigeno and his colleagues were employed to write official history, but they had their own agendas as well as that of their employers. They had embarked on their task as government officials no different from their colleagues in other offices, but those who remained in the Office of Historiography gradually became specialists: Japan's first professional historians. They claimed to be searching for historical truth and their claim must be taken seriously as well as examined critically. We no longer share their optimism about the possibility of establishing historical truth once and for all; we may even doubt the desirability of attempting it. As Herbert Butterfield points out: 'If history could be told in all its complexity and detail it would provide us with something as chaotic and baffling as life itself ...';[36] Butterfield suggests that the basic problem underlying difficulties in the study of history is how to abridge without changing the 'meaning and purport of the historical story' (p.102), and certainly one of the most difficult problems faced by Shigeno and his colleagues was how to present the increasing amount of evidence, unearthed in their travels around the country, in a manageable form that would show 'meaning and purport'.

For Shigeno and his colleagues the question of meaning seemed straightforward. They believed that if they recorded the historical facts as they were (*ari no mama*) their meaning would become apparent. They do not seem to have been sufficiently aware of the distinction between discovery and representation.[37] One need not go as far as Hayden White and claim that there is no significant difference between historical and other forms of narrative to concede that the way in which historians represent the past they aim to reconstruct in their writings is far from given and a subject of investigation in its own right.[38] In fact, the members of the Office of Historiography did give some thought to the form of historical writing. Nevertheless they ended up staying in the old mould of the chronological enumeration of events. Thus the work of these scholars had little impact on the way history was written; nor did it provide any innovations in the realm of historical interpretation, beyond the affirmation that historiography should be free from Confucianist bias. This concentration on the collection and examination and arrangement of sources and the preoccupation with historical facts rather than their representation and interpretation is often cited as one of the reasons why academic history was in no position to resist the official distortion of history for political ends in the 1930s.[39] This may be in part true, but the isolation of historical research as it was practised at the Historiographical Institute was the result of a consensus among scholars and statesmen that historical research, also termed 'pure history' (*junshō shigaku*), must be kept separate from other forms of history, known as 'applied history' (*ōyō shigaku*), such as history for educational purposes. This separation was finalized in the textbook controversy of 1911 (Chapter 6.6), when a historical question was decided by an imperial edict.

It has already been outlined that the close relationship between the emergence of the nation state and of the historical discipline in the nineteenth century is characteristic of other countries beside Japan. This is not a comparative study, and at present research in Japan has not progressed sufficiently to allow a full-scale comparison. However, some references to Germany in particular will be made for three reasons. First, German historical scholarship provided a model for other European countries and North America before it was introduced into Japan. Second, it directly influenced historical studies in Japan through the persons of Ludwig Rieß and of several Japanese who studied history in Germany and returned to teach it in Japan. In fact Germany became a model for Japan in many areas, including the introduction of a parliamentary constitution. Third, national unification came later to Germany than to the other great European powers. The German Empire was founded in the year the Meiji government achieved control over the whole of Japan by abolishing the feudal domains (1871). Thus the relationship between historiography and the search for national identity is particularly evident in these two countries. However, historical scholarship as practised by Shigeno and his colleagues did not have the same influence on the emerging Japanese national ideology as the Prussian school of historiography on that of the German Empire. Despite the fact that modern historical scholarship in Japan originated as a government-sponsored project, it was much more distinct from national ideology than in Germany.

The idea for this book was conceived at a time when the problems both countries have had with their national past since their defeat in a world war they had provoked and fought with extreme cruelty became particularly acute. In both countries there was a feeling among conservative intellectuals that a sense of national identity needed to be reinforced and that history could provide it. In Germany these discussions became mixed with the perennial debates about the Third Reich, culminating in the 'Historikerstreit' in summer 1986. In Japan similar attempts at resorting to the past to remedy a perceived lack of national consciousness occurred at the same time as the debates about the responsibility of Emperor Shōwa for the war reached a new height in the months preceding his death.

Since then, both countries have experienced changes. In Japan, the end of the Shōwa era (although it may seem like no more than a change in name, it nevertheless was perceived as a significant break), the prolonged economic recession from the end of 1991 and the fall of the LDP, which had dominated Japanese politics for almost 40 years, have highlighted the changes Japan has undergone since 1945. In Germany, the events of 1989–90 showed even more clearly how transient ideas about national identity and national history can be.

How the changes in both countries and in the world at large following the dissolution of the Soviet communist bloc and the resurgence of nationalist sentiment in eastern Europe will influence historiography remains to be seen. What seems certain is that for some time to come the story of history and national identity will be an ongoing one.

2

Historiography in the Service of the Meiji Government

Nothing shows the link between historiography and the state as clearly as the fact that the Meiji government, soon after it came into power, established an office with the aim of compiling an official national history. From 1872 to 1888 this office was part of the Council of State (*Dajōkan*), the highest executive organ, and the Cabinet that succeeded it in 1885.

2.1 The Meiji Restoration and the Revival of Historiography by the Government

In the years between the Meiji Restoration in 1868 and the abolition of the domains in 1871, the leaders of the Restoration, the court nobles Iwakura Tomomi and Sanjō Sanetomi, together with samurai from the domains of Satsuma, Tosa, Hizen and Chōshū, tried to concentrate political power in the hands of the new government. Military resistance from the shogunal government was broken by the spring of 1869 in the Boshin War. In January 1868 the restoration of imperial rule was decreed and in April an Imperial Oath containing a general policy was issued. It was followed by a fundamental law establishing the Council of State as the locus of supreme political power under the emperor. The Council of State consisted of a legislative, an executive and a judiciary organ. In the summer of 1869 it was reorganized. In theory, the new Department of Rites (*Jingikan*) became the highest government office. The most important government posts were the ministers of the left and of the right and the state councillors. There were initially six ministries, but a seventh was added later. The new government was modelled after the centralized bureaucratic state of the Nara period (704–84).

Little is known about the beginnings of historiography initiated by the

Meiji government and of the early education system in general. Some of the documents might have been lost when the building of the Council of State, which included the Department of History (*Rekishika*: Chapter 2.2), burnt down in 1873. The few surviving documents are contained in the compilations of government decrees, *Dajō ruiten* and *Hōki bunrui taizen*.[1]

A major concern of the new government was education. The first state schools were established in Kyoto in 1868. In summer 1868, following the transfer of the capital to Tokyo, the former bakufu schools of medicine (*Igakusho*), Western studies (*Kaiseijo*) and neo-Confucian studies (*Shōheikō*, the former academy of the Hayashi) were reopened.[2] A few months later, the *Shōheikō* school was placed under the jurisdiction of the Executive Council (*Gyōseikan*) in the Council of State. At the beginning of the following year the reopening of the school was authorized. Yamanouchi Toyoshige, the lord of Tosa, Akizuki Tanetatsu, formerly an adviser to the shogun, and Matsuoka Tokitoshi, adviser to Yamanouchi, became officials of the school. The *Shōheikō*, renamed *Shōhei gakkō* or *Gakkō* was not only a school but also an administrative office responsible for the entire education system. In the summer of 1869 it was renamed *Daigakkō* or University; it received the status of a ministry of education, and the schools of medicine and Western Learning were placed under its jurisdiction. When the school was closed down the following year and most of the teaching staff were dismissed, the University retained its administrative functions until the Ministry of Education was established in 1871. The schools of medicine and Western Learning once again became independent; the government attached more importance to the Western knowledge taught there than to the Confucian studies that had been taught at the former *Shōheikō*, which had only been reopened in consideration of the more conservative views of Iwakura Tomomi.[3] The closure of the *Shōheikō* or University was a result of the conflicts between scholars of National Learning (*kokugaku*) and Chinese Learning (*kangaku*), who competed for influence in the new education system and for political power. Moreover, there were tensions between the teaching staff and the students, most of whom came from samurai families and had been educated in their domains. The *Daigakkō* was not so much a university in the modern sense as a place where students met and exchanged ideas while freely pursuing their studies. The rivalries between the scholars of National Learning and Chinese Learning cannot be treated in detail here. They are significant, however, for they continued throughout the Meiji period and affected the fate of official historiography considerably.[4]

It was the *Gakkō* from which the first known attempt to revive official historiography originated. Little is known about this initiative, but at the beginning of 1869 the *Gakkō* drew up a proposal for the establishment of an office for the compilation of a national history. The proposal lamented that, since the decline of imperial rule, the Six National Histories (*Rikkokushi*) had been discontinued. Now however, imperial rule had been restored and the tradition of official historiography should be revived in honour of the emperor. For this purpose an office should be established and suitable officials appointed. A member of the *Gakkō* should be named as director and work should begin at once.[5]

The author of the proposal is not known, but we know who was in the *Gakkō* at the time. According to Ōkubo, the members were scholars of Chinese Learning, only two of whom had belonged to the former bakufu school.[6] Ōkubo (p.184) states that the reasons for their appointment are not obvious and are likely to have included self-promotion and recommendation by others. Some of them were later in the Office of Historiography (*Shūshikyoku*): Rai Matajirō, Okamatsu Ōkoku, Fujino Masahira, Gamō Keitei. Aoyama Nobumitsu was the author of various historical works and had been involved in the compilation of the *Dainihonshi* (*History of Great Japan*) in the Mito domain; his brother Nobuhisa later became a member of the College of Historiography (*Shūshikan*). Mizumoto Seibi was a friend of Shigeno Yasutsugu who later became prominent in the Office of Historiography. Together they had compiled a chronological history of Japan based on the *Dainihonshi*.[7] It is likely that the idea to compile an official history of Japan came from these men or, possibly, from Akizuki Tanetatsu, who is supposed to have revised the draft of the Imperial Rescript on Historiography issued a few weeks later.

Whoever was responsible for the proposal seems to have had in mind the bureaucratic state of the Nara period, which had produced the Six

National Histories mentioned in the proposal. The historian Sakamoto has pointed out the close link between the imperial bureaucratic *ritsu ryō* state of the Nara period and the Six National Histories.[8] It is therefore not surprising that the historiographical tradition of the Nara period was resumed at a time when the models for political institutions were taken from that period.

The proposal was accepted, and in the following month an Office for the Collection of Historical Materials and Compilation of a National History (*Shiryō henshū kokushi kōsei kyoku*) was established. However, it was established not in the office in Yushima (*Gakkō*), from which the original proposal had come, but in the Institute of Japanese Studies (*Wagaku kōdansho*), another former bakufu institution. The Institute of Japanese Studies had been ceded to the new government by Hanawa Tadatsugu, the grandson of its founder Hanawa Hokiichi, the year before and had presumably been placed under the jurisdiction of the Schools Administration Office (*Gakkō*).[9] At the same time three men were appointed Officials for the Collection of Materials and the Revision of the Six National Histories (*shiryō henshū Rikkokushi kōsei goyō kakari*). They were Kimura Masakoto, Konakamura Kiyonori, and Yokoyama Yoshikiyo. In addition to these men Hanawa Tadatsugu was appointed as assistant (*Shiryō henshū Rikkokushi kōsei kenshū*). All these men were scholars of National Learning and had formerly been at the Institute of Japanese Studies. The choice of place and of people suggests an attempt to resume the tradition of National Learning from the Edo period and in particular to continue the work of Hanawa Hokiichi. His compilation of documents (*Shiryō*) became the starting point for historiography initiated by the Meiji government.

The revival of historiography by the imperial government was sanctioned in April 1869 (Meiji 2.4.4) by the imperial rescript passed to Sanjō Sanetomi (Chapter 1). Its wording was similar to that of the proposal by the *Gakkō*; it deplored the decline of historiography together with imperial rule and stressed the importance of reviving the tradition. According to Numata, the Emperor wrote the edict himself. Hérail states that Akizuki Tanetatsu revised the rescript but gives no source for this information.[10] However, the ideological tradition in which the rescript stands is clear enough. The Imperial Rescript on Historiography (*Shūshi no choku*) was quoted repeatedly to justify official historiography; it is regarded by historians as the beginning of official historiography in the Meiji period, although it did no more than confirm a previous initiative. Two months after the Office was established, it was transferred to the *Shōheikō* and two more officials were appointed for the revision of the National History (*kokushi kōetsu goyō kakari*). They were Hirata Kanetane and Tanimori Yoshiomi, both scholars of National Learning.

In addition, three officials were appointed for the compilation of a National History (*kokushi henshū goyō kakari*). Rai Matajirō was a Confucianist Scholar from Kyoto and a son of Rai San'yō. The other two were Fujino Masahira and Okamatsu Ōkoku. These men were the first Scholars of Chinese Learning to be appointed. It is not clear whether work on a national history was begun at this time. The office was renamed 'Office for the Compilation of a National History' (*Kokushi henshū kyoku*) in the autumn of 1869. The new name indicated its purpose for the first time. However, at the end of that year the office was closed, probably as a result of the rivalry between the scholars of National Learning and Chinese Learning.

The first attempt to resume the tradition of the Six National Histories by the Meiji government had failed. The government had more pressing concerns than writing history. It is remarkable that it took an interest in writing history at all while it was so busy, as it were, making history. The explanation lies in the claim of the Meiji leaders that they had effected a return to direct rule by the emperor after more than 700 years in which imperial rule had been usurped by the shoguns. Resuming the tradition of the National Histories compiled under the imperial bureaucratic state served to emphasize the legitimacy of this claim.

Many of the officials were appointed to other government posts, and of those appointed to the task of compiling a national history, only Hanawa, Fujino and Tanimori were later appointed to the Office of Historiography. Kimura Masakoto became an official in the Department of Rites, then in the Ministry of Education, where he compiled a history textbook for schools: later he held appointments in the Ministry of Justice and in the Imperial Household Ministry. In 1891 he became a professor at the Imperial University. Konakamura Kiyonori was first in the Council of State. In 1878 he became a lecturer and in 1882 a professor of the University. He had considerable influence on the development of academic history. Yokoyama Yoshikiyo also became a government official and spent his last years teaching legal history at the University. Hanawa Tadatsugu joined the Ministry of Education and the Department of Rites. Hirata Kanetane became a teacher for the Ministry of Religious Affairs (*Kyōbushō*). Tanimori Yoshiomi joined the Department of Rites. Rai Matajirō returned to Kyoto. Fujino Masahira and Okamatsu Ōkoku also left the capital for some years. Okamatsu taught in Kumamoto, but later became a professor at the University.

The closure of the Office for the Compilation of a National History did not mean that interest in history had faded. Various offices were involved in some kind of historical research even before the Department of History (*Rekishika*) was established in 1872. One of them was the Department for the Examination of the Imperial Genealogies (*Gokeizu torishirabe kakari*), established in the autumn of 1870 in the Department of Rites. It became part of the Department of History in 1872.

In 1871 the Ministry of Education (*Monbushō*) was established in the location of the former office (*Gakkō*) in Yushima. Etō Shinpei became the minister of education, and many officials of the *Gakkō* found posts in the Ministry. An Office for the Compilation of Textbooks (*Henshūryō shuppan kakari*, from 1872 *Kyōkasho hensei kakari*) was set up in the Ministry of Education. Some of the members of this office were later transferred to the Department of History.

Before the Department of History was established in 1872, the Meiji government appointed an official of the Council of State, Nagamatsu Miki, to write a history of the Meiji Restoration with the title *Fukko ran'yō* (Brief Account of the Meiji Restoration), which was to serve as a reference book for the members of the Iwakura Embassy when they travelled to the United States and Europe in 1871.[11] Nagamatsu was the son of a doctor from the Hagi domain and had studied in Kyoto before being appointed to the Office of Compilation (*Henshūkyoku*) in his domain. There he wrote an account of the Restoration entitled *Sonnō jiseki* (Achievements of Reverence for the Emperor). The *Fukko ran'yō* provided the starting point for the compilation of the *Fukkoki* (*Chronicle of the Restoration*), the official account of the Meiji Restoration. For this purpose a Department of History (*Rekishika*) was established in the Council of State in 1872.

2.2 Centralization of Government and the Department of History

In 1871 the Meiji government abolished the domains, which had retained much of their independence in the years immediately following the Meiji Restoration. The domains were replaced by prefectures. This measure consolidated the central government's jurisdiction over the entire country and its populace, as well as its control of the revenues and military power of the former domains. At the same time the government inherited the problems of the former domains, the most important of which was regulating land ownership and securing taxes. In 1873 a new system of taxation was introduced, according to which landowners were to pay 3 per cent of the estimated value of their land. It took eight years for the system to be enforced.[12] Following the introduction of the prefectural system the Council of State was reorganized around the Central Chamber (*Seiin*) through which the emperor was to rule in person. The most important government posts were the minister of state, the ministers of the left and the right and the councillors.

The Department of History was set up in 1872 within the Central Chamber, which was the highest government office. The preface to the Chronicle of the Restoration (*Fukkoki*) suggests that the establishment of the Department of History was a result of the centralization of the government.[13] It may have been seen as a way to facilitate the introduction of the new system of taxation, as the Department was mainly concerned with collecting and organizing information as a basis for administration. In order to govern efficiently, the central government attempted to learn as much as possible about the country. For this purpose, prefectures as well as the ministries and other government offices were repeatedly ordered to collect and submit written documents (Chapter 3.3).

The attempts of the Meiji government to collect information as a basis for administration are illustrated by the fact that a Department of Topography (*Chishika*) was established at the same time as the Department of History.[14]

The Department of Topography compiled the *Kōkoku chishi* (Topographic Descriptions of the Empire), which were probably inspired by the *Fudoki* (provincial topographies) of the Nara period, as well as similar attempts in the Edo period. The topographies included descriptions of the economic and social situation of each region at the time,[15] whereas the *Fuken shiryō* (Historical Materials of the Prefectures) compiled in the Department of History described the historical development. The director of the Department of Topography was Tsukamoto Akitake, who had formerly been in the service of the bakufu and worked as a military instructor. The Department of Topography was later housed within the Interior Ministry for some time before it became part of the Office of Historiography.

In 1873 the tasks of the Department of History were defined and extended to include the compilation of a history of Japan (*kokushi no henshū*). The following year, Kawada Takeshi and his disciples, who had been compiling a National History ordered by the Ministry of Education in 1873, were transferred to the Department of History. Kawada became an Official in the Department of History (*rekishika goyō kakari*) and was entrusted with the compilation of a history of the period from the Emperor Gokomatsu (1382–1411) to the Emperor Ninkō (1817–45). It seems, however, that the compilation of an official history of Japan was not attempted in earnest in the Department of History.

It is impossible to be certain who the members of the Department were. Miyachi states that there were 18 men in the Department besides Nagamatsu, but he does not mention any sources for this information. Ōkubo names eight followers of Kawada, some of whom were later in the Office of Historiography. Chō Hikaru, Yotsuya Tsune, Nakamura Teigo and Hirose Shin'ichi, who had formerly been in the Education Office or in the Council of State, were also appointed to the Department of History; they were transferred to the Office of Historiography in 1875.[16] The Department for the Examination of the Imperial Genealogies was attached to the Department of History and later to the Office of Historiography. These three groups of men, officials from the Council of State, Kawada's followers and those engaged in examining the imperial genealogies, formed the departments within the Office of Historiography, established in 1875.

With the exception of Kawada, no one at this stage was engaged in writing history. The Chronicle of the Restoration, on which Nagamatsu was working, was not so much a history as an account of the most recent events. Apart from the Chronicle, the officials concentrated on collecting documents from the prefectures and on investigating the imperial genealogies. The Department of History was an administrative office for the prefectures while also functioning as an archive. Thus recording current affairs and writing history were not clearly distinguished. It was not until the Office of Historiography had been established that the work on a National History was seriously attempted.

2.3 The Osaka Conference and the Office of Historiography

In 1871 several of the Meiji oligarchs left Japan for America and Europe with the Iwakura Embassy. While they were away, the remaining government leaders, Saigō Takamori, Soejima Taneomi, Gotō Shōjirō, Itagaki Taisuke and Etō Shinpei, planned to provoke a war with Korea, with whom relations had been strained since 1868. The return of the Embassy prevented a war with Korea, but the Meiji government fell apart and Saigō, Soejima, Gotō and Itagaki resigned in October 1873. Itō Hirobumi, Ōkuma Shigenobu, Ōkubo Toshimichi and Iwakura Tomomi became the most influential members of the government.

The Meiji leaders who had left the government began to organize discontented samurai in their former domains and then nationwide.[17] Itagaki founded the Public Party of Patriots (*Aikoku kōtō*); Gotō, Soejima and Etō became members. On 17 January 1874, they and four other members of the party submitted a petition for the establishment of an elected assembly. This marked the beginning of the People's Rights Movement (*Jiyū minken undō*), supported mainly by samurai, wealthy farmers and merchants. The party leaders took advantage of popular discontent with government reforms to fuel opposition to the government leaders. Etō led an armed revolt of discontented samurai, but it was soon suppressed and Etō was executed. A punitive expedition against Formosa was planned, partly to placate the samurai, but had to be abandoned after Ōkubo had reached an agreement with China. Consequently tensions increased. In protest against the expedition Kido Kōin left the government and joined Itagaki and Gotō. They were powerful and their opposition was a serious threat to the government. Ōkubo therefore organized a meeting with Kido and Itagaki to re-establish unity. The meeting was held in Osaka in February 1875. The participants agreed to work towards a constitutional government and their resolution was sanctioned with an imperial edict on 14 April 1875 (*Rikken seitai no shōchoku*). Kido and Itagaki were readmitted to the government. As a result of the meeting, a senate, an assembly of prefectural governors and a Supreme Court were established and the Council of State was reorganized.

The Osaka Conference put an end to a series of crises beginning with the return of the Iwakura Embassy in 1873. The collapse of consensus within the government in conjunction with increasing popular demands for democratic rights challenged the Meiji government.[18] On 14 April 1875 an imperial edict promised a constitutional government. It was not a coincidence that the Office of Historiography (*Shūshikyoku*) replaced the former Department of History (*Rekishika*) on the same day. *Shūshi* means 'compilation of history' and the name of the new Office indicated the intention to produce a national history. It was significant that this change occurred after a power struggle among the Meiji leaders, which had resulted in a further consolidation of the government's authority. The government needed to assert its authority in the face of the People's Rights Movement.

The former Department of History was completely reorganized. On 4 May 1875 the Office of Historiography sent a document entitled *Shūshi jigi* (*Right Compilation of History*) to the ministers of the Council of State, requesting their opinion.[19] According to the *Shūshi jigi*, the completion of the *Fukkoki,* the *Chronicle of the Restoration,* was to be expected shortly and it was necessary to plan the future course. The lack of an official standard history of Japan (*seishi*) and the importance of compiling one were pointed out. Some suggestions about how to proceed followed. The document went on to state that historical facts had not always been transmitted accurately, especially in the time of feudalism (*hōken jidai*); in order to bring the facts to light, the authority of a central government was needed. Furthermore, a president should be appointed, a person of high rank who was well-esteemed. The former president Sanjō Sanetomi had too many other commitments to concern himself with history. In response to this request Ijichi Masaharu was appointed on 24 June 1875.[20]

The new office was divided into four departments, two of which continued the work of the Department of History, while the other two began preparations for a national history. From this period we have the first complete account of who was employed in the Office (Chapter 3.1).

On 20 September 1875 the Department of Topography (*Chishika*) which had been within the Ministry of Home Affairs for a while, was once again transferred to the Council of State and became a separate department in the Office of Historiography.

Work on a national history began with the establishment of the Office of Historiography. It was much larger than the Department of History had been; its tasks were clearly defined, as was the way in which work was to proceed. Twice a year the Office submitted an account of the progress made in the preceding months and of the officials employed in the Office.

However, the Office of Historiography did not exist for long. At the beginning of 1877 the Central Chamber of the Council of State, of which the Office of Historiography formed a part, was abolished to make the government function more efficiently in the face of its financial difficulties on the eve of the war against Satsuma. The Office of Historiography was abolished on 18 January and replaced by the College of Historiography (*Shūshikan*) on 26 January. The yearly budget was fixed at 25,000 yen, which, according to later documents, was only half the amount the Office of Historiography had received.[21] The number of staff was reduced from 74 to 59; the Department of Topography was most affected. Nagamatsu was entrusted with drafting rules for the staff. Ijichi Masaharu was appointed vice president, then president (19 August; at the same time he became an official of the Imperial Household Ministry). The different posts were renamed; administration was assigned to a separate department. The former departments of the Office of Historiography were merged; one was dissolved and its members transferred to a new department in the Imperial Household Ministry a few months later.

Work in the College of Historiography suffered from lack of resources. The president, Ijichi Masaharu, complained to the minister, Iwakura

Tomomi, more than once.[22] Disagreements among the members of the College also impeded progress. The departments differed not only in their tasks but in character. The department for the imperial genealogies was transferred to the Imperial Household Ministry as a result of these differences; it seems that Ogawa (Ogō) Kazutoshi was the spokesman for this department, as several memoranda and letters by him have been preserved.[23] The transfer did not resolve all the differences in the College.

In spite of these difficulties the College of Historiography was entrusted with new tasks. When the war against the samurai rebels under Saigō Takamori in Kumamoto and Kagoshima ended in 1877, the College was commissioned to compile an account of the war with the title *Seisei shimatsu* (*Account of the Pacification of the West*). This again illustrated the close link between historiography and the description of recent events, shown by the *Fukkoki*. However, the government had more important problems to deal with than writing history and did not show much interest in the work done at the College. In the following years progress was slow. Nevertheless, the belief that the compilation of a national history was a task to be carried out by the government prevailed. In 1881, when another political crisis led to reforms, official historiography was reorganized once again.

2.4 The Political Crisis of 1881 and the Reorganization of the College of Historiography

The political crisis of 1881 was similar to the one in 1875, in that the government was threatened by disunity within and widespread protest without. As the League for the Establishment of a Diet (*Kokkai kisei dōmei*), which had emerged from the former People's Rights Movement, gained strength, the Hokkaidō Colonization Assets Scandal provided fuel for opposition to the government. Within the government, Ōkuma Shigenobu campaigned for the immediate opening of a parliament. But before opposition inside and outside the government could unite, Itō Hirobumi's ally Inoue Kowashi acted. Ōkuma was expelled from the government on 11 October 1881, and on 12 October an imperial edict announced that a parliament was to be opened in 1890, after the proclamation of a constitution. Once again the government had secured the authority to determine the political fate of the country by decisive action coupled with compromise.

In the political crisis of 1881, the conservative forces in the government prevailed. In the first years following the Restoration the government had been the driving force behind reforms, but after 1881 its efforts concentrated on securing what had been achieved. Armed rebellions no longer posed a threat after the successful suppression of the Satsuma rebellion. Instead, pressure was put on the government by the prefectural assemblies established in 1878 and the now-legitimized political parties demanding constitutional government. By promising to establish a parliament within ten years the government had in part ceded to these demands, and it now stepped up the preparations for a constitution. On 21 October 1881 a new council headed by Itō Hirobumi was established to draft new laws. At the same time measures were introduced with the object of containing the powers of a future parliament. As the Meiji oligarchs had a deep suspicion of political parties, they took steps to limit their influence. The bureaucracy was strengthened so that it would be independent of short-term politics. A new peerage was created; its members constituted the major element in the Upper House and acted as a counterbalance to the political parties. In 1885 a cabinet system was introduced; the cabinet ministers were responsible only to the emperor. The financial position of the imperial household was also secured in order to make it independent of budget debates in parliament.[24]

In education steps were taken to counteract the extreme Westernization and reformatory enthusiasm of the early Meiji years. Under Mori Arinori, who became education minister in 1885, the education system, which had already been systematically reorganized, was placed more securely under government control.[25] Tokyo University became the Imperial University in 1886. It served the state by training government and business leaders and offset the influence of private universities such as the *Tōkyō senmon gakkō* (now Waseda University), founded by Ōkuma Shigenobu in 1882 after his expulsion from the government. Mori had studied in England and the United States and had been an envoy to China and Britain. In his reforms he followed Western models. However, the underlying claim, that the state alone should decide what is best and that education should primarily serve the state, was reactionary and brought Mori close to the National Scholars and Confucianists who wanted their doctrines alone to be treated as authoritative. From the 1880s onwards the political and intellectual climate was increasingly influenced by conservative tendencies, and the representatives of traditional learning were able to regain some of their former influence, much of which they had lost in the years after the Restoration. The study of classical texts was revived in new institutions; a Department of Classics (*Koten kōshūka*) was established at Tokyo University in May 1882. Although it only existed until 1887 it brought forth many notable scholars. An Institute for Japanese Literature (*Kōten kōkyūjo*) was also established in 1882, the present Kokugakuin University.

The reorganization of the College of Historiography in December 1881 formed part of these general efforts to secure what had been achieved and to re-emphasize Japan's own cultural traditions. Moreover, it was an immediate result of the political crisis of 1881, as is evident from a document in the papers of Sanjō Sanetomi, in which the anonymous author expressed his views on the reform of the College of Historiography.[26] The document is not dated, but from the subtitle *Shūshikan kaikaku no gi* (*On the Reform of the College of Historiography*) and the reference to the planned establishment of a parliament in 1890 we can conclude that it was written in 1881. The document stated that the new parliament would debate the budget, and if the College had nothing to show for itself, its funding might be withdrawn. Therefore, it was imperative for an authoritative history of Japan to be written as soon as possible.

At the same time, reorganization of the College of Historiography was probably also motivated by problems within the College itself. Work on the national history was not progressing satisfactorily. It had not even been decided what kind of history was to be written, and officials in the College disagreed about many issues (this is hinted at in a proposal from the College to appoint a vice-inspector, dated 4 November 1881).[27] To put an end to arguments the College was organized on hierarchic lines. The chief editors (*henshū chōkan* and *henshū fukuchōkan*) supervised the work of the four editors (*henshūkan*). Their task was for the first time defined as 'compilation of a chronological history' and took precedence over all other assignments. Work on the chronological history entitled *Dainihon hennenshi* (*Chronological History of Great Japan*) was begun the following year. It was based on the sources that had already been collected; new sources were added, as the collection of sources remained a major task of the College of Historiography. By examining and organizing newly discovered documents, the officials increased their historical knowledge and refined their methods of textual criticism. This, however, was not conducive to producing quick results. Lack of funding and continuing frictions among the officials further impeded progress.

Nevertheless, with the *Dainihon hennenshi* the official national history decreed by the imperial rescript in 1869 was at last begun. But the timing, after the political crisis of 1881, gave the official history a new significance. The *Dainihon hennenshi* became part of the preparations for the proclamation of the Meiji Constitution; later sources indicated that it was expected to be completed by 1890, to coincide with the opening of the first parliament.

However, work on the *Dainihon hennenshi* still did not progress satisfactorily. As the date for the first parliament drew nearer, the future of official historiography once more became an object of debate.

2.5 On the Way to the Meiji Constitution: From Government Office to University Institute

The renewed interest in Japanese traditions, including Japanese history, in the 1880s did not only affect the College of Historiography; two new projects for a definitive history of Japan were initiated in this period.

In June 1883 the History Society (*Shigaku kyōkai*) was established, and it published a review (*Shigaku kyōkai zasshi*). The president was Soejima Taneomi and the secretary was Maruyama Sakura, who had played a prominent role in the disputes between Scholars of National and Chinese Learning, which resulted in the closure of the Education Office in 1870. Among the members of the Society were Konakamura Kiyonori and Kimura Masakoto, who had both been in the first office of historiography in 1869. Maruyama gave a speech at the first meeting, in which he stated that the aim of the Society was to publish a history of Japan written in Japanese. Although no mention of the College of

Historiography was made, Maruyama complained that there were few good histories of Japan and deplored the idea that one could write a history of one's own country in a foreign language (meaning *kanbun*; see Chapter 4.3), thereby indirectly criticizing the work of the College of Historiography. The History Society, however, published only a few articles in its review.[28]

The second project to write a history of Japan was initiated by Iwakura Tomomi. Iwakura had become one of the most conservative statesmen in the Meiji government. While preparations for a constitutional government were progressing, Iwakura's main concern was to make sure that the emperor's supremacy would not be threatened by parliamentary intervention. Moreover, Iwakura feared that by adhering to Western models Japan might not be doing justice to its own political and cultural heritage. While Itō was in Europe to study the constitutional laws of different countries, Iwakura ordered that a history of Japan be compiled that illustrated Japan's special qualities and made them clear to the foreign advisers, who were to receive a translation of the work.[29]

Iwakura may have been influenced by Itō Hirobumi's reports on his conversations with Lorenz von Stein, who gave Itō lectures on constitutional history and constitutional law in Vienna in October 1882.[30] In his lectures Stein stressed that a constitution must be seen in the context of the society in which it evolved. He compared the constitutions of Britain, France, Prussia and Austria to demonstrate that different circumstances produced different constitutions. Legal systems must be studied by taking the historical development of society into account. Stein even urged his Japanese audience to have departments of Latin and Greek established at Japanese universities, as studying the Classics was indispensable in order to understand Western culture. Itō would have liked Stein to come to Japan as an adviser, but Stein declined because of his age. Responding to Itō's invitation in a letter of 15 November 1882, Stein once again stressed the importance of studying constitutions as part of society as a whole and warned him that Japan should not simply adopt the legal system of another country.[31] After the proclamation of the Meiji Constitution, Stein received the text of the Constitution and the commentary in an English translation prepared by Itō Myōji, who had accompanied Itō Hirobumi on his study trip to Europe. In two letters to Japan (the recipient of the letters is unknown), one dated 22 April 1889 and one undated but probably written in the autumn of 1889, Stein discussed the characteristics of Japan's new constitution and urged the Japanese to study the history of their country as a guide to how its articles should be interpreted. When Kaneko Kentarō visited him in Vienna at the end of 1889, Stein, almost on his deathbed, once again mentioned the Japanese constitution and recommended that the Japanese publish a history of the evolution of their constitution to ensure that the account became known abroad as well as in Japan. He also stressed the importance of national history in education to promote love of one's country.[32]

It is not known to what extent Stein's views influenced Iwakura. There is no direct evidence that they did or that they directly inspired the establishment of a department of Japanese history at the Imperial University in 1889, but the similarities in the line of argument as well as the timing make it seem likely. At the very least, Stein confirmed what the Japanese themselves believed. Similar ideas were voiced independently in Japan. Miura Yasushi, for example, Inspector in the College of Historiography, was the author of two memoranda, one addressed to Sanjō Sanetomi in 1880 and one to Itō Hirobumi on the eve of his departure for Europe in 1882.[33] In both memoranda Miura emphasized Japan's special qualities (*koyū no gokokushitsu*), the unbroken line of emperors and the differences between Japan and Western countries. One fact that distinguished Japan from Western countries, according to Miura, was that in Japan parliamentary government was not a result of revolution as in England or France. Miura, therefore, advised Itō to look to Prussia, where the constitution had been granted by a monarch, as a model.

Iwakura set up an Office of Compilation (*Henshūkyoku*) in the Imperial Household Ministry on 2 April 1883, and an outline for a history of Japan was drafted. Two volumes were planned, the first one comprising the history of Japan from its beginnings to the Meiji Restoration and the second volume from the Meiji Restoration to the present. The editor of the first volume was Fukuba Bisei.[34] Fukuba was a scholar of National Learning. The editor of the second volume was Nishi Amane. He was a Confucian scholar, but had studied in the Netherlands. Both the editors and the other men involved in the project were government officials, except for Konakamura Kiyonori, who taught at the Imperial University. None had anything to do with the College of Historiography. The two volumes were entitled *Taisei kiyō* (*Outline of the Imperial Rule*) and organized on the basis of imperial rulers. They were to be written in Japanese in a style that could be generally understood.[35] The history was intended to describe the origins and the evolution of the imperial institution in order to demonstrate the legitimacy of the Meiji restoration of imperial rule. Implicit throughout was that the emperor should hold a dominant position under the new constitution. The work was to be completed within six months, in time for Itō's return from Europe.

Iwakura died on 10 July 1883, before the *Taisei kiyō* could be completed. Although work was continued under the supervision of Yamagata Aritomo, the history was abandoned and the Office of Compilation closed on 11 December 1883. At first the idea was that Inoue Kowashi should complete the history, but he found that the parts already written were full of errors and he was already too busy drafting the constitution. Transferring work on the *Taisei kiyō* to the College of Historiography was also considered, and the College received a printed copy of the parts that had been finished, but, like Inoue Kowashi, the College discovered many errors.[36]

The *Taisei kiyō* was a product of the reaction against the Enlightenment and the Movement for Democratic Rights and served to justify the position of those political leaders who wanted a gradual transition towards constitutional government.[37]

Why did Iwakura order an official history, when such a history was already being written in the College of Historiography? Iwakura's initiative suggests discontent with the way work on chronological history *Dainihon hennenshi* was progressing. The differences between the *Taisei kiyō* and the *Dainihon hennenshi* were significant: the former was written in Japanese, not Sino-Japanese (*kanbun*) and it was not strictly chronological, but arranged according to imperial rulers. Most importantly, it clearly revealed the political aim of the compilers, to demonstrate the uniqueness of Japanese political culture. The focus was on the most recent period. The interpretation of the Meiji Restoration was not fundamentally different from that in the chronicle *Fukkoki* compiled by the Office of Historiography, but the account was more tendentious. In order to serve as a reference for the statesmen drafting the constitution it was to be completed within the short period of six months.

One of the main problems of the College of Historiography was that it failed to produce visible results in the short term. In 1881 its goal had been clearly defined and it had been organized more efficiently. However, the slow rate at which each section of the chronological history was submitted may have finally convinced Iwakura that not much was to be expected from the College. Even the *Fukkoki,* begun ten years before, had not yet been completed.

The History Society and the compilation of the *Taisei kiyō* by Iwakura were only two indications of discontent with work on the *Dainihon hennenshi*. Other sources, too, suggest that the officials in the College of Historiography were subjected to criticism. The College was not fulfilling the expectations of the government at the time the Council of State was abolished and the cabinet system (*naikaku seido*) was introduced in 1885. The immediate reason for this measure was that no successor to Iwakura as minister of the right could be found after his death, but it was also a step on the way to a parliamentary constitution. The imperial advisors were replaced by ministers and a prime minister with considerable powers, Itō Hirobumi.[38] The imperial household minister did not belong to the Cabinet, as the imperial household was separated from the government. Within the cabinet were several offices; one was the College of Historiography, which was renamed the Temporary Office of Historiography (*Rinji shūshikyoku*) in January 1886. The organization remained the same, but the addition of *rinji* (temporary) to the name suggests plans to close the Office in the near future. It is likely that the Office was seen as having fulfilled its purpose once the *Fukkoki* and the *Dainihon hennenshi* were completed, although no documents to that effect have been found.

Another consideration may have been that no office of historiography would be provided for under the new constitution; certainly none of the Western models had a government office for the compilation of an official history. The first draft of the Meiji Constitution was completed in April

1888 and revised in the following months. In October 1888 the transfer of the Temporary Office of Historiography to the Imperial University was discussed. The draft for the cabinet order states that the *Dainihon hennenshi* was expected to be completed in just over a year, in 1890. Attached to the draft were two plans for the budget, one for the year 1889 (23,686 yen) and one for 1890 and the following years (12,000 yen).[39] Both plans formed part of a memorandum submitted by the president of the Imperial University, Watanabe Kōki, and dated October 1888. In his memorandum, Watanabe stressed the importance of history and the necessity of research into Japanese history. He proposed establishing a Department of Japanese History at the Imperial University and transferring the Office of Historiography to the University. The expertise of the men in the Office as well as the documents they had collected would be a great asset to a Department of Japanese History; it would also resolve the problem of what to do with them after the closure of the Office.

Watanabe's views were similar to those expressed by Lorenz von Stein. He believed that the study of history (and geography) formed the key to understanding the laws, politics and economy of any country. According to Watanabe, Japan was studying the history of Western countries, but in this period of profound change Japanese history should also be studied as a basis for reform, and a department of history should be established for that purpose.[40] Watanabe had studied with representatives of the Japanese enlightenment, Mitsukuru Rinshō and Fukuzawa Yukichi, and had been a member of the Iwakura Embassy. Like Iwakura, but not necessarily for the same reasons, he believed Japanese history should be studied as a prerequisite to reform. Presumably this view was widespread enough for a proposal expressing it to be acceptable.

It is obvious from Watanabe's proposal that the Office of Historiography would be closed soon. One can surmise that Watanabe's proposal was the result of previous consultations with members of the Office or other cabinet members. The transfer of the Temporary Office of Historiography (*Rinji shūshikyoku*) to the University, where it became the Temporary Department for the Compilation of a Chronological History (*Rinji hennenshi hensan kakari*), known in English as the Historiographical

Institute, was effected on 30 October 1888. It is unlikely that the transfer was simply a result of Watanabe's proposal (as some Japanese accounts seem to suggest). One day before the move, two editors from the Office, Kume Kunitake and Hoshino Hisashi, were appointed professors of the Imperial University. The appointment of Shigeno followed on 9 November. The year before, 1887, a Department of History (*Shigakka*) had been established. The Department of Japanese History (*Kokushika*) did not come into being until 1889, the year the Meiji Constitution was promulgated. The timing was not coincidental. The constitution marked the beginning of a new era, but at the same time Japan's future development was to be based on its own traditions.[41] Among the ceremonies to celebrate the promulgation of the Meiji Constitution on 11 February 1889 was one held at the Imperial University, during which Shigeno Yasutsugu gave a lecture with the title *Wagakuni korai no kenpō oyobi daigaku no keikyō* (The Constitutions of Our Country since Ancient Times and the Situation of the Universities). In the lecture he compared the texts of the 17 Articles (604) and the *Taihō* Code (701) with that of the Meiji Constitution and concluded that in essence the laws were similar, merely adapted to the times. The tradition of universities, according to Shigeno, also dated back to the seventh century.[42]

In the same month, Shigeno published an essay outlining the causes of the Meiji Restoration in the journal *Bun,* which summarizes Shigeno's views on the Restoration.[43] For Shigeno the causes dated as far back as the establishment of the Kamakura Bakufu by Minamoto Yoritomo in the twelfth century, when the usurpation of imperial rule began. Among the immediate causes, he emphasized the role of the scholars of the Mito domain in demonstrating the legitimacy of imperial rule in their *Dainihonshi* (*History of Great Japan*).

It seems that many officials of the former Office of Historiography were not happy to move to the Imperial University and hoped to return to government service after completing the history. Hoshino is said to have hoped so for years.[44] Some of the officials, among them Miura Yasushi, remained in the government and the new Historiographical Institute had fewer members than the Office of Historiography.[45] Apart from that, work went on as before. Presumably the newly appointed professors had few teaching obligations until the Department of Japanese History was established in June 1889. The new Institute retained the character of a government office and the Imperial University itself was close to the government. It is said that the Institute was known as the History Office (*Shikyoku*) as late as the 1920s, long after its function had changed and it had become a research institute.

For the time being the Historiographical Institute continued to compile an official national history as its predecessors had done. The word *rinji* (temporary) in its name still indicated the temporary nature of its existence, and it seems that it was expected to close when the history was completed.

3

The Activities of the Office of Historiography

Although the compilation of a national history was the main task of the office, it was not the only one. As a government office the Office of Historiography had various functions connected with government administration in the widest sense. Nor was it the only government office in which history was compiled in some way.

3.1 Organization and Staff up to 1881

Little is known about the first office of historiography, so not much can be added to what has been said in the previous chapter. It is unlikely that the national history was begun at the time. The Department of History (*Rekishika*) did not directly succeed this first office, although there was some continuity in Kawada's appointment by the Ministry of Education to write a history of Japan since the emperor Gokomatsu (1392–1412).[1] In the Department of History three different projects were combined, rather arbitrarily it would seem: the compilation of the Chronicle *Fukkoki* by Nagamatsu and his colleagues from the Council of State; the examination of the imperial genealogies by officials from the Department of Rites; and the compilation of a history of Japan by Kawada.

Work on these three projects was continued in the departments of the Office of Historiography (*Shūshikyoku*), which succeeded the Department of History in 1875. The Council of State was informed about the organization of the Office in a document entitled 'Regulations for the Office Organization and the Methods of Compilation in the Office of Historiography' (*Shūshikyoku shokusei oyobi henshū chakushu no hōhō o sadamu*); it confirmed the document's contents by a decree on 19 September 1875.[2] According to the Regulations the Office had four departments; two were responsible for preparing the compilation of a national history by taking the facts from existing histories and collecting the relevant sources. The third department was expected to complete the *Fukkoki* and then compile a chronicle of current events, while the fourth department was to continue work on the imperial genealogies and on the manuscript *Shiryō* begun by Hanawa Hokiichi. There were three different positions in the Office: editor (*shūsen*), co-editor (*kyōshū*) and clerk (*shoki*), and three ranks (*ittō, nitō, santō*; first, second and third). The document mentions 29 names; I found biographical details for 22 of them. The following table gives details of the men employed in 1875: [3]

a.   Name, date of appointment, name of position with rank (the first name of each department is that of the director)
b.   Home, description of rank or profession, dates of birth and death, if known
c.   Positions held before appointment to the Office, if known
d.   Last mention as official in the Office or its successors

President:
a.   Ijichi Masaharu 24.6.1875 *Shūshikyoku sōsai*
b.   Satsuma *hanshi* (vassal), 1828–86
c.   1874 in *Rekishika*
d.   1879 returned to his native province

Department 1
a.   Kawada Takeshi 28.8.1875 *ittō shūsen*
b.   Bitchū (Okayama) Matsuyama *hanshi*, Scholar of Chinese Learning, 1830–96
c.   2.7.1874 *Rekishika goyō kakari* (commissioner)
d.   1882 Imperial Household Ministry, 1884 (in addition), professor at the Imperial University

a.   Takezoe Shin'ichirō 28.8.1875 *nitō shūsen*
b.   Higo (Kumamoto) diplomat, Scholar of Chinese Learning, 1841–1917
c.   29.4.1874 *Shūshikyoku goyō kakari*
d.   1875 Ministry of Finance, 1880 Consul in Tientsin

a.   Gamō Keitei 4.10.1875 *santō shūsen*
b.   Echigo (Niigata), Scholar of Chinese Learning
c.   Official of the Schools Administration (*Daigaku*)
d.   1876

a.   Itō Sukeo 28.8.1875 *ittō shoki*
d.   1879

a.   Watanabe Akira 28.8.1875 *nitō shoki*
d.   1876

a.   Horiguchi Shōkai 28.8.1875 *santō shoki*
d.   1876

Department 2

a.   Shigeno Yasutsugu 20.9.1875 *ittō shūsen* (and *fuku kyokuchō*: deputy director of the Office)
b.   Satsuma *hanshi*, Scholar of Chinese Learning, 1827–1910
c.   14.4.1875 *fuku kyokuchō* (in the Council of State since 1872)
d.   1893 (dismissed)

a.   Yoda Hyakusen 28.8.1875 *santō shūsen* (1876 Department 1)
b.   Shimōsa (Chiba) Sakura *hanju* (Confucian scholar in the service of the domain lord), Scholar of Chinese Learning, 1833–1909
c.   1872 Secretary of the Conference of Prefectural Governors
d.   1881 Ministry of Education

a.   Oka Senjin 28.8.1875 *ittō kyōshū*
b.   Sendai *hanshi*, Scholar of Chinese Learning, 1833–1914
c.   1870 Schools Administration (*Daigaku*)
d.   1877 Director of the Library of Tokyo

a.   Hagiwara Seichū 28.8.1875 *ittō kyōshū*
b.   Edo Confucian scholar, 1830–98
d.   1877 Compilation of a history of diplomacy in the Council of State

a. Kihara Genrei 28.8.1875 *nitō kyōshū*
d. 1878

a. Gokyū Hisabumi 28.8.1875 *santō kyōshū*
b. Bigo (Hiroshima) Scholar of National Learning 1823–86
c. Worked as a teacher before and after his appointment
d. 9.12.1875; succeeded by Hoshino Hisashi

a. Gōmoku Chōhō 4.10.1875 *santō shoki*
d. 1876

Department 3
a. Nagamatsu Miki 20.9.1875 *ittō shūsen* (and *kyokuchō*: Director of the Office)
b. Suō (Yamaguchi) Hagi *hanshi*, 1834–1903
c. 1873 *Rekishikachō* (Director or the Department of History); 14.4.1875 *kyokuchō* (Director of the Office of Historiography)
d. 1884 *genrōin gikan* (Member of the Senate)

a. Chō Hikaru 28.8.1875 *ittō shūsen*
b. Bungo (Ōita) Scholar of Chinese Learning, calligrapher, 1833–95
c. Schools Administration, Ministry of Education, 5.11.1874 *Rekishika goyō kakari* (commissioner in the Department of History)
d. 1878 resigned from government duties after the death of his patron Kido Kōin 1877

a. Hirose Shin'ichi 18.8.1875 *ittō shūsen*
b. Buzen (Fukuoka) Confucian scholar, 1819–84
c. Official in Iwate, then in the Council of State
d. 1879 teacher

a. Yotsuya Suihō 2.9.1875 *ittō kyōshū*
b. Hyōga (Miyazaki) Nobeoka *hanshi*, Scholar of Chinese Learning, 1831–1906

  c. Council of State, 19.6.1874 *Rekishika goyō kakari*
  d. 1881 Secretary of the Senate, lecturer at the Imperial University

  a. Nakamura Teigo 28.8.1875 *nitō kyōshū*
  b. Ōmi (Shiga) Minakuchi *hanshi*, 1822–97
  c. Schools Administration; Council of State; 1874 *Rekishika*
  d. 1879 teacher in Saitama, Shiga

  a. Fujikawa Shōgen 28.8.1875 *santō kyōshū*
  b. Sanuki (Kagawa) Takamatsu *hanshi, kinnōka* (loyalist), expert in fisheries, 1818–91
  c. Council of State, founder of a private school, 1874 *Rekishika*
  d. 1878; 1888 School of fisheries in Osaka; author of many works including one on the Meiji Restoration (*Ishin jikki*)

  a. Hirano Shigehisa 28.8.1875 *ittō shoki*
  b. Shimōsa (Chiba) Sakura *hanshi*, 1814–83
  c. Teacher in Sakura
  d. 1875 compiled a history of Sakura domain

  a. Sawato Kōkō 28.8.1875 *nitō shoki*
  d. 1884

Department 4
  a. Tanimori Yoshiomi 28.8.1875 *santō shūsen*
  b. Kyoto Courtier of the house of Sanjō, 1817–1911
  c. Office of Historiography in the School (*Gakkō*), Examination of the imperial genealogies, *Rekishika*
  d. 1886; since 1877, mainly in the Imperial Household Ministry; author of various works, some on history

  a. Ogawa (Ogō) Kazutoshi 28.8.1875 *santō shūsen*
  b. Bungo (Ōita) Oka *hanshi* 1813–86
  c. Department for the Examination of the Imperial Genealogies; 1873 *Rekishika*

d.   1877 Imperial Household Ministry

a.   Ōtani Hidezane 28.8.1875 *nitō kyōshū*
b.   Iwami (Shimane) Tsuwano *hanshizoku*
c.   1874 *Rekishika*
d.   1877

a.   Shioda Ekisui 28.8.1875 *santō kyōshū*
b.   Izumo (Shimane) Mori *hanshi*
c.   *Rekishika*
d.   1877

a.   Juge Shigekuni 4.10.1875 *santō kyōshū*
b.   Ōmi (Shiga) *kinnōka*, 1822–84
c.   Pupil of Tanimori; Department of Rites; 1874 *Rekishika*
d.   1877

a.   Matsuura Chōnen 4.10.1875 *santō kyōshū*
c.   1874 *Rekishika*
d.   1876 (13.6.) dismissed because of illness

a.   Kajiyama Yoshikado 18.8.1875 *ittō shoki*
b.   Tōkyō-fu *kizoku, shizoku* (peer)
d.   1877

Although it is not always possible to discover details about the men named, some tendencies emerge. Most officials came from a few regions: six from Kyushu, five from southern Honshu (three from the San'in, two from the San'yō district), three each from the Kyoto and the Tokyo areas. These are also the regions from which most of the Meiji leaders came.[4] The officials were usually former vassals of the lord of their native domain. They had been educated in the Chinese classics, whether or not they were known as *kangakusha* (Scholars of Chinese Learning). Most of them were between 40 and 60 years old in 1875. Many had studied in Edo at the bakufu school *Shōheikō*: Gokyū, Kawada, Hirano, Gamō,

Fujikawa, Yotsuya, Oka, Hagiwara and Yoda; some of them had been there at the same time, during the Kaei era (1848–53). It is known that some of them were friends since their student days, for example Shigeno and Oka, and Fujino and Miura, who were appointed to the Office later.

Only comparatively few of the men in the Office of Historiography are known to have studied or written history prior to their appointment. The most experienced were probably Nagamatsu and Shigeno. Nagamatsu had compiled a history of loyalist achievements in the Meiji Restoration for his domain just after the Restoration. Shigeno had compiled a history of Japan for the lord of Satsuma, Shimazu Hisamitsu, before the Restoration. Some of the men are characterized as loyalists (*sonnōka* or *kinnōka*: Nakamura, Chō, Oka, Fujikawa) or their biographies are included among those of the heroes of the Meiji Restoration (*Kokuji ōshō hōkō shishi jinmeiroku*; Ijichi, Yoda, Juge, Fujino). They were engaged in activities described as *kokuji ni tsutometa*, that is, they fought for the loyalist cause in the years leading up to the Restoration. These men were probably no different from other government officials. Certainly they were not specialists in the field of historical research and writing. Some of them might have been appointed because of their literary talents, others because the government had no better use for them.

The four departments of the Office of Historiography corresponded to the projects in progress in the former Department of History. There were some differences between the departments and there is evidence that this caused friction.[5] Most of the members of Department 4 were scholars of National Learning, as opposed to Chinese Learning; the men in Department 3 had been particularly active before the Meiji Restoration and had probably been appointed as a reward for their political loyalty rather than for their literary or scholarly talents. The ranks listed above do not correspond to those given in later sources; obviously many of the high-ranking officials classified as editors (*shūsen*) did not rise to any position of importance (Takezoe, Chō, Hirose) and in some cases soon left the Office. Presumably the position someone held initially had more to do with his rank by birth and his political background than with his role in the Office.

Most of the men in the Office of Historiography in 1875 did not remain there for long. Only 5 out of 29 were still in the Office after its major reorganization at the end of 1881. Even of those who were appointed as editors in 1875, that is, to the highest position, only Shigeno, Nagamatsu and Tanimori remained in the office after 1881, and only Shigeno was influential. In fact, he was the most important man in official historiography until its abandonment in 1893.

Shigeno Yasutsugu (1827–1910) was the son of a vassal of the house of Shimazu, the lord of the Satsuma domain.[6] He studied at Satsuma domain school and from 1848 to 1854 at the *Shōheikō* in Edo. He was politically active during the Restoration years, following which he became an official of the Council of State. Shigeno was one of the few men with previous experience of writing history. While teaching in Satsuma, he was ordered by Lord Shimazu Hisamitsu to compile a chronological history of Japan entitled *Kōchō seikan*. An office (*Shikyoku*) was established in the domain school. Shigeno and his assistants closely adhered to the history of the Mito school, and their work was little more than a chronological version of the *Dainihonshi*. However, Shigeno attempted to correct some of the errors in the *Dainihonshi*. His critical examination of this work marked the beginning of his historical scholarship.[7]

Until 1881, Kawada Takeshi (1830–96), head of Department 1, rivalled Shigeno in importance. He came from the Matsuyama (Takahashi) domain (Okayama prefecture), and his master had sided with the shogun during the Restoration. In spite of this, Kawada became an official in the new Ministry of Education. He was later favoured by statesmen from Chōshū, who regarded him as a victim of the Satsuma clique.

Kawada was soon joined by his friend Yoda, who moved to Department 1 in 1876 and from whose diaries we learn something of the conflicts between Shigeno and Kawada.[8] Yoda was replaced by Fujino Masahira (Kainan; 1826–88), who was first appointed commissioner (*goyō kakari* – his name appears in second place after Shigeno's) and then, in 1877, editor. Fujino was a friend of Shigeno's from *Shōheikō* times.[9] He came from the Matsuyama domain (Ehime prefecture) and, like Shigeno, had been politically active in the years leading up to the

Restoration, persuading his domain to side with the new government. After the Restoration he was appointed professor to the *Shōheikō* and commissioned to compile the national history, and so was one of the few men who had some experience of compiling history before joining the Office. After his appointment he and Shigeno compiled the sources of the Ashikaga and the Tokugawa period and wrote an account of the reign of the last emperor before the Restoration, entitled *Senchō kiryaku*. Fujino seems to have been a respected scholar and Shigeno thought highly of him, but little is known about him. According to Shigeno this was true even in his lifetime;[10] he died in 1888, before the Office of Historiography was transferred to the Imperial University and its members began to publish the results of their work.

Over the next few years the members of Departments 1 and 2, who were engaged in compiling sources for the national history, described as an urgent task in the imperial rescript of 1869, came to dominate the Office.

Sanjō Sanetomi, who had been appointed president of official historiography by the emperor in 1869, did not have the time to concern himself with it; in fact there is no evidence that he was at all interested. A vice president was therefore appointed in response to the Office's submission *Shūshi jigi* (Chapter 2.3).[11] This was Ijichi Masaharu, a vassal of the former lord of Satsuma, who had played a leading role in the Restoration and held various high offices since 1871. In 1877 he became president, but in 1879 he asked to be relieved of his duties and returned to his home in Satsuma. He had less authority than Sanjō, but may have been more active, for when he fell ill, members of the Office wished that he would recover soon and resume his duties.[12] Sanjō was reappointed president once again on 21 May 1879. Neither the regulations of 1877 nor those of 1881 provided for a vice president, but on 22 December 1883 a new one was appointed: Date Munenari.

When the Office of Historiography was abolished in 1877 and replaced by the College of Historiography, it was in response to the financial needs of the government, but at the same time, work in the College became focused on the national history. Department 4 (imperial genealogies) was dissolved and its members transferred to Department 1 and then to the

Imperial Household Ministry. This meant that most of the scholars of National Learning left the Office, although one or two remained as commissioners (*goyō kakari*; Chapter 6.2). The Departments 1 to 3 became the Departments 2a and 2b and 3a; 3b became the Department of Topography. The most important post in the College of Historiography was that of editor (*henshūkan*).[13] The editors were Nagamatsu, Chō, Shigeno, Kawada, Ogō, Yoda, Fujino as well as Tsukamoto and Kawada Higuma from the Department of Topography.

For the first time administration was separated from the scholarly work and became the new Department 1. The first official to be appointed to the task was Miyajima Seiichirō, who became a commissioner in 1876. In October 1877 Miura Yasushi was appointed inspector (*kanji*). Miyajima Seiichirō (1838–1911) was a vassal of the lord of Yonezawa in Dewa (Yamagata prefecture).[14] He was appointed to the Council of State after the Restoration, where he was very active and wrote a memorandum concerning a constitution for Japan. He did not gain much influence, however, and his appointment to the Office of Historiography in 1876 represented his removal from the centre of political activity. Miura Yasushi (1829–1910) from Iyo (Ehime prefecture) had been an associate of Shigeno and Fujino at the *Shōheikō*. He too had been politically active in the years before the Restoration.[15] He was an administrator in the Office until it was transferred to the Imperial University, when he remained in the government. The third official responsible for administration was Iwaya Osamu (Ichiroku; 1834–1905), a government official. He was appointed editor (*henshūkan*) in 1879 and deputy inspector (*fuku kanji*) in 1881 and proofread the chronicle *Fukkoki* (1882–24).[16]

We can get a picture of the work done in the Office of Historiography from 1876 to 1888 from the reports on its progress which were submitted twice a year.[17] According to the first report, for the first half of 1876, Department 1 completed three manuscripts with a chronological table and the sources relating to each event (*shiryō kōhon*) for the period from 1392 to 1394. In Department 2, work was done simultaneously on the beginning, the middle and the end of the Edo period, and 14 manuscripts were completed: four for 1612–13, five for 1716 and five for 1863. In

Department 3, two volumes of the *Fukkoki* were completed for the year 1867, as well as the first part of *Meiji shiyō* (1867–70). In Department 4, four volumes of documents in chronological order for the year 1025 were completed. Work on all these tasks was continued in the following years. The figures given above show how slow progress was; a few years, sometimes only months, were covered at a time. New assignments were added; in the second half of 1876, Department 2 compiled a history of the domains (*Hanshi kō*) and a chronicle of the reign of the previous emperor (*Senchō kiryaku*).

After the reorganization, Department 2a (formerly 1) compiled sources from the period of the Northern and Southern Courts to the beginning of Tokugawa rule and investigated the imperial genealogies. Department 2b worked on the Edo period and 3a on the Meiji Restoration, compiling the *Fukkoki* and the *Meiji shiyo*. 3b was the Department of Topography. The reports for the following years record additional assignments. In 1879 the departments 2a and 2b had to compile an outline of Japanese History (*Nihon shiryaku*). Even the administrative department had to compile a record of the men who lost their lives during the Meiji Restoration (*Junnan jinmeishi*) in 1877–8. With so many diverse tasks to complete, it is hardly surprising that work on the official history did not progress. This changed in 1881.

3.2 Organization and Staff after 1881

The reorganization of the College of Historiography in 1881 marked a decisive step towards the compilation of an official history, which at last became the central task of the Office. A more hierarchic organization than previously was introduced to prevent continuous disputes from impeding progress. At the same time it appears that certain men, led by Shigeno, had successfully asserted themselves. It was at this time that Kawada left the Office. According to Kume, the immediate cause was an inquiry by President Sanjō about the progress made in the Office. Shigeno wished to start compiling the national history at once, while Kawada favoured leaving it to a later date and concentrating on collecting and arranging documents. Shigeno's opinion, which was shared by Kume, won the day.[18] In fact, there had been friction between Shigeno and Kawada for a long time and Kawada's friend Yoda saw the reorganization as a takeover by Shigeno.[19] Kawada entered the Imperial Household Ministry where he was employed until his death. His work there included historical research, but he was not involved in the compilation of the history *Taisei kiyō* ordered by Iwakura. Kawada taught at the Imperial University from 1884 to 1888 and then at the Institute of Japanese Literature, but he taught Chinese Learning, not history.[20]

Kawada and Shigeno were equally respected during their lifetimes; they were two of the so-called 'Three Literary Masters of the Meiji Era' (*Meiji no Sandai bunsō*).[21] However, Kawada's achievements are virtually unknown today. He published less than Shigeno and there is no edition of his collected works.[22]

After the reorganization, the chief editor and his deputy (*henshū chōkan, henshū fukuchōkan*) determined how the history would be compiled and supervised the work of the editors (*henshūkan*). No chief editor was appointed, so Shigeno Yasutsugu, the deputy editor, was formally in charge for all practical purposes. Nagamatsu Miki, though higher in rank than Shigeno, only worked on the *Fukkoki* and was made inspector (*kanji*). Shigeno may well have influenced the shape and progress of official historiography more than anyone else. His colleague Kume later emphasized the bureaucratic character of his scholarship, calling him a scholar with the character of a politician and stating that he always remained a 'history official' (*shikan*).[23] While his scholarship was deeply rooted in the tradition of the Edo period, he became one of the foremost representatives of historical scholarship in the Meiji period. His strength was his critical examination and correction of scholarly works using refined methods of textual criticism. He was very exact, almost pedantic, but not particularly creative. When it came to actually writing the official history, he was not directly involved, leaving it to the editors.[24]

The editors arranged the material collected by the archivists (*shōki*) and wrote the commentaries to the quoted documents. In addition, copyists (*zenshasei, shajisei*), often former samurai, were employed.[25] The editors' task was for the first time described as 'compilation of a chronological history' (*hennenshi o sen su*).[26] Other tasks such as the completion of the *Fukkoki* were treated as minor. The former departments were dissolved and the work done so far became the basis for the chronological history; the report submitted in December 1881 includes a list of the periods for which the sources had already been collected and arranged in chronological order. While the compilation of source materials was continued, four editors started to write the chronological history in 1882. This was entitled *Dainihon hennenshi* (*Chronological History of Great Japan*). The four editors were Kume Kunitake, Fujino Masahira, Ijichi Sadaka and Hoshino Hisashi. Only two of them had been in the Office for a number of years: Fujino and Hoshino. By now several officials who had held high-ranking positions in 1875 were no longer in the Office.

What kind of men then were the four new editors? Fujino we already know to have been an important member of the Office since 1876. Hoshino Hisashi (Tsune, Hōjō; 1839–1917) was appointed the same year as Fujino. Hoshino's regional and social background was different from that of his colleagues. He came from Echigo (Niigata prefecture), from a family who had been farmers for generations.[27] Although Hoshino was his parents' eldest son, he was permitted in 1859 to leave the farm to his brother and study in Edo. He spent eight years at the private school of the Confucian scholar Shionoya Tōin. After Shionoya's death, Hoshino returned home and taught Confucian classics at the local school, where he became headmaster.

In 1875 Hoshino returned to Tokyo. He became acquainted with Shigeno and was appointed to the Office of Historiography. It is said that Hoshino knew nothing about Japanese history; an anecdote records that when he was the guest of influential families in his home province and the conversation turned to Japanese history, Hoshino always went very red with embarrassment.[28] It is true that Chinese and Confucian studies (*kangaku*) were limited to Chinese history.

Hoshino remained in the Office of Historiography and its successors until 1899. When the Historiographical Institute (*Hennenshi hensan kakari*) was temporarily closed after Kume's and Shigeno's dismissals in 1893, it was Hoshino who administrated the Institute until its reopening in 1895. He was director of the reopened Institute until 1899. In 1888 he was appointed professor at the Imperial University and taught Japanese history and Chinese and Japanese literature. His historical writings were published in two volumes in 1909.

Kume Kunitake (1839–1931) was appointed to the Office of Historiography in 1879 and became its most influential member after Shigeno. He was from Hizen (Saga prefecture), one of the domains that had played a leading role in the Meiji Restoration. Kume was a member of the Iwakura Embassy and an archivist in the government before he became a member of the Office of Historiography. Like Shigeno and Hoshino he was made a professor in 1888, but was dismissed in 1892. Kume's importance in the development of modern Japanese historical scholarship rivals Shigeno's.[29]

The fourth and least important of the editors appointed in 1881 was Ijichi Sadaka (1826–87), who had only become a member of the College of Historiography a few months previously. He was a vassal of the lord of Satsuma.[30] Ijichi Sadaka had studied at the *Shōheikō* at the same time as Miura and Shigeno. Together with Shigeno and Ijichi Masaharu he took part in the negotiations between the Satsuma domain and Britain following the killing of a British merchant, Charles Richardson, and wounding of two British men by vassals from the Satsuma domain in 1862 (the Namamugi Incident). After the Meiji Restoration, Sadaka conducted reforms in Satsuma. In 1871 he was ordered to conduct negotiations with the king of the Ryukyu Islands and to report to the Meiji government about the killing of inhabitants of the Ryukyus by men from Formosa (Taiwan). In the following years he was in charge of Ryukyu affairs until he was dismissed in 1876; perhaps the government had no more use for him after the affairs of the Ryukyu islands had been temporarily dealt with.[31]

When Sadaka became a member of the College of Historiography in June 1881, he first edited a work on the Ryukyus (*Okinawa shi*) before he became an editor of the *Dainihon hennenshi,* which he remained until his death in 1887. Compared to his achievements before the Restoration his later career was not remarkable. Nor is he known to have possessed any literary talents. Presumably he was appointed to the College because he came from Satsuma and was on good terms with Ijichi Masaharu, Shigeno and Miura. The editors of the *Dainihon hennenshi* (with the possible exception of Hoshino) were not very different from the other officials. They became the most important men in the Office, while the editors of the *Fukkoki,* which had been the starting point for official historiography, had little influence. In 1882 work on the *Fukkoki* was almost abandoned, but Nagamatsu prevented this.

In 1883 another vice president was appointed: Date Munenari (1817–92), who had taken Masaharu's place for a while in 1877.[32] He had been the last lord but one of Uwajima (Ehime prefecture). In 1858 he retired following the Ansei purges. He then tried to mediate between the court and the bakufu. After the Meiji Restoration he held high-level positions in the government, but he wielded little political influence, and it is significant that biographical dictionaries such as the *Konsaisu jinmei jiten* and the *Meiji ishin jinmei jiten* have nothing to say about him after 1871.

Date Munenari became vice president of the Office at retirement age, but his journal *Shūshikan bibō* testifies that he went to work nearly every day. He read among other things the chronicles *Fukkoki* and *Seisei shimatsu* (the latter inspired him to write a poem in the journal) and was obviously involved in the activities of the Office. He was relieved of his office in 1886.

Date Munenari is another example of a member who had served the cause of the Meiji Restoration, but had failed to gain much political influence after 1868 (though in his case that could have been partly due to his age). Most members of the Office of Historiography had no particular qualifications to write history beyond the education usual for members of their class and worked in the Office for no longer than a few years. Only three members came to play a decisive role not only in official historiography but, after the transfer of the Office to the Imperial University, in historical scholarship: Shigeno, who by then had been in the Office longest, and two of the editors appointed in 1881, Hoshino and Kume.

The reorganization in 1881 did not resolve all the conflicts among the members of the Office. In 1884 Shigeno and Iwaya addressed a letter to President Sanjō Sanetomi, in which they stressed that the work of the College of Historiography demanded scholarly abilities (*gakuryoku*) and literary talent (*bunsai*). They went on to say that the officials appointed recently were not only not suited to the task, but because of their high rank behaved as if they were superiors, interfered with the teamwork of the others and impeded progress.[33] Enclosed with the letter was a list of officials recently transferred by the Council of State. The list included people like Matsudaira Noritsugu and Maeda Toshichika, who came from families that had been powerful in the Tokugawa period, but also Juge Shigekuni (1822–84) who had been in the Office of Historiography in 1875. Juge came from a family of priests of the Hiyoshi Shrine in Sakamoto (near Kyoto). He had studied National Learning with Tanimori Yoshiomi and had been politically active at the end of the Edo period, supporting Iwakura Tomomi. After the Restoration he became an official in the Department of Rites, the Council of State and the Imperial Household Ministry. It is remarkable that he was appointed to the Office of Historiography a second time, even though he had not distinguished himself there before.[34]

The immediate reason for the letter appears to have been that the compilation of sources by the prefectures had been given up. The money saved was used to pay for additional staff in the Office of Historiography. The men were transferred from other offices, where they were no longer needed. This is hinted at in a memorandum presumably written by Shigeno in 1885, in which he emphasizes the importance of collecting primary sources. Additional funds, wrote Shigeno, should be spent on collecting documents, not on superfluous staff. In two letters addressed to Vice President Date Munenari on 3 June and 6 June 1885, Shigeno was more outspoken.[35] In particular he complained about Chōno Tōkage, the first name on the list in the letter to Sanjō Sanetomi, whom he regarded as extremely inefficient and generally a nuisance and wanted to see transferred as soon as possible. Chōno Tōkage (Tanzan; 1831–1916) was a former samurai from the Kōchi domain. His biography is again typical of an official in the Office of Historiography. He had worked for the imperial cause during the Meiji Restoration, but after 1868 was not strong or not competent enough to gain an important position in the new government. However, while Chōno and the other men appointed around that time came from the same background as the other officials, the latter had by now gained considerable experience on the job and had become specialists. That the Office of Historiography was regarded as a place to accommodate people for whom no better use could be found shows how little importance was attached to official historiography.

When the College of Historiography was replaced by the Temporary Office of Historiography (*Rinji Shūshikyoku*) in the Cabinet in 1886, there was no reorganization. The staff was reduced; the lists submitted by the College of Historiography name around 40 men, the list for January 1886 only 36.[36] Work continued as before. Nor did its task change when it was transferred to the Imperial University in 1888. It became the Temporary Department for the Compilation of a Chronological history (*Rinji hennenshi hensan kakari*), known in English as the Historiographical Institute.[37] Many officials remained in the government, and the report submitted at the end of the year 1888 lists only ten names. Shigeno was made chief editor (*hensan iinchō*); Kume and Hoshino were editors (*hensan iin*). They are named as the editors of the *Dainihon hennenshi*, together with Kusaka Hiroshi (Shakusui; 1852–1926), a clerk (*shoki*). There were eight more clerks, among them Tanaka Yoshinari and Kan Masatomo, and a few men whose duties were described as 'dealing with the remaining tasks' (*zanmu toriatsukai*).

In the following years university graduates came to be recruited, first from the Department of Chinese and Japanese Classics (*Koten kōshūka*) and then from the departments of history. Among them was Mikami Sanji, appointed assistant (*hensan joshu*) in September 1889, who later became director.[38] This was more than a generational change; the gradual replacement of officials by specialized scholars represented a new departure in the history of the Institute.

3.3 'Applied History'

The term 'applied history' was used by the historian Tsuboi Kumezō (1858–1936) in his article 'On History'. In analogy to the natural sciences he spoke about *ōyō shigaku* (applied history) and *junshō shigaku* (pure history).[39] Similarly, Kume, in his article 'Insight in History', distinguished between *ōyōsha,* who apply historical knowledge, and *senshūsha,* specialists.[40] The dangers of such a distinction are evident from the way Japanese historical scholarship developed from the late

Meiji period onwards. The nature of official historiography facilitated the distinction. The Department of History and the Office of Historiography were part of the government and involved in various tasks broadly related to the past, but not directly to writing history.

The collection of documents, especially recent ones, had more to do with administration than with historiography; it served to provide necessary information for the government. Immediately after the Restoration the government had to know which domains it could rely upon, for it had still to break the resistance of former supporters of the bakufu. This is probably why, in 1869, the Meiji government twice ordered the domains to conduct investigations on people who had died during the Restoration and their families.[41] In the following year the lords and the court nobles were ordered to submit their documents dating from 1853 onwards. The Shizuoka domain (formerly part of the shogun's home domains) had to submit the records of the old government. In 1872 the ministries were ordered to submit their records since the Boshin war in 1868. A few months later, the ministries, other offices and the new prefectural governments were ordered to collect their own records. The former feudal lords and families of the nobility were told to do the same and also to compile genealogical tables of their families to supplement the tables in the *Zoku hankanpu* (*Sequel to the List of Daimyō Family Trees*) compiled by the bakufu. A similar order was issued to the court nobility and the Shinto and Buddhist priests in 1874.

On 5 May 1873 the buildings that housed the Council of State burnt down and most of the documents collected to that date were lost. What remains of the collections is now in the Historiographical Institute. In February 1874 the prefectures were once again ordered to submit documents to replace the ones lost in the fire. In addition, orders were issued to investigate the achievements of certain men for the compilation of *Fukko kōjin,* a record of subjects who had served the cause of the Restoration (Iwakura Tomomi, Sanjō Sanetomi and another 21 men), as well as the *Kokuji kinrō,* a record of people who had served the state (Yamagata Aritomo and 31 other men). It seems that the government was attempting to compile a kind of canon of the heroes of the Restoration.

In 1873 the former feudal lords had been ordered to submit documents for the compilation of the *Fukkoki,* the official chronicle of the Meiji Restoration. In 1874 the prefectures were asked to record the development of their regions up to 1875; the records were then to be continuously updated. The Department of History had previously suggested that an editor for a history of each former domain (*hanshi henshū*) be appointed in the prefectures, but this had been rejected because of the high cost.

As well as information about the historical development of the regions, topographical data were compiled. For this purpose a separate office (*Chishika*) was established in the Council of State in 1872, and in 1875 the prefectures received funds for the compilation of *Kōkoku chishi* (Topographies of the Empire).[42] Most of the topographical compilations were in the library of the Imperial University when it burnt down in 1923, and only a few have been preserved in local archives.[43]

The orders issued to the prefectures were usually accompanied by instructions on how to proceed. The ones for the genealogies were brief and left the families some freedom, such as whether to write in Japanese (*wabun*) or Sino-Japanese (*kanbun*).[44] The instructions for the histories of the prefectures (*fukenshi),* issued in 1873, were more detailed.[45] They began with a few general remarks on historiography followed by a list of things that should be included in the histories. For the biographies similarly specific instructions were issued, which included the treatment of the various first names and what kind of information about the family of a given person was required.[46] In 1876 new guidelines for the compilation of the prefectural histories were issued, but they were not much different from previous ones except that they were more specific. They also advised the prefectures to appoint a chief editor, to whom the Department of History could address queries and requests to examine the work.[47] Some attempts were made to ensure that the resulting histories possessed some degree of uniformity. In the following years some of the prefectures submitted manuscripts; they are preserved in the Historiographical Institute. However, in 1885 the whole project was abandoned and the Office of Historiography itself assumed responsibility for the compilation of sources in the regions. Some local histories were also compiled in the Office (in Department 2b), guidelines for which were drawn up in 1877.[48] The focus was on the domains that had played a decisive role during the

Meiji Restoration, and the question of which domains to single out, seven or eight of them, gave rise to some discussion.[49]

More important than the histories compiled in the prefectures are the sources collected there. They are preserved as *Fuken Shiryō* in the library of the Cabinet (*Naikaku bunko*) in the National Archives.[50] In 1962 microfilms were made of them and a catalogue with a short introduction was published.[51] Many prefectures made duplicates of their compilations, so that a second copy is preserved in some prefectural archives (Kyoto, Yamanashi, Nagasaki). After the Second World War the value of these documents as sources of local history was discovered and they were used for the publication of prefectural histories. Beside the sources compiled by the prefectures, the *Fuken Shiryō* collection includes the documents collected between 1877 and 1883 by the Office of Historiography; documents concerning the prefectures from the central government offices, copied on paper marked '*Shūshikan*' (indicated in the catalogue). The collections by Fukui and Mie prefectures include their correspondence with the Office of Historiography, which gives an idea of how the task was performed. The compilations vary considerably from prefecture to prefecture, but the collection as a whole offers valuable information on the political, economic and social situation in most regions around the time of the Meiji Restoration.[52]

Collecting information was one important task; controlling the dissemination of information was another. In September 1873 the Department of History was asked to check two historical works submitted to the Ministry of Education before publication in accordance with the publishing regulations (*shuppan jōrei*) issued in 1869 and 1872. The request apparently caused consternation. In a draft document preserved in *Shimatsu* the Department pointed out that the number of works they had to deal with was more than its few members could manage. Besides, the Ministry of Education could not refuse permission to publish on the grounds of factual errors, since the publishing regulations did not provide for publication to be prohibited for this reason. In any case, unless the regulations were changed, examining works intended for publication was the responsibility of the Ministry of Education. Eventually the Department of History declined to examine the historical works.[53]

In this document, the Department referred to a work they had been asked to examine the previous year. This was *Kinsei shiryaku* (*Outline of Modern History*) by Yamaguchi Ken, which dealt with the period from the arrival of Commodore Perry in 1853 to the end of the conflict between the Restoration army and the troops of the shogunate in 1869. It contained many factual errors and its sale was prohibited in 1872. It was then submitted to the Ministry of Education because the author wished to publish a revised edition. The Ministry passed it on to the Department of History, which said it could not point out and correct every single error. *Kinsei shiryaku* was not much different from other works of its kind. However, it was translated into English by the British diplomat and Japan expert Sir Ernest Satow and thus became known abroad; this was noted with concern by members of the Office of Historiography.[54]

Another work passed on to the Department of History was the *Dainihon yashi* (*Private History of Japan*) by Iida Tadahiko (1799–1861), who had been in the service of the family of court nobles Arisugawa no Miya. The *Dainihon yashi* was conceived as a sequel to the history *Dainihonshi,* covering the period up to Emperor Ninkō (1817–46). The author had spent 40 years working on it and the preface is dated 1851. In 1870 a representative of the Arisugawa family had written to the Council of State for permission to publish the work of his vassal. In 1873 an application was submitted to the Ministry of Education, which passed the work on to the Department of History for examination. The Department concluded that the *Dainihon yashi* contained numerous errors. Several errors were mentioned, most of them relating to the period of the two imperial courts (*Nanbokuchō*).[55] Moreover, the Department claimed that the work was strongly biased in favour of the Tokugawa shogunate. Nevertheless it recommended publication on the condition that errors directly concerning the moral principles governing the relationship between ruler and subjects (*taigi meibun*) be corrected.[56]

More significant than the examination of manuscripts for publication was the collaboration between the Department of History and the Ministry of Education to compile school textbooks, and this will be treated later in this chapter.

The Ministry of Education was not the only government body to address inquiries to the Department of History or its successors. Many inquiries concerned the imperial genealogies. On 4 February 1876 the Ministry of Religious Affairs inquired about the tomb of one of the sons of the emperor Godaigo, and the Office of Historiography answered on 15 February. The Office often had to deal with similar inquiries from the Ministry of Religious Affairs or the Senate (*Genrōin*). Sometimes they sparked off a lengthy dispute, such as the one with the Imperial Household Ministry about Iitoyo-ao-no-himemiko. [57]

In 1877 the Office received an inquiry from the Department of Rites in the Office of Ceremonies (*Shikiburyō*) in the Ministry of Home Affairs. It concerned the date of the festival at the Fujishima shrine, which had been built on the site of the death of Nitta no Yoshisada, a fourteenth-century hero.[58]

In 1879 the Office examined the classified register of nobles (*Kazoku ruibetsu roku*) compiled by Iwakura and wrote a commentary (*Kazoku rui betsu roku kōan*).[59] The genealogies of the nobility occupied the members of the Office several times, for in 1884 a law regulating the ranks of the peerage (*kazoku rei*) was promulgated. In addition to the existing nobility, rank was given to men considered to have rendered great service to the country or the descendants of such men. Many fourteenth-century heroes posthumously received ranks and often monuments were erected in their memory.[60] It was up to the scholars in the Office of Historiography to determine who was the most deserving, namely who had fought on the 'right' side, that is on the side of the emperor Godaigo and his successors in the conflicts between the divided courts and with the shoguns. Thorough investigations were required for the case of Nanbu Moroyuki (?–1338), whose descendant Nanbu Toshichika proposed in December 1883 that his ancestor receive honours similar to those bestowed on Nitta Yoshisada. The Office of Historiography acknowledged Moroyuki's merits, but denied he was Toshichika's ancestor, asserting that the genealogical tables were forged.[61] The Office also dismissed the application of one Kōno Bukichirō from Tokushima, who wished honours to be bestowed on his ancestor Kōno Michimori or Michiharu (?–1364). He claimed that Michimori had fought for the Southern court together with Doi Michimasu (?–1336) and

Tokunō Michitsuna (?–1337). The Office had carried out thorough investigations on both of them in 1882–83 and not deemed them worthy of a rank.[62] According to the Office of Historiography, Michimori had sided with Ashikaga Takauji and fought against Doi and Tokunō.[63] In another case it was the Office of Historiography which took the initiative; in 1882 it proposed with reference to the example of Kojima Takanori to build a shrine in memory of Kitabatake Chikafusa, the author of the history *Jinnō shōtōki* (Chapter 1).[64]

On a few occasions members of the Office of Historiography were entrusted with the composition of inscriptions for the tombs of deceased leaders of the Meiji Restoration; in 1877 Kawada was asked to do this for Kido Kōin and in 1878 Shigeno was asked to do so for Ōkubo Toshimichi. The inscriptions were not completed until 1881.[65] In 1881 Kume was ordered to compile the record of the imperial journey to the provinces on the Pacific coast (*Tōkai tōsan junkō nikki*).[66] Tasks of this kind show that historiography was not yet regarded as separate from other activities involving the recording of events for future generations.

The Office of Historiography was also called upon to represent Japan abroad. At the world exhibition in Philadelphia in 1876 the first volume of the *Meiji shiyō* (*Outline of the Meiji Restoration*), which the Office had recently published, was shown together with publications from the Department of Topography.[67] More importantly, for the world exhibition in Paris in 1878 the Office prepared specially a history of Japan with the title *Nihon shiryaku* (*Outline of the History of Japan*). Work on it was begun in 1877.[68] The history was not much more than a chronicle of events arranged according to the reign of the emperors. It was later revised and published as the *Kokushi gan* (*View of Our National History*), which was used as a textbook in the newly established Department of Japanese History at the Imperial University.

In fact official historiography and education were linked in several ways from the beginning. The standard history was, according to the Rescript of 1869, to serve education, and immediately after the Meiji Restoration historiography and education were both under the control of the same office, the Schools Administration (*Gakkō*). The Ministry of Education, which succeeded the Schools Administration Office, had an

Office for Compilation (*henshūkyoku*), which subsequently became part of the Department of History.

Certainly history was regarded as an important subject to be taught in schools. This was not new, for in the Edo period the study of history had formed a significant part of Confucian education.[69] History, usually Chinese history, had provided the examples for the moral principles taught in Confucian classics, and historical events were judged according to Confucian principles. Towards the end of the Edo period history, including the history of Japan, gradually became a field of study in its own right. The first historical textbooks were published, usually digests of the history *Dainihonshi* or other highly regarded works. This trend continued into the Meiji period. In 1872 the Education Law (*gakusei*) treated history (which included world history and Japanese history) and moral education (*shūshinka*) as two separate subjects. In the first years after the Restoration history was usually taught in the spirit of the Enlightenment and not so much as part of the Confucian tradition. The history of Western countries dominated.

The general trend in education in the Meiji period was towards a greater standardization on a national scale of both the system and what was taught.[70] The textbooks reflected the trend; up to 1881 the publication and use of textbooks was hardly regulated at all. The textbooks published by the Ministry of Education only served as examples to encourage private initiatives. The first textbook published by the Ministry in 1872 was entitled *Shiryaku* (*Outline of History*), like many of its kind. 130,000 copies were sold between 1872 and 1877, more than of any other history textbook published by the Ministry. In addition, it was reprinted by the prefectures and served as a model for similar publications.[71] The first two volumes on Chinese and Japanese history were written by Kimura Masakoto, who had been in the Office of Historiography in 1869. The volume on Japanese history consisted of a list of the reigns of the emperors and was probably only intended as a reference book and for memorizing dates. Kimura was also the author of the first textbook dealing exclusively with Japanese history and published in 1875, entitled *Nihon ryakushi* (*A Short History of Japan*) and of two subsequent textbooks.

In 1873 Tanaka Fujimaro, the highest-ranking official in the Ministry of Education, addressed a letter to Iwakura Tomomi, the minister of the right. Tanaka wished to have points made clear concerning the imperial lineage for the history textbook that his Ministry was compiling. Tanaka's inquiry was passed on Nagamatsu in the Department of History, who answered it in 1874.[72] On the same day Nagamatsu proposed an imperial decree on the matter. The importance attributed to the imperial lineage and the idea that the questions it raised could be resolved by an imperial decree is significant in the light of later events (Chapter 6.6). One of Tanaka's questions was, which of the imperial courts in the period of division was the legitimate one. Nagamatsu answered, the Southern court.

The Office's own history *Nihon shiryaku,* compiled for the world exhibition in Paris, became the basis for some school textbooks; this is mentioned in Shigeno's lecture on methods of historical compilation given in 1879. The revised version of the *Nihon shiryaku,* the *Kokushigan,* was also adapted for use in schools.[73]

Members of the Office of Historiography were also directly involved in textbook compilation by the Ministry of Education. In the 1880s the Ministry increased its control over the teaching of history. The emperor himself was involved in defining ethical goals: reverence for the emperor and love for the nation (*sonnō aikoku*). Emphasis was to be given to periods when the imperial house had enjoyed its greatest power and influence. Biographies were to form the core of history teaching. Certain terms for historical events were altered: *Nanbokuchō no ran* (the conflict of the two imperial courts) became *Nanbokuchō no ryōritsu* (the existence of the two imperial courts). More attention was given to the mythical age of the gods. After 1886 the use of textbooks was subject to permission from the Ministry, but this was intended to ensure a minimum standard, and private publications still predominated. Guidelines for the examination of textbooks were publicized and a competition organized to encourage authors. The invitation for contributions was drawn up by a committee presided over by Shigeno Yasutsugu and Suematsu Kenchō, who had just returned from England and held a post in the Ministry of Home Affairs.[74] Other members were Isawa Shūji from the Office of Compilation in the Ministry of Education and Toyama Masakazu and

Mozume Takami, both professors at the Imperial University. The invitation suggested a list of themes to be included in the textbook. This list, drawn up by distinguished scholars of the period led by Shigeno Yasutsugu, became the basis for the competition. Moreover, after the Ministry nationalized the publication of textbooks in 1902, the same list provided the framework for the first standard history textbook published by the Ministry in 1903, and for all the following textbooks up to the 1940s. Shigeno Yasutsugu's influence on the compilation of school textbooks and on history education was therefore highly significant. Shigeno also talked about teaching history in schools in his lectures.[75]

For the compilation of a textbook in 1903, the Ministry of Education again commissioned distinguished scholars. One was Satō Jōjitsu, who had become chief editor of the collection of sources *Koji ruien* (Chapter 3.4); another was Mikami Sanji, then director of the Historiographical Institute.[76] Mikami and his colleague Tanaka Yoshinari became members of the committee for the revision of textbooks established in 1904. In 1908 the committee prepared a revised edition of the 1903 textbook and published it in 1908. The second edition had to be in part rewritten after the textbook controversy in 1911; this meant that the views of the historians involved, Mikami, Tanaka and Kita Sadakichi, who had written the book, were disregarded in favour of official ideology. The idea that education was governed by different standards from scholarship thus became official policy. Even Mikami accepted this distinction between education and scholarship. In the following years the influence of historical scholarship on the history taught in schools declined.[77]

Even after moving to the Imperial University the former government office performed some functions reminiscent of its former character as the highest authority in matters concerning history. Its members continued to be involved in the compilation of history textbooks. Mikami Sanji, then the director of the Historiographical Institute, was once called upon to testify in court about legal matters in the Tokugawa period.[78] The publications of the Institute were sent to institutions abroad, partly in order to represent Japanese achievements. Every year, when the emperor visited the University to attend the graduation ceremony, a special exhibition of valuable documents was prepared for him at the Historiographical

Institute and shown to him by its director. However, 'pure history' and 'applied history' increasingly went their separate ways.

3.4 The Office of Historiography and Its Rivals

The work carried out in the Office of Historiography was not unique. The Edo and the Meiji periods saw several projects involving the collection of sources and the compilation of historical works.[79]

Of the different historical compilations of the Edo period the history *Dainihonshi* and Hanawa Hokiichi's *Shiryō* must be regarded as direct predecessors of the projects undertaken in the Office of Historiography. Another project begun by the bakufu which continued after 1868 was the collection of documents concerning foreign relations. It was initiated in 1865, and Tanabe Ta'ichi (1831–1915) became the editor of the compilation, which was entitled *Tsūshin zenran* (*Complete Overview of the Correspondence*). After the Restoration the Ministry of Foreign Affairs continued the compilation under the title *Zoku Tsūshin zenran*. This is a good example of continuity from the Edo to the Meiji period.[80] The compilation of documents on foreign relations was transferred to the Historiographical Institute in 1907.

Documents resulting from the actions of the Meiji government were collected in the compilations *Kōbunroku, Dajō ruiten, Kōbun ruishū* and *Hōrei zensho* (imperial decrees). *Hōki bunrui taizen* (a classified collection of government decrees) contains short accounts on how each law came to be passed, quoting related documents and summaries of the ensuing developments.[81]

In the 1870s and 1880s the ministries published histories and collections of historical documents of their fields of responsibility in response to government orders; for example, the Ministry of Education compiled *Nihon kyōikushi shiryō* (*Materials on the History of Education in Japan, 1883*).[82]

The Ministry of Education also initiated another compilation: the *Koji ruien,* begun in 1879, was an encyclopaedic collection of sources of Japanese cultural history in the Chinese fashion; for each entry the source in which its subject was first mentioned and relevant decrees were quoted. Work on it was continued for many years until it was provisionally completed in 1907 and printed in 1914. By then the project had been transferred, first to the Academy of Sciences (*Tōkyō gakushi kaiin*), then to the Institute for Japanese Literature (*Kōten kōkyūjo*) and finally to the Department of Shrines (*Jingū shichō*). Members of the Office of Historiography were involved in the compilation of the *Koji ruien* from time to time.

One of the most important groups of official or semi-official historical compilations in the Meiji period includes the various attempts to produce a comprehensive and definitive history of the Meiji Restoration, based on the sources. The *Fukkoki,* the chronicle compiled in the Department of History, was the first of these. The *Taisei kiyō,* the work commissioned by Iwakura Tomomi, was intended to be brief and for a specific purpose. More important was the establishment of the *Shidankai* (Society for Historical Narration). Shimazu Hisamitsu, the former lord of Satsuma, had suggested such a society to the Imperial Household Ministry in 1889, just before his death. The Ministry was already compiling biographies of Sanjō Sanetomi and Iwakura Tomomi, and in 1890 the representatives of the former ruling houses from the domains which led the Restoration, Shimazu (Satsuma), Mōri (Chōshū), Yamanouchi (Tosa) and Tokugawa (Mito) were ordered to produce a history of their domain from 1848 to 1871 within three years. Later the Imperial Household Ministry also asked the descendants of the shogun and of the lords of Owari, Aizu, Kuwana and Aki to write a history. An office of compilation was established in the Ministry for the purpose of producing a history of the Meiji Restoration entitled *Meiji chūkōshi* (*History of the Meiji Restoration*).[83] In 1892 Date Munenari of Uwajima and Hachisuka Mochiaki, the former lord of Tokushima, were made directors, and all the former ruling houses were invited to participate. The *Shidankai* society was intended as a forum for exchanging documents and information and for discussions. Contributions by individual members were published in the 'shorthand notes' of the society (*Shidankai sokkiroku*). The history of the Restoration was never compiled; only the biographies of heroes and martyrs of the Meiji Restoration were published in two collections from 1907 onward (*Senbō junnan shishi jinmeiroku* and *Kokuji ōshō kōko shishi jinmeiroku*). The members of the *Shidankai* society, representatives of the former ruling houses, had lost their political influence to their former vassals. Their account of the Restoration was directed against the new political powers, the so-called *hanbatsu* government of former samurai from the domains who had led the Restoration. These active statesmen were not much interested in writing history and refused government support to the society, reducing it to a private undertaking. It became a society for storytelling in the literal sense of its name, where memories of a glorious past were exchanged.[84]

Significantly, towards the end of the Meiji period, when their own influence was waning, the same statesmen who had not been interested in the work of the *Shidankai* society began to collect documents for their own history of the Meiji Restoration. The former *hanbatsu* leaders had become elder statesmen (*genrō*) and in 1910 established the *Shōmeikai* society. In 1911 it became the *Ishin shiryō hensankai* (Association for the Compilation of a History of the Meiji Restoration), established in the Ministry of Education. Inoue Kaoru was its president. The establishment of the *Ishin shiryō hensankai* was motivated by a sense of crisis. In 1909 Itō Hirobumi had been assassinated in Harbin; the Meiji oligarchs realized that the times were changing rapidly and that they no longer had much part in events, and they began to reflect on their past glories. Their interpretation of the Meiji Restoration as *ōsei fukko*, restoration of imperial rule, was not much different from the one adopted by the members of the *Shidankai* society or even the one expressed in Iwakura's *Taisei kiyō* or the *Fukkoki*. Distinguished historians were employed to compile a history of the Restoration. They produced the *Gaikan ishinshi* (*Outline of the Meiji Restoration*; 1940) and the *Ishinshi* (*History of the Meiji Restoration*; 1936–41); both were published during the Second World War, when the ultra-nationalistic *kokutai* ideology was at its peak, and they are probably more influenced by notions of the superiority and uniqueness of the Japanese Empire than the initiators intended. Nevertheless, the *Ishinshi* is of considerable value as a scholarly account of the Restoration.[85] The materials collected by the *Ishin shiryō hensankai* were transferred from the Ministry of Education to the Historiographical Institute in 1949 and are preserved there as *Ishin shiryō hikitsugibon*.

Besides producing the biographies of Sanjō Sanetomi and Iwakura Tomomi (*Sanjō Sanetomi kō nenpu*, 1901 and *Iwakura kō jikki*, 1906), between 1901 and 1905 the Imperial Household Ministry edited a biography of the last emperor of the Tokugawa period, the *Kōmei tennō ki*, published in 1906. In the same way a biography of the Meiji emperor was begun after his death; the *Meiji tennō ki* was completed in 1932. Among the authors was Mikami Sanji, formerly director of the Historiographical Institute. All these biographies are in an annalistic style. Many documents were accumulated during the compilation, and they are now in the archives of the Imperial Household Office.

Several former ruling houses compiled their own histories, either because they were urged to do so by the *Shidankai* society or the *Ishin shiryō hensankai* or independently. Many of them were published around 1930; examples are the *Nanki Tokugawa shi* of the Kii branch of the Tokugawa, the *Kagahan shiryō* of the house of Maeda, the *Mitohan shiryō* of the Mito Tokugawa, or the *Kaitei Higohan kokuji shiryō* of the Hosokawa.[86] One of the most important of its kind is the *Bōchō kaitenshi* (*History of Suō and Chōshū in the Restoration*), compiled by the house of Mōri, of which the first edition was published between 1911 and 1920.[87] The Mōri had begun work on a history shortly after the Restoration and had established an office for the purpose, which was transferred to Tokyo in 1883. Thanks to the *Shidankai*, the Mōri, like other houses, received support from the Imperial Household Ministry. When the last lord of Chōshū, Mōri Motonori, died in 1896, Inoue Kaoru became the representative of the family and reorganized the office. As president he appointed Suematsu Kenchō, recommended to him by Itō Hirobumi; this was a remarkable choice, for Suematsu came from the domain of Kokura, which had been at war with Chōshū when Suematsu was a child. Suematsu had researched Western historical methods for the Office of Historiography in 1879 (Chapter 4.4). He took an active part in the compilation of the Mōri history, even continuing work on his own when the office was closed down in 1899, before the history was completed, and Suematsu himself was relieved of his duties as president in 1911 after completing the first draft. He thoroughly revised the first version, which was published in 1921, after his death.

These are just some of the compilations undertaken from mid- to late Meiji. I have limited my examples to official or semi-official publications. An example of a private one is Taguchi Ukichi's *Kokushi taikei* and *Zoku kokushi taikei* (*Compendium of Japanese History* and *Continuation of the Compendium of Japanese History*), published by his company *Keizai zasshi sha* from 1897 to 1902 and later revised and supplemented by Kuroita Katsumi, professor of history at the Imperial University, in 1929. Nor was this enthusiasm for compilation limited to the field of history. From the 1880s the publication of literary anthologies became popular, and in 1890 the *Nihon bungaku zensho* (*Complete Works of Japanese Literature*) were published. Incidentally, the literary review *Waseda bungaku* in 1893 reported, among other social 'fevers' or crazes, a 'complete works fever'.[88] History compilations often served to justify the political position of those who commissioned them, but works such as the *Kokushi taikei* also contributed to the formation of a canon of historical texts, just as the *Nihon bungaku taikei* helped form the canon of literary works. However, above all, the preoccupation with the country's past and with its cultural heritage was part of formulating Japan's national identity (Chapter 7.2).

For the work of the Office of Historiography, all this means that the *Dainihon hennenshi,* far from holding an exclusive position as an official record of the past, was not even the most successful product of these various ventures. As a means of legitimation for the government the compilation of a history in the tradition of the ancient imperial histories lost its significance once the Meiji Restoration and the establishment of a new government had become accomplished facts. The Restoration itself became a focus of interest and a source of legitimation of political power. By the late 1880s it had 'so diminished in meaning that it had practically to be reinvented'. Like the Tokugawa period it had 'receded sufficiently to qualify for the time-honoured tradition of using the past to serve, esteem or blaspheme the present'.[89] It is significant that the waning interest in the *Dainihon hennenshi* coincided with the establishment of the *Shidankai* Society and its attempt to compile a definitive history of the Meiji Restoration.

4

The Form of Official Historiography

When the Office of Historiography was first established, the form the official history should take was not determined. Over the next years the members of the Office had to decide what kind of history to write and for whom.

4.1 Recording the Restoration

One of the tasks of the Department of History established in 1872 was the compilation of a chronicle of the Meiji Restoration, the *Fukkoki*. The new government wanted a record of the events leading to its establishment, similar to Chinese dynastic histories, which record the downfall of the previous dynasty to show the legitimacy of the new one. Thus, although the imperial rescript suggests a history continuing where the Six National Histories left off, that is, covering the whole period of rule by the shoguns, the first attempt to write a history by the government focused on the immediate past. The chief editor of the *Fukkoki*, Nagamatsu Miki, had already written an account of the Restoration, entitled *Fukko ran'yō*, for the members of the Iwakura Embassy in 1871.

The preface to the first printed edition of the *Fukkoki*, which was not published until 1930, states that in 1873 Nagamatsu and his colleagues had compiled over 30 volumes of documents for the *Fukkoki* and over 20 for the *Fukko gaiki*, a chronicle of the armed conflicts during the Restoration. That year the building which housed the Council of State burnt down; most of the documents were lost and Nagamatsu had to start collecting again. Although completion of the *Fukkoki* was supposedly imminent in 1875,[1] Nagamatsu was still working on it in 1882, and only his petition to Sanjō Sanetomi prevented work on the *Fukkoki* being abandoned after the reorganization of the Office of Historiography. According to the preface of the printed edition, the *Fukkoki* (together with the *Fukko gaiki* 289 volumes) was completed in December 1889.[2]

The introductory remarks to the *Fukkoki*, dated 1 June 1876, describe its organization. It treats the period from the resignation of the last shogun in 1867 to the dismissal of the Commander for the Subjugation of the East (*tōsei taisōtoku*) in 1868. For each event the year, month and day were given and the relevant sources quoted verbatim. As there were hardly any documents from central administrative offices for the beginning of the period in question, the editors had to rely on materials from the domains, from families of warriors and court nobles, from military institutions and from private individuals. When the evidence was not conclusive, the persons concerned were questioned wherever possible. If a point remained unclear a note to that effect was made. Events and documents that could not be dated precisely were listed at the end of the month or, failing that, the year they related to. The appointment and dismissal of important officials was always noted.

The introduction also explains the choice of certain terms and the use of personal and place names. The sources consulted are listed; most of them were journals of various central and regional administrative offices, accounts by important individuals or biographies of them, documents from temples and shrines and lists of personnel. The number of documents consulted is given: 1,212. The table of contents consists of 42 pages and amounts to a chronological outline of events. These are again chronicled in the main part with short notes stating where the persons involved came from and their different titles; then the relevant sources are quoted.

In short, the *Fukkoki* is no more than a list of events and a collection of relevant documents in the *kōmoku* format (Chapter 1). The value of the *Fukkoki* lies in the rich material used, not in the chronological outline (*kō*), which hardly attempts to explain or interpret events. The title does however imply an interpretation; it characterizes the Restoration as a return to imperial rule as it was supposed to have been in the past (*fukko*). The original sources used that have not been lost are now preserved in the Historiographical Institute and have only recently been subjected to detailed investigation.[3]

What was the *Fukkoki* compiled for? Of course it was partly intended as a legitimation of the new government in the tradition of the Chinese dynastic histories.[4] But this was probably not the only motive and not even the most important one. The *Fukkoki* only deals with the Restoration itself, including the years immediately preceding it, not the entire period of Tokugawa rule (the preceding 'dynasty', as it were). It was not so much a history as a review of recent events for stock-taking and justification, perhaps also for the very practical purpose of providing orientation for the new government.[5] This may be why work on it was almost abandoned in 1882: the government no longer felt a need for it.

The *Meiji shiyō* (*Outline of the History of Meiji*) was based on the *Fukkoki* and is a chronicle of the same events but without quotations from the documents. It was published in six volumes between 1876 and 1886, soon after its completion.[6] The first volume was presented at the world exhibition in Philadelphia in April 1876, together with the works produced by the Department of Topography. In May it was presented to the Imperial Household Ministry as evidence that work in the Office of Historiography was carried out in honour of the imperial house. Foreign representatives in Japan also received copies.[7]

The *Seisei shimatsu* (*Account of the Pacification of the West*), like the *Fukkoki* and the *Meiji shiyō*, was an account of recent events. It dealt with the war against Satsuma in 1877, in which the government troops defeated the rebellion of Saigō Takamori and his followers. The government ordered the compilation of the *Seisei shimatsu* immediately after the event, in December 1877.[8] Although it was probably in part intended as legitimation, it was a detailed description of the events of the war against Satsuma, mainly as a record for future reference. Apparently it was not intended for publication; the regulations for its compilation state that secret actions of the government should be included in the account. The facts and materials in the *Seisei shimatsu* were arranged much in the same way as in the *Fukkoki*. According to the regulations drafted in March 1878 it was to be a chronological account of the events between 15 February and 10 October 1877, that is, from the beginning of Saigō Takamori's attack to victory by the government troops. The sources for the information, chiefly government records (*jitsuroku*), were to be quoted. Government offices were asked to submit relevant material. The table of contents submitted to the government shows that the planned account was not so much a historical narrative as a comprehensive compilation of facts, although it could possibly serve as a basis for a history of the war.[9]

Work on the *Seisei shimatsu* had already begun when in 1879 Suematsu Kenchō, researching Western methods of historiography in London for the Office of Historiography (Chapter 4.4), sent Augustus Henry Mounsey's book *The Satsuma Rebellion,* which had just been published, to Japan. The book was immediately translated into Japanese and Shigeno, at least, read it. Nothing, however, suggests that Mounsey's account influenced the compilers of the *Seisei shimatsu*.[10]

The first compilations by the Office of Historiography were not histories in the sense of historical narratives, but chronicles of the most recent events, which had barely come to a conclusion. The guidelines for the compilation of the *Fukkoki* state that it would be continuously kept up to date. However, the format of these early works was the same as that used for the annals begun in the following years.

4.2 Collecting Materials and Writing History

For the first years after the Meiji Restoration there are hardly any sources to tell us what exactly the proponents of an official history of Japan had in mind. The two earliest documents, the proposal by the schools administration and the Imperial Rescript on Historiography, both refer to the Six National Histories and express the idea that, since imperial rule had been restored, historiography (*kokushi henshū, shūshi*) in the emperor's name should also be resumed. Both describe the task with the word *taiten*, which can mean a state ritual or a great, norm-giving work. Historiography was viewed as part of creating order after the restoration of imperial rule to the supremacy it had held before the ascendancy of the warrior class.

For the next few years, however, the plan to continue the Six National Histories was not put into practice. The Department of History did not work on a national history, although the regulations for the Department mentioned the compilation of an official national history (*kokushi, seishi*).[11] The collection of documents from the prefectures and the histories written by the prefectures served the immediate needs of administration and taxation (Chapter 3.3). The prefectures were supposed to continue them on a yearly basis, which also suggests that they were intended for practical purposes. Nevertheless the guidelines for the prefectures drawn up in August 1873 and issued to the prefectures the following year began with a definition of history.[12] History, they said, deals with political development and the rise and fall of humans and of things. The prefectures should describe their development since their establishment, avoiding everything that was superfluous; events should be recounted in chronological order and the relevant documents quoted. If something was not clear, a comment should be added. Five of the eight regulations prescribed what was to be included in the account; the focus was to be on administration and taxation, including information about households, temples and shrines, harbours, markets, military installations, but also historic monuments and inscriptions. The chronological arrangement by year, month and day with quotations from the relevant sources, the concentration on political events and the use of brief and simple language expected from the prefectures all characterized the historical compilations begun by the Office of Historiography in the following years.

The compilation of a history of Japan in the tradition of the Six National Histories was begun in earnest in 1875, after the establishment of the Office of Historiography. The two memoranda *Shūshi jigi* (*Proper Historiography*) and *Henshū chakushu no hōhō* (*Methods of Beginning the Compilation*), as well as the regulations concerning personnel give an idea of the kind of work that was planned. According to the accompanying letter by Shigeno and Nagamatsu, the memoranda were presented to Sanjō Sanetomi and the members of the Council of State in May 1875.[13] The papers of Shigeno Yasutsugu contain copies of the documents: he probably drafted them himself, because some of the phrases used are to be found in his lecture on the methods of historiography given in 1879. The *Shūshi jigi* stated that now the *Fukkoki* was nearing completion it was time to consider the future work of the Office, and the following proposals were made: The official histories of the empire (*kōkoku no seishi*), the Six National Histories, were never continued. The history (*seishi*) *Dainihonshi* only covers the time until the end of the period of the two imperial courts (1336–92). For the 500 years after that there exist only unreliable private histories. Therefore an official history (*seishi*) must be compiled. – In other words the *Dainihonshi*, produced by one of the collateral houses of the Tokugawa, is accorded the status of a standard history, but the official annals of the shogunate, such as the *Honchō tsugan*, are not.

According to the *Shūshi jigi*, the historical facts were collected in three departments: in the first from Emperor Gokomatsu to Emperor Goyōzei (1382–1610), in the second from Emperor Gomizunoo to Emperor Kōmei (1611–1867) and in the third for the period after 1868. In the first two departments the documents should be collected and arranged according to the example given by Hanawa Hokiichi. The work should be divided so that each member was responsible for a short period. In the third department the official documents should be collected and edited in addition to work on the *Fukkoki*. The *Fukkoki* was not a historical narrative in the strict sense of the word, but a detailed chronicle of events quoting the original sources. Work in the Office of Historiography should be divided into collection of documents and compilation.

The reference to Hanawa Hokiichi indicates that the author of the *Shūshi jigi* was not much concerned with the actual writing of the history. The aim was less a definitive history than the provision of reliable sources that could become the basis of such a history, but had a value in their own right. Hanawa used this format for his *Shiryō*, as did his contemporary Hayashi Jussai (1768–1841), under whose auspices the *Chōya Kyūbun hōkō* (draft collection of official and unofficial old documents) was begun.[14] Since the latter centred on shogunal rule, it was obviously not mentioned by the members of the Office of Historiography who, like Hokiichi, were working on a history centred on imperial rule.

The ultimate aim was, however, a *seishi,* a correct and definitive history. Moreover, this task was not to be left to unspecified future generations, but to be undertaken as soon as possible. For this reason the author of the *Shūshi jigi* stressed the need to appoint someone who would be in charge and make the final decisions. This was also necessary because the misrule of the feudal age had prevented the historical facts from being brought to light. The author pointed out that when the Six National Histories were compiled, a relative of the emperor was in charge. This time too, a supreme authority was considered necessary.

The *Shūshi jigi* also includes comments on the language to be used for the history and on the value of referring to Western examples of historical writing, but the emphasis is on providing a work in *kōmoku* format. It ends with a promise to submit details on the procedure after receiving the order to begin. These were laid down in a document entitled *Henshū chakushu no hōhō* (*Methods of Beginning the Compilation*). The document begins with the list of the members of each department quoted in Chapter 3.1 and the tasks of each department. There follow instructions on how to proceed. Here is a summary of the most important ones.

In the first two departments each member is responsible for a period of 20 to 30 years. The facts derived from the literature are arranged so that the date (if possible, to the exact day) comes first, then the event followed by quotations from the sources, first primary sources, then secondary accounts and then dubious accounts.

The passages to be quoted shall be copied out by the scribes. Examples of events to be included are natural disasters, progress and decline, lives and deaths, wars, rewards and punishments, money and provisions, building work; in the case of religious affairs and court ceremonies a selection shall be made. Decisions on what to include and other questions are to be made by consultation among the members. When a part is finished it shall be examined and corrected by the editor, the chief inspector and the president. Twice a year a report on the work completed shall be prepared.[15]

From the document it would seem that the main task of compilation was carried out by the co-editors (*kyōshū*), who collected the facts and the documents, and the editors (*shūsen*), who compiled the text from them. The chief inspector (*sōetsu*) examined the resulting compilation. The president (*sōsai*) supervised the work. The clerks (*shoki*) organized the collected material. Historiography was an administrative act organized in a similar way to government business in other offices.

Although these guidelines defined the course to be taken in the Office, they did not put an end to the discussions about how to proceed. Nothing was said in them about the actual history and how to write it; we can assume that this was discussed, but there are hardly any documents to tell us for certain. Some evidence is provided by a lecture given by Shigeno

Yasutsugu in 1879 at the Tokyo Academy (*Tōkyō gakushi kaiin*), entitled 'Discussing the Methods for Compiling a National History' (*Kokushi hensan no hōhō o ronzu*). Here he introduced his ideas to a general audience for the first time. He described the issue he wanted to discuss as urgent and asked for opinions from his audience. According to Shigeno, it was necessary to study past events as lessons of moral behaviour for the present. Shigeno mentioned the different forms of Chinese historiography, annals (*hennentai*), biographies (*kiden*) and treatises (*kiji honmatsu*). Then he spoke about Japanese historiography. He pointed out that although Japan had adopted its literary forms from China, it had no *seishi*. He briefly discussed some of Japan's most famous histories, but accepted none of them as a *seishi*. As the Office of Historiography had no Japanese precedent, the question of what form to adopt for the planned history was open to discussion, and Shigeno mentions that such discussions were indeed taking place. In their search for a form for the *seishi*, the members referred to Western as well as Chinese works, and Shigeno discusses the merits of both.

That a *seishi* was both desirable and possible, Shigeno did not doubt. Most of the difficulties in the office he blamed on lack of resources and personnel. However, his insistence that one person, whose opinion must be decisive, must be in charge of the project indicated a crucial problem. If there are different opinions on how the history is to be written, whose opinion is to be final and how can this choice be justified as the only correct one? How definitive how objective can any history be? Even if it is no more than a string of loosely connected facts, the necessity of selecting the facts themselves as well as the words to describe them will make bias inevitable. An attempt to produce not just an annalistic record but a narrative, establishing connections between events, compounds the difficulties. That Shigeno had such a narrative in mind is evident from his lecture, from his criticism of mere annals and his remarks on the Satsuma rebellion. Shigeno reminded his audience that he was a native of Satsuma and therefore could speak with authority. The necessity to establish this suggests that his colleagues had different ideas.

Shigeno's views on writing history are better documented than those of any other member of the office. However, in the papers of Sanjō

Sanetomi, there is an anonymous memorandum that gives a different view. It is entitled, *Bo gakushi shiseki henshū ron: Shikan kaikaku o kou no gi* (*A Certain Scholar's Discussion of Compiling Histories: A Request for the Reform of the History Office*). The anonymous author was apparently not a member of the Office. Like Shigeno, the author stresses the importance of writing history and laments the absence of a history (*shijō*: history, annals), describing Japanese histories as unsatisfactory. Like Shigeno, and for similar reasons, he praises Western examples of historical writing. He demands that the scholars in the Office produce a good history (*ryōshi*) as soon as possible, looking to Western histories as a model. For this purpose experts in Japanese, European and Chinese Learning should be employed and a commander (*teitoku*) appointed, who should select the members and be solely responsible.

The differences between the memorandum and Shigeno's lecture are mainly in emphasis. The anonymous author is more specific about the aims of the planned history: it should be read by the people, who would become educated without noticing and learn to love their country, which in turn would contribute to strengthening and enriching Japan (*fukyō*). He is also more insistent than Shigeno that the history be completed soon, in view of the intended parliament. If, by the time the parliament debated the budget, the Office did not present results that justified the expense and the employment of so many scholars, the reputation of the imperial house would suffer.[16]

The author seems to have been well informed about historiography and mentioned having heard lectures on history. It seems that he knew what was going on in the Office of Historiography without working there himself. More than Shigeno, the author of the memorandum concentrated on practical considerations. This reflects the different priorities of a scholar himself involved in the project and an official outside the Office who was mainly interested in quick results. No fundamental difference in their views of history is discernible.

From the documents discussed we gain some insight into the process of compiling the planned official history. The compilation in *kōmoku* format was to lay the foundations for the *seishi*, which was the ultimate goal. What form it was to take seems to have been the subject of disagreement between members of the Office, but we have little information on the nature of these discussions. Among the things discussed seems to have been the format of the history; strictly chronological, or biographical (like the *Dainihonshi*).[17] Another question was whether to continue from where the Six National Histories ended, or from the *Dainihonshi* ended, or whether to start from scratch. However, the most contentious issue appears to have been that of the language to be used.

4.3 The Language of Official Historiography

Why was the issue of language so important? To answer this question, we must know what choices the members of the Office had and the implications of these choices.

Two characteristics of the Japanese written language are relevant here: the wide range of written styles and the distance between most of them and the spoken language until well into the Meiji period. Both are a consequence of the adoption and adaptation of the Chinese script by the Japanese from the fifth century onwards. The two languages are entirely different in structure, and at first texts were written with Chinese syntax and read in Japanese, a style known as *kanbun*. From around the eighth century the Japanese tried to adapt the Chinese script to their own language. Chinese characters were used to express sounds as well as meanings, and two syllabaries evolved, making it possible to write Japanese as it was spoken. Over the centuries a variety of styles emerged, absorbing elements of Chinese to a varying degree; from 'pure' Chinese, (*kanbun*) read as Japanese (*kundoku*), to 'pure' Japanese (*wabun*), which most closely reflected the spoken language.

However, while the spoken language changed over time, the written form remained much as it had been in the Heian period (ninth to twelfth centuries), when it had originated. Thus, at the beginning of the Meiji period, most written forms of Japanese were far removed from the spoken language of the time. Chinese or a Sino-Japanese style heavily loaded with Chinese words and syntax (*kanbun*) was regarded as the norm for official documents and scholarly writing – indeed for all 'serious' writing.[18]

In the course of the Meiji period this began to change.[19] The Japanese realized that Western writings were in a style close to the spoken language. Representatives of government and press saw that in order to communicate information effectively to the masses (who as a result of the education system were increasingly literate), they had to use a language that was comprehensible to Japanese all over the country and not just to a small elite with a monopoly on education. From around mid-Meiji, especially after the Sino-Japanese war, nationalistic ideology influenced the discussion, which had at first been fairly pragmatic. The process of standardizing the written language in a form close to the spoken language continued into the twentieth century and was not completed until after 1945.

What were the consequences for the writing of an official history? Obviously, a choice had to be made and the choice had implications for the readership. Essentially two options were discussed: *kanbun* and *kokubun* (national written language), which in this case probably meant a mixed style, still far from the spoken language. *Kanbun* had a long tradition as the language of learning, perhaps comparable to Latin in Europe. It was the language of the *Dainihonshi* and this was not seen as being in contradiction to its nationalistic contents. The use of *kanbun* implied respect for Chinese erudition and morals. It was also considered more precise. The preface of scholarly works was often written in *kanbun* in the Meiji period, even if the main body was not.[20] The mixed style was also an accepted style for scholarly works; it is strongly influenced by Chinese, yet easier to understand.

The first mention of a proposed language for the official history is in *Shūshi jigi* in 1875; the author, probably Shigeno, proposed the mixed style. His main consideration was that the writing be clearly understood. In his lecture in 1879 Shigeno did not talk about language, but of the Japanese histories he praised apart from the *Dainihonshi*, the *Jinnō shōtōki* and the *Tokushi yoron* were written in the mixed style, while there existed editions of *Nihon gaishi* in this style. It seems that Shigeno preferred the mixed style.

The anonymous author of the memorandum *Shikan kaikau o kou no gi* was more explicit. He claimed that now Western knowledge and

(Western-style) civilization were gaining ground, most people were no longer able to read *kanbun*.

Other scholars argued that a nation with an advanced civilization like Japan should be able to write its history in its own national language. They included members of the History Society (*Shigaku kyōkai*; see Chapter 2.5). This opinion had already been expressed by Motoori Norinaga (1730–1801) and was shared by many Japanese scholars. As nationalistic ideology gained ground from the 1880s onwards, it naturally became a powerful argument. By the time the anonymous author stated his views on the language of the official history, the decision had already been made in favour of *kanbun*. It was by no means undisputed and was defended in a lengthy document drawn up by a member of the Office of Historiography, probably at the time of the reorganization. The author is not known, but he quotes numerous sources, most of them from the Muromachi period (1338–1573), so we can assume that it was someone working on those sources, probably Kume Kunitake.[21] The author rejects two main objections against *kanbun*: that it cannot be understood by most people and that it is a foreign language and therefore unsuitable for writing the history of Japan. The claim that it was more economical to write in Sino-Japanese was probably more a concession to the bureaucratic minds of government officials than a real consideration by the scholars, although the argument of conciseness was often used by defenders of *kanbun*.[22]

Apart from the language of the history, the author of the document defended the course taken by the Office in general. He explained why the Office had finally decided not to follow Western models: Western knowledge had not been sufficiently digested and there were not enough translations. The author also defended the collection of sources and stressed that the members of the Office had not been idle. He argued that the aim was not a history to entertain the people like the war tales (*gundan senki*) but one that would form the basis of historical scholarship (*wagakuni rekishigaku no kihon*) and further historical writing.

This defender of *kanbun*, however, admitted the possibility of rewriting the history if the Sino-Japanese style were sometime in the future replaced by a standard Japanese style, or after Western historiography had become more widely known as a result of translations. This, whether or not the author intended it that way, amounted to a negation of the *seishi*.

The decision to use *kanbun* meant a departure from the intention laid down in the Rescript of 1869 in another way: it limited the readership of the work. The history would not serve the education of the populace, but, as the author of the document pointed out, it was intended as a scholarly work, addressed to a specialist audience.

The defensive character of the document suggests that it was drawn up in answer to criticism from outside. It may have been a reply to the memorandum on the reform of the Office discussed in the previous chapter, as it takes up all the points mentioned there. In fact the decision to write in *kanbun* was continuously criticized and became one of the reasons for abandoning the whole project in 1893. Although *kanbun* flourished in the first years of the Meiji period, it increasingly lost its importance, since the formal education system, introduced in the 1870s, stressed Western learning and neglected the study of *kanbun*. By the time the Office of Historiography began to write the national history, *kanbun* was already regarded as obsolete.

4.4 Studying Western Methods (1): Zerffi

In their search for a suitable form for the national history the members of the Office of Historiography were attracted by Western methods of historiography. The *Shūshi jigi* cited above mentions Western histories. They are said to include analysis, maps and tables in the text as well as describe the geographical situation and general conditions at the time the events took place and to discuss causes and effects. These remarks sound rather vague, but at the time it was difficult for the scholars of the Office of Historiography, who did not understand foreign languages, to obtain more precise information.

In 1878 an opportunity to learn more about Western historiography presented itself when Suematsu Kenchō set off for London to become a secretary to the Japanese legation and to observe the political situation in Europe for his mentor Itō Hirobumi. Suematsu Kenchō was a native of Buzen (Fukuoka prefecture), where he had been educated in Chinese Learning before going to Tokyo to study English and write articles for the newspaper *Tōkyō nichinichi shinbun*. After being introduced to Itō

Hirobumi, he embarked on a career in government service. From 1875 onwards Suematsu held various government posts.[23] The Office of Historiography asked Suematsu to investigate English and French historiographical methods (presumably because the translated works they knew were by English and French authors). A letter from the Office to the Ministry of Foreign Affairs stated that traditional histories only treated domestic politics, political systems and wars, but not economic developments, customs and religion, flora and fauna, agriculture, commerce and the situation of the general populace. The members of the Office wished to study Western historiography, but they lacked suitable translated works. Therefore Suematsu should be ordered to research into English and French historiography (*ei-futsu rekishi hensan hōhō kenkyū*) in his spare time.[24] What exactly he was expected to do is not clear. Possibly this was discussed with Suematsu, but it is equally likely that the members of the Office of Historiography were not sufficiently well informed to express their wishes in more detail.

Two letters to Shigeno from Ōkubo Toshimichi and Nakai Hiroshi deal with Suematsu, both of them dated 6 February 1878 (Meiji 11).[25] Ōkubo Toshimichi mentioned a conversation with Itō Hirobumi and concluded that Suematsu was the right man for the task and should be appointed immediately. Like Shigeno, Nakai Hiroshi came from Satsuma and had served in the Japanese legation between 1874 and 1876. He also recommended that someone be appointed to the task as soon as possible, but he expressed doubts whether Suematsu would have the time to perform such a difficult task in addition to his work for the legation. Nakai added remarks about the shortcomings of Japanese historiography and about what he expected of a good history; his views were similar to those expressed by the Office of Historiography.

Suematsu received a sum of 1,500 yen. He was expected to buy books to read himself and to send to the Office of Historiography. Most of the documents preserved in the Historiographical Institute deal with the financial side of Suematsu's appointment.[26] They include the correspondence between Miura Yasushi, the administrator of the Office, and Ueno Keihan, the Japanese representative in London, as well as some letters from Suematsu himself.

Suematsu arrived in England on 1 April 1878. He wrote letters to his family, which give us some information about his arrival and his stay in London. Suematsu also wrote long letters to Itō Hirobumi, in which he dealt with Britain's domestic and foreign politics.[27] Unfortunately, none of his correspondence tells us much about the nature of his historical studies. He must have started his investigation for the Office of Historiography soon after his arrival, for by December he had drawn up a list of items for investigation, entitled *Shiyō monmoku* (*Catalogue of principal topics on history*). This document is a Japanese translation of the English original and consists of a letter to an unnamed English historian dated 7 December 1878 and instructions for a book on European historiography, divided into eight parts. According to Suematsu's letter to the Office of Historiography, dated 5 January 1880, he sent the English version to the Office to have it translated.[28] As stated in a summary by a member of the Office, Suematsu also reported that he had written down his own investigations and thoughts concerning the war with Satsuma (Suematsu had taken part in it himself as a secretary to the war minister Yamagata Aritomo). He was studying hard, but Western historiography was difficult to comprehend, so he had asked the scholar George Gustavus Zerffi for an introductory work on the basis of the queries he had drawn up.

The content of the letter to an unnamed addressee in *Shiyō monmoku* is as follows: Suematsu thinks it would be useful to provide Japanese historians with an outline of the most important Western historians and their works. Japanese and Chinese histories are different from Western ones, because they present the facts without any philosophical reflections. Now Japan is learning much from Europe, and Japanese scholars would like to take the best examples of European historical writing as their model. However, most European histories are not accessible to them, so a general outline would be very useful. Suematsu, therefore, wished the addressee to write such an outline in order to present Japanese scholars who want to write a history of their country with suitable models. The author should take care to stress the advantages of Western histories, which combine the representation of facts with theoretical considerations and point out causes and effects. The finished work will be translated and made available to Japanese scholars.

Suematsu then gives instructions for the planned outline of European historiography, asking that special attention be paid to the following points:

1. The importance of historical research and the qualities a historian should possess.
2. A critical survey of the most important historians and their work, beginning with the authors of ancient Greece.
3. The authors of ancient Rome.
4. The greatest modern British, French and German authors and, as far as they are of interest, the medieval authors.
5. The different kinds of history: universal history, national history and their subdivisions.
6. Another critical survey of the most important histories in chronological order and by country of origin in their historical context.
7. The methods of the historian, the difficulties he faces, especially in the times before freedom of speech was introduced. Statesmen who wrote history and historiography in the service of rulers should also be mentioned. The structure of European histories should be treated as well.
8. What the historian has to take into account; especially that he should not lose himself in details, but should attempt to examine the general course of development and point out causes and effects. History should deal not only with politics but also with society as a whole. Description of the facts should be combined with theoretical reflections. A good history should enable its readers to learn from past experience by pointing out general laws. Historiography should contribute to the progress of mankind.

These instructions, although somewhat unsystematic and repetitive, show that only a few months after arriving in England, Suematsu not only planned to commission a work outlining European history, but also knew what he expected from such a work. The man he asked to write the outline was George Gustavus Zerffi. A native of Hungary, Zerffi had fled to

England after the revolution of 1849 and had been naturalized.[29] In response to Suematsu's request Zerffi wrote a book entitled *The Science of History*. The preface to the book is dated 15 October 1879. It is followed by the letter Zerffi received from Suematsu, dated 6 March 1879, and Suematsu's instructions to Zerffi. Comparing the instructions Zerffi received to those Suematsu sent to Japan in December 1878 is difficult, because we have only the Japanese translation of the latter and cannot be sure how accurate it is. It is clear that they represent two separate versions, but there is no significant difference in content.

According to Suematsu, a good history should deal with the evolution of society in all its aspects. It should not only name the events, but connect them by explaining causes and effects and draw conclusions for them as lessons for the present and the future. Past experience should contribute to the progress of mankind. Suematsu named several historians to illustrate his arguments: Thucydides, Caesar, Frederick the Great, Napoleon, Clarendon, Thiers, Guizot, Macaulay and Buckle; this again shows that Suematsu must have studied quite intensively before writing his instructions.

It is evident from *Shiyō monmoku* that Suematsu had plans to ask a local scholar to write a work on historiography as early as autumn 1878. Whether he already had Zerffi in mind is not clear, nor how Suematsu came to ask Zerffi. Zerffi taught at the University of London and was a member of the Royal Historical Society and the Royal Society of Literature. Apart from various works on religion, history and philosophy, he also published an annotated edition of Goethe's *Faust*. Zerffi was well known as a lecturer on historical subjects.[30] Suematsu may well have heard about Zerffi soon after arriving in London and met him at one of his lectures. We can assume that Suematsu attended lectures on historical subjects to learn more about European historiography, and the Royal Historical Society would have been an obvious choice. Zerffi was a member of its committee and gave many lectures there; in 1875 he had talked about the study of history and between 1876 and 1880 he gave a whole series of lectures entitled *Historical Development and Realism*. Suematsu might have attended some of these lectures, which dealt with the history of European philosophy. In the fourth lecture of the series

Zerffi mentioned Suematsu's instructions.[31] In 1879, at the annual dinner of the Society, one of its members (Dr Rogers) praised the growing importance of the Society in his speech and named the book commissioned by Suematsu as an example. However Suematsu came to approach him, Zerffi was a lecturer at the University and a well-known figure in intellectual life in London, so there was some reason for Suematsu's choice.

Suematsu might have been impressed by Zerffi's personality too. A glance at biographies of the two men reveals that they had some things in common, although they were a generation apart in age. Both of them had been journalists and were prolific writers, both had a wide range of interests, of which history was a special one, and both translated a great literary work: Zerffi produced a translation of *Faust* and Suematsu the first English translation of parts of the *Tale of Genji*.

Zerffi's views on history are evident from the title of *The Science of History*. To call history a science was characteristic of the optimism of the nineteenth century. It was believed that in any branch of knowledge it was possible to create an ultimate body of facts answering all questions and enabling scholars to derive laws that would always remain valid.[32] It is evident from *The Science of History* that Zerffi shared this optimistic belief. He also believed that history was subject to universal laws and that it was the historian's task to show that individual facts were merely the effects of general laws, because the same causes invariably brought forth the same effects. The aim of historiography was to educate and encourage virtue and to promote a better knowledge of humans as the actors in history.[33] Ultimately the study of history should promote awareness of mankind 'as the one great and mighty agent of history' and 'make us acquainted with the final aim', which is civilization (4–5), defined by Zerffi as the balance between acting and reacting, dynamic and static, intellectual and moral forces (17). Zerffi believed that all facts and the laws that defined their relations could be discovered and that this knowledge would lead to progress (760, 765). He had already expressed these ideas in his lecture 'On the Possibility of a Strictly Scientific Treatment of Universal History', and they dominate all 773 pages of *The Science of History*.[34]

Japanese scholars have pointed out that *The Science of History* did not take into account the wishes of the members of the Office of Historiography, for whom Suematsu commissioned it. But before examining that question we must first ask whether the content of Zerffi's book was in accordance with Suematsu's wishes. This is not too difficult, since Zerffi included Suematsu's instructions in his book, which enables us to compare them with what Zerffi wrote.

Zerffi begins his book with an introductory chapter in which he outlines the importance of studying history and discusses some of the difficulties of writing history and the qualities a historian should possess. He emphasizes the contribution of historiography to civilization by providing a better knowledge of human actions. Zerffi discusses the qualities of a good historian (26–8, 34–6) and states that the greatest difficulty lies in not only recognizing the truth but representing it faithfully (27). According to Zerffi, a historian should think logically, write clearly and engage in philosophical reflections. He should act as a supreme judge on the basis of unchanging laws of human morality and human intellect (36); for this he needs a comprehensive love for humanity, a love of the truth as well as courage, freedom and independence in his thoughts. Zerffi then mentions the qualities of a good history and stresses that it should discuss causes and effects (28, 34–5), a demand he repeats throughout his book.

In the following four chapters Zerffi discusses the historians of ancient Greece and Rome and their works. In his sixth chapter he treats the historians from the Middle Ages to the sixteenth century. As he explains, he regarded a brief treatment of these historians as sufficient, believing that they had not contributed anything new to the knowledge of fundamental laws (554). According to Zerffi, later historians achieved perfection only insofar as they attained the high level of Greek and Roman historiography (633). It is obvious that Zerffi concentrated on the ancient world in his survey on purpose.

Zerffi's book is essentially a chronological account of historians and their works, but he includes some discussions of the common people, the arts, religion, customs and ideas, as well as auxiliary and related disciplines (30–4) necessary to the historian. Throughout his book, Zerffi discusses the different kinds of historical writings and stresses the importance of presenting causes and effects (151, 362, 494, 771–2). He stresses the importance of philosophical questions and sometimes treats philosophers in the same way as historians. He mentions the difficulties different historians have encountered and the limitations they have suffered in different periods, especially in times of strict censorship (707). At the end of his book, Zerffi reiterates some of his points about the importance of philosophical reflection, the usefulness of successful historical writing and the lessons to be learnt from history. He does not offer a final summary and conclusion.

The Science of History represents a critical discussion of the most important European historians. They are treated as products of their own times and judged according to whether their work meets the standards of a 'scientific' history, whether it is completely objective and relates past events to causes and effects, showing them to be examples of general laws. Zerffi's comments included hints for future historians. Characteristic of Zerffi was also his view of history as universal 'history'; his brief remarks on Asian history can be seen in this light, although they might also represent a concession to his Japanese readers. Another feature of Zerffi's book is his emphasis on religion, especially Christianity, which he attacks sharply, making it responsible for what he perceived as a lack of historical studies in England (484, 502, 505, 511). Apart from historians, Zerffi also discusses poets and philosophers (Shakespeare 658–9, Rousseau 735–6, Kant 759).

A comparison with Suematsu's instructions shows that Zerffi followed them faithfully, including the treatment of all the historians and statesmen named by Suematsu in the second version of his instructions (Caesar 299, Frederick the Great 640, Napoleon 735, Clarendon 673, Thiers 739, Guizot 741).

Japanese historians, usually quoting an essay by Imai Toshiki, have pointed out that *The Science of History,* while treating ancient authors in great detail, hardly mentions the compilation of historical sources in Britain, Germany and France in the nineteenth century and that the book, therefore, did not conform to the wishes of the scholars at the Office of Historiography.[35] As a reason for the shortcomings of the book these historians cite the short time in which it was completed, assuming that

Zerffi wrote it between the dates of Suematsu's letter (6 March 1879) and his preface to the work (5 October 1879). However, even if Zerffi did not start the book before receiving the written instructions, the fact that he wrote it in six months does not suffice to explain its alleged weak points. They are inherent in Zerffi's plan for the work. Greek authors were accorded so much space in it because he saw their contributions as fundamental to all subsequent historiography, which only repeated the principles once defined (554, 633). The allegation that he gave too much attention to Asia is not justifiable, since he only mentioned it occasionally, usually in comparisons. That Zerffi hardly treated modern methods of historiography at all is true and can be explained with his view that a philosophical treatment of history as a whole was more important than dealing with details. Zerffi even claimed that the greatest enemy of the historian beside the theologian was the pedant (769). His very brief treatment of nineteenth-century German historians, despite stressing their merits, might be explained by the fact that their merits lay outside his main area of interest.

Suematsu did not mention methods of compiling documents or other more technical matters in his instructions; Zerffi's book undeniably conformed to his wishes. He expressed his satisfaction with it in a letter to Itō Hirobumi with the following words: 'Although a scientific work may to some Chinese scholars not be as pleasant to read as San'yō's historical writings, it should be of considerable merit to them if they have it translated by a competent translator.'[36] The question is: did Suematsu's instructions express the wishes of the Office of Historiography? We know virtually nothing about what Suematsu was told to do; nor do we have any evidence that Suematsu studied much history before he left Japan. However, it seems that he did so once in London, and within six months he was able to draw up instructions that were remarkably in tune with Zerffi's interpretation of history. The likeliest explanation is that he had already been strongly influenced by Zerffi's views when he drew up the first set of instructions in autumn 1878.

Similarly, Zerffi could have started work on the book before he received the instructions he quoted. In any case he probably used some of his previous works, such as 'On the Possibility of a Strictly Scientific

Treatment of Universal History' and 'The Historical Development of Idealism and Realism'.[37] All the same, to produce a lengthy work such as *The Science of History* in only a few months, beside his many other obligations, was no mean feat. However, was the book suited to meet the needs of the scholars for whom it was written? Considering its intended purpose, the work had several drawbacks, its length being one of them. To be of any use, the 773 pages had first to be translated and then carefully studied by several members of the Office of Historiography. It would therefore take time until the knowledge it conveyed could be applied. Nor was its content of the kind that could be put to immediate practical use. Suematsu might not have been interested in the latest methods of compilation and historical research, but for the Office of Historiography such information would have been more relevant. Moreover, many of the underlying ideas must have been alien to them. For writers of a national history, Zerffi's concentration on universal history must have been beside the point and was perhaps not even comprehensible. At the same time, Zerffi's Eurocentrism, evident despite his examples from Asia, would have made *The Science of History* harder to understand; furthermore it cannot have escaped the notice of Shigeno and his colleagues that this kind of 'universal' history, as well as Zerffi's notion of progress, relegated Asian countries to the place of backward nations. Zerffi's preoccupation with Christianity and the church might have seemed irrelevant to his Japanese readers.[38]

In fact, *The Science of History* failed to fulfil its intended purpose. Suematsu had 200 copies printed and sent half of them to the Office of Historiography. The Office asked Nakamura Masanao to translate it; he had translated Samuel Smiles' *Self-Help,* one of the bestsellers of the early Meiji period. However, Nakamura translated only one chapter before giving it up, apparently because he was too busy. Only after Suematsu's return in 1886, and perhaps because he insisted, was the translation resumed, this time by Saga Shōsaku. It was completed in 1887, eight years after Zerffi had written it.[39] Shigeno and his colleagues had probably soon realized that *The Science of History* was not the kind of work they had hoped for. However, little is known about their reaction to it. It is certain that Shigeno studied at least parts of it carefully; his papers in the

Historiographical Institute include excerpts from Nakamura's translation of the first chapter on paper marked 'Office of Historiography' (*Shūshikyoku*) and from Saga's translation, with Shigeno's comments in the margins.

The documents from the Office of Historiography deal mainly with the cost of Zerffi's book. This was much higher than the budget allowed Suematsu and more than could be paid from the regular budget of the Office or the Council of State. After sending the book, Suematsu informed the Office in January 1880 that he had not yet heard from them. The new consul in Britain, Mori Arinori, had told him that the book had met with satisfaction. Suematsu wanted to know whether it had been translated; it was a bit long to be sure and therefore expensive, but the content was of great importance. Suematsu then gave instructions about the distribution of the copies and advised that the members of the Council of State should each receive one. In a second letter, written in the same month, Suematsu again mentioned the cost of the book. He wrote that he had taken pains to ask a well-respected scholar; he was sure Zerffi was worth the money. Then he gave a detailed account of the costs. It seem that the Office took its time over paying the bill, for Suematsu mentioned the transaction more than once in his letters to Itō Hirobumi.[40]

Why did the members of the Office of Historiography show so little interest in *The Science of History* after having spent so much money to learn something about European historiography? The main reason was probably the shortcomings of the book, which did not conform to their wishes and may well have been almost incomprehensible to them. The first chapter, translated by Nakamura Masanao, expressed a view of history entirely alien to Japanese scholars not acquainted with Western ideas and could not readily be understood without some familiarity with Western modes of thought.[41] The disappointed scholars may not have thought it worthwhile to find a second translator immediately after Nakamura had laid down the work, especially as it had already cost them more than they could afford. By then the Office of Historiography had been transferred to the Imperial University and its members had the opportunity to gain first-hand knowledge of Western historiography from their German colleague, Ludwig Rieß.[42]

Zerffi's book had some limited influence on Japanese historiography. Shigeno's colleagues must have at least looked at the translation briefly. Iwakura seems to have borrowed the manuscript of Nakamura's translation for the editors of the history *Taisei kiyō*.[43] Saga Shōsaku himself wrote a book about the study of history in 1888, which was strongly influenced by Zerffi.[44]

Thus Suematsu may well have benefited most from the encounter with Zerffi and his ideas on history. Suematsu spent eight years in Britain and studied law and literature in Cambridge. After returning to Japan he became a politician, member of parliament and minister in Itō's cabinets. He wrote and translated and was active in the movement to reform Japanese theatre. Among his many interests history may well have been the most enduring.[45] In the last years of his life he made a significant contribution to Japanese historiography with the *Bōchō kaitenshi* (*History of the Great Achievements of Chōshū and Suō*; Chapter 3.4), which he edited in the service of the house of Mōri from 1897 to 1911 and revised on his own initiative in the last years before his death.[46] This history is still highly regarded today.

Perhaps Suematsu himself benefited more from his historical research than the scholars who commissioned it. *The Science of History* had little influence on the work of the Office of Historiography. The chronological history begun in 1882, the *Dainihon hennenshi*, did not mark a fundamental departure from traditional historiography.

4.5 The *Dainihon hennenshi*

In early 1882, following the reorganization of the Office of Historiography, writing the national history was at last begun and became the central task of the Office. The actual writing was done by the four editors (*henshūkan*), Kume, Fujino, Hoshino and Ijichi. Shigeno, the deputy chief editor, was in charge of the compilation and proofread passages as they were completed. When the period of the divided imperial courts caused problems, it was left to Shigeno to complete.[47]

The title of the national history, *Dainihon hennenshi* (*Chronological History of Japan*), indicates its affinity with the *Dainihonshi* of the Mito school. The Imperial Rescript of 1869 had envisaged a sequel to the Six

National Histories, but the *Dainihon hennenshi* was conceived as a continuation of the *Dainihonshi,* which was accorded the status of a standard history (*seishi*) on the grounds of having received imperial sanction in 1809. Shigeno refers to the *Dainihonshi* as a *seishi* in the *Shūshi jigi.*

However, the *Dainihon hennenshi* did not start where the *Dainihonshi* ended, with the reconciliation of the Northern and the Southern courts in 1392, but with the reign of emperor Godaigo, who attempted the Kemmu Restoration and brought about the schism. It seems that the decision to include the Kemmu Restoration and the period of the Northern and Southern courts was made at short notice and not by Shigeno. Kume later claimed it was his suggestion.[48]

Like the *Dainihonshi*, the *Dainihon hennenshi* centred on the imperial house and was written in Sino-Japanese, but it was organized differently, following a strictly chronological format (*hennentai*), while the *Dainihonshi* was arranged by different sections, like the Chinese dynastic histories (Chapter 1). Various guidelines for the collection of sources and the compilation of the history tell us what was to be included. They were probably drawn up by Shigeno because there is usually one version in his papers and another, with amendments, in *Shimatsu*. Not all of them are dated, but they appear to have been drawn up between 1879 and 1882. The documents are:

- *Shiryō hanrei* (general remarks about materials).[49]
- *Henshū reisoku* (guidelines for compilation).[50]
- Untitled, begins with 'Daini kyoku ...' (Department 2); regulations for the compilation of sources in Departments 2 and 3.[51]
- *Shishiryō sanshū kisoku* (regulations for the compilation of materials for the historical treatises) for the sub-departments (*bu*).[52]
- *Henshū reisoku* (guidelines for compilation); about the compilation of the history on the basis of the sources collected so far.[53]

The guidelines were intended to ensure that all the officials would proceed in the same way; in the case of uncertainty they had to reach some kind of agreement. The regulations concerning the collection of materials had been in force for some time and were confirmed after the reorganization. They prescribed what should be included in the history and what should be left out as well as the words that should be used to describe certain events. The main themes were the imperial court, the careers of high court officials, ceremonies and other events; then the shogunate and the relations between shogun and emperor. Other information to be included concerned harvests and taxes, natural disasters and rebellions. Some of the regulations concerned the use of the documents; the relevant passages from the sources were to be quoted for each event, another feature characteristic of the *Dainihonshi*. At the beginning of each year the sources used were to be named. If there were discrepancies between two sources, both accounts should be carefully examined, taking the context into account. Here are a few examples of the guidelines from the first version of *Henshū reisoku*:

- In general the emperors should be referred to as 'tennō', not as 'mikado' or 'in'. Abdicated emperors [daijō tennō] should be called 'jōkō', but after Zōsen 'hōō'. When there were two abdicated emperors at once, the terms common at that time should be used and 'hon'in' or 'shin'in' should be written; the same applies to the case of three or more abdicated emperors.[54]
- The death of a foreign sovereign should be called 'sosu' if he is Chinese and 'shussu' if he is Korean; for the kings of the Ryukyu Islands, although they were part of a feudal domain [Satsuma], 'shussu' should be used.[55]
- Generally, when accounts of the same event differ, thought should be given as to which one can be regarded as the earliest one (even if the same event is reported in the same way, it should not be taken for granted that it is correct). When incomplete accounts throw light on each other, both should be quoted to make them available for further research. If the dates or the facts are different or doubtful and lacking in detail, they should be set side by side for comparison and added at the end.[56]

As these examples show, the guidelines were quite technical and mainly concerned with reporting isolated facts accurately. The importance given to selecting the right terms to denote a ruler's status show that, although overt evaluation was not allowed, the aim was nevertheless to distinguish between the 'alien and the proper' in accordance with the rescript of 1869.

Of the documents cited, the second version of *Henshū reisoku*, dated January 1882, directly concerns the *Dainihon hennenshi* and is the most important source of information about what the editors had in mind. According to this document, the Six National Histories and the *Honchō tsugan* merely chronicle the emperor's activities and do not explain the historical situation. The new history would be different from the previous histories. The structure was to be based on that of the *Spring and Autumn Annals* in the commentated version by Zuo Qiuming (Jap. Sakyūmei) and the *Comprehensive Mirror for Aid in Government* (*Zi shi tang jian,* Jap. *Shiji zukan*), written in 1085 by Sima Guang (1019–89).

The reference to these works as models shows that the *Dainihon hennenshi* was conceived in the old Confucian annalistic tradition. The *Spring and Autumn Annals* of Confucius' home province Lu are regarded as the oldest Chinese history and are a concise, strictly annalistic record of events. The commentary by Zuo Qiuming from the third century BC is the most recent one, and, like the other commentaries, it sets out Confucian principles in carefully chosen words.[57] The *Comprehensive Mirror for Aid in Government* was written in the same Confucian tradition, strictly annalistic and covering the whole history of China spanning the period from 481 BC to 959 AD. Sima Guang attempted to present the history of China in a continuous narrative. In his commentary, he explained the process by which he compared variant statements in his sources and chose one rather than the others. The history is written in the form of annals on the basis of excerpts from the collected materials arranged chronologically (*chang bian,* Jap. *chōhen*). This procedure was often imitated and, as Naitō points out, the *Dainihon shiryō* compiled by the Historiographical Institute (Chapter 7.1) follows the same method.[58]

However, the document goes on to emphasize that the new history would not necessarily follow older examples in every respect. Rather, it would include sections to illustrate the historical circumstances and provide information on social and economic history and would also include descriptions of political rule, the conditions of the people and the times (*chitai minjō jisei*). The guidelines (*Hennenshi reisoku*) suggest an effort to combine the advantages of chronological and thematic arrangement. Certain themes would be treated in a series of essays, and the document includes guidelines about what was to be treated in the main part and what in the essays. For example, only the broad outlines of foreign relations would form part of the main body; the details were to go in an essay on foreign relations. Other essays were entitled: 'Astronomy'; 'Geography'; 'Shrines and Temples'; 'Offices'; 'Rites and Music'; 'Military Affairs'; 'Punishment'; 'Food and Money' (economic affairs); 'Art and Literature'; 'Customs'; 'Crafts'; 'Foreign Affairs'; and 'Clans and Families'.[59]

Regulations about what was to be included and what words were to be used can be found in the introductions to earlier histories such as the *Honchō tsugan* and the *Tokugawa jikki*. The broader range of subjects to be treated and the plan to combine chronological and thematic treatment marked a new departure, however. Ōkubo sees this as a new tendency and the germination of a modern approach to historical writing.[60] Nevertheless, the essays were not without precedents. Plans for the *Dainihonshi* included essays entitled 'Gods of Heaven and Earth' (i.e. Shintō rituals and shrines); 'Clans and Families'; 'Offices'; 'Provinces and Counties', 'Food and Money' (i.e. economic affairs); 'Rites and Music'; 'Military Affairs' (including institutions of the shogun's government); 'Punishment'; 'Yin and Yang' (with a section on the calendar and chronological lists of portentous national phenomena); and 'Buddhist Affairs'.[61]

If, as Webb states, the organization and content of the Essays in the *Dainihonshi* had largely been decided upon by 1709, then clearly this shows once again how much the *Dainihon hennenshi* owed to the *Dainihonshi*, because many of the titles are the same. However, by the time the Essays of the *Dainihonshi* were completed in late Meiji, influence may well have been reciprocal. Certainly the general preface to the Essays of the *Dainihonshi,* written in 1897, tells us more about the political ideas of late Meiji than of the Mito school. The close connection between the *Dainihonshi* and the *Dainihon hennenshi* is moreover evident in the fact that some of the members of the Office of Historiography had formerly worked on the *Dainihonshi* in the Mito office, most notably Kan Masatomo, who worked on the Essays there,[62] and Kurita Hiroshi, the scholar who is credited with having completed the *Dainihonshi*.

Although Shigeno and his colleagues had shown an interest in Western historiography, there are hardly any signs of its influence in the *Dainihon hennenshi*. The editors endeavoured to establish the facts – but not their relative importance in the development of events – by carefully examining the sources, and to represent them without any kind of bias. They made some attempt to go beyond enumerating isolated facts by providing thematic descriptions in the Essays and possibly the arrangement and content of these was in part inspired by Western works, which they admired for including social and economic developments and making causes and effects clear. However, none of this was more than the attempts by the editors of the *Dainihonshi* in the Edo period carried one step further.[63]

The first parts of the manuscript were completed in 1882. There are six different manuscript versions, completed between 1882 and 1891, in the Historiographical Institute, together with a table of contents drawn up in 1897, which gives the number of fascicles covering each period: 24 fascicles edited by Kume cover the period of the Northern and Southern courts; 76 cover the following period up to 1663 and were edited by Kume, Hoshino; Fujino, Ijichi Sadaka and Kusaka Hiroshi (a member of the Office since 1877). Some of the manuscripts show signs of repeated, thorough revision, reflecting the changing views held by the editors as their work progressed. The manuscripts show that work on the *Dainihon hennenshi* progressed a long way; nevertheless, it was finally abandoned and never published.

How does the *Dainihon hennenshi* compare with previous histories? A detailed comparison is beyond the scope of this book, but it would seem that it marked no new departure. It was claimed that the Meiji Restoration made a fundamental break with the preceding period of shogunal rule. The impact of Western civilization resulted in profound changes, necessitating a reassessment of Japanese traditions. Even the scholars of the Office of Historiography, who were more conservative than the representatives of the Japanese Enlightenment, looked critically upon the achievements of previous generations and were selective in what they retained. Nothing was taken for granted, nothing was inviolable; even the Six National Histories, treated almost as a sacred text in the Imperial Rescript on Historiography, were criticized by Shigeno. At the same time Shigeno and his colleagues were steeped in the traditional learning of their Confucian education. They had had minimal exposure to Western civilization before 1868. The *Dainihon hennenshi* is essentially a product of the kind of scholarship that had grown in Japan during the Tokugawa period; the influence of the *Dainihonshi* and other works is far more evident than that of Western historiography, despite the efforts made by Shigeno and his colleagues to learn more about it.

In theory, the *Dainihon hennenshi* was to be a *seishi*, a standard history, but we have already seen that the memorandum on the language of official historiography (*Shūshi buntai ron*; Chapter 4.3) suggests that the history would not be definitive. Shigeno does not mention the word *seishi* in the regulations for compilation of 1882 and criticizes the Six National Histories as inadequate for providing a survey of historical developments. As past generations had obviously failed to produce a satisfactory *seishi,* how confident were Shigeno and his colleagues that they could do better? They had amassed an unprecedented amount of documents, which made selection vital, and they had to agree on what was to be selected.[64] They then had to find a way to fulfil their aim of representing the historical facts in a way that provided both a comprehensive chronological survey of events and analyses of historical circumstances and developments. Neither the problems of selection nor of representation were solved. The documents do not say so, but presumably the members of the Office realized that a *seishi* that met their standards was impossible.

Thus, by the time the *Dainihon hennenshi* was abandoned in 1893, the idea of a definitive history, in the tradition of the *seishi*, had become not only a political anachronism but also a conceptual impossibility.

5

History as an Academic Discipline

Writing history has a long tradition in Japan; the oldest written works that we have are histories. In the Tokugawa period something like scientific historical research emerged; the compilers of the *Chōya kyūbun hōkō, Shiryō* and *Dainihonshi* strove to collect and examine the evidence and establish historical facts. However, in Japan, as in the West, history as an independent academic discipline with a defined area of study, its own canon of methods and organizational structures is a product of the late nineteenth century. Through being transferred to the Imperial University, the leading members of the Office of Historiography became part of this development.

5.1 Scholarly Traditions

The members of the Office of Historiography derived their methods from the *kōshōgaku* school of textual criticism, which was originally a branch of Confucian scholarship, but became the basis for National Learning (*kokugaku*) as well as Chinese Learning (*kangaku*) during the Edo period. Shigeno Yasutsugu was one of the foremost scholars of Chinese Learning in his time as well as a historian, and his description of the methods of *kōshōgaku* can be regarded as authoritative. He gave a lecture entitled 'All Scholarship Is in the Final Analysis *kōshō* Textual Criticism' at the Tokyo Academy on 9 March 1890.[1] In his lecture he dealt especially with scholars who had used the methods of *kōshō* in their critical study of Japanese texts, and named Arai Hakuseki, Motoori Norinaga, Ise Sadatake, Hanawa Hokiichi, Kariya Ekisai, Ban Nobutomo, Kurokawa Harumura and Okamoto Yasutaka. According to Shigeno, the method consisted of collecting all the sources of written evidence and comparing them to establish the facts. Shigeno compared this to the Western concept of induction; however, he explained this term with the etymology of the

Sino-Japanese *kinō* with which 'induction' was translated and does not seem to have been aware of the meaning of 'induction' in the Western sense of inferring a general law from particular instances. Shigeno went on to say that in China the method had been practised for 200 years, in Japan for 100 years and in the West for 50 years. The method enabled scholars to examine the evidence critically by collecting all the sources and comparing them; thus what was true and what was false would become clear immediately. For Shigeno, the *kōshō* method formed and would continue to form the basis of all scholarship.

Applying the *kōshō* method to history meant collecting and comparing all the sources to determine the historical facts.[2] Their relative importance within the historical process was not considered. The selection of facts to be included in the chronological history *Dainihon hennenshi* was made according to fixed rules, not context, and the editors were not free to decide what was significant and what was not.

The members of the Office of Historiography, especially those who later became the most influential, had studied the methods of *kōshō*, and work in the Office was based on these methods. The main task was the compilation of documents. At first these were either collected by the prefectures or government offices for the Office or came from collections in Tokyo: the Institute of Japanese Learning (*Wagaku kōdansho*), the former *Momijiyama bunko* library of the shogunate, established in 1602, or the *Asakusa bunko* public library. In the 1880s members of the Office travelled all over Japan in search of documents. Chronological tables were drawn up and the documents relevant to each event cited. To obtain a reliable chronology the members of the Office at first referred to the traditional histories.

The chronological history was centred on the reigns of the emperors, and establishing a definitive line of legitimate emperors was therefore crucial. We have evidence of several discussions about whether certain rulers were legitimate emperors or not. For many years after its establishment in 1875 the Office of Historiography included a department for the investigation of the imperial genealogies, first established in 1870 and incorporated in the Department of History in 1872. Among the questions discussed were the beginning of the imperial line, the legitimacy of the Northern or Southern courts in the fourteenth century, the legitimacy of Iitoyo-ao-no-himemiko and Chōkei as emperors, the official names of the emperors, duration of their reigns and their ages. To settle these matters once and for all, Nagamatsu Miki twice appealed to the emperor for a decision, in 1874 and 1875.[3] However, in 1876 the discussion had still not come to an end. In Department 4, the department for the imperial genealogies, Ogō Kazutoshi made himself spokesman and expressed his opinions in various memoranda including the two addressed to Iwakura Tomomi at the beginning of 1876.[4] Ogō also appealed for an official decision and stressed the importance of being able to tell the exact place of the present emperor in the imperial line – especially for the benefit of foreigners (he mentioned the preparations for the world exhibition; Chapter 3.3).

The reign of Iitoyo-ao-no-himemiko, mentioned in Chapter 3.3, is a good example of the discussions concerning the imperial line.[5] According to the *Nihongi,* Iitoyo-ao reigned from 484 until her death the following year, because each of her two brothers wanted to leave the throne to the other. After her death the younger brother ascended the throne as Emperor Kenzō; in 488 he was succeeded by his elder brother, who became Emperor Ninken (488–99). The *Nihongi* counts the year 484–5 as part of Kenzō's reign, and this was decisive for those who were against counting Iitoyo-ao among the emperors. The problem of how to treat her reign was discussed several times, and at the end of the year 1881 the department for the imperial genealogies (which had been in the Imperial Household Ministry since 1877) attempted to obtain an imperial decision. The scholars of National Learning in the Ministry based their argument on moral grounds such as the good customs of ancient times.[6] In contrast, the arguments of the scholars in the Office of Historiography were typical of the positivist approach of the *kōshō* school of textual criticism; the oldest sources, the *Kojiki* and more importantly the standard history *Nihongi,* were regarded as the most reliable ones, while later sources were not even consulted. As the *Nihongi* did not name Iitoyo-ao as an empress in so many words she was not one. No agreement had been reached by 1883, and around 1890 the discussion was once again resumed.[7]

Discussions such as these revolved around isolated problems without any attempt to reconstruct a whole chain of events. Only when the scholars at the Office began to concentrate on the *Dainihon hennenshi,* after 1882, were they able to treat past events more systematically. The decision to begin the history with the reign of Emperor Godaigo (1318–39) meant that the period of the Northern and Southern courts, which was covered by the *Dainihonshi,* would be dealt with again, both because the scholars had already discovered flaws in the account given by the *Dainihonshi* and because of the significance of this particular period for the history of the imperial house. Ōkubo describes this revision as the beginning of the New School of Textual Criticism (*shin kōshōgaku*), which developed from the *kōshō* tradition of the Edo period.[8] Shigeno himself had corrected errors in the *Dainihonshi,* when he based his history for the lord of Satsuma on the *Dainihonshi,* and in the Office of Historiography similar efforts had been made to revise traditional historiography (e.g. Kawada's correction of the *Nihon gaishi*).

This in itself was not new. What was new was the extent of the revision. All the available sources were collected and examined with a view to completely rewriting the parts in question. Moreover, the scholars stressed that they would not be led by any moral bias, unlike the editors of the *Dainihonshi.*[9] As the *Dainihonshi* gave what was at the time the official interpretation of the period of the Northern and Southern courts, it must be assumed that the members of the Office genuinely wished to establish what they regarded as the truth and not substitute the interpretation in the *Dainihonshi* with a new one.

A further indication that the interest of the scholars in the Office went beyond the immediate task of producing the official history is the introduction of regular informal meetings to discuss historical themes. Thirty-three meetings were held between January 1882 and June 1885, in a restaurant in what is today Ueno Park, and the minutes are preserved in the Historiographical Institute.[10] According to the statutes passed at the third meeting, the arrangement was at first very casual, but became so successful that the director of the Office (Shigeno) joined in and it was decided to put it on a more permanent footing.

At the first meeting ten people were present, more at some of the later meetings. In every meeting about ten short reports were given on various subjects. Usually they dealt with one specific point which probably arose from the work of the speaker. Biographical notes were common: Kan Masatomo twice spoke about Fujita Yūkoku, a representative of the later Mito school, and Tanaka Yoshinari about Yasui Sokken, a Confucian scholar, who had taught several members of the Office, and Hoshino Hisashi about Yasui's letters.[11] Other subjects were the Japanese writing system (Kusaka) and even potatoes (Kume).[12] Oka Shigezane, who worked with Nagamatsu on the Chronicle of the Restoration, talked about themes from the history of the Meiji Restoration.

At the third meeting, on 20 April 1882, Kume gave a report entitled 'Some demands concerning the compilation of sources' (*Shiryō sanshū ni tsuki seikyū no ken*), which can be regarded as the programme of the new school of textual criticism. Kume stressed the importance of using the sources as a basis for research and establishing the facts, and then urged his colleagues to keep certain points in mind when they worked with the sources. His report amounts to a summary of the principles expressed in the guidelines drawn up in the Office. The fact that Kume mentioned them once again shows not only their importance, but also the difficulty of adhering to them.

In May 1882 Kinoshita Masatomo, who had apparently travelled in remote parts of the country to look for sources and found many collections that he had not known to exist, urged that they be dealt with immediately before they were lost. Local officials could not be relied upon. The task was so important that money for it should be saved elsewhere, if necessary. Tanaka Yoshinari also stressed the importance of examining more sources in a report entitled 'Primary Documents in Chronological Order' (*Hennen komonjo*) in December 1884.[13]

Shigeno, Hoshino and Kume discussed various historical writings. Among the histories Kume discussed in his report on 3 March 1885,[14] was the *Taiheiki*. He criticized the fact that it was widely regarded as a reliable history, although only 20 to 30 per cent of its contents was supported by other evidence. Kume presented many examples of its unreliability, anticipating the content of his later article 'The *Taiheiki* Is of No Use for Historical Scholarship'.[15]

The reports illustrate some of the characteristics of the new school of textual criticism. Its representatives were very much influenced by their background in Chinese Learning; they concentrated their efforts on isolated facts; they believed that official historiography was reliable and deserved to be continued; they closely examined traditional accounts of events and made collecting sources an end in itself. The first field trips for this purpose were made before 1882. In March 1876 Kawada and one of his colleagues went to Mito to see documents kept in the *Shōkōkan*, the history office of the former Mito domain, for the compilation of the *Dainihonshi,* on which work continued even after the Meiji Restoration until its completion in 1906. The same trip had already been made by Ogō the year before. The documents had probably been collected in connection with work on the *Dainihonshi*. In the same year, Department 4 applied for permission to send members to Yamato and Yamashiro (near Kyoto and Nara) stating that some questions concerning the imperial genealogies could only be answered by experts examining the original documents. The questions referred to the fourteenth century, when the imperial court was split. According to Tanimori Yoshiomi, the head of the department, the trip, though expensive, was necessary because the issues were important not only for the genealogies but also for the compilation of sources. Permission for the trip was granted, and in August Ogō and Shioda set out expecting to be away for 70 days.[16]

While the field trips mentioned above served to clarify specific points, the extensive trips undertaken after 1885 had the purpose of discovering and collecting all the documents in a given area. In 1884 the task of collecting sources on a local level had been transferred from the prefectures to the Office of Historiography, and on that occasion the Office had stressed the necessity of collecting the documents and suggested that the money which had previously been paid to the prefectures be used for this purpose. In 1885 a memorandum about the search for primary documents was drawn up in the Office. It stated that historiography relied on two types of sources: journals and primary documents (*nikki monjo*) for fundamental evidence (*konkyō*) and military and war tales (*gunki senki monogatari*) for reference (*sankō*). As the latter were recorded by later generations, they were less reliable, but they were referred to more often because they were easier to obtain. The Office intended to send representatives out, both to negotiate the transfer to the Office of the work formerly done by the prefectures and to investigate new sources. It included a list of provinces and other places to which the Office wished to send members, together with the number of days required and the costs. According to the budget attached to the document, the total itinerary would be 3,420 *ri* (c. 8345 miles), the duration 652 days, the cost of travel was estimated at 3,420 yen and the cost of accommodation at 4,164 yen.[17]

In the summer of 1885 some of the members of the Office did in fact travel extensively in search of sources. Shigeno went to Ibaraki, Tochigi, Saitama, Kanagawa and Chiba prefectures on a journey lasting 81 days, and collected 8,900 documents.[18] That same year the Office addressed a memorandum (probably drawn up by Shigeno) to President Sanjō Sanetomi, in which it once again stressed the necessity of field trips to search for documents. The apologetic tone of the memorandum suggests that the Office had to defend itself against criticism. Nevertheless, Shigeno's trip was only the beginning of extensive trips by members of the Office. Vast numbers of documents were collected, which form the basis of work in the Historiographical Institute to this day.

The search for new documents proceeded as follows: the scholars from the Office either visited a temple, shrine or private home themselves or they ordered the local officials to invite the inhabitants of a village or town to a meeting on a given day with their documents. The scholars would then borrow the documents or order them to be copied. In 1887 Kume travelled to Kyushu and brought hundreds of documents back with him, which he had borrowed or had had copied. He submitted a detailed report in February 1888 with a list of the sources he had collected.[19]

Collecting documents from all over the country and work on the *Dainihon hennenshi* were undertaken simultaneously. It is hard to imagine that the masses of documents were examined in any detail and used as a basis for the chronological history. Rather than being part of the preparation for writing the history, the collection of sources had become an end in itself.

However, although the unprecedented scale of the undertaking, made possible by the centralization of government and administration, was new, the idea of making historical sources available for future researchers was not. It can be traced back to the *Chōya kyūbun hōkō* and the *Shiryō* compiled under the Tokugawa shogunate in the late eighteenth and early nineteenth centuries. The aim of these works was not to formulate a definitive version of history, but to provide a collection of sources, selected and commentated on critically and arranged in chronological order, which could serve as the basis for a standard history, to be written by later generations.[20]

At the same time the resulting compilation was regarded as authoritative in a similar way that a *seishi* was. The citation of sources deemed good was given enormous significance, without their value being sufficiently examined. This is a problem that will become even more apparent when we look at the *akademizumu* school of historical scholarship (Chapter 5.4), which owed much to *kōshōgaku*. Nevertheless, this concentration on the sources, rather than on the writing of history, was an important stage in the formation of an independent academic discipline. The most significant organizational step was the establishment of a history department at the Imperial University.

5.2 History at the Imperial University

Before the establishment of the Department of History at the Imperial University on 9 September 1887, neither universal history (de facto European and North American history) nor Japanese history were taught as independent subjects. European and Japanese history were taught in the faculties of law and literature, but not by specialists.[21] In 1886, when the University was named Imperial University (*Teikoku daigaku*),[22] two lecturers taught history: Tsuboi Kumezō, who was by training a scientist, and the Scotsman James Main Dixon (1856–1933), lecturer in English at the Faculty of Engineering. For textbooks, translations of foreign books were used.[23] It seems that foreigners played at least a small part in encouraging the Japanese to study their own history. The German Adolf Groot (1854–1934), who taught at the preparatory school of the University, suggested to the headmaster that Japanese history should be included in the curriculum, and the German doctor Erwin Bälz, who taught medicine at the University, criticized the Japanese for not taking more interest in their own history.[24] In 1877 a department of history, philosophy and politics was established but soon abolished. At that time the president of the University, Katō Hiroyuki, stated that there was no one qualified to teach history and philosophy of the East and the West. Instead, following his suggestion, the Department of Classics (*Koten kōshūka*) was established. Scholars of National Learning taught Japanese literature and Japanese history: Konakamura Kiyonori, Naitō Chisō, Kurita Hiroshi, Kurokawa Mayori and Iida Takesato. Thus the study of Japanese history was not neglected; history had just not yet been organized into a separate discipline. The same was still true for most European universities until the end of the nineteenth century (Chapter 7.2).

At the Imperial University, the first step towards a permanent department of history was taken when the German historian Ludwig Rieß (1861–1928) was appointed professor of history at the University. He took up his post on 3 March 1887 and probably acted as an adviser when the Department of History was established in September 1887. In June 1887 Tsuboi Kumezō, who had been teaching history, was sent to Europe by the Ministry of Education to study history. He studied in Berlin, Prague, Vienna and Zurich, received his PhD from the Imperial University in 1891 and was appointed the second professor at the Department of History when he came home the same year.

The Imperial University now had a department of History and a specialist historian as professor, but Japanese history was still only taught as part of other disciplines, for the Department of History was in fact a department of European history. Apparently there were already plans for a department of Japanese history. Watanabe Kōki, the president of the University, referred to these plans when in 1888 he proposed transferring the Office of Historiography to the University. His memorandum was almost certainly the result of discussions on the subject. Apart from the necessity of studying the history of one's own country, Watanabe also stressed the importance of scientific methods. Like Katō before him, he stated that these were still lacking in Japan and even suggested that this might be why work in the Office of Historiography was not making sufficient progress. At the same time he mentioned that the documents collected by the Office and the experience and knowledge of its members would be a great asset to the new department.

The Office of Historiography was transferred to the University on 30 October 1888. The day before, Kume Kunitake and Hoshino Hisashi were appointed professors. Shigeno's appointment followed on 9 November. The Office was now named 'Temporary Department for the Compilation of a Chronological History at the Faculty of Arts of the Imperial University' (*Teikoku daigaku bunka daigaku rinji hennenshi hensan kakari*). On 31 March 1891 it was merged with the Department of Topography (*Chishi hensan kakari*), which had been transferred from the Ministry of Home Affairs (*Naimushō chirikyoku chishika*) the year before, and became the 'Department for Historical and Topographical Compilation' (*Shishi hensan kakari*). Possibly the new name (without the attribute 'temporary') suggests that the collection of materials, and not so much the compilation of the chronological history, was now seen as the main task of the Institute.

One month after the transfer of the Office to the University, on 30 November 1888, Rieß, in accordance with Watanabe's wishes, submitted a memorandum proposing the establishment of a department of Japanese history. Rieß treated Japanese history as a subsidiary discipline to general history. Students were expected to apply the methods learnt from Rieß to the study of Japanese history. Special attention should be given to the auxiliary disciplines, which Rieß described in detail in his memorandum, and students should learn to do research independently through lectures and seminars. The two departments of history (*Shigakka* and *Kokushika*) were to be treated as one for as long as the foundations for both subjects still had to be laid. After completing their studies students should be capable of conducting research in both Japanese and European history. The materials in the Historical Institute should be accessible to students and form the subject of lectures.[25]

It is not clear how much of Rieß's proposal was suggested by Watanabe himself, but the details and the postscript, in which Rieß drew attention to documents relating to Japan in the archives in The Hague, were probably Rieß's own idea.

Several months passed before the Department of Japanese History was established, on 27 June 1889. Lectures and seminars did not start until 1890, because there were no students. Apart from the newly appointed professors, Shigeno, Kume and Hoshino, the professors and lecturers from the Department of Classics, abolished the year before, taught history, namely Naitō and Konakamura. This alone indicates that the way Japanese history was taught cannot have changed significantly. In his lecture 'The Abuse of *kōshō* in Historical Scholarship' (Chapter 5.4) in 1901, Kume self-critically admitted that he and his colleagues from the Historiographical Institute had given priority to their work there and not devoted enough attention to teaching. The system of chairs (*kōzasei*), introduced in 1893, reflected the traditional view of Japanese history; while there were two chairs for history, Japanese history was represented by four chairs for Japanese language, literature and history. It did not get a chair of its own until 1901, when Japanese language and Japanese literature received one chair each and Japanese history two (in 1911 a third was added). That Japanese history was not yet fully recognized as an independent scholarly discipline is also suggested by the term *kokushi*, 'national history', in contrast to *shigaku*, 'historical science'. Only in 1904 did the term *kokushigaku* come into use, when the courses were reorganized and Western, Chinese (the course in Chinese history developed in a similar way to Japanese history) and Japanese history were grouped together as one subject area.[26] In 1919 the three courses became independent departments. Thus the Department of Japanese History marked only the first step in the development of Japanese history as an independent discipline.

Another step was the founding of the Historical Society (*Shigakkai*) on 1 November 1889, which began publishing a historical journal, *Shigakkai zasshi* (Journal of the Historical Society), renamed *Shigaku zasshi* (Journal of History) in 1892. The first issue appeared on 15 December with an introduction by Watanabe Kōki. Different stories are told about the founding of the Society and the publication of the journal.[27] According to Shigeno's account in his inaugural lecture, Shigeno and Rieß first discussed the matter, and their colleagues and students agreed that it was a good idea.[28] Rieß would have had European examples in mind. In Germany, the *Historische Zeitschrift* had been published since 1859 and the *Historisches Jahrbuch* since 1880; France had a *Revue Historique* since 1876 and England the *English Historical Review* since 1886, to name but a few. Japan itself was not without precedents: a historical society, the *Shigaku kyōkai* established in 1883, had existed a few years previously and published its own journal. More recently, a philosophical society had been established.[29] From its foundation, older students supported the Historical Society and became active members.[30] Rieß became a member of the Society as did his foreign colleague Basil Hall Chamberlain (1850–1935). Among the members were many from the Historiographical Institute and from the former Department of Classics.[31] The Society was open to anyone interested in history.

On 15 November 1889, Shigeno was appointed president of the Historical Society, and remained so until his death in 1910. No successor was appointed.

The establishment of the two departments of history, the transfer of the Office of Historiography to the University and the foundation of the Historical Society and its journal created the necessary framework for the development of historical research as an independent discipline. At the same time the history of Western countries and the history of Japan were institutionally separate from each other and taught by different people. At the Department of History (*Shigakka*) Rieß taught; in 1891 he was joined by the former scientist Tsuboi Kumezō, who had returned from his studies in Germany. The Department of Japanese History (*Kokushika*) was dominated by scholars of National Learning from the former Departments of Classics and scholars of Chinese Learning from the Historiographical Institute. The scholars teaching Japanese history had been educated before the Restoration; they belonged to an older generation than Rieß and Tsuboi and Mitsukuri Genpachi, who later succeeded Rieß.

Turning the Office of Historiography into the Historiographical Institute did not immediately change its character and its task too remained the same. But its members were now part of an educational institution. By becoming professors Shigeno, Kume, Hoshino and later Tanaka Yoshinari joined the ranks of those for whom scholarship was a profession, including specialists in history. They published the results of their research in the new journal. The new opportunities for exchange with other scholars included the chance to learn more about Western historical scholarship from the German professor Ludwig Rieß.

5.3 Studying Western Methods (2): Rieß

As early as 1878 the members of the Office of Historiography had attempted to learn something about European historiography to help them with their own work. The encounter with Ludwig Rieß at the Imperial University gave them the opportunity to gain first-hand knowledge about European methods or, more precisely, the historical methods of textual criticism pioneered in Germany. To what extent did they profit from this opportunity and what influence did Rieß have on the work carried out at the Historiographical Institute?

Ludwig Rieß was born in Deutsch-Krone in what is now Poland.[32] His father Julius was a factory owner and merchant. Ludwig attended gymnasia in Deutsch-Krone and Berlin. Then he studied history and geography at the University of Berlin. It is said that he became an assistant to Leopold von Ranke around 1883; this may be the reason why Japanese scholars often describe him as Ranke's disciple. By then Ranke had been retired for many years and Rieß is only supposed to have met him twice, but he was trained in the historical methods taught by Ranke in his seminars in Berlin, where Ranke's students and successors continued the tradition. There is evidence that Rieß greatly admired Ranke; in the printed notes of his lectures on universal history at Tokyo University Rieß adopted Ranke's definition of world history and described Ranke as 'the greatest historian of all times'. Rieß also published an article about Ranke in the journal *Shigaku zasshi*.[33]

In February 1884 Rieß conducted research in England and Ireland. After his return in June he wrote his dissertation 'Geschichte des Wahlrechts zum englischen Parlament im Mittelalter' (History of the Parliamentary Franchise in Medieval England) and passed his PhD examinations in July.[34] His supervisor was Hans Delbrück, and Rieß expresses his high respect for him in the dedication of his thesis. Delbrück was not strictly a Rankean. He had a strong interest in British history and in his writings attempted a universalist approach which went beyond Ranke's.[35] In February 1885 Rieß passed the entrance examination to teach at gymnasia, but instead of taking up a post he went to England for a second time (until June 1885). At the beginning of 1886 he made a third trip to England. There he received the invitation to teach at the Imperial University in Tokyo.

The decision to appoint a German historian is attributed by Kanai to Zerffi's praise of German historical scholarship in *The Science of History*. The contribution by Ranke and his seminars to the training of historians would have been well known in Japan. Besides the reputation of German scholarship, the importance of Germany as a model for the Japanese Constitution and of the German advisers on constitutional matters may well have played a role in the decision. The study of history was regarded as necessary to understand the constitution of a country. Why Rieß was selected, who first had to be called back from England, is not clear. He may have been recommended by his supervisor Hans Delbrück (1848–1939), when Shinagawa Yajirō, the Japanese ambassador in Berlin, inquired at the University in Berlin.[36] Delbrück's brother Ernst and his cousin Felix had been teaching in Tokyo at the School of the German Studies Society (*Doitsu gaku kyōkai*; now *Dokkyō daigaku* or Dokkyo University) since 1885, and they may have been consulted by the Japanese.[37] Though it is likely (as is stated in the *Encyclopedia Judaica* and repeated by Kanai and other Japanese scholars) that Rieß chose to go to Japan because as a Jew his prospects of becoming a professor in Germany were not good, this hardly explains the motives of his Japanese employers.[38] Rieß's specialization in constitutional history might have made him interesting to the Japanese, although the question remains as to why they did not select a specialist in German constitutional history. Some hints as to what the Japanese expected of a professor of history are given in a letter by the minister of education, Mori Arinori, to the foreign minister Inoue Kaoru on 13 May 1886. Mori wrote that the prospective candidate should be able to teach European and American modern history, especially political history, economic history and changing social structures. He should be a good teacher and scholar, capable of laying the foundations of historical science in Japan. Moreover he should be able to teach in English, the usual language for courses taught by foreigners; Rieß's excellent knowledge of this language may well have been one of the main reasons why he was chosen.[39]

When Rieß arrived in Japan (it is said that he studied Japanese history during his voyage) he received a contract for three years. This was extended four times, the last time in 1899. Rieß taught at the Imperial

University from 1887 to 1902. In 1893 he took seven months leave to do research in Europe. During his 15 years in Japan, Rieß also taught at the private Keiō University during 1891–92.[40]

While in Japan Rieß sent articles about Japan to German newspapers, and some of them were later published in his book *Allerlei Japanisches* (*Various Things Japanese*). He became a member of the Asiatic Society of Japan and its German counterpart, the Gesellschaft für Natur- und Völkerkunde Ostasiens (OAG), and gave lectures on Japanese history at both of them, most of which were translated into Japanese and published in *Shigaku zasshi*. When he left, the OAG made him an honorary member.[41]

What did Rieß teach at the Imperial University? More is known about this than most Japanese scholars would lead us to suppose. Not only have handwritten notes of his lectures been preserved (for example, of his lectures on universal history in 1899, preserved by the descendants of the historian Tsuji Zennosuke), but his lecture notes were published: *Methodology of History*, n.d., 2nd edition 1896; *Universal History*, 1893; *English Constitutional History,* 1897–8; *A Short Survey of Universal History*, 2 vols, 1899–1901. The *Methodology* is a short introduction to the study of history. Rieß emphasized the scientific character of historical research and described the methods of the historian, auxiliary disciplines and criticism of historical sources. He classified different types of historiography according to Johann Gustav Droysen. The philosophy of history is mentioned briefly in the introduction, but Rieß did not treat it in any detail. Rieß used many examples from Japanese history, presumably to help his Japanese students. In his *Universal History,* Rieß referred to Ranke's *Weltgeschichte,* describing the relations between the states, mostly European states; the colonial empires and the United States are only treated briefly. In his *English Constitutional History,* Rieß attempted to show 'synthetically' how the contemporary government system had evolved. Rieß used a wide definition of constitutional history as the history of political and social systems, not merely of the legal system. At the beginning of each new chapter Rieß gave information about sources and bibliography. The lecture notes were partly compiled by Rieß himself, partly by the students and edited by Rieß.

We also have some descriptions of Rieß's lessons by former students. Between 1958 and 1960 the magazine *Rekishi kyōiku* (*History Education*) published a series of reminiscences by old historians about their teachers, including Ludwig Rieß. The historians who talked about Rieß were Segawa Hideo (graduated 1896), Nonomura Kaizō (1901), Chō Jukichi (1905) and Abe Hideo (Rieß's grandson). The historian Mikami Sanji also wrote about Rieß in his memoirs.[42]

Rieß's lectures are said to have been easy to comprehend, despite his German accent and many Germanisms – unlike those of his colleague, the philosopher Raphael von Koeber (1848–1922). However, subjects like the ancient cultures of Assyria and Babylonia were a little too remote for his Japanese students (*'dōmo pin to kimasen deshita yo'*). In addition to the lectures, Rieß gave seminars; for example, in one of them the students read and interpreted the texts of the American declaration of independence, passages of John Locke's writings and Jefferson's speech in Georgia. Methods of textual criticism were practised with Japanese sources. Segawa related that in the summers of 1899 and 1900 he collected materials in the Southwest of Japan (Aki, Suō and Nagato) and visited historic sites. These districts had already been visited by Tanaka Yoshinari of the Historiographical Institute, but he had only collected materials and drawn up lists and had not done any detailed research on their content.[43]

Some idea of how he taught is given us by Rieß himself in one of his lectures at the OAG. He mentioned the help he received from his Japanese colleagues and students. The students translated Japanese documents, which Rieß then studied with them in his seminars. About the handwritten documents on the Shimabara uprising in 1637–38, the subject of one of his lectures, Rieß wrote:

They were available to me, because the Historiographical Institute of the Imperial University directed by Professor Shigeno has collected the sources relating to Japan's national history from Kiushiu and united them in one place. I am obliged to Shigeno for the generosity with which he lent the valuable manuscripts to the students of history M. Isoda and T. Urai, who translated them for me. My critical analysis of the sources is based on the research done together with my students in historical seminars, especially work done by Mr M. Isoda.[44]

Rieß's lectures show that he practised himself what he taught his students.[45] He did research on Japanese history using the methods he had learnt in the historical seminars at Berlin University. Most of them deal with the relations between Japan and the Europeans in the sixteenth and early seventeenth centuries, showing Rieß's interest in world history in its Eurocentric form of the time.

Many of Rieß's students wrote their final dissertations on themes from Japanese history, even some who later became specialists in European history. Segawa (1960: 33) was encouraged to do so by Professor Tsuboi Kumezō, who pointed out that a dissertation on European history would be little more than a summary of European historiography. Students of Rieß's not only succeeded him in the Department of Western History, as it was named in 1904, but also became professors of Chinese and Japanese history at the Imperial University of Tokyo and other universities. Many of them were pioneers in their respective fields.[46] One of his first students was Shiratori Kurakichi, who was already in his second year when Rieß arrived. After graduating in 1890 he taught at the Peers' School (Gakushūin) and at the same time began to take an interest in Oriental history (tōyōshi).[47] From 1901 to 1903 he studied in Europe. When in 1904 Chinese history, like Western and Japanese history, received its own department (in 1910 it became the Department of Oriental History), Shiratori and Ichimura Sanjirō became the first professors there. Ichimura had taught Chinese history at the Imperial University since 1898 and had also been Shiratori's colleague at Gakushūin. Until 1925 both of them exercised a decisive influence on the new department.

At the Historiographical Institute, Rieß's students gradually succeeded the older members. Miura Hiroyuki, who graduated in 1895, was a member of the Historiographical Institute before he moved to the newly established department of history at Kyoto Imperial University in 1907. He became a professor there in 1909. Kuroita Katsumi, who graduated in 1896 and became a lecturer at Tokyo University in 1902, was employed by the Historiographical Institute in 1905, when he also became assistant professor. From 1919 to 1920 he was the director of the Institute and from 1919 to 1935 he was a professor of Japanese history at the University. His successor at the Institute was Tsuji Zennosuke, who graduated in 1900 and became a member of the Institute in 1902. He was its director from 1920 to 1938. In 1911 he became assistant professor and from 1923 to 1938 was a professor at Tokyo Imperial University.

Once Rieß had trained historians fit to succeed him, he shared the fate of most of the foreign teachers in the service of the Japanese government. When his contract expired for the fifth time in 1902, it was not extended. In the same year Mitsukuri Genpachi, who had returned from Germany, was appointed to succeed Rieß as a professor. Whether Mitsukuri was favoured because the minister of education, Kikuchi Dairoku, was his brother or whether Rieß had complained that his salary was lower than that of his colleague Karl Florenz is not significant.[48] He had done what was expected of him and made himself dispensable.

Rieß returned to Berlin in 1903, where he taught and published. In 1909 he visited Japan once more, and his family, colleagues and students gave him a warm welcome.[49] In 1926 he travelled to Springfield, Ohio to become an exchange professor at Wittenberg University, but he had to return before he could start teaching because of ill health. Rieß died in Berlin in 1928. His son-in-law Abe Hidesuke taught at Keiō University from 1907 onward and Hidesuke's son Hideo also became a professor of history.

In Germany, Rieß's scholarship was soon forgotten, but in Japan his importance is emphasized to this day. Rieß approached Japan and his Japanese students with a relatively open mind, perhaps because he was young and had lived abroad before. Although Rieß, like his foreign colleagues, was convinced that Western scholarship was superior and that European history (and even the history of the ancient cultures of Assyria and Babylonia) was important for his Japanese students, he encouraged them to study Japanese history as well and even did so himself. Rieß also contributed to the organization of Japanese historical scholarship at the Imperial University. By the time he left Japan in 1903 his students were teaching at all the imperial universities and at several private universities.[50]

Nevertheless, Rieß's contribution to modern historical scholarship in

Japan is often overrated. Rieß was strongly dependent on his Japanese employers, and his initiatives could not overcome the limits imposed by them. He had a low status; although he was one of the two professors at the Department of History he was not treated as the holder of the second chair, because he was a foreigner.[51] Moreover, when assessing Rieß's influence, we must distinguish between Western history and Japanese history, since they have different origins.[52] For many years Japanese history was taught by scholars educated in the Tokugawa period and by their students. Shigeno and his colleagues of the first generation at the Historiographical Institute and the Department of Japanese History were succeeded by Mikami Sanji (1893 assistant professor, 1899–1926 professor) and Hagino Yoshiyuki (1899 lecturer, 1901–23 professor). Both had graduated from the Department of Classics. Their colleague Tanaka Yoshinari (1892–93, 1895 assistant professor, 1905–19 professor) had worked his way up in the Office of Historiography. They were succeeded by Rieß's students Kuroita Katsumi and Tsuji Zennosuke. Thus it was only in the third generation that Rieß' students became influential at the Historiographical Institute.

Of course Shigeno and especially Kume had learnt from Rieß, but they were older than Rieß and at the height of their careers and their own commitments would hardly have allowed them to sit next to undergraduates in Rieß's lectures and seminars, even had they wished to do so. Mikami Sanji, who had attended some of Rieß's courses, became a friend and helped him with his research on Japanese history.[53] When the collection of foreign documents relating to Japan was envisaged, Mikami sought Rieß's advice.[54] This was Rieß's idea and possibly his most significant contribution to the Historiographical Institute. However, on the whole, work at the Historiographical Institute continued in much the same way as in the two decades before Rieß's arrival.

5.4 The *akademizumu* School of History

The term *akademizumu* or *kangaku akademizumu* usually refers to the kind of scholarship first practised at the Imperial University (*kangaku akademizumu* is a tautology, since *akademizumu* by itself means the quasi-official scholarship practised chiefly at state institutions).[55] The University had been established as a place of training for future bureaucrats and scientists to serve the needs of the state. As the Imperial University Ordinance of 1886 put it, it was to 'provide instruction in the arts and in the sciences and to inquire into the mysteries of learning in accordance with the needs of the state'.[56] It was modelled, like new universities in Europe and North America, after the Prussian universities, but the Japanese tradition of government schools tended to emphasize more strongly the influence of the state. Emphasis was also on communicating knowledge that could be practically applied, with natural science and technical subjects predominating. From the Imperial University of Tokyo, *akademizumu* spread to other state universities and private institutions, and so had considerable influence, which is still noticeable today.

Akademizumu was the mainstream of historical scholarship as history became an independent academic discipline. Current scholarship tends to emphasize the differences between *akademizumu* and the other important school of the period, the Enlightenment school, as well as the objective, scientific nature of *akademizumu*. However, there were important similarities, and the characterization of *akademizumu* as objective is problematic. *Akademizumu* shared with Enlightenment history the belief that historiography should be rational and progressive and that society was the primary unit of analysis, and both emphasized gradual change. The claim to be scientific was also characteristic of both schools, although Enlightenment history based its claim on its search for universal laws and *akademizumu* on its strict canon of methods for the verification of historical facts. *Akademizumu* historians were affiliated with public institutions of learning and this contributed to the image of *akademizumu* as objective.[57]

The institutional requisites for the academic discipline of history were created by appointing Ludwig Rieß, establishing the two departments of history and transferring the Office of Historiography to the Imperial University. The two departments encompassed the three intellectual traditions from which modern historical scholarship evolved. National and Chinese Learning were first represented by scholars in the Department of Classics and then in the Department of Japanese History and the Historiographical Institute. The members of the Institute had refined the methods of textual criticism (*kōshōgaku*), which formed part of both these traditions. Western history and German methods of historical scholarship were taught by Rieß and Tsuboi. At first National Learning, Chinese Learning and Western historiography existed side by side and often their representatives were hostile to each other; but they had much in common and together contributed to the development of *akademizumu*.

Akademizumu stressed the collection of primary documents and the verification of facts. It emphasized methodology and claimed to be 'objective', that is, free from political or moral bias. These characteristics are apparent in the early articles in *Shigaku zasshi*. Most of the articles in the first issues of *Shigaku zasshi* were written by scholars from the Historiographical Institute; 47 of the 64 articles in the first 6 issues (the proportion is even higher if articles appearing in several parts are only counted once). It is often said that the first contributions to the journal dealt with theoretical questions until Rieß, in the fifth issue, advised his Japanese colleagues to concentrate on the more important task of publishing sources. It is true that the ten contributions to the first four issues have fairly general themes. However, one should not imagine that they discussed great philosophical questions in depth.

The first article, after the preface by the president of the University, Watanabe Kōki, was the inaugural lecture by Shigeno Yasutsugu, 'Those Who Engage in Historical Research Must Be Impartial and Fair-Minded'.[58] A historian who takes sides, said Shigeno, is prejudiced and hinders the progress of scholarship. Shigeno emphatically denied that historiography should teach moral principles such as the proper relationship between ruler and subjects (*meibun*). The historian should concentrate on describing the facts; the moral implications would then become clear of their own accord. The task of the historian was to establish the facts beyond doubt and to record them truthfully. Shigeno spoke about his experience in the Office of Historiography; it had shown him how difficult the task was. He expressed the wish that the materials collected by his Office and the Western methods, taught by Rieß, would help research into and writing of Japanese history.

This is hardly a profoundly theoretical discussion. Like most articles by members of the Institute, the issues he raises appear to be closely connected to his work at the Institute. Another example is Hoshino Hisashi's article 'For Historical Research and Compilation the Sources Should Be Selected with Care'. Hoshino emphasized the importance of using the most reliable sources, giving priority to primary documents (*monjo*) as Hoshino and his colleagues at the Institute were doing already.[59] In an article entitled 'The Application of History', which appeared long after Rieß had allegedly caused him and his colleagues to stop discussing theoretical questions, Hoshino defended the investigation of primary documents with the methods of *kōshō* textual criticism. In answer to the criticism of the way he and his colleagues debunked legendary heroes he stressed that historical scholarship should be independent of moral claims.[60] In a lecture about public opinion on history Hoshino again defended the independence of historical scholarship and stressed that historiography should be based on the sources, which should be made available for the purpose. He also stated that this was what the Historiographical Institute was trying to do, despite insufficient resources.[61]

Only one article by a member of the Historiographical Institute actually dealt with the philosophy of history. Yamagata Shōzō, in his article 'The Main Points of the Philosophy of History' calls it the nerves of historical scholarship and stressed that it was important for placing the knowledge gained by historical research into a wider framework.[62]

Most of the more theoretical discussions of historiography did not come from members of the Historiographical Institute and not even from scholars writing history themselves. Ueda Kazutoshi was a student of Basil Hall Chamberlain, and later, having studied in Germany, became a professor of linguistics. He stated that historiography provided examples, which philosophy set in order and gave meaning to. Ueda stressed that history should not be governed by morals (*dōtoku*), politics (*seiji*) and loyalty to the emperor (*kinnō*). He defended the use of historical research to deny the existence of well-known figures (such as Kojima Takanori; see Chapter 6.3) and to describe negative traits of heroes. Ueda criticized two extremes of historical scholarship: the history of civilization (*bunmeishi*) was too theoretical and neglected the facts; scholars writing in the tradition of Chinese and Japanese Learning (*wakangaku*) put too much emphasis on the facts.[63]

Katō Hiroyuki, in his article 'Natural History and History', demanded that history take into account the influence of nature on human society and named Montesquieu, Buckle, Spencer and Herbart as models.[64]

Ueda and Katō, whose articles were more theoretical than those of Shigeno and his colleagues, were not engaged in historical research themselves. Both of them were strongly influenced by Western ideas. Katō had studied in Germany and Ueda went there in 1890. It would seem that Rieß's proposal to concentrate on the task in hand was very much in tune with what the members of the Historiographical Institute were trying to do anyway.[65]

On the other hand, articles dealing with general issues appeared in *Shigaku zasshi* even after Rieß's memorandum. Several of them were written by Kume, perhaps the most original of the three leading scholars at the Institute. Kume used examples from his practical work to illustrate his points, but he attempted to discuss wider issues. The articles were usually the result of lectures at meetings of the Historical Society and Kume's style is lively, using not only examples from history but also from everyday life.[66] Kume's colleague Hoshino, whose views were similar, also spoke about general questions, but his lectures were not as interesting as Kume's and he presented few original ideas.[67] The articles cited here are evidence of the historians' preoccupation with collecting sources and using text-critical methods. In his last lecture before the closure of the Institute in 1893, Hoshino emphasized the importance of collecting documents, which had become the most important activity of the Institute, even before it was made its only aim when it was reopened in 1895.

Certainly the members of the Institute devoted a great deal of energy to this task, as they had in the former government office. While the appointed editors worked on the *Dainihon hennenshi,* other members of the Institute continued their field trips all over Japan.[68] For example, Hoshino and two other members accompanied Watanabe Kōki (the president of the University) on an official journey to North East Japan and collected documents in Ibaraki, Miyagi, Fukushima and Iwate prefectures, regions which had been neglected so far.

Shigeno and his colleagues also participated in new initiatives for collecting evidence from the past. They were involved in a project initiated by the Historical Society. This was the *Kyūji shimon kai* or Committee for Inquiring into Ancient Matters, set up in 1890. Its aim was to ask survivors from the Edo period about matters which were not mentioned in the written sources. For the young generation of scholars the Edo period had receded so far into the past that they did not know it from their own experience. For their teachers it had become the object of nostalgic reminiscence. In 1889 an Edo Society was founded in Tokyo to preserve Edo culture, before it was lost; the committee set up by the Historical Society was part of a trend.[69]

In the twelfth issue of *Shigaku zasshi* the programme of the committee was outlined by its secretary Ogawa Ginjirō, a student in his second year. The society would collect details about the Edo period which were not in the written documents from people who were old enough to remember them. The professors Shigeno, Toyama, Konakamura, Kume, Hoshino and Miyazaki Michizaburō (1855–1928) and the graduates Mikami, Takatsu, Isoda and Shiratori had held a meeting and decided to draw up a set of questions, pick suitable candidates and to hold questioning sessions, of which the minutes would be printed. The project would be financed by contributions (54–7).

Members of the committee met regularly to question one or two people, usually former officials of the shogunate. Once (April 1892), two women were questioned: they had served in the private quarters of the shogun at the time of Shogun Iemochi's marriage with the emperor's sister Kazunomiya. The minutes of each session were printed and distributed among the members of the Historical Society, who were also encouraged to express wishes for questions or to contribute their own memories.[70] The minutes of eleven sessions between January 1891 and April 1892 were published and accounts of three further sessions can be found in *Shigaku zasshi*.

Clearly the project did not aim to collect information about those parts of the population who rarely feature in written records (the focus of oral history when it became a widely used approach from the 1960s onwards). The idea was to fill information gaps in the existing written documents after they had been examined. The project can therefore be seen as part of the attempts to establish the facts in the *kōshō* tradition practised at the

Historiographical Institute. At the same time the project had a strongly antiquarian character. Many of the facts recorded seem of little significance by themselves. The records were distributed to all the members of the Historical Society. They have been reprinted several times and read not only by scholars but also by interested amateurs and have served authors of historical novels and film scripts as a valuable source of information.[71]

More significant in the history of the Historiographical Institute is the collection of foreign documents relating to Japan, because it still forms an important part of the Institute's activities today. The idea was suggested by Rieß, who may well have been inspired by the German initiative to collect the sources of German history in the archives of the Vatican, which had recently been made available. A German historical institute was established in Rome in 1888; in 1881 a similar institute had been established by Austria (Chapter 7.2). In Rieß's memorandum about the establishment of a Department of History at the Imperial University, he had mentioned documents relating to Japanese history in the Imperial archives in the Netherlands in a postscript. Rieß himself brought back copies of documents in The Hague from his two trips to Europe in 1893 and 1900. As early as 1888, President Watanabe Kōki had reacted to Rieß's remarks and had had some documents copied. Documents were copied until 1892, when the project was abandoned.[72] The extent of the task had probably been underestimated, and anyway the Historiographical Institute was closed in 1893. Rieß published an article about sources of Japanese history in the archives in The Hague in *Shigaku zasshi*, describing his own efforts and stressing the importance of these sources for the history of the Tokugawa period.[73]

Murakami Naojirō likewise made an effort to collect documents while he was studying in Europe from 1899 to 1902, and some of the documents he collected were incorporated into the compilation *Dainihon shiryō*, which the Historiographical Institute began publishing in 1901. Great interest in the foreign documents was shown by Mikami Sanji, who, at the international conference of academies of science, suggested making accessible sources on Japan's relations with European countries on an exchange basis. A plan was submitted to the conference in the following year by Inoue Tetsujirō and Minobe Tatsukichi, both professors at the Imperial University. A committee was established, but work did not proceed systematically. Research in foreign archives was limited to sporadic efforts by Murakami and others. Beside the Netherlands, preliminary investigations in France, Italy and the Vatican were made. Not until 1954 were foreign documents collected systematically. From then onward they were microfilmed and work on a catalogue was begun.

The new projects for collecting yet more sources were very much in the tradition of *kōshōgaku*. As new documents were made available and subjected to critical analysis, the result was often a re-evaluation – or devaluation – of previous historical writing. Every issue of *Shigaku zasshi* had a section on *kōshō* (textual criticism) and *kaidai* (bibliographical notes), in which historical works were introduced: for example, the fourth issue introduced the *Honchō seiki,* an annalistic account in the tradition of the Six National Histories from the twelfth century (by Hoshino) and the *Baishōron,* a historical tale comparable to the *Taiheiki,* presenting the Ashikaga viewpoint, from the fourteenth century (Kan Masatomo).[74] Of the articles dealing with textual criticism, those by Kan Masatomo and Kume Kunitake, which questioned the reliability of the *Taiheiki,* received the most attention. Kume even went so far as to describe it as useless to the historian. The infamous *massatsu ron* (obliteration theories; Chapter 6.3), debunking well-known and well-loved heroes of Japanese history and attributed to Shigeno, were the result of critical, often over-critical examination of the sources by the members of the Historiographical Institute. They did much to damage the reputation of academic history, since the public associated it with the obliteration theories.

The 'obliteration theories' highlight a problem inherent in the methodology of *akademizumu*. With the methods of *kōshōgaku* it is far easier to falsify existing assumptions than to offer positive proof. Kume's condemnation of the *Taiheiki* as worthless for the historian illustrates the overly critical attitude, which accepts nothing that is not mentioned in the primary documents. Historians today credit the *Taiheiki* with more value as a historical source than Kume did.[75] Kume's critics at the time, who stated that in periods of unrest, such as the one described in the *Taiheiki,* many primary documents would have been lost, had a valid point.

Nevertheless, the 'obliteration theories' are an expression of *akademizumu*'s claim to objectivity. But the emphasis on primary documents, verifiable facts and scientific methodology obscures a crucial issue that arises when the results of research have to be presented, whether in editions of sources or in the writing of a historical narrative. Sources and facts have to be selected and arranged: in short, choices have to be made, and these are determined by the values of the editors and writers. As Stefan Tanaka points out, 'someone (or some body) must decide, which part should be highlighted for the good of each social unit'.[76] *Akademizumu* was neither as objective as its proponents claimed nor as devoid of ideology as modern scholars have alleged, but this fact is further obscured by the general consensus at the time that scholarship was to serve nation and state (Chapter 6). If Shigeno and his colleagues did not recognize the inherent potential for conflict in the contradiction of their position[77] it was due to this consensus and because they did not sufficiently distinguish between historical research and writing. German historicism in the Rankean tradition failed in a similar way to reflect on the issue of historiographical presentation, thus succumbing to the illusion that the knowledge gained from the sources would speak for itself (just as Shigeno claimed in his lecture cited above; see Chapter 7.2). Both *akademizumu* and historicism overlooked the fact that the way history is presented plays a decisive role in determining its function in political culture.[78] Thus, while seemingly objective, historiography could end up being abused in the service of politics, propagating political values without examining or discussing them.

It may well be that it was this failure to distinguish between research and writing and to reflect on the problems of representation, rather than the alleged objectivity and paucity of ideas in themselves, that resulted in *akademizumu* failing to combat the abuse of history for the purpose of political propaganda.

Some of the problems of *akademizumu* were recognized by contemporaries. Twice, in 1892 and in 1893, the literary review *Waseda bungaku* described the main currents in historiography, outlining the strengths and weaknesses of each. In 'Shigaku no fūchō' (*Trends in Historiography*), three groups were identified: a traditional faction (*kyūha*), an enlightenment faction (*bunmei ha*) and the academic historians (*kokkaha, kōshōha, risōha*). These last, the commentator said, had learnt from Rieß or developed historical methods themselves and tried to combine the best of all currents of scholarship, but tended to be too preoccupied with textual criticism and establishing facts.[79]

A year later, in 'Shiron yonha' ('Four Factions in Historical Discussion') the author distinguished between a Textual Criticism Faction (*kōshōha*), an Applied History Faction (*ōyō shiha*) influenced by Seeley and other Western scholars, an Oriental version of the same represented by traditional scholars, and a Literary Faction (*bungakuteki shiha*).[80] Again it criticized the academic historians (here described as the Textual Criticism Faction) for being too strongly fixated on textual criticism and the verification of facts.

Yamaji Aizan, a representative of the *Min'yūsha* group of historical writers, pointed out the differences between historical narrative and positivist research:[81] works such as the *Kokushigan* by the Historiographical Institute had a high standard, but were of little interest save for preparing for examinations, while a good read like the *Nihon gaishi* by Rai San'yō was very popular. Kawada, a former member of the Office of Historiography and author of an article pointing out the errors in the *Nihon gaishi*, attacked what he perceived as the abuse of textual criticism and the tendency to regard official documents as more reliable than literary sources, as well as the hasty abandonment of existing interpretations by scholars. In a lecture in 1890 he distanced himself from his own statements about the *Nihon gaishi*, stating that its factual errors were less significant than the author's moral stance.[82]

Even some proponents of *akademizumu* recognized how problematic the obsession with textual criticism and isolated facts could be. In his lecture 'The Abuse of *kōshō* in Historical Scholarship' (1901), Kume Kunitake emphasized that textual criticism was the means, not the end, of historical scholarship and should serve as the starting point for further research and for interpretation by the individual historian.[83] Kume rejected the idea of waiting until all the facts were established before beginning independent research. Although Kume once again defended the 'obliteration theories', he added that historical scholarship must not stop there. Moreover, historical interpretations should no longer rely on outdated moral values, or new knowledge would be worthless. Kume's ideal was historiography contributing to the progress of human society by helping to avoid the mistakes of former generations. He rejected the idea that the study of history should serve to emulate the heroes of former times; this would make progress impossible.

Kume attributed the dominance of textual criticism to political suppression of historical research, alleging that research in Japanese history alone did not enjoy academic freedom. Therefore the historians had concentrated on textual criticism to obtain indisputable results. But it was precisely by doing so that they had encountered difficulties (910–11).

Tanaka Yoshinari, another member of the Historiographical Institute, also criticized the excessive reliance on textual criticism in the *kōshō* tradition. In his lecture 'The Application of History' ('Shigaku no katsuyō'), he blamed the increasing specialization of modern scholarship. Tanaka stressed that the historian must serve state and society.[84] Through history the memory of the spirit in which the state had been founded was preserved and the strength of the state depended on remembering its origins. The *Nihon shoki* (720) was compiled in imitation of Chinese models, but the aim of the compilers was to demonstrate Japan's independence from China. Japan had adopted the benefits of foreign civilizations but had at the same time preserved its own heritage. Tanaka pointed out the relation between the Nara state and the Six National Histories and mentioned further examples of historical writings and their political significance, including those that had influenced the leaders of the Meiji Restoration. Of course, Tanaka and his colleagues must concentrate on discovering historical truth. However, if their insights were not put to any use they were meaningless, and statesmen without knowledge were like travellers without a map.

Tanaka concluded his lecture by urging his colleagues to voice their opinions in the discussions of the day. If a Sugawara no Fumitoki (899–981) had been able to do this, how much easier must it be in the present age where freedom of speech prevailed ('genron no jiyū naru gendai'; 1049).

It is interesting that Tanaka, who gave his lecture in the wake of the textbook controversy in 1911 (Chapter 6.6), stresses that freedom of speech was not a problem, while Kume blames the lack of it for the excesses of textual criticism. Of course, Kume had suffered more directly than Tanaka from the consequences of government intervention in historical research. He was not, however, the only one who saw freedom of expression under threat. In 1893, an anonymous article in the *Min'yūsha* journal *Kokumin no tomo* stated that new approaches in historical scholarship were suppressed by the nobility, the military and scholars with an outdated view of history, and that this lack of academic freedom hampered its development. Freedom to discuss even topics relating to the imperial house was a necessary condition for fruitful debate. At the same time the new historians (*shin shigaku ka*) were criticized for being too preoccupied with textual criticism and not contributing to the progress of society.[85]

A commentator in *Waseda bungaku* spoke of a general climate which discouraged freedom of research and expression,[86] although a commentator in *Kokugakuin zasshi,* responding to the first expressed doubts about the alleged lack of freedom without being able to deny it.[87] Instead he spoke about nationalistic research in the service of the state (*kokugakuteki kenkyū*) and scientific research (*kagakuteki kenkyū*), but stressed that the two did not necessarily have to conflict. In the following issue of *Kokugakuin zasshi* he repeated this point and emphasized that scientific research need not be disloyal to the state, but that criticism of the imperial house and the state must not be expressed without careful examination of the evidence.[88]

Clearly, academic freedom, or the lack of it, was an issue, but present-day historians would seem to overstate the case when they claim that historians took refuge from the threat of political suppression in positivist studies in the wake of the Kume Affair. It is wrong to assume an extent of political pressure in the Meiji period comparable to that of the 1930s. Although topics relating to the imperial house were almost taboo,[89] the suppression of historical scholarship did not initially come from the government, as we shall see in the Kume Affair (Chapter 6.4). The retreat of historical scholarship into the mere accumulation of facts began before political pressures made themselves felt. While the historians at the

Imperial University did experience some political suppression, the character of the *akademizumu* school cannot be explained by external pressure alone.

The question remains: why did the age that saw the development of historical scholarship based on objective and scientific criteria and positivist studies in state-sponsored institutions also witness the propagation by the state of a view of history based not on critical research, but on myth? The usual reason given by historians is that *akademizumu,* because of its lack of ideas and theoretical concepts, was not able to provide a defence against the political distortions of history for political ends. I have already suggested that the problem was not so much the alleged lack of ideas or 'objectivity' of *akademizumu* as the prevailing consensus between historians and statesmen about the role of history in the state, as well as the absence of reflection on the relationship between research and writing and between history and political culture. Closely connected with this was the belief that a definitive and complete history, free from any bias, could ultimately be written. The concept of a *seishi,* although it ceased to be important, was never explicitly dismissed.

Finally, neither *akademizumu* nor any other kind of scholarly history can meet all the external demands made on history, including the demand for political legitimation and the strengthening of national identity. It was the tension between historical scholarship and these external demands that led to conflict, which resulted in a further rift between 'objective' history and myth-history.

6

History and Ideology in Conflict

The measures to establish history as an independent academic discipline and to write history free from bias in the late 1880s came at a time of increased ideological activity in order to create a sense of nation among the people.[1] History had an important role to play in fostering national identity. However, the often conflicting demands placed on the writing of history caused problems.

6.1 History and the Public

In 1889 the Meiji Constitution was promulgated and in 1890 the first parliament elected. The country's political framework was thus determined. In the following decade the most pressing issue of foreign policy, the revision of the unequal treaties, was accomplished, and with its victory over China in 1895 Japan embarked on its course of expansion that made it the only non-Western colonial power. The years around 1890 are recognized as a 'major watershed in modern Japanese history'.[2] The pace of change had slowed down since the early years of Meiji: the following years were 'a time of settlement', when the leaders of the Restoration now sought stability and order.[3]

Political, administrative and educational centralization as well as increasing communication, including the popular press, enabled the growth of collective national sentiment.[4] Whereas the audience of the early Meiji proclamations of political statements and nationalist ideas had been limited to the feudal aristocracy and the exceptional commoner, late Meiji rhetoric claimed that the forty million countrymen had to be turned into citizens. During the run-up to the first parliament, the nation state (*kokka*) and its people (*kokumin*) were frequently invoked as the necessity of national unity was stressed.[5]

In the same year that the first parliament was elected, the Imperial

Rescript on Education was promulgated. It was the result of a complicated drafting process and provided a national text, vague enough to be used by ideologues of different persuasions.[6] It stressed Confucian virtues – although they were not described as such, and Shigeno Yasutsugu was attacked when he did so[7] – and civil morality. However, by representing both as 'the teaching bequeathed by Our Imperial Ancestors', who are described as the founders of the empire, the Rescript also emphasized continuity from the distant past and shared, unique tradition. The uniqueness of Japanese culture was a major focus in the efforts to define the nation, and the formulation of ideas of national distinctiveness centred on the belief that the Japanese shared a unique history.[8] This found expression in the different attempts to study and write the history of Japan in the 1880s (Chapter 3.4). The widespread interest in history reached a peak in the years from 1890 to 1893, when the journal *Waseda bungaku* diagnosed 'historical fever' or 'history fashion fever' (*rekishinetsu* or *rekishi no ryūkōnetsu*).[9] A number of historical journals, mostly short-lived, were launched; the big dailies carried history sections; and *Waseda bungaku,* although mainly devoted to literature, regularly reported on the latest developments in historical scholarship and debate and discussed the progression of 'historical fever' and its decline into an 'appearance of desolation'.[10]

The most popular history journal of these years was *Shikai,* published by Taguchi Ukichi between 1891 and 1896. Taguchi was one of the representatives of the Japanese Enlightenment and writers of the history of civilization (*bunmeishi*) of the 1870s, and aimed to stimulate the interest of educated Japanese in their own history, as well as the history of other countries.[11] A special feature of the journal was the last few pages: they contained reviews of the preceding issue and its articles which had been published in newspapers or were submitted by readers. These pages became a place for lively exchanges of opinion between readers of *Shikai*. Comments on most articles were printed in the following issues. In *Shikai* most of the historical debates of the day were reflected, but general discussions of the nature of history and its study were comparatively rare and more likely to appear in the more academic *Shigaku zasshi*.[12] *Shikai* was very popular and its practical contribution to historical information for a wider educated public was great. Kuroita Katsumi, who later became a director of the Historiographical Institute, is said to have enjoyed reading it while he was at high school.[13]

The 'historical fever', of which *Shikai* was a symptom, reflected both the general transition of the early 1890s and the transition of historical scholarship from a branch of literature to a modern academic discipline. Different views on what the study of history was about and approaches to writing history existed side by side and in contention with each other; a lively interest not just in history itself, but also in the way it should be written characterized 'historical fever'.

At the same time, the compilation of an official history by the government had, like other government business, been the subject of newspaper reports from the start.[14] The members of the Office of Historiography, moreover, were public figures and often in the news, whether as receivers of ranks and titles,[15] as founding members of new societies[16] or as guests at important public events, for example Shigeno's presence at the inauguration of the Russian Orthodox Nikolai Church in Tokyo.[17]

The members of the Office of Historiography and Historiographical Institute, Shigeno, Kume and Hoshino especially, frequently published articles, mainly, but not necessarily, on historical subjects and often for a non-specialist audience. Shigeno gave lectures at the Tokyo Academy and other associations.[18] Kume was a regular contributor to *Shikai*.

Being the focus of attention could mean being the target of criticism. Newspapers and journals carried articles criticizing the idea that the compilation of a national history could be carried out by a government office, or, more often, the way this task was being carried out. An example of the first kind of criticism is an editorial in *Tōkyō akebono shinbun* in 1876. The anonymous author questioned both the kind of history that was written in the Office and the fact that there was an Office at all. Although, like the authors of the Imperial Rescript of 1869, he regarded history as a means to educate the people, he denied that official historiography could fulfil this purpose. His criticism was not limited to historiography. Using a style close to *kanbun* and many literary allusions and similes, he lamented the suppression of freedom of speech on the eve of the war with Satsuma.

Criticism of the way history was written in the Office was more common than questioning official historiography as such. On 14 March 1881 Fukuchi Gen'ichirō published an article discussing history in the newspaper *Tōkyō nichinichi shinbun*.[19] Fukuchi had been in government service after the Meiji Restoration and taken part in the Iwakura Embassy before he became the editor of the *Tōkyō nichinichi shinbun*. Fukuchi expressed indirect criticism of official historiography in general. He criticized historiography in the Chinese tradition. Since the national customs (*kokufū*; in one place Fukuchi added the reading '*nashonarichii* = nationality' to the Chinese characters) formed the basis of any political system, Fukuchi stressed that Japanese history should acquaint the Japanese with their own special traditions, a task made all the more important by the expected constitution.

Directly concerned with the work of the Office of Historiography was a memorandum by Kodama Shōsuke, a secretary in one of the ministries.[20] Kodama mentioned a conversation with an unnamed member of the Office. To give weight to his opinions he quoted a passage of Zerffi's *The Science of History* in translation, which is signed by Kodama himself and Narishima Ryūhoku, the director of the newspaper company *Chōya shinbunsha*. In the memorandum Kodama criticized the accounts of the Meiji Restoration produced by the Office, the *Fukkoki* and the *Meiji shiyō*, because they only recorded facts one by one. Moreover, a history of one's own country should be written in the language of the country and instead of imitating Chinese histories the historiography of all countries should be studied and the best examples taken as models. In any case the materials should be collected first and their arrangement begun later.

The opinion that a history of Japan should be written in Japanese was often expressed, as we have seen, but Kodama's suggestion that the history should not be written until the material had been collected was exceptional, since critics outside the Office tended to demand speedy results.

The study of foreign historiography was also urged by Okamatsu Ōkoku in a memorandum drawn up in April 1882[21] which reflects the sense of crisis in the face of the Movement for Freedom and Democratic Rights. If activists studied the history of Europe they would realize how disastrous the French Revolution was and no longer admire its power. Okamatsu did not directly criticize the work of the Office of Historiography. His views were similar to Shigeno's.[22]

Undated, but probably written at around the same time was a memorandum by Yano Gendō and Inoue Yorikuni.[23] It is significant as a memorandum by representatives of National Learning. The authors did not mention the language of a national history but stress the importance of using sources in the Japanese language. The *Dainihonshi* and the work done by the Office of Historiography were both criticized and some of their faults enumerated. The decision by the Office to compile a history in continuation of the *Dainihonshi* and not of the Six National Histories was rejected.

Other critics focused on the methods of scholarship. In summer 1889 a certain Fujiyama Bun (or Yutaka), writing for the journal *Bun* and obviously influenced by Western ideas of history, criticized the representatives of National Learning and other scholars, who only studied Japanese history. He stated that because there were similarities in the histories of all countries one should not limit one's study to one country.[24] Another author, Tōichi Makoto, attacked the hair-splitting methods of the *kōshō* scholars.[25] An anonymous author styling himself Nōgensei also rejected the methods used by Shigeno and his colleagues, including Shigeno's statements about Kojima Takanori.[26] Criticism of the leading members of the Institute could even come from their own colleagues. Suzuki Shigeaya, a member of the Office and the Historiographical Institute from 1882 to 1889, wrote a contribution to *Shikai,* in which he claimed that the *Taiheiki* was not a work of fiction but a reliable historical account (*jitsuroku*). It seems that the views publicized by Shigeno, Hoshino and Kume were not shared by all their colleagues.[27]

In the early 1890s, the former Office of Historiography and its members, who had always been in the public eye and often the subject of criticism, experienced new pressures. Formerly, criticism had posed less of a threat to them than official indifference and the lack of funding that tended to accompany it. However, this changed when the preoccupation with ideology became more widespread and national pride and national unity were increasingly invoked. The need for a unified nation with a strong sense of its cultural identity was felt all the more in the face of the drafting of the new legal codes and the negotiations to revise the unequal treaties. The two issues were intertwined, with opponents of the draft reforms warning against destroying the unique values of Japan's heritage by adopting Western laws based on European customs and Christian beliefs.[28] The prospect of foreigners living among the Japanese after the revision of the treaties (*naichi zakkyō*), was also seen as a threat to Japanese identity, and some historians referred to it in their writings.[29] Taguchi Ukichi published an article on the subject in October 1893.[30]

This atmosphere of perceived foreign threat and increasing nationalism produced a series of controversies provoked by self-appointed defenders of national pride. They were not the result of government attempts to systematically suppress freedom of opinion, but government institutions tended to react with sanctions against the victims.[31] In 1891 the Christian Uchimura Kanzō (1861–1930) had to resign from his post as a teacher at the First High School because he had refused to bow before a copy of the Imperial Rescript and was therefore accused of *lèse majesté*; the following year, Inoue Tetsujirō, the first Japanese professor of philosophy at the Imperial University, attacked Japanese Christians and in his commentary to the Imperial Rescript accused them of a lack of loyalty towards the emperor. A vehement dispute ensued, and many articles on the subject were written. Also in 1892, the Presbyterian clergyman Tamura Naoomi (1858–1935) was denounced by the press and by other Christians because he criticized the Japanese family system in his book *The Japanese Bride,* published in America. In the 'liberal seventies', criticism of things Japanese had been common and, despite censorship, had not had any negative consequences for the critics.[32]

Shigeno and Kume (and to a lesser extent their colleagues) became the targets of similar attacks for their dismissal of national heroes and well-known stories about the past as legendary. The attacks culminated in the Kume Affair in 1892 and the temporary closure of the Historiographical Institute a year later. The members of the Institute failed to meet the expectations of statesmen and ideologues. Among their severest critics were the representatives of National Learning.

6.2 National Learning versus Chinese Learning

In the changed climate of the 1880s, the Shintoists and scholars of National Learning were able to regain some of the influence they had lost in the preceding decade. Immediately after the Restoration there had been attempts to establish Shinto as a state religion while the National scholars, who claimed a leading role in the Restoration for themselves, dominated the first institutions of higher learning in Tokyo.[33] It was the National scholars who first called for the resumption of official historiography (Chapter 2.1). After the closure of the *Gakkō* in 1870 the National scholars lost their influence in higher education for a while. In the Office of Historiography they dominated only in the department for the imperial genealogies, which was moved to the Imperial Household Ministry in 1877. After that, scholars of Chinese Learning dominated the Office, but their approach to writing history did not go unchallenged.

The National scholars, in reasserting national tradition, also denounced foreign ways. Mostly this was directed against excessive Westernization, but Chinese Learning was also under attack. National scholars accused its representatives of being too much influenced by foreign ideas and displaying a lack of love of their own country. The deterioration of relations between Japan and China also contributed to the loss of prestige for Chinese studies. Shigeno gives an example in his lecture 'History and Education'.[34] According to a newspaper report, law students had demonstrated in front of the Chinese consulate and denounced Confucianism.

Disputes between representatives of Chinese and National Learning may well have continued within the Office, as well as in the form of external attacks, since scholars of National Learning were never entirely absent from the Office. Some were always there as commissioners (*goyō gakari*); their names usually appear at the end of the lists, suggesting low rank. One of them was Hanawa Tadatsugu, grandson and heir of Hanawa Hokiichi. The materials collected by Hokiichi formed the basis of the documents in the Office and his *Shiryō* served as a model for its work. Tadatsugu's name is on the list of officials from 1876 to 1879 and from 1882 to 1884.

Konakamura Kiyonori, like Hanawa Tadatsugu, had been among the National Scholars first appointed to compile a national history. He was one of the most influential representatives of National Learning and a firm opponent of Shigeno and his colleagues. He was employed in the Office from 1877 to 1879. Inoue Yorikuni and Kurita Hiroshi are named on the lists for 1877 and 1878. Inoue Yorikuni was a disciple of Hirata Kanetane, another National scholar appointed in 1869, and was later in the Imperial Household Ministry and the Institute of Japanese Literature. Kurita Hiroshi came from Mito, where he had studied before participating in the work on the *Dainihonshi,* which he eventually completed. From 1882 he taught at the Imperial University and from 1894 at the Institute of Japanese Literature. When the Historiographical Institute was reopened in 1895, he became one of its members for a short time.[35] Another scholar from Mito was Aoyama Nobuhisa, who had worked on the *Dainihonshi* in the 1850s. He was a member of the Office from 1876 to 1879 before he returned to Mito.[36]

Iida Takesato, another disciple of Hirata Kanetane, worked in the Office from 1878 to 1884, as commissioner and as archivist. From 1881 to 1886 and in 1896 he taught at the Imperial University and from 1888 at the Institute of Japanese Literature. He was one of the founding members of the History Society (*Shigaku kyōkai*) and wrote a commentary on the *Nihon shoki,* the first of the Six National Histories.

When the Office of Historiography became a University Institute and Shigeno, Kume and Hoshino were appointed professors, several National scholars were already teaching at the Imperial University, usually in the Department of Classics and its successors, the departments of Japanese and Chinese literature.[37] Konakamura Kiyonori and Naitō Chisō are said to have taught history. Naitō, who had become professor in 1886, was another representative of the eclectic late Mito school. He published a history of the Tokugawa shoguns.

Konakamura Kiyonori was probably the most influential representative of National Learning at the University. A native of Edo, he became a government official after the Restoration and was employed in the History Office in 1869. From 1878 he taught at the Imperial University, where he was actively involved in establishing the Department of Classics in 1882. At the same time he was one of the chief compilers of the *Koji ruien* (Chapter 3.4). He was among the founding members of the History

Society (*Shigaku kyōkai*) and, in 1883, one of the editors of the history *Taisei kiyō* in the Imperial Household Ministry. In 1886 Konakamura became a professor of the Faculty of Law at the Imperial University, and later he was a member of the Faculty of Literature. He was also on the textbook compilation board in the Ministry of Education. Konakamura's influence on intellectual and cultural life was considerable. He contributed to laying the foundations of legal studies in Japan as well as dealing with practical problems concerning the legal system in the government. He played an important role in the formulation of state Shinto. The Department of Classics owed much to him, and he taught at the Imperial University and the Institute of Japanese Literature for many years, educating several distinguished scholars.

Konakamura's views on the writing of history are evident from his *Kokushi no shiori* (*Introduction to National History*), originally a series of articles for the periodical of the Institute of Japanese Literature, *Kokugakuin zasshi*. Konakamura stressed that classical literature was just as important as the histories for learning about the past and about society and its customs (*setai fūzoku*).[38] He recommended some works which, although not histories, threw light on the origins of the imperial house and explained the ancient customs as well as the soul of ancient Japan (*Yamato damashii*); at a time where Japanese had to live side by side with foreigners, this was vital.[39] Konakamura discussed the chief narrative sources of Japanese history. He criticized the *Nihon shoki,* the first of the Six National Histories, for its strong Chinese influence. He emphasized the popularity of the *Taiheiki* since ancient times and mentioned the assumption of Shigeno and Hoshino that the *Taiheiki* had been written by the priest Kojima, but he did not discuss its reliability. Konakamura insisted that the study of a new area must begin by reading and being guided by the secondary literature (45); this may have been a dig at Shigeno and his colleagues who stressed the importance of studying the primary sources.

Although *Kokushi no shiori* was not completed, it shows some significant differences between the views of Konakamura and the Chinese scholars in the Historiographical Institute: Konakamura's high esteem for the literary, narrative sources as opposed to primary documents and the importance he gives to the ancient way of life. His mention of the *Yamato damashii* is a hint that he saw a moral purpose in the study of history, though he did not elaborate on it. Konakamura's (indirect) criticism of the kind of historical scholarship that neglected the literature and ignored society as a whole is not without justification.

Konakamura's views on history were also expressed in the review *Nihon bungaku (Japanese Literature)*, first published in 1889 and renamed *Kokubungaku (National Literature)* in April 1890. Here, National scholars such as Konakamura Kiyonori, Kurokawa Mayori, Kurita Hiroshi, Komiyama Yasusuke (a scholar from Mito) and their disciples Takatsu Shūsaburo, Ochiai Naobumi, Hagino Yoshiyuki and Mikami Sanji published. Konakamura believed that National literature (*kokubun*) included history, law and the art of writing. He regarded the Department of Japanese History as redundant and called for its abolition. Mikami Sanji later claimed that Konakamura was largely responsible for the closure of the Historiographical Institute in 1893.[40] Certainly, there was continuous opposition from Konakamura and like-minded scholars to the Institute. The fact that Mikami himself, who had studied under Konakamura in the Department of Classics, became one of its most influential members when it reopened, suggests that Konakamura played at least some part in the affair. He may have been backed up by scholars like Kimura Masakoto, who had been his colleague at the History Office in 1869 and became a professor at the Imperial University in 1891.

By the time the former Office of Historiography had moved to the Imperial University, it was clear that the compilation of the *Dainihon hennenshi* was not a task of major political significance. The controversies between Konakamura and Shigeno were as much about methods of writing history as they were about influence on political ideology. But in the early 1890s the political climate was on Konakamura's side.

6.3 'Dr Obliterator'
One of the most disputed periods in Japanese history is the period of the Northern and Southern courts (*Nanbokuchō jidai*) and it was the interpretation of this period that gave rise to the most controversial pronouncements of Shigeno and his colleagues.

At the beginning of the fourteenth century, disputes surrounding imperial succession and frictions between the imperial court and the bakufu weakened the position of the imperial court. Emperor Godaigo (r.1318–39) attempted to seize political power from the shoguns and restore it to the imperial court. He failed, however, and Ashikaga Takauji, fighting for the bakufu, instated a rival emperor (Kōmyō, r.1336–48). In 1337 Godaigo fled to Yoshino near Nara, where he and his successors maintained a second imperial court, the Southern court, in opposition to the Northern court in Kyoto. In 1392 an agreement between the two emperors was reached and the emperor of the Northern court, Gokomatsu (r.1382/92–1412), became the sole ruler.[41]

The discussion about which of the two courts was the legitimate one is as old as the division itself. At first, the Northern court, which had finally asserted itself, was usually regarded as the legitimate one. However, when the history *Dainihonshi* of the Mito school represented the Southern emperors as the legitimate rulers, this view became the dominant one, although some scholars maintained that the question could not be decided.

The *Dainihonshi* played a significant role in forming the ideology that led to the Meiji Restoration, and in the Meiji period the Southern court continued to be regarded as the legitimate one. The *Dainihonshi* ended with the reconciliation of the two courts in 1392 and, by deciding to compile the *Dainihon hennenshi* as a sequel to it, the Office of Historiography confirmed its status as an official history. But the members of the office had started to doubt the *Dainihonshi*'s account of this crucial period of imperial history and decided to include the period of the Northern and Southern courts already covered by the *Dainihonshi*. The scholars of Mito had relied on the *Taiheiki,* but the scholars in the Office of Historiography discovered that the information they obtained from the primary documents they had collected often failed to substantiate the account given in the *Taiheiki* and similar narratives. Shigeno and his colleagues began to regard the *Taiheiki* as unreliable and Kume even denied it had any value as a historical source.[42]

The *Nanbokuchō* period was not only of significance to historians. The Meiji Restoration was interpreted as the successful conclusion of the failed attempt by the emperor Godaigo to reassert imperial sovereignty in the Kemmu Restoration.[43] Loyalists who had fought for the Southern emperors were posthumously honoured,[44] and when in the 1880s a new peerage was created to provide members for the future Upper House, their descendants were among those promoted. If their claim was doubtful, it was referred to the Office of Historiography.

When famous and popular heroes were involved, the doubts raised about them by the Office of Historiography attracted considerable public attention. Two fourteenth-century characters whose 'obliteration' particularly provoked widespread indignation were Kojima Takanori and Kusunoki Masashige. Both were regarded as models of devotion to the imperial cause and every schoolchild knew them from lessons in history, Japanese and ethics.[45]

Nothing is known about Kojima Takanori except what we read about him in the *Taiheiki*. There he is mentioned for the first time after the defeat of Emperor Godaigo in Kasagi and of the Kusunoki in Akasaka. Kojima, it is said, wished to free the emperor from captivity while he was on his way to exile. However, as he did not succeed in getting close to Godaigo he carved a Chinese poem into the bark of a cherry tree in front of the emperor's lodging place to give him courage. Only the emperor himself understood the message. When the emperor returned from exile, Kojima fought on his side and, after the Kemmu Restoration had failed, on the side of the Southern court. He is last mentioned as having led an army to the North-East in the service of Emperor Gomurakami.

It is not certain when the reliability of the *Taiheiki* was first questioned; probably sometime between 1882 and 1888. In 1882 the Office of Historiography received an inquiry from Okayama prefecture, which contained a proposal to honour Kojima Takanori with a title. Shigeno answered it himself and described the honour for Kojima as justified (*tōzen*).[46] It seems that in 1882 Shigeno did not question the existence of Kojima. In the first manuscript of the chronological history *Dainihon hennenshi* Kojima is mentioned in the main text; but in the second manuscript he is relegated to a footnote. According to Kume it was Kan Masatomo who first discovered the contradictions in the *Taiheiki,* and he may well have been the first to question Kojima's existence. In Kan's collected works there is an undated passage concerning Kojima.[47] Kume himself was also held responsible; when he had an eye complaint around 1888, his former colleague Kawada Takeshi jeered and said it must be Kojima's revenge.[48] In 1909 the newspaper *Yomiuri shinbun* reported that the real 'Dr Obliterator' had been Kume, not Shigeno. Obviously the 'obliteration theories' were worth a headline even 20 years after they had first been publicized.[49]

Kan Masatomo worked directly with the primary sources, providing the basis for the writing and revising done by Kume and Shigeno. But if Kan and those working with him were responsible for uncovering the contradictions surrounding traditional heroes, Shigeno was the first to make their discoveries publicly known. In his lecture about the errors in the traditional histories given in 1884, Shigeno criticized Rai San'yō's *Nihon gaishi* and the *Taiheiki*. He attacked the latter even more strongly in his lecture about the *Dainihonshi* in 1886.[50] Kojima Takanori was the subject of one of Shigeno's lectures at the Historical Society in 1890.[51] It is evident from the lecture that Shigeno had spoken on the subject before and had been attacked in the newspapers. He defended his view by pointing to contradictions in the *Taiheiki* itself. For example, he stated that it was unlikely that the Chinese poem Kojima carved into a tree would have been understood by the emperor alone, since several of the 500 men of his entourage were known to be highly educated. Shigeno also drew attention to the different names given to Kojima and to the fact that he always seemed to act in isolation. He added that there were no primary documents to prove that he had existed at all. He expressed agreement with Hoshino's view that Kojima Takanori might be the same person as the author of the *Taiheiki,* a monk named Kojima.[52] Finally, Shigeno claimed that the legends about Kojima did not lose their value because they had no basis in fact.

Evidently Shigeno's statements had aroused considerable indignation. Again and again the newspapers reported the latest contentions by 'Dr Obliterator', as Shigeno was nicknamed.[53] Sometimes criticism was humorous; a series of fictitious letters from historical characters to living public figures of the day, entitled *Meido no tayori* (*Mail from the Other World*) and published in the newspaper *Tōkyō nichinichi shinbun,* included a letter from Kojima Takanori to Shigeno Yasutsugu, which ran as follows:

> Preliminaries omitted. I have heard that you are a great scholar of your time, but that you assert that the single-heartedly loyal Kojima Takanori is a fictional person invented by writers in ancient times. This absolutely outrageous assertion I cannot ignore. [I,] Takanori did indeed frequently steal my way to the Emperor's camp and did carve, 'Ten Kōsen no munashu suru nakare … [Heaven will not destroy Kou-chien…]' into the bark of the *sakura* tree. This is not only proven by the entire *Taiheiki* but also through the legends told by old people since ancient times. Surely these cannot be mere fabrications. On what grounds do you state your eccentric views, which impinge upon my honour? If it were granted me to live on in this corrupt world, I would certainly rise up and face you and appeal to have my honour restored. Unfortunately I have joined the ranks of the ghosts, and I cannot entrust an attorney with fighting for my rights in court. Tears of chagrin soak the sleeves of my armour. If you repent immediately and retract the above perverse statement, I will forgive you and let it pass. If you do not, I will haunt the rear of your privy and frighten your daughters. That, then, is the bargain. Enough said.

This piece appeared several years after Shigeno had publicized his views; it seems that the author could still count on his readers' interest; the letter may well have reflected their own indignation.

Years later the question of whether Kojima Takanori had existed or not could still be worth a newspaper article. In 1909 Kojima was posthumously given a title. As his heirs could not be determined, a certain Miyake from the Tsushima shrine in Aichi prefecture received the document. On this occasion a journalist asked a few historians about their views on Kojima Takanori, including Shigeno and Hoshino. Hoshino and an unnamed 'distinguished historian' expressed their doubts about Miyake being the legitimate heir of Kojima Takanori.[55]

The same article mentioned that the descendants of Kusunoki Masashige were still unknown, because no candidate had been able to prove his claim. Kusunoki Masashige was one of the most celebrated heroes, whose loyalty to the emperor was treated as exemplary in all Japanese schools. As early as 1871 the Minatogawa Shrine (in Kobe) had been erected at the site of his death. Kido Kōin mentions in his diaries several visits to the shrine of Kusunoki Masashige to worship him.[56] Ochiai Naobumi wrote a poem about Kusunoki's farewell to his son Masatsura at the post station of Sakurai on the way to his last battle at the Minato river; Okuyama Tomoyasu set the poem to music in a song which was sung in every school in Japan.[57] Masashige remained a model of loyalty to the emperor until the end of the Second World War; Tōjō Hideki, prime minister and army minister during the Second World War, identified with him, and he inspired many of the kamikaze pilots.[58]

Kusunoki's existence was not denied by Shigeno or his colleagues. Unlike Kojima Takanori's name, his was mentioned in other tales and in primary documents. Instead they claimed that some of the famous stories about him were mere fiction. In the *Taiheiki,* Kusunoki Masashige (?–1336) is first mentioned in 1331, when the emperor Godaigo allegedly had a dream which made him search for a warrior named Kusunoki. From then on Kusunoki fought against the Kamakura shogunate on the emperor's side. His successful defence of the Chihaya fortress (Osaka prefecture) against the troops of the shogun in 1332 was decisive for the victory of the imperial side. The most famous episode in the story of his life as it is told in the *Taiheiki* is his farewell at Sakurai before meeting his death in battle in 1336. Kusunoki sent his son Masatsura home after admonishing him to remember what he had been taught and to serve the emperor loyally. Masatsura and his younger brothers Masatoki and Masanori also appear to have died later for the imperial cause (the records relating to the lives and fates of these warriors are few and contradictory).

The death of these three heroes was the subject of a play written by Yoda Hyakusen, formerly a member of the Office of Historiography and author of history plays (*katsureki mono*). His play *Yoshino jūmeika no homare* (*Praise of a Celebrated Poem Found in Yoshino,* 1886), was based on their deeds as narrated in the *Taiheiki*. The play was read and discussed at a meeting assembled for the purpose, at which Itō Hirobumi, Yamagata Aritomo, Shigeno Yasutsugu and Suematsu Kenchō, who, like Yoda, was involved in the reform of Japanese theatre, were present.[59] The newspaper report pointed out that the play was based on the standard historical account of events (*seishi*) and that the discussion, which resulted in a few suggestions to improve the play, stressed the differences between expounding history (*seishi kōshaku*) and playwriting. The example illustrates the importance of heroes like the Kusunokis in popular historical imagination. Shigeno's attendance at the reading suggests that he agreed to the role ascribed to historical figures in popular entertainment and education. Even though he described certain heroes and events as fictitious, he did not deny their importance as role models.[60] In his lecture on Kojima, Shigeno stressed that the value of legends for educating the people could not be diminished by scholarship. He said the same when he spoke about Kusunoki while visiting a school.[61]

Given Kusunoki Masashige's popularity, it is easy to imagine what it meant when Shigeno dismissed Godaigo's dream and the farewell at Sakurai as mere fiction. Again it is not quite clear when he expressed his views for the first time. In the lecture in 1888 mentioned above he also spoke about Kusunoki Masashige (23–5) and as late as 1902 he published an essay about Sakurai.[62] There he quoted primary documents and pointed to contradictions in the chronology to prove that the event could not have taken place. Shigeno, Kume and Hoshino seem to have enjoyed shocking their contemporaries by their arguments, because they repeat them so often, but perhaps they merely did so because they were forced to defend themselves against vehement criticism.

Kojima Takanori and Kusunoki Masashige were the most prominent among several victims of Shigeno's 'obliteration theories' (*massatsu ron*), which did much to discredit the work of the Office of Historiography and the Historiographical Institute. After Shigeno's inaugural lecture at the first meeting of the Historical Society, an anonymous author accused him of lacking in loyalty to the state, and Shigeno defended himself in a reply that emphasized his love for his country.[63] At a time of increasing nationalism the unmasking of national heroes caused great concern and gave fuel to the suspicion concerning the work of the Institute and to the opposition to it. Finally, only a spark was needed to cause it to explode. This was provided by Kume in 1892.

6.4 The 'Kume Affair'[64]

On 25 January 1892 Kume Kunitake published an article entitled 'Shintō wa saiten no kozoku' ('Shinto Is an Outdated Custom of Heaven Worship') in Taguchi Ukichi's journal *Shikai*. The article had previously been published in the historical review *Shigaku zasshi* without drawing much attention, though there had been some criticism.[65] However, when Kume's pronouncements on Shinto became known to a wider audience, they created a storm that ended with Kume's suspension as a professor of the university and editor of the *Dainihon hennenshi*, and ultimately with the closure of the Historiographical Institute. The Kume Affair is usually cited as the first of several instances of historical scholarship being suppressed by government intervention.

Kume was perhaps the most original scholar in the Historiographical Institute. He was the only one with experience of foreign travel, as a member of the Iwakura Embassy, and this may partly account for it. His articles in *Shigaku zasshi* express his ideas in a vivid style and he did not limit himself to pure textual criticism, but tried to place his research in a wider framework. He emphasized the scientific character of historical scholarship and repeatedly asserted that it must be free of political and moral bias. He saw the use of historical research in providing information about the collective experience of a society, represented by history. He called for a rigorous methodology and is regarded as one of the founders of Japanese diplomatics, which he taught when he became a lecturer at *Tōkyō senmon gakkō*.[66]

'Shintō wa saiten no kozoku', however, is not a prime example of scholarship in the *kōshō* tradition. Kume wished to examine modern religious practices and the origins of heaven worship in the Orient. He discusses the general phenomenon of religious worship, not merely its manifestation among certain people at a given time in the past.

The content of Kume's article was provocative, for he claimed that Shinto was not a religion but merely a primitive cult of heaven worship that had evolved during the infancy of mankind. While in other countries heaven worship had been superseded by religions with a dogma and a moral code of behaviour, Japan had still retained its primitive cult.[67] The Japanese government at the time claimed that Shinto was no religion because it stood above and could encompass other religions, but Kume maintained that Shinto represented a primitive stage of religious development that preceded other religions and as such was something less than a religion.[68]

The article marked a bold departure from traditional scholarship. Kume's interpretation of Shinto was rationalistic; he set Shinto in the context of world religions and viewed it critically. But by the strict standards of the positivist school, the article contains serious flaws.[69] For example, Kume offers no evidence for his remarks about religious customs in contemporaneous Japan. To support his statements about the past he quotes from the Chinese and Japanese classics, without discussing their value as evidence. His line of argument and his use of sources are somewhat arbitrary and he appears to have lacked an adequate understanding of Shinto. Kume's representations can be regarded as an awkward attempt to explain religious customs rationally in the tradition of the Enlightenment; at the same time he upholds the myth of Japan's uniqueness based on the unbroken line of emperors and on religious practices that unite ruler and subjects. He praised the customs of heaven worship and the national polity (*kokutai*) founded on them. This was more than a concession, for Kume genuinely wished to reconcile the ideas of the Enlightenment and the *kokutai* ideology in a way similar to Fukuzawa Yukichi and Taguchi Ukichi.[70] Kume's assertions were not new; much harsher criticism of Shinto had been published in the 1870s.[71]

Reaction to the publication of the article in *Shikai* was not immediate and when it came was often positive.[72] Readers expressed their agreement in letters that were printed in the following issues of *Shikai* together with warm reviews from several newspapers.[73] Some writers described Kume's ideas as entirely new. But the question was also raised as to whether respect for the imperial house allowed this kind of investigation.[74]

Kume's critics relied on moral rather than scientific arguments, and after the publication of the article some Shintoists demonstrated in front of his house.[75] But the real confrontation occurred on 28 February 1892, when four members of the private school *Dōseikan*[76] called on Kume at his home; they were Kuramochi Jikyū, Hongō Sadao, Fujino Tatsuji and Hagyūda Morio. They discussed the article with its author for no less than five hours and Kume's visitors published a brief account of the discussion in *Tōkyō nichinichi shinbun* (4 to 6 March), our only source of information on the meeting.[77] Their discussion with Kume seems to have become heated and the same arguments were repeated several times.

Kume's visitors accused him of abusing his responsibility as a scholar and a professor at the Imperial University, of lacking in reverence for the imperial house, of harming the national polity (*kokutai*), and of causing confusion among the people. Kume conceded that there were some weak points and ill-chosen expressions in his argument, but he strongly denied charges of irreverence towards the emperor and the state. Kume may have been associated with Christianity because Taguchi Ukichi, the publisher, had received baptism.[78] Equating Shinto with a hated foreign doctrine could not have served to ingratiate Kume with the Shintoists. Christians were accused of being disloyal to their emperor and country, and associating Kume with Christianity made his arguments all the more open to suspicion. As a professor of the Imperial University, the Shintoists told him, he should first and foremost serve his own people. They accused Kume of misleading the general public. One of them remarked that he had in his youth heard scholars of Chinese Learning (*kangakusha*) refer to the punishable offence of fabricating lies for one's own convenience and leading the people astray (*zōgen ranmin no kei*) and now he finally understood what this meant.

In sum, the dispute was about ideology rather than historical scholarship, even though some of the arguments in Kume's article were discussed. Kume's adversaries were not so much interested in this one particular article as in his entire way of treating the nation's history. The Shintoists and scholars of National Learning resented the position and authority that Kume and his colleagues held as professors at the Imperial University and as authors of what was to be a definitive, state-sanctioned history of Japan.

The meeting ended with Kume's promise to retract his statements, not because they were wrong, but because they had caused misunderstanding. He repeated this partial concession in a letter to the Shintoists[79] and his retraction duly appeared in several newspapers on 3 March.[80] However, the Shintoists were not content with mere discussion, for they had protested to the Ministry of Home Affairs, the Imperial Household Ministry and the Ministry of Education.[81] On 4 March the Ministry of Education informed Kume of his suspension, and at the end of the month he was dismissed. The further distribution of the relevant issues of *Shigaku zasshi* and *Shikai* was proscribed. Kume seems to have taken this and his dismissal in his stride and, as far as he was concerned, the matter ended there; a party organized to comfort him owed its success to his cheerful mood.[82] After his dismissal he travelled around the country giving lectures, until in 1895 he was invited by his friend Ōkuma Shigenobu to teach at his school, *Tōkyō senmon gakkō*, later renamed Waseda University. Kume became a lecturer and in 1922 a professor there.

The Shintoists quoted Kume as having attributed the misunderstanding to Taguchi's provocative preface to his article, which had allegedly surprised even Kume himself. Taguchi's words were indeed outspoken. Expressing his enthusiasm for Kume's ideas, he boasted that if certain Shinto fanatics read them and remained silent, then he would assume that they had been silenced for good. After Kume's retraction, Taguchi continued the dispute by himself. On 12 and 13 March, he published an article 'Shintōsha shoshi ni tsugu' ('Proclamation to All Shintoists') in several newspapers and *Shikai,* calling for more scientific research into Japan's ancient history. This, he noted, was not being disloyal; on the contrary, it was proof of patriotism because it increased knowledge of Japan's history. Taguchi ended by censuring the Shintoists' behaviour and demanding freedom of research in ancient history.[83] Kuramochi Jikyū answered Taguchi's article, dismissing his call for a discussion as a mere pretext; he went on to accuse him of sympathy for Christianity and of blindly accepting Western concepts of history.[84]

The Shintoists continued to abuse both men. Even writers sympathetic to their cause admit that the Shintoists were so preoccupied with defending their beliefs that they did not really take up the issues raised in Kume's article.[85] The Shinto ideologues published much on the subject of Kume's article in several magazines, and special issues of their journals *Kokkō* and *Kamunagara* were brought out. Most of the authors were not interested in the individual statements Kume made. Among the few Shinto scholars who did attempt to refute his arguments in an objective discussion was Saeki Ariyoshi, who published an article in *Kokkō*.[86] Not content with general accusations of disrespect for the imperial house and the state, Saeki pointed out methodical weaknesses in Kume's arguments. He showed that Kume's arguments could be refuted without resorting to general moral accusations.

Those who accused Kume on moral grounds also attacked Shigeno and Hoshino.[87] They alleged that Shigeno's textbook *Kokushigan* was full of false statements. As for Hoshino, his statement in *Shigaku zasshi*, that the imperial ancestors came from Korea, was seen as proof of his lack of loyalty. The contents of newspapers, magazines and books in general and their negative influence outside Japan were deplored. It was said that Kume's dismissal would not put an end to the objectionable type of historiography he represented as long as his colleagues continued to exercise their influence and even compile textbooks. Historiography should serve the state, it was asserted, and too much textual criticism and Western theories were harmful since Japanese history could not be compared to Western history.[88]

Taguchi's intention may have been an academic debate, but the dispute quickly degenerated into an exchange of insults. Some considered Kume as a victim of Taguchi's quarrelsome disposition, although Kume himself denied this and later claimed to have been grateful to Taguchi for supporting him.[89]

How did Kume's colleagues and students at the Imperial University react to the Affair? There is little evidence that they reacted at all, although the dismissal of a professor and colleague following his publication of a scholarly article constituted a dangerous precedent.

Only a few students expressed doubts. One of them was the historian Ōmori Kingorō, who relates that after hearing about Kume's suspension, he and several other students went to see Katō Hiroyuki, the president of the Imperial University. Katō told them that the suspension was an informal measure; he had heard of the anger Kume's article had caused after its publication in *Shigaku zasshi* and had therefore looked at it briefly. When public indignation increased, Katō had decided to suspend Kume for the time being.

The students then asked whether to discipline a professor as a result of public opinion did not affect the dignity of the University. Katō replied that it was not a question of discipline; the University was entitled to suspend someone temporarily while there was no employment for him. When the uproar had subsided, Kume could be reinstated. However, the students soon realized that there was no intention of re-employing Kume, for a successor had already been appointed.[90]

It is worth asking what the students meant by the dignity (*songen*) of the University.[91] That same year a dispute occurred between one of the students who had called on Katō and Tanaka Yoshinari, who had been appointed assistant professor one day before Kume's suspension. Tanaka finally resigned from his new post, although he was later reappointed. The reason for the dispute lay in Tanaka's career, which he had begun as a copyist in the Office of Historiography. The students, proud of belonging to the academic elite, appear to have considered it beneath their dignity to be taught by a former scribe.[92] The dignity of the University meant not so much academic freedom as the power of a privileged institution to form its own policies independently of the uneducated masses.

Although Katō's justification was far from convincing, there is no evidence of further protest. Indeed, the reaction or, better, the absence of it, to this interference with academic freedom is surprising and was noted by contemporaries. The newspaper *Asahi shinbun* not only criticized Kume for revoking his statements but went on to remark that Shigeno and Hoshino had made no attempt to come to his rescue, although they had collaborated with him in bringing new aspects to historical research.[93] This was all the more surprising, because attacks on Kume often included his colleagues. Moreover, Kume's dismissal resulted in a lack of qualified teachers, when in the same year a course on diplomatics was planned.[94]

The professors were quite capable of defending their interests against government intervention; they successfully did so ten years later in the Tomizu Affair.[95] In 1905, Tomizu Hirondo, professor of law at Tokyo Imperial University, and six other professors (all except one from that University), the 'seven doctors', publicly attacked the government's foreign policy and Tomizu was dismissed. Strong protest from the academic community led to his reinstatement. In making their criticism, Tomizu and his colleagues interfered with government policies and even jeopardized Japanese diplomacy by undermining its credibility.[96] Nevertheless they were defended by their colleagues, who acted in unison and successfully invoked the values of university autonomy and academic freedom.

It is true that Kume's statements concerned the very identity of Japan and its imperial house, in many ways a more delicate issue than that of foreign policy, but Kume's publication in no way affected government policies. The nature of the dispute, therefore, does not suffice to explain why Tomizu was backed by his colleagues and Kume was not. Certainly, Tomizu represented views that turned out to have popular support, but the fact that they acted as a unified body and were able to 'invoke a well-articulated set of values to sanction their social function as an intellectual elite in the service of the nation' probably decided their success.[97]

This unity may well have been lacking at the time of the Kume Affair. The academic elite at the Imperial University was then less homogenous and the representatives of different scholarly traditions opposed each other. Some of Kume's colleagues may well have been glad to get rid of him. The scholars of National Learning had long opposed him and the other members of the Historiographical Institute. Men such as Konakamura would not have been sorry to see Kume go.

Konakamura and the other advocates of National Learning represented the traditional type of Japanese scholar; so did Kume and his colleagues educated in Chinese Learning before the Meiji Restoration. However, in the 1890s a new type of academic was emerging: the young specialist who had usually been educated in the West or by Western teachers.[98] Inoue Tetsujirō (1856–1944), whose attacks on Japanese Christians have been mentioned (Chapter 6.1), is a good example. He had studied in Germany and become the University's first Japanese professor of philosophy. Inoue expressed his views on history in an article in *Shigaku zasshi* at around the same time as Kume published his statements on Shinto in that journal. According to Inoue, history had an important role to play, because knowledge of the past promoted love for the nation. He praised the scholars of National Learning and criticized Taguchi Ukichi, the publisher of *Shikai*. Kume published an attack on Inoue's views.[99]

Katō Hiroyuki (1836–1916), whose dubious role was mentioned above, belonged to Kume's generation, but he had studied Western Learning before the Restoration. There is little evidence concerning his position in the Affair, apart from his conversation with the students who came to see him, but a statement by Ludwig Rieß gives us some idea of his attitude:

With withering scorn he [Katō] rebuked the Japanese historians, who by their over-confident hypercriticism had exposed themselves to ridicule and, when they experienced public indignation fuelled by the priests, did not have the courage to stand by their convictions, and reminded them of the fact that their methods were not the ones imported from abroad.[100]

Whether or not Rieß fully understood the Kume Affair, Katō may well have considered the kind of scholarship represented by Kume and his colleagues outdated, and other Western-educated scholars perhaps shared his view. In fact, although some of Kume's critics associated Kume with Western scholarship, Kume and his colleagues were just as often criticized for being stuck in the scholarly tradition of Chinese Learning.

The Kume Affair was just as much a confrontation between different traditions of learning and methods of scholarship as between scholarship and political ideology.[101] At least one contemporary interpreted it in this way: the commentator in *Waseda bungaku* called the Kume Affair a clash between representatives of conservative and progressive historiography (*hoshu shigaku* and *kaishin shigaku*).[102] Certainly, it cannot be regarded solely as repression of academic freedom by the state. It was at the same time an expression of the disputes and rivalries between scholars of different backgrounds in a period of transition. But in the course of these conflicts the Shintoists and the scholars of National Learning took advantage of the political climate to rid themselves, with the backing of the government, of an ideological adversary. The professors of the Imperial University consented by their silence, perhaps because they were relieved at the departure of a colleague whose views disturbed them. Thus they accepted that what should have been a scholarly controversy was conducted on a political level and that their academic freedom was threatened.[103]

The contrast between the 'Kume Affair' and the 'Tomizu Affair' was noted by contemporaries. In the Christian magazine *Shin kigen* one author asked whether the same professors who so vehemently defended Tomizu would do so if a 'second Kume' emerged, and answered flatly, 'No'.[104] The textbook controversy about the legitimacy of the imperial line (*Nanbokuchō seijun ron*) five years later proved him right.

6.5 The End of the Official History

One year after the 'Kume Affair', on 10 April 1893, the Historiographical Institute was closed down. Most of its members were dismissed, including Shigeno. Hoshino Hisashi and Tanaka Yoshinari were appointed to deal with such tasks as remained (*Shishi hensan kakari zanmu toriatsukai*).

The closure was ordered by the minister of education, Inoue Kowashi. Inoue had supported Mori Arinori's educational reforms and had participated in drafting the Imperial Rescript on Education. Although he was education minister for only a short time, from 1893 until his death in 1895, his influence on the education system was considerable. He was especially interested in Japanese language and literature as well as Japanese history.[105]

Inoue addressed a proposal to Itō Hirobumi, giving the following reasons for closing the Historiographical Institute. (1) In the 20 years since it was first established it had not produced the expected results. (2) The history was being written in Chinese (*kanbun*), although this language was no longer used in administration and education.[106] Inoue planned to suspend official historiography at the Institute and to resume it when a new course had been decided upon. In a letter addressed to Itō Hirobumi, however, he gives another reason for closing the Institute. Writing about his plans as education minister to reform education in Japanese language and history, he remarked about the history textbooks:

> ...when I looked into one or two of them I saw that they contained impossible statements, such as that the ancestors of the imperial family were Indians or were of the same lineage as the Koreans. Therefore I have crushed the Office of Historiography. The root of the disease lies there I believe.[107]

Miyachi, quoting the passage, emphasizes the pressure exercised by state authority and the representatives of state Shinto at the time Inoue became education minister. For him the closure of the Institute in the wake of the Kume Affair is part of the ideological consolidation of the authoritarian emperor state (*tennōsei kokka*) and the defeat of the emerging scientific history.[108] Nevertheless, the reasons given in the official proposal are more than a pretext. In the same letter Inoue describes *kanbun* as a dead language (*shibutsu*). The language of the history and the slow progress of the work had long been criticized. Inoue had himself been involved in planning the *Taisei kiyō,* the history initiated by Iwakura Tomomi with the intention of producing an official history in a short time.[109]

Inoue may well have been influenced by scholars of National Learning, first and foremost Konakamura Kiyonori, who continued to present their views to the Ministry of Education after the Kume Affair and demanded that the Historiographical Institute be closed. Mikami Sanji, a disciple of Konakamura Kiyonori and on friendly terms with Inoue, later told his student Ōkubo Toshiaki about Konakamura's role in the affair. Mikami himself was involved in the discussions about the future of the Institute and later became its director. He was accused of being in league with Konakamura but denied this.[110]

The closure of the Institute can therefore be attributed both to the official and the unofficial reasons. Incidentally, none of the reasons were made known publicly and in the newspaper reports speculation was rife. The *Yomiuri shinbun* published an article in three parts (14–16 April) criticizing Inoue's decision. It praised the achievements of the Institute and defended its course of concentrating on the collection of documents. After reopening, it argued, the Institute should continue on the same lines. The article also criticized the Institute's lack of openness, which had led to misunderstandings and ultimately to its closure. A different view was expressed in the newspaper *Nihon* (14 April 1893); Konakamura Yorikata, disciple and adopted son of Konakamura Kiyonori, condemned the course pursued by the Institute. Yorikata alleged that the Institute had cost a lot of money without producing any results. Such histories as it had written were merely a collection of dates; moral issues were neglected and the importance of literature and of social evolution not acknowledged. The members of the Institute were behind the times or they would not compile a history in a foreign language (*kanbun*). They had also ignored the spirit of the Imperial Rescript on Historiography of 1869.

Some newspapers published suggestions for the future course of official historiography, among them proposals that a new office be established in the Imperial Household Ministry.[111] The closure also provoked derision. A caricature in the satirical magazine *Marumaru chinbun* (see Fig. 6.1) shows three men with a cart loaded with the kind of boxes in which written documents are stored. The two men pulling the cart have an ink stick and an inkstone for faces, the third man pushing the cart a calligraphy brush. The three have halted because the way is barred and a notice tells them that carts must stop. The caption reads:

> Damn! If only we had known that we would be stopped so suddenly we would have taken a byway, how annoying! Now nothing can be done, oh, one mistake and everything ends up like this. We tried a fresh start, but then the thought/Chinese Learning [a somewhat clumsy pun with *kangae* (thought) and *kangaku* (Chinese Learning)] – oh what a hateful business![112]

Inoue had closed down the Institute planning to reopen it and even to have it continue to compile an official history. He consulted with Katō Hiroyuki, Hamao Arata, who had succeeded Katō as president of the University, and Toyama Masakazu, the dean of the literature department, and asked for proposals to be submitted.[113] The earliest proposal was from Kurita Hiroshi and was submitted on 27 March, before the Institute was closed. On the whole, Kurita's suggestions amount to a continuation of historiography much in the same way as before, except that the history should be written in Japanese. One man who was in charge should be named; Kurita suggested Kawada Takeshi. He also named other possible candidates for the Institute; apart from Hoshino, mainly representatives of National Learning such as Konakamura Yorikata, Ochiai Naobumi, Naitō Chisō and Hagino Yoshiyuki. Kurita wished to see scholars appointed who could write well.

Caricature from the magazine *Marumaru chinbun* (22 April) relating to the closure of the Historiographical Institute in 1893.

In another proposal on 7 July 1893 Kurita discussed the amount of time necessary to complete the task and the difficulties of finding suitable specialists for each historical period. Kurita also suggested that strict rules be laid down concerning the information given to outsiders about the work in progress, stating that this had been the case at the *Shōkōkan* academy in Mito.

The other proposals were submitted in April 1893. They were from Toyama, dean of the literature department, Hoshino Hisashi, Kan Masatomo and Ikeda Kōen from the Historiographical Institute, Takatsu Shūsaburō, a graduate of the Seminar for Classical Studies and lecturer at the University, Kawada Higuma from the Topographical Department of the Institute and an anonymous author. Apart from Kawada, who only mentioned the topographical materials, the authors all agreed on one point: the compilation of historical documents was the greatest achievement of the Institute and should become its main task. While in Hoshino's and Kan's opinion a history of Japan should be written at the same time, the other authors thought that the actual writing of history was best left to private authors. Kan Masatomo proposed that the Institute, which should never have been transferred to the University in the first place, be re-established in the Imperial Household Ministry. The others proposed that the documents collected remain in the University and be accessible to researchers. For this purpose an institute or department should be established; Toyama and the anonymous author cited science laboratories as a model.

Toyama's proposal is the most succinct in its formulation of the problem and its solution: in a not yet fully civilized society only the state can write a history of the country. However as culture becomes more widespread there are private individuals capable of writing history. No historian can be completely impartial and everyone judges differently, including historians appointed by the state. Official historiography is therefore dangerous since by its very authority it suggests a degree of objectivity which it cannot possess. But the collection of documents is an immense task and should therefore continue to be pursued by the state.[114] Toyama then dealt with the particulars of collecting the historical documents, referring to Hoshino's letter, which he enclosed with the proposal. The collection of documents had already been the main preoccupation of the Historiographical Institute for some time, and its importance was recognized by the authors of the other proposals.

Inoue was obviously convinced by the arguments set forth in the proposals and finally decided that the main task of the Institute after its re-establishment should be the collection and publication of historical sources. Two memoranda as well as four draft proposals to reopen the Institute show us how Inoue came to reach this decision.[115] The first draft contains the plan to continue the official history starting with Oda Nobunaga and Toyotomi Hideyoshi. The following drafts mention only the compilation of sources. Before Inoue reached his decision, he attempted to gather as much information as possible.[116] He consulted with members of the Imperial University. Mikami Sanji, Tsuboi Kumezō and Tanaka Yoshinari discussed the matter in autumn 1893 and reported to Toyama and Hamao, who presumably informed Inoue. Since Inoue and Mikami were on friendly terms, it can be assumed that they also talked about it informally.

Inoue's fourth draft, the proposal which was debated in parliament, contained the following plan. The Institute should be set up for five years.[117] It should receive a yearly budget of 12,900 yen, 65,400 yen in all. The Institute was expected to improve the existing collection, adding documents especially for the period between 1037 and 1317 (covered by the *Dainihonshi* but not the *Dainihon hennenshi*). The publication of the documents was planned. Professors from the literature department of the University were to be selected as members of the Institute and paid for the extra work; the Ministry of Education would draw up an appropriate Imperial Rescript.[118] Inoue's proposal included an inventory of the material collected so far and of the tasks that had yet to be completed. This was based on the information Hoshino had submitted to Toyama.

The proposal was accepted at the beginning of 1895.[119] Inoue Kowashi died on 15 March 1895, and his successor Saionji Kinmochi notified the University of the decision. The Institute was expected to resume work beginning with the fiscal year, in April 1895. In March Hamao and Toyama consulted with Kurita, Hoshino, Tanaka and Mikami, who were appointed editors (*hensan iin*).[120] Kurita declined on the grounds of old age and Konakamura Yorikata, who replaced him, left for France in 1898. Nominally Hoshino was the director of the Institute until 1899 (or interim administrator; his precise title was *Buppin kanrisha*). But his ill health soon prevented him from coming to work and it was Mikami Sanji who took his place, even before he formally succeeded Hoshino as director (until 1919). According to Mikami, Konakamura was responsible for the period up to 1317 and Tanaka for the following period. Mikami himself worked on the Tokugawa period.[121] There were three clerks (*shoki*), 13 assistants (*join*) and 40 scribes. Many of the members, such as Ikeda Kōen, the author of one of the proposals mentioned above, had been members of the Institute before its closure.[122]

Of the four editors, Hoshino and Tanaka had previously been in the Institute and were by now among its most senior members. Tanaka's career is remarkable, for he first entered the Office of Historiography as a scribe in 1876.[123] In 1885 he accompanied Shigeno on his long field trip. In the Office of Historiography he rose to the position of an archivist (*shōki*). At the Historiographical Institute he became editor (*hensan iin*) while teaching at the University. Among his historical writings are works on the Ashikaga period, the times of Oda Nobunaga and Toyotomi Hideyoshi and a history of the two imperial courts in the fourteenth century.

The most influential man in the Institute after 1895 was Mikami Sanji (1865–1939).[124] Mikami had studied Japanese literature at the Department of Classics. While pursuing postgraduate studies he became an assistant at the Historiographical Institute. In 1891 he began to lecture in history; in 1892 he became assistant professor and in 1899 professor. That same year, at a comparatively early age, he was awarded a doctorate. Mikami also lectured at the Women's High School, at Waseda University and at the Institute of Japanese Literature, but gave up these commitments when he was appointed to the Historiographical Institute. Until his retirement from the University in 1926 he devoted much of his energy to the Institute (although he had resigned from his formal position there in 1919). After retiring he took part in editing the biography of the Meiji emperor (*Meiji tennō ki*) until 1933. Twice Mikami travelled to Europe. He and Ludwig Rieß, some of whose courses he had attended, were friends and Mikami visited Rieß in Berlin. Among Mikami's publications is a history of the Edo period in two volumes (1943–4). Mikami himself stated that he conducted hardly any research while he was employed by the state, because he did not want to become so engrossed in his own work that he neglected his official duties as his predecessors had done.[125]

In fact the rnembers of the re-established Historiographical Institute restricted their own freedom considerably. In April 1895 regulations to the following effect were issued: (1) to avoid public indignation, members should not publish their own interpretations and textual criticism; (2) members should only conduct research of their own in their free time and as long as it did not affect their official duties; (3) outsiders should not be told under what name and by what methods the documents were arranged; (4) articles should only be published in periodicals edited by the Imperial University or the Institute of Japanese Literature; and (5) exceptions were poems, literary works and school textbooks.[126]

On 3 July the new members of the Institute assembled and the president of the University, Hamao, gave a speech composed by Mikami. He advised the members to collect documents concerning not only political history but also Japanese society. Since they did not have much time to complete the task in hand they were urged to look after their health.[127] The introduction to the regulations cited above also stressed the limited amount of time and advised members to work together. Evidently every attempt was made to ensure speedy progress and avoid conflicts and obstacles.

At the end of the first five years, in 1900, an extension of another five years was granted. In 1905 the Institute became a permanent one. Publication of the documents began in 1901.

The re-establishment of the Historiographical Institute involved a complete change of course. The Institute was no longer a *historiographical* institute (though it has retained this English title to this day); its only task was the collection, arrangement and publication of written sources on the history of Japan.

The new beginning represented a retreat. The members of the Institute gave up the ambition to fulfil a public role, which had motivated Shigeno and Kume. In order to avoid confrontation with outsiders they did not publicize their findings even if they did conduct research of their own. Nevertheless, even Mikami, who was in his own way no less of a 'history official' than Shigeno, did not escape confrontation. Fifteen years after the Institute had been reopened, the controversy about the legitimacy of the imperial house in the period of the two imperial courts provoked a much greater uproar than the Kume Affair.[128]

6.6 Scholarship versus Education: The Textbook Controversy of 1911

The controversy in 1911 concerning the two imperial courts in the fourteenth century (*Nanbokuchō seijun ron*) and their representation in the school textbooks is the second spectacular instance of historical scholarship being suppressed by semi-official ideology.[129] As in the Kume Affair, the government reacted to pressure from nationalist groups to suppress a historical debate. What might have been a scholarly debate became a political crisis and was resolved by a political decision.

The existence of two imperial courts in the fourteenth century raised the question of which of them was legitimate and challenged the assumption of an unbroken imperial line from the first emperor to Emperor Meiji. In the question of legitimacy, the official view after 1868 followed the interpretation of the *Dainihonshi*, that the Southern court was the legitimate one, and at first the scholars in the Office of Historiography shared this view; this is suggested by Nagamatsu's answer to the inquiry sent by the Ministry of Education (Chapter 3.3) and the fact that the Office supported the posthumous honours for heroes who had fought for the Southern court. They took the initiative in proposing honours for Kitabatake Chikafusa, the author of the *Jinnō shōtōki* (1339), one of the earliest works to treat the Southern court as legitimate. However, the question of legitimacy was not definitively decided as long as there was no official statement from the Imperial Household Ministry. The *Taisei kiyō* compiled under Iwakura's orders was sanctioned by imperial edict and therefore later regarded as the official imperial statement, but the work was never completed or published.[130] In the *Taisei kiyō*, the Southern court was depicted as the legitimate one but the emperors and era names of the Northern court were also given. The same method was used by the Office of Historiography for the history textbook *Kokushigan*. But the issue was far from clear; Ogō's trip to Yamato and Yamashiro in 1876 was justified with the argument that more sources on the period of the two imperial courts had to be examined.

When the members of the Office began revising the *Dainihonshi*'s account of the *Nanbokuchō* period, their views changed. Shigeno criticized the version given in the *Dainihonshi* in a lecture in 1900 entitled 'Dainihonshi no tokuhitsu ni tsuki shiken o nobu' ('Private View on the Innovations of the *Dainihonshi*').[131] Shigeno stated that the discussion about legitimacy was not appropriate to Japan since it had originated in China, where the historical situation was fundamentally different (in China the period of the 'Northern and Southern courts' describes the time of the second divided empire from 420 to 589). At the time he gave the lecture Shigeno was no longer a member of the Historiographical Institute, where the editors were preparing the collected sources for publication as *Dainihon shiryō*. Tanaka was responsible for the period in question and Mikami, in his lecture in memory of Tanaka and in his own memoirs, described the difficulties he faced.[132] The scholars finally decided to leave the question of legitimacy open and only named the Southern court before the Northern one because this is the order in which the four directions are usually named in Japan (*tōzai nanboku*). The decision was justified by emphasizing the character of *Dainihon shiryō*: it was a collection of sources without any kind of judgement. According to Mikami, the Imperial Household Ministry, the Ministry of Education and the president of the University were informed and no one expressed doubts. Five years later, the Ministry of Education received an inquiry about the imperial house from an American publisher planning to compile tables of all the world's sovereigns. The Ministry of Education passed the question on to the Imperial Household Ministry, where a committee had been established to examine the chronological tables of imperial succession. Mikami was also a member. The committee did not make a final decision on the legitimacy of the two courts.

It was therefore consistent that the first standard textbook issued by the Ministry of Education (*Jinjō shōgaku Nihon rekishi*) acknowledged the existence of two courts between 1337 and 1392 and left the question of legitimacy open. The manuscript was written in 1903 by Kita Sadakichi, a graduate of the Department of Japanese History.[133] He was assisted by members of the Historiographical Institute, who like him had been appointed by the Ministry of Education: Mikami Sanji, who proofread the manuscript, Tanaka Yoshinari and Hagino Yoshiyuki. In 1911 Kita stated that he and his colleagues had been fully aware of the difference between scholarship and education; however, they had judged it wise to acknowledge the existence of two imperial courts and not to pass any judgement.[134] The textbook was used from 1903 to 1910 in all Japanese primary schools and no one objected.[135]

Why then did the same textbook cause a heated controversy in 1911? Towards the end of the Meiji era the emperor was gradually elevated to the position of a sacred ruler. He no longer travelled around Japan to visit his people but became more and more remote. At the same time the social tensions accompanying industrialization and urbanization increased and were aggravated by the economic crises following the Russo-Japanese War. Socialist groups formed since the 1890s became more and more radical. The climax and for the time being the end of the socialist and anarchist movement came with the 'High Treason Incident'. In 1910 the police questioned several hundred socialists and anarchists and accused 26 of conspiring to assassinate the emperor. Of these, 24 were sentenced to death, and 12 of them, among them the socialist and pacifist Kōtoku Shūsui, were executed on 24 January 1911. The political situation was already unstable; governments changed frequently, cabinets succeeded each other under Yamagata Aritomo's protégé Katsura Tarō and Itō Hirobumi's protégé Saionji Kinmochi (*Kei-En-jidai*) and could only stay in power with considerable effort by negotiating compromises (*jōi tōgō*).

Against this background of social and political tensions a primary school teacher and two professors provoked the controversy.[136] In 1910 Kita Sadakichi, having just completed the draft for a teacher's handbook to go with the standard textbook, introduced it to an assembly of primary school teachers. Justifying the viewpoint the textbook committee had adopted concerning the period of the two imperial courts, Kita maintained that the existence of two courts was a historical fact. The legitimacy of one or the other could not be decided upon, because although the Southern court was generally regarded as the legitimate one, there was as yet no final statement by the government.[137] Kita explained himself very carefully; obviously he was conscious of the fact that he was dealing with a highly sensitive issue.

On 19 January 1911, the day the papers reported the sentences passed in the High Treason trial on 18 January, the newspaper *Yomiuri shinbun* published an editorial by Toyooka Hanrei.[138] The author lamented the ambiguous standpoint adopted by the authors of the textbook. If moral principles were not clearly set forth and taught in the schools, argued the author, individualistic and nihilistic ideologies could spread unhindered. Thus the author constructed a link between the interpretation of history offered by the textbook and the kind of ideas propagated by men such as Kōtoku Shūsui and the others condemned in the High Treason trial. The article drew the attention of two professors at Waseda University, whose subsequent actions turned the question of the textbook into a government crisis: Makino Kenjirō and Matsudaira Yasukuni. They persuaded Fujisawa Genzō, a relative of Makino and a member of parliament, to bring up the matter at the next session, which he did on 4 February 1911.

Was it not lamentable, he inquired, that a textbook authorized by the Ministry of Education caused the people to confuse loyalty and treason and right and wrong, violated the dignity of the imperial house and destroyed the principles of education? Fujisawa then announced that he would treat the problem in detail in a statement on 16 February.

The Katsura Cabinet felt threatened by Fujisawa's announcement; feelings were aroused by the High Treason Incident, lack of respect for the emperor was the gravest offence one could be accused of and the government was already in a precarious position. Prime Minister Katsura himself, together with General Terauchi Masatake, a former student of Genzō's father, the Confucian scholar Fujisawa Nangaku, persuaded Fujisawa not to make his statement and promised in exchange to have the textbook revised. Fujisawa, not equal to the critical situation and the sudden shower of attention to his insignificant person, gave in, much to the disappointment of his allies. In a melodramatic speech in parliament, which became the subject of several newspaper cartoons, he announced his resignation.[139]

But the embarrassment of the Katsura Cabinet did not end there.[140] Several individuals and organizations demanded a definite answer to the question of legitimacy of the Northern and Southern courts. The most insistent group was the *Dainihon kokutai yōgodan* (Assembly for the Protection of the National Polity of Great Japan), established in the aftermath of Fujisawa's defeat; among its members were Makino and Matsudaira.[141] This association sent its programme to all leading newspapers. One of its members, Inukai Tsuyoshi, who was the leader of the Kokumintō party, attacked the government in parliament. In a resolution that was almost passed he established a link between the textbook issue and the High Treason Incident. Yamagata Aritomo, elder statesman and together with the late Itō Hirobumi one of the most influential political figures, personally intervened, requesting the emperor to take a firm stand in favour of the Southern court.[142] The emperor (himself a descendant of the Northern court) replied that he had always regarded the Southern court as the legitimate one and the Meiji Restoration as the fulfilment of the Kemmu Restoration of the emperor Godaigo. An imperial edict on 3 March 1911 declared the Southern court alone to be legitimate. The textbook was revised: the Southern court was renamed Yoshino court and the existence of the Northern court suppressed. Thus, on the political level, the controversy was resolved; the Katsura Cabinet was however soon replaced by a Saionji Cabinet.

Discussions about which of the two courts was legitimate continued and became the subject of numerous publications predominantly by advocates of the Southern court.[143] Not all the most outspoken participants were historians; indeed these often remained silent, such as Tanaka Yoshinari, who lectured on the period of the two courts and was presumably one of the most competent scholars in the field.[144] Kume on the other hand, in his outspoken way, condemned the whole controversy as a children's squabble (*yōji no kenka*) and the discussion about the three imperial regalia (*shingiron*) as play-acting (*oshibai*). [145] He told the self-appointed defenders of the imperial house that they were themselves irreverent to indulge in such a discussion at all and stated sarcastically, 'unfortunately there were indeed at that time two suns in heaven and two monarchs on earth' (157).

The controversy was a cause for vehement attacks on the scholars in the Office of Historiography and the Historiographical Institute. One critic, Mishio Kumata, alleged that the main cause of the controversy was the aversion of Shigeno Yasutsugu and Kan Masatomo to the *Dainihonshi* of the Mito school and Shigeno's virtual monopoly in the Office of Historiography.[146]

For the historians directly involved in the controversy, the consequences were not limited to verbal attacks by their opponents. Kita was dismissed from his post in the Ministry of Education on 27 February and Mikami resigned. Tanaka was forced by the head of his faculty, Ueda Kazutoshi, to change the title of his lecture from *Nanbokuchō shi* (History of the Northern and Southern Courts) to *Yoshinochō shi* (History of the Yoshino Court), despite his protest that an academic lecture was different from a primary school textbook.[147]

The historians at the Historiographical Institute also came under pressure. The historical documents concerning the period of the Northern and Southern courts were published in Volume 6 of *Dainihon shiryō*. The editors had finally decided to treat the two courts in an equal manner. The head of the faculty, Ueda, and the president, Hamao, who had not objected at the time, now demanded that the possibility of a revision be examined. An undated 'Answer to the inquiry concerning the revision of the representation of the period of Northern and Southern courts in *Dainihon shiryō*' is preserved in the Historiographical Institute.[148] The authors state that the *Dainihon shiryō* was purely a collection of sources without evaluation. The sources clearly showed that two rival courts had existed. The authors then discussed a few possibilities for renaming the two courts in a way that showed the Southern court to be legitimate, but discarded them. The authors refused a revision and reiterated the difference between a collection of sources and a historical narrative. From the contents of the document we can conclude that it was drawn up in March 1912. It seems that it was never submitted; possibly the death of the Emperor Meiji on 30 July 1912 put an end to the discussion.[149]

The controversy of 1911 is generally viewed as having sealed the separation of historical scholarship and education. In the terms used by Tsuboi Kumezō in 1894 (Chapter 3.3), scholarship was *junshō shigaku,* pure history, while education fell into the realm of *ōyō shigaku,* applied history. The idea that history for educational purposes was different from academic history was shared by prominent historians such as Shigeno and Mikami. Shigeno used the term 'education history' (*kyōiku rekishi*) in his lectures. Mikami's attitude is illustrated by the following two anecdotes.

The historian Inoue Kiyoshi relates that at a party to welcome freshmen Mikami told them that they must not teach in schools what they were to learn at university. For example, the foundation of the Japanese Empire by Emperor Jimmu had not occurred in 660 BC as they had learnt, but around 600 years later, a fact which was already known to scholars in the Edo period. They would learn about the historical events at university, but as school teachers they would have to stick to the mythical date. Ōkubo also remembers that Mikami emphasized the distinction between teaching in schools and at university. In his lectures, before beginning to talk about the period of the Northern and the Southern courts, he would instruct one of the students to close all the windows. This symbolic gesture was supposed show the divergence between public opinion and the view held by the scholars, which the common people could not understand. Mikami related this episode himself, but claimed that he was genuinely threatened.[150] The controversy in 1911 may well have been another reason, besides the Kume Affair and the ensuing closure of the Institute, why Mikami conducted hardly any private research and published little.

It seems then, that the government decision to revise the textbooks was received without protest because it was accepted that history education had a different purpose to serve than historical research. The anecdote about Mikami suggests that he may even have taken a certain pride in the distinction between what the masses learnt about history and what he revealed to a chosen elite.

There is little evidence that the controversy was seen as a threat to academic freedom. Men who had attacked the government's position in the Tomizu Affair now sided with the government. Tomizu himself demanded that the professors involved in the textbook controversy be dismissed.[151] Like the behaviour of the students in the Kume Affair, Tomizu's attitude suggests that, to the men at the Imperial University, 'academic freedom' was primarily about securing the privileges of an elite. Of course the sacrosanct position of the imperial house and the fact that the High Treason Incident had cost probably innocent victims their lives may provide some explanation, but it does not seem sufficient. In the course of the controversy, opinions opposing the official line were expressed and even published by opponents. Kita, dismissed by the Ministry of Education, later became professor at the second Imperial University in Kyoto (1920). Mikami and Tanaka remained at the Historiographical Institute and Mikami even became one of the editors of the official chronicle of Emperor Meiji (*Meiji tennō ki*). In the more liberal climate of the following years various opinions could be publicized without restriction. This was the time when Tsuda Sōkichi published his theories, which cost him his chair at Waseda University in the 1930s – the third famous instance of historical research being suppressed by state intervention before the Second World War.

Tanaka Yoshinari, in his lecture 'Shigaku no katsuyō' ('The Application of History') given in the year following the textbook controversy,[152] characterized the age as one where freedom of speech prevailed and urged his colleagues to voice their opinions in discussions of the day (Chapter 5.4).

It is therefore an over-simplification to regard the textbook controversy merely as an instance of historical truth suppressed by government intervention and to explain the development of historical scholarship solely in terms of its reaction to government suppression. Rather, it would seem that academic historians accepted that history should meet the extra-academic demands placed on it by the government and by nation-minded people. The problem was how to respond to the different, often conflicting, demands on the writing of history.

Mori Ōgai, in *Kano yō ni* (*As If*), which was inspired by the textbook controversy and published in January 1912,[153] tells the story of a young scholar, Gojō Hidemaro, whose life ambition it is to write a history of Japan. Hidemaro is preoccupied with the contradiction between myth and reality. For him, the distinction between myth and historical fact is crucial. However, he does not want to rebel against his father, a peer and a loyal servant of the imperial house (Ōgai's friend Yamagata Aritomo probably provided the model for him) and a defender of the myths. When Hidemaro reads Hans Vaihinger's work *Die Philosophie des Als Ob* (*The Philosophy of As If*, 1911), he believes he has found the solution to his dilemma. However, his friend Arakoji contradicts him and tells him that conflict with his father is inevitable.

The historians at the Historiographical Institute did not give themselves to philosophical speculations like Ōgai's Hidemaro. Their answer to the problem was avoidance. Ignoring Tanaka's call to take a responsible role in society, they continued their retreat into the collection of primary sources and textual criticism. The tradition of the Historiographical Institute, which for years had emphasized the collection of documents and the verification of isolated facts, encouraged this kind of attitude.

7

Conclusion

7.1 The Legacy: The Historiographical Institute since 1895

In 1895 the Institute was reopened after a break of two years under the new name *Teikoku daigaku bunka daigaku Shiryō hensan kakari* (Department for the Compilation of Historical Materials at the Faculty of Arts at the Imperial University). Its aims were much the same as they are today: research (*kenkyū*), compilation (*hensan*) and publication (*shuppan*) of historical documents (*shiryō*). The evolution from a government office to a university research institute was complete. The Institute received its present name, *Shiryō hensanjo*, in 1929. Since 1950 it has been under the direct administration of the University rather than the Faculty.

When the Institute was reopened, financial support was approved by the Diet for five years, and the period was extended for another five years in 1901, the year publication of *Dainihon shiryō* and *Dainihon komonjo* began.[1] The assumption still seems to have been that the Institute would complete its task and become redundant within a few years. However, five years later the Institute proposed that its work be financed as an ongoing project.[2] The proposal cited the example of Western countries, a common rhetorical device in the Meiji period (and sometimes to this day) and also mentioned the insecurity of the scholars working at the Institute. A second document proposed a system of full-time posts, which was sanctioned by imperial edict on 28 March 1905.[3] Tanaka Yoshinari became the chief editor, and Mikami Sanji became editor and administrative director. Tanaka was the only member who had occupied a high-level post in the Institute before 1895.

At the beginning of the twentieth century some of the members of the former office still remained, including Hoshino Hisashi, who died in 1917. He was probably less influential than his younger colleague Tanaka

Yoshinari, who died in 1919. New members usually were graduates of the Imperial University. Mikami, who succeeded Hoshino as director from 1899 to 1919 (Chapter 6.5), had graduated from the Department of Classical Studies. The subsequent directors, Kuroita Katsumi (1919–20) and Tsuji Zennosuke (1920–38) were graduates of the Department of Japanese History (*Kokushika*) and had studied under Rieß.

In 1924 the number of members was more than doubled, and at the end of 1925 there were 137. The higher number of members made it possible for them to specialize, and there was separate administrative and technical staff.[4]

Today (1995) the Institute has 83 members, 19 of whom are women, and since 1954 they no longer have the status of officials in the Ministry of Education, but are professors, assistant professors and research assistants like other members of the University; 26 of the 83 members (11 of the women) are administrative and technical staff. There are departments for ancient history, medieval history, early modern history, documents (*komonjo*, *kokiroku*) and special materials.[5]

In 1911 the Institute received its own building for the first time, by the 'Red Gate' (*Akamon*) of the former Kaga residence. In 1916 a fireproof storage building was added, which still stands inside the gate today. In 1920 the building was extended. It survived the great earthquake in 1923, during which the main library burnt down. In an exhibition, members of the Institute presented copies of documents, the originals of which had been lost in the earthquake, proving the importance of preserving valuable documents by producing duplicates. A 14-volume collection of photographs of documents was also published.[6] In 1928 all the holdings of the Institute were housed together in a new building next to the new library. This building survived the Second World War (most of the documents were removed to safety during the war). It was extended in 1973, and now the Institute has a basement and seven storeys with a total surface of 8,000 square metres.[7]

Even before 1895, the collection of documents had become the most important task of the Institute, and after 1895 it was continued in much the same way. In July 1895 field trips were resumed and many followed over the following years.[8] Today members of the Institute travel to different regions several times a year to work on particular documents or photograph them for the Institute, but their trips tend to be shorter. Members also increasingly travel abroad.

In 1895 it had been decided to begin publishing documents as soon as possible, and from 1901 onward the first volumes of *Dainihon shiryō* (historical materials) and *Dainihon komonjo* (official documents) were published. To cover some of the high costs, the members of the Institute tried to enlist subscribers at home and abroad. In a lecture at the *Shidankai* society, Mikami mentioned noble families, high schools, public institutions and wealthy private individuals as potential buyers.[9]

According to Mikami (408: 73), there was talk of involving Shigeno Yasutsugu in the publication, but the idea was abandoned. His 'obliteration theories' were still in the public mind, and the house of Shimazu refused to lend their documents as long as Shigeno was involved in the project. He had angered the family of his former feudal lord by denying that they were descended from the first shogun, Minamoto Yoritomo, as they themselves claimed.

In the compilation *Dainihon shiryō* events are recorded chronologically with year, month and day, and the relevant primary sources cited; later illustrations and photographs of objects were also included. If the exact date of a source is unknown, it is cited at the end of the respective month or year. This structure goes back to Hanawa Hokiichi's compilation *Shiryō* at the end of the eighteenth century. Some details in the method are also reminiscent of earlier compilations: for example, in notes referring to the emperor, the subject of a sentence is omitted.[10] Although the procedure for including documents has not fundamentally changed since Meiji, younger generations of scholars have attempted to take into account new trends in historical scholarship, such as the increased interest in the history of the common people (*minshūshi*).[11]

The compilation *Dainihon komonjo* has three parts. The first (*hennen monjo*) consists of decrees by the emperors and abdicated emperors, the Council of State (*Dajōkan*) and the shoguns, as well as documents from military commanders and other individuals. The second part (*iewake monjo*) contains documents arranged according to provenance, from major families or temples; it includes, for example, eight volumes with documents from the Kōyasan temple complex and the documents from the house of Date in ten volumes. The third part (*Bakumatsu gaikoku kankei monjo*) contains documents concerning the foreign policy of the shogunate since 1853. These documents were taken over from the Foreign Ministry in 1907. Both *Dainihon shiryō* and *Dainihon komonjo* are still being continued.

It soon became clear that the publication of *Dainihon shiryō* would not be completed for several years, and so, in 1923, a condensed version was begun by excerpting the annalistic sections (*kōbun*) and listing the relevant sources. For the 23-part volume one (Heian period I) this resulted in a single volume. The series was entitled *Shiryō sōran* (*Overview of the Historical Materials*). It bore the same relationship to *Dainihon shiryō* as the *Meiji shiyō* to the *Fukkoki* (Chapter 4.1).

After 1945 further series were added: *Dainihon ishin shiryō* (documents of the Meiji Restoration) and *Dainihon ishin shiryō kōyō* (essential materials of the Meiji Restoration). Both series were based on documents taken over from the *Shōmeikai* society and its successor, the *Ishin shiryō hensankai,* which had an office in the Ministry of Education (Chapter 3.5). It began the compilation of *Dainihon ishin shiryō* in 1938, and the *Shiryō hensanjo* took over in 1949. The structure is the same as that of *Dainihon shiryō,* and the period covered is 1846 to 1871 (although only part of this work was published). There is also a separate part, which consists of documents classified by provenance, such as the documents of the Ii family. *Dainihon ishin shiryō kōyō* is organized in the same way as *Shiryō sōran*.

The *Dainihon shiryō* only cites excerpts of documents; to publish important chronicles and diaries in their entirety a new series was begun, *Dainihon kokiroku* (old journals). The first volume appeared in 1952. This series includes documents from the tenth to the sixteenth centuries. Documents of the Edo period are treated in the same way in the series *Dainihon kinsei shiryō,* begun in 1953. The amount of materials for the Edo period is so vast that the editors have to choose which ones to include.

Apart from these major series, various smaller ones are published as special materials (*tokushu shiryō*). They include the printed catalogue of the Institute's library and a collection of signatures of famous historical figures (*Kaō kagami*). At the time of the 100th anniversary of the Meiji Restoration the diary of the statesman Sasaki Takayuki (1830–1910) was published (*Hoko hirohi Sasaki Takayuki nikki*; 12 vols, 1970–7), unfortunately without notes or subject index. In addition, two volumes of selected documents on the Meiji Restoration (*Meiji ishin shiryō senshū*) were published.

The collection of foreign documents relating to Japan, first suggested by Ludwig Rieß, has been pursued systematically since 1954. All the unprinted documents in foreign archives are recorded on microfilm and a printed catalogue is published (15 volumes in 1988). Some of these have been printed with Japanese translations, such as the journals of the captains of the Dutch and English trading posts (*Oranda shōkanchō nikki* and *Igirisu shōkanchō nikki*).

More recently, since 1984, the Institute has been developing databases to widen access to its materials. In 1990 the database of *Ishin shiryō kōyō* was made publicly available on site and since 1991 it has been open to users all over Japan.[12]

Despite such innovations, some features are reminiscent of the Institute's origins. It took the research institute a long time to shake off the characteristics of a government office. The former Office of Historiography continued to be known as the *Shikyoku* (history office) as late as the 1920s, probably in part because of its bureaucratic character, which is still noticeable today.

The first volumes of *Dainihon shiryō* and *Dainihon komonjo* were dedicated to the emperor, just as former compilations had been. Some activities of the Institute were also reminiscent of its former close links to the imperial house and government. When the Meiji emperor visited the University for the graduation ceremony, as he did from 1899 onwards, a special exhibition of valuable documents was always prepared for him at the Institute, and Mikami and his colleagues would show him round and explain their significance.[13] The visits were abandoned under the Taishō emperor, who soon became too ill; moreover, the imperial visits necessitated security measures, which the University saw as a threat to its autonomy. Today there is a permanent exhibition in the entrance hall of the Institute.

Representation abroad is another task the Institute continued to fulfil to a certain extent. Some of the Institute's publications were donated to foreign institutions to give an impression of Japan's cultural heritage. According to the explanation on a list of such publications dating from 1905, just after the Russo-Japanese war, the Institute wanted to demonstrate that Japan could boast cultural as well as military achievements. The Institute was also represented at the Japan-British Exhibition of 1910, with the published volumes and portraits of historical figures.[14]

The Institute continued to be the official authority on matters relating to the past, at least in Mikami's time. He was sometimes asked to examine the genealogies of families to be elevated to the ranks of the nobility. Once, two candidates claimed to be heirs of the hero Kusunoki Masashige, and alleged heirs of Kojima Takanori were also common.[15]

For a while, members of the Institute continued to be involved in the compilation of school textbooks, and in 1907 they also planned to publish illustrations from the Institute's documents as teaching materials.[16] After 1911 this role lost its importance, but immediately after the Second World War members of the Institute were involved in compiling a primary school textbook for the Ministry of Education, as well as materials for middle schools, including a compilation of illustrations.[17]

In 1895 the freedom of members of the Institute to publish their own research was severely limited, and Mikami adhered to these instructions. However, it seems that not everyone did, and Mikami had to mediate when Hoshino and Tanaka published in *Rekishi chiri*, a new academic journal, which was not on the list of journals the members were permitted to publish in (407: 85). Mikami himself was criticized for his views concerning Ii Naosuke, expressed in the first official history textbook for primary schools, published in 1903. One of the critics was Yamagata Aritomo – until Mikami reminded him that a preface written in his name by Inoue Kowashi for Shimada Saburō's book on the opening up of Japan expressed similar views.[18] However, the organizer of a memorial service for the samurai who had died in 1860 in the attack on Ii Naosuke tried to have Mikami removed from his post. The president of the University, Hamao, defended Mikami and pointed out that such a measure was against the autonomy of the University.[19]

Tsuji Zennosuke, director of the Institute from 1920 to 1938, encouraged his colleagues to conduct their own research.[20] However, when in the 1930s freedom of expression came under increasing threat, the members of the Institute responded by avoiding public attention. While, at the Department of Japanese History, Hiraizumi Kiyoshi (1895–1984) rose to become a prominent exponent of the emperor-centred interpretation of history (*kōkoku shikan*; Chapter 7.2) in the 1930s, work at the Institute continued much as before.[21] In 1934 the 600th anniversary of the Kemmu Restoration was celebrated, and the question of the two imperial courts once again became the subject of debate. To avoid confrontation the members of the Institute postponed further work on the relevant volumes of *Dainihon shiryō*.[22]

Even after 1945, members of the Institute hesitated to conduct their own research and especially to publicize it outside the University. During the student unrests of the 1960s, this attitude provoked criticism, and in response attempts were made to reorganize the Institute with a view to making it more open and to promote the integration of research and teaching. Vacant posts were for the first time advertised publicly, and members now are no longer necessarily graduates of Tokyo University. Since 1967 yearly reports have informed the public about the work of the Institute (*Tōkyō daigaku Shiryō hensanjo hō*). Members of the Institute publish their own work, give lectures and seminars outside Tokyo University or assist institutions throughout Japan in the publication of regional and local histories. The Institute accepts visiting scholars from Japan and abroad and strives to promote scholarly exchange.

The striking contrast between the former restrictions and the freedom its members enjoy today was demonstrated during the last illness of the Shōwa emperor. Members of the Institute were among the most vociferous critics of the emperor's role in the Second World War and conservative attempts to revive the 'emperor system'. In the winter of 1988–89 posters outside the Institute, put up by some of its members, showed copies of foreign newspaper reports attacking the semi-official attitudes towards the imperial house. Some members published topical articles; for example, the then director, Takagi Shōsaku, in an article in a widely circulated journal, discussed the ideology of Japan as the land of the gods and the divine descent of the emperors from a historical perspective and contended that the Japanese had not yet fully overcome these ideas. This, he claimed, placed a burden on international relations.[23] Another example is a publication containing critical discussions of the enthronement ceremonies for the new emperor, which contains contributions from a former member and a present member of the Institute about the enthronement ceremonies of medieval and early modern Japan.[24]

In sum, the Historiographical Institute continues to collect and publish documents in much the same way it has done since the times of Shigeno and Hoshino. The bureaucratic character of the former government office still lingers, for example, in the numerous regulations regarding the use of its materials by outside visitors, which is still fairly restricted. At the same time, the Institute has become more open. Its members are less of a homogenous group and are more independent. The fact that a director of this Institute, the origins of which go back to an imperial rescript, could criticize the role of the emperor in a journal for the general public without having to fear sanctions shows that, despite continuities, the times have changed since Kume was dismissed because of his article about Shinto.

7.2 History and the Nation in Germany and Japan

'Sanctus amor patriae dat animum' (Holy love for the fatherland gives the spirit), was the motto of the Society for the Study of Early German History, established in 1819 with the aim of publishing what subsequently became the great national collection of sources of medieval Germany, the *Monumenta Germaniae historica* (MGH). Perhaps more than any other work it has become an example of the achievements in the collection and publication of sources inspired by rising German nationalism, in the wake of the Wars of Liberation (1813–15).[25] No wonder that Japanese scholars claim that the MGH inspired the *Dainihon shiryō*, although in fact the two collections have hardly anything in common, and the *Dainihon shiryō* clearly owes its format to Hanawa Hokiichi's *Shiryō*.

Germany exemplifies the relationship between the rise of nationalism and of historical scholarship in nineteenth-century Europe. In Germany, romantic nationalism, which emerged under the influence of European romanticism, was particularly strong. It was a reaction to French hegemony and above all a kind of nationalism of peoples not living in a state. Culture, language and literature had to define the nation; political nationalism followed and expressed itself in the concern with creating a nation state. History in particular served to define the identity of a nation and emphasize its uniqueness, showing the nation to be the result of a process.[26] Individuality and organic development characterized historicism, which contributed so much to the organization of historical scholarship. German historical scholarship was a model for other countries up to the end of the nineteenth century.[27] Leopold von Ranke is credited with having laid the foundations of a specialized academic discipline, when he started training students in techniques of historical research in his seminars in Berlin.[28] Other universities followed his example, such as Breslau from 1832.

Ranke's oldest disciple and one of his most famous ones was Heinrich von Sybel (1817–95), who introduced historical seminars in Marburg and, more importantly, in Munich.[29] Munich became a centre for historical research under King Maximilian II, who had studied with Ranke and had Ranke give lectures to him in 1854. With the King's support, Sybel established a department of history at the University of Munich in 1857. He initiated the first professional historical journal, the *Historische Zeitschrift*, in 1859. The collection and publication of documents also owes much to Sybel. He became the first secretary of the Historical Commission of the Bavarian Academy, established by King Maximilian and directed by Ranke, who had suggested it, until his death in 1886, when Sybel succeeded him.[30] The Commission's aim was to collect and publish sources of German history in a definitive text and correct chronology and, if possible, establish the causal relationships. Apart from Ranke and Sybel, its members included Georg Heinrich Pertz, director of the MGH, and Johann Gustav Droysen. While the MGH was a private enterprise, albeit subsidized by several German states and the German Confederation, the initiative for the Historical Commission came from a monarch. Another new feature was that it employed scholars from all over Germany. The Commission was to publish the Acts of the Imperial Diet and the Chronicles of the German Towns of the fourteenth to sixteenth centuries. Another task was the compilation of historical annals, the *Jahrbücher zur deutschen Geschichte*. The suggestion had come from Ranke, who was already working on them with his students: 'Would it not be a wonderful thing, if we could unite critically verified annals of German history in a single great work?' Ranke's intention was not so much a definitive history as a reliable basis for further research and writing.[31] This is reminiscent of the *Dainihon hennenshi*, as it was conceived by the author of the memorandum on its language (Chapter 4.3).

The aims of the Commission were not only scholarly. In addition to the publication of sources, it was to encourage historical writings, which 'through stimulating form and ethical content will excite patriotic feelings and national consciousness, bring to the mind of the people the rich abundance of its past and thus provide the spirit of the nation with strong and fruitful nourishment.'[32]

Sybel's contribution to the organization of historical scholarship was even greater than Ranke's. The advance of the historical seminar at German universities owes much to him, and several projects to publish documents were initiated by him: *Publications from the Prussian State Archives*, *Acta Borussica*, *Political Correspondence of Frederick the Great*, *Acts of the German Imperial Diet*.[33] Moreover, it was Sybel who, after becoming Director of the Prussian Archives, proposed the establishment of a historical institute in Rome in 1883, together with Georg Waitz, Wilhelm Wattenbach and Julius von Weizsäcker.[34] In 1880–81 Pope Leo XIII had opened the secret archives of the Vatican, and in 1881 the Austrian Historical Institute had been founded. The Prussian Academy of Science set up a committee, of which Sybel was a member, to determine the aims of such an institute, and in 1888 the German Historical Institute was founded to conduct research into German history and to publish documents.

Historical studies in Germany developed in parallel to the nation state and were inspired by the search for national identity, that is, by political and ideological concerns, rather than scholarly ones. National unification came later to Germany than to its neighbours. The foundation of the German empire in 1871 created the framework for the development of a national state that was accepted by its citizens.[35] For Sybel, who was himself politically active (1848 member of the pre-parliament in Frankfurt, 1862–64 and 1874–80 member of the Prussian House of Representatives, 1875–95 Director of the Prussian Archives in Berlin and semi-official historian of the German empire), political decisions had to be directed by historical tradition.[36] Sybel saw history as a continuous chain of causes and effects and concluded that objective knowledge of the past and its complete reconstruction were possible. He thus had a reliable standard for making decisions: historical success. Sybel recognized early on the potential of history for legitimizing the wish for German unity among the educated middle classes.[37] The close relationship between historical writing and the concerns of the day was a characteristic of historicist writing. This relationship was expressed, for example, in the idea that a German constitution had to be appropriate to German tradition and the German national character. Not only Sybel but other historians of the time too viewed it as their task to influence the political actions of their contemporaries. Many German historians were politically active themselves: Droysen was a representative of the Prussian government at the Bundestag (the assembly which managed the affairs of the German Confederation) in Frankfurt; Ranke, Theodor Mommsen, Sybel, Droysen, Treitschke and others were active publicists. They endeavoured to discuss political and social problems of the day from the perspective of their historical knowledge. Their collected essays appeared in books that stood on the shelves of educated citizens.[38] Ranke himself had taken the importance of historical writing for politics for granted.[39] Droysen, the first representative of the Prussian school of historiography, went even further, describing his intention in the *History of Prussian Politics* as representing the past in order to provide orientation for the present and future. The historian's task was to provide principles for action in foreign politics.[40] Heinrich von Treitschke (1834–96), in his *German History in the 19th Century* (1871), stated that he wished to 'give the political consciousness of the Germans a protestant Prussian identity'.[41]

Historians collaborated in the construction of monuments to celebrate the Prussian state. Treitschke was a member of the advisory committee for planning the national monument to Emperor Wilhelm. The historical interpretations of Sybel and other Prussian historians formed the basis for the murals in the upper hall of the Imperial Palace in Goslar, which was remodelled into a national monument between 1878 and 1897.[42]

Similarities in the historical situation made Germany the prime model for Japan in the late nineteenth century.[43] While Japan did not have to be politically unified to become a nation state, the feudal domain, the village community, the neighbourhood, not the country as a whole, had been the prime focus of loyalties and attachments before 1868. Nationalist sentiments were confined to intellectuals, especially the scholars of National Learning, and part of the ruling class.[44] Not until after the centralization of government and increasing communication did nationalism become a collective sentiment.

Confrontation with the West played a major role in this process, as did Western ideas of the nation state. Meiji Japan followed Western example in most areas of life. As a result, many Japanese feared Japan would lose its special characteristics. The 1880s, which saw the height of Westernization, symbolized in the Rokumeikan, the Western-style hall in which political leaders and their wives attended balls in Western evening dress, also saw a revival of Japan's own cultural traditions (Chapter 2.5). As in Germany, culture, not the state, was the source of nationalism. The new constitution was to be firmly rooted in Japan's own cultural heritage. The Japanese state was regarded as an organism (*kokutai*) with individual characteristics (*kokushitsu*),[45] which expressed themselves in language and literature and which history served to explain. The belief that Japan was the 'land of the gods' and that the imperial house was divine in its origins gave Japanese nationalism its religious character.[46] The enshrinement of historical figures such as Kusunoki Masashige as deities shows even more clearly than the German monuments the close relationship between nationalism and religion. The connection between ancestor worship in Japan, worship of founding heroes and of 'ancestors of the nation' in the 'family state' is a topic well worth further research.

Although the origins of cultural nationalism in Japan can be found in the Tokugawa period, its ideas were directly influenced by German thought, brought back to Japan by Japanese students. For example Inoue

Tetsujirō, one of the leading ideologues of late Meiji, studied in Germany from 1884 to 1890 before teaching philosophy at the Imperial University. On the other hand, Lorenz von Stein, who heard much about Japan from his Japanese students, concluded that German and Japanese history had many striking parallels and called on Germans to study Japanese history in cooperation with Japanese scholars.[47]

The 1880s, the years of preparation for Japan's first constitution, were also the years when Japan increasingly turned to Germany in search of a model. Germany had won a military victory over France in 1871 and formed its first nation state, rapidly advancing to become economically powerful. The new state was authoritarian. Military and economic strength, a constitutional monarchy and state control of many areas of life; these were characteristics that appealed to the Japanese, but they were particularly impressed by the way nationalism had been the driving force for these developments. During the Iwakura Embassy, Iwakura was impressed by the way Bismarck referred to history to legitimize the German nation state, and he and other Meiji leaders insisted that the Japanese constitution must be rooted in Japanese history, a message reinforced by Lorenz von Stein (Chapter 2.6).[48]

Education was another area where German thought and practice played a major role. When Itō Hirobumi travelled to Europe to study constitutional systems, he also met Mori Arinori, who was to become his education minister in 1885, in Paris to discuss the reform of the Japanese education system. This discussion resulted in the decision to imitate the dual Prusso-German structure and remodel the system, so that it should serve the state.[49]

In the 1880s the government increased its control over education. The teaching of Japanese and Chinese literature and history was given more attention. At the same time the interest of many Japanese intellectuals in German thought expressed itself in the establishment of the *Doitsugaku kyōkai* (Association for German Sciences) in 1881. Besides Ludwig Rieß, several Germans taught at the Imperial University.

My purpose in summarizing German influence in Japan is not to emphasize its extent, but to demonstrate how similar challenges, a newly formed nation state that had to be filled with meaning and define its position among the powers, caused Japan to look to Germany. Japan was highly selective in importing from abroad, and what it imported was often determined by Japan's own cultural traditions. Historiography is a good case in point. German historical scholarship was most influential where it confirmed existing tendencies. It attracted the Japanese because of its role in shaping the new German nation state. The historicist emphasis on individuality and historical development potentially offered an alternative view to the Enlightenment view of history; a view in which Japan was not in an earlier stage on the way to 'universal' progress than the West, but progressed in its own particular way. In Germany, historicism had led to a reappraisal of the Middle Ages, which for the Enlightenment historians had been the object of contempt. However, German influence shaped not so much Japanese interpretations of history and historical writing as the organization of historical scholarship and the development of research techniques. It did not help Shigeno and his colleagues solve the problem of representing their national history or stimulate thought about the meaning of history.

Perhaps the most significant difference between Germany and Japan was that the historians at the Historiographical Institute did not become interpreters of the nation; their lives and works did not help shape the Japanese empire as those of the German historians shaped the German empire. Of course, today, these German historians are remembered for their contributions to the edition of sources and the organization of scholarship, not for their narrative histories, and their role as supporters of the authoritarian state is criticized.

From today's point of view the failure of Japan's first professional historians to fulfil this role is perhaps no loss. However, the Imperial Rescript of 1869 stated that history was important to the state, and the scholars who spent a great part of their working lives trying to produce a national history saw themselves as playing an important role in the new nation. Shigeno's and Kume's writings show that they perceived themselves as having a contribution to make to educating the nation. It is therefore legitimate to ask why they failed not only to complete their task but also to exercise significant influence on the shaping of a national historical consciousness.

In part it was precisely their official position that limited their influence. They were engaged in government business; they served first of all the government, rather than seeing themselves as spokesmen for the citizens; in the tradition of East Asian political thought, which distinguishes sharply between officials (*kan*) and people (*min*), this means they were far removed from the people. Even when they became professors they were still representatives of the government. Their role was not to 'profess' as German professors were expected to do.[50] Deep knowledge was the privilege of an academic elite, not to be imparted to the masses, as is illustrated in the anecdotes about Mikami Sanji (Chapter 6.6). Closely related to this role of the professor is the issue of academic freedom, or lack of it, often cited as reason for the isolation of professional historical scholarship. As professors interpreted it as institutional autonomy and the preservation of their privileges, they did not necessarily defend their right to publicize their opinions freely (Chapter 6.4). To what extent government intervention stifled scholarly debate is not altogether clear, and the opinion of contemporaries on the issue was divided, but the Kume Affair and the textbook controversy of 1911 show that at the very least discussion about the imperial house was severely restricted. For the historians writing an official history centring on the imperial house this posed a problem, for which the retreat into 'objectivity', concentrating on editing sources and verifying facts, may have seemed like the only solution.

German historical scholarship as it was brought to Japan by Rieß and by Japanese students returning from Germany, such as Tsuboi Kumezō, strengthened the tendency to retreat into 'objectivity'. Ranke combined a firm methodological basis with his aim to intuitively understand the ideas that shaped history. His disciples, while adhering to Ranke's code of research, expressed their political standpoint in their works.[51] But as historical thinking became more 'scientific', the focus shifted from historical knowledge in narrative form to the techniques of research and textual criticism and to the auxiliary disciplines of history. Droysen's lectures on *Historik* since the late 1850s illustrate this new emphasis. Speculation about the meaning of history was relegated to philosophy, from which historians distanced themselves. Ernst Bernheim's *Lehrbuch der historischen Methode*, first published in 1889, did not include a section on the philosophy of history until the fifth edition (1908).[52] Even then, Bernheim did not consider speculation part of the historian's task. Perhaps the historian Theodor Mommsen exemplifies this development. His *Roman History* (1854–6) was based on sound research, but also reflected his political commitments and his brilliance as a writer, in recognition of which he received the Nobel Prize for literature in 1902. However, Mommsen ended his history with the fall of the republic and never wrote a history of the following imperial period. Berding suggests that he gave up writing narrative history because he could not resolve the tension between research and narration. Only detailed research on isolated questions, the mosaic stones that would form the whole picture, could he reconcile with his high standards of 'scientific' research. Instead, Mommsen's work as a scholar concentrated on numismatics, epigraphy and philology. [53]

Japan imported German historical scholarship as it manifested itself in the late nineteenth century, that is, as historicism in the narrow sense of positivism, aiming to produce factual knowledge, but losing sight of the inner connection between historical thinking and contemporary experience and problems of orientation.[54] Rieß's teaching on methodology, in which he had a special interest,[55] may well have impressed his Japanese students more than anything else he taught. Certainly his teaching provided confirmation for the historians at the Historiographical Institute. Tsuboi Kumezō, who joined him in the Department of History in 1891, also emphasized methodology. His *Shigaku kenkyūhō* (*Research Methods of Historical Science*, 1893) was based on Bernheim's *Lehrbuch der historischen Methode*.[56] When Ranke is represented as the founder of modern historical scholarship in Japan by describing Rieß as his disciple and overemphasizing the importance of his legacy, it is Ranke the 'quasi-positivist' (Breisach) who is invoked, not the Ranke who saw God's plan behind the whole of history and who wrote narrative history that was indebted to the universalist tradition of Christian and Enlightenment historiography. This partial reception of Ranke is not unique to Japan.[57] However, invoking Ranke as the ancestor of modern historical scholarship in Japan served to legitimize its characteristics by making it part of the story of the rise of 'scientific' history in the context of 'universal' human progress.

The emergence of a 'scientific' history, which neglected to address the representation of knowledge in the historical narrative and the function of historical knowledge in educating society and left speculation about the meaning of history to non-historians, resulted in similar problems in Germany and Japan. Historical scholarship could be and was taken into the service of politics to propagate unexamined political values, while still appearing to be 'objective'.[58]

Because it ignored the problem of representation, 'scientific' history as it came to Japan in the late 1880s and early 1890s did not offer Shigeno and his colleagues working on the official national history any solution to one of their greatest problems: the problem of form. The document *Shūshi jigi* and Shigeno's lecture on the compilation of history (Chapter 4.2) show that Shigeno perceived the traditional forms of historical writings as inadequate; the annals merely enumerated facts; the narrative histories on the other hand were unreliable. His interest in Western historiography was motivated by the search for a new form; in his lecture he stated: 'Unlike Japanese and Chinese histories, which confine themselves to factual statements, Western histories inquire into causes and consider effects, provide detailed accounts of their subjects and vivid pictures of conditions of the time with which they are concerned.' [59] His notes on Zerffi's *Science of History* show his particular interest in Zerffi's statements about cause and effect. Shigeno, it appears, was searching for a form that was objective, but also revealed meaning; the meaning he assumed to be given by the events themselves; hence the search for ever more evidence in the hope that one day all the evidence would be assembled and the meaning would become clear. Ultimately this concentration on accumulating evidence resulted in the issue of representation being avoided.

The problem of form was at the same time a problem of meaning, for although narrative history claims to relate 'things just as they really happened', it implies 'an interpretation, an authentic philosophy of history'.[60] For this reason the form of historiography has recently become a much-debated question of historical theory and of the history of historiography; not just as writing but as historical thinking.[61] Jörn Rüsen in particular stresses that writing history does not merely represent the results of research but has a fundamental function in creating meaning.[62]

The typical form of historical writing of the German historicist school was the epic narrative; Ranke, Sybel, Mommsen, Droysen and others wrote in this form. The narrative detailed the historical development of people and institutions or the events of a given period. It was more than an admission that history was still seen as an art as well as a science; it expressed the historicist concept of the past as a coherent entity, which the narrative strove to present.[63] The inspiration was provided by nationalism, and historians at the time were conscious of the fact.[64] The creation of a German nation state marked a new departure and a break with the past. However, there was enough continuity to enable historians to interpret the events of 1866–71 as a culmination of a process leading towards the new nation state.[65]

The characteristic form of the *akademizumu* school, on the other hand, is the positivist article. Shigeno, Kume and their colleagues published their lectures and wrote articles, most of them narrow in focus. But 'such articles form the skeleton of history and are not true history'.[66] Moreover, broad narrative histories, rather than narrowly focused analytical articles, are the means of reaching a non-specialist audience. As a contemporary observer expressed in the wake of the mid-Meiji 'historical fever' (Chapter 6.1): '...textual criticism which just enumerates the facts without any logical connection nor appeal; historical discussions which are filled with speculation and conjecture; textbook-like works which cannot narrate more than the usual facts; all these surely make the public react with scorn'.[67] He and other commentators were aware that the right form for writing a national history had yet to be found. When commentators in *Waseda bungaku* repeatedly described the state of historical scholarship as 'chaotic and backward', it was above all the state of historical writing that was being criticized. A commentator discussing the historiography of the previous years in 1896 remarked that neither publicists (*hyōronka*) nor specialists (*senmonka*) were capable of producing a complete work of history.[68] Similarly, Yamaji Aizan criticized the specialists for not producing narrative histories and concluded that the advances in historical scholarship had not served the people.[69] Citing Macaulay as an example, he said that research had to be combined with art (*geijutsu*) to produce a history that was both accurate and readable.

If narrative implies interpretation, the inability of the scholars at the Office of Historiography to find a suitable form for the national history they were trying to write may well be the reflection of their failure to formulate an interpretation of Japan's history that did justice to the upheavals Japan was experiencing. The Office of Historiography, established in an attempt to revive the ancient tradition of history written by rulers to legitimize their position, soon became an anachronism. The Six National Histories and the *Dainihonshi*, which were the main models for its members, were written to strengthen the position of the imperial house within Japan. Even the fourteenth-century history *Jinnō shōtōki*, which begins with the assertion that Japan is the land of the gods (*shinkoku*) and attempts to demonstrate Japan's superiority over all other countries, was not primarily concerned with Japan's position in the world. This was, however, an issue that historians writing after the enforced opening of Japan had to confront. The ideas of Japan's uniqueness and superiority developed by the National scholars in the Tokugawa era stood in obvious contrast to reality. Japan was weak and threatened by the Western powers.

The problem with building the Japanese nation state was that it involved disowning Japanese culture and adopting an alien culture.[70] Japan had to find a new way not only to relate to its own past, but also to the West.[71] The sense of crisis brought about by the confrontation with an alien culture and the rapid pace of change after 1868 is evident in documents such as Miura's memoranda (Chapter 2.5). The collapse of the old order and the upheavals in the first 20 years of the Meiji era necessitated a new conception of history. As Pyle puts it:

Disorientated by the accelerated progress of history, she [Japan] required some meaningful way of relating her past to the present and future, some clear perspective and sense of direction that would function as a binding and integrative force, enabling her people to act in concert and deal effectively with her domestic and international problems.[72]

Cultural identity was not just an issue for the 'new generation': Shigeno's generation was educated in the Confucian tradition, before Japan was forced to open itself to the West, but after 1868 they experienced the passing of the world they had known. Shigeno's writings show his attempts to reconcile the old and the new. They are the testimony of a man deeply rooted in the tradition of Chinese Learning but also open to new ideas. Shigeno stressed that Japan must go with the times (*jisei*) by combining Western achievements with Japanese traditions. Nevertheless he did not cease to look upon China as the source of true learning; this is evident from his lecture on the compilation of history in 1879 (Chapter 4.2) and his lecture on *kōshōgaku* (Chapter 5.1); China provided his frame of reference for considering Japan and the West. His own knowledge of the West was limited; he was an old man when he travelled abroad for the first time in 1907. Kume reports that he regretted not having gone earlier, when he was asked to accompany the Iwakura Embassy.[73]

The Enlightenment historians had attempted to make sense of Japanese history by writing 'universal' history, applying Western notions of progress.[74] The problem was that this Enlightenment history did not accommodate Japan as an equal.[75] Such a view of Japanese history no longer seemed appropriate when Japan began to find itself a place among the great powers. In 1895 the revision of the unequal treaties had at last been accomplished, and Japan won a military victory over China, the country it had for centuries looked to as a model. Commentators celebrating the victory in the new journal *Taiyō* (*Sun*), among them Kume, announced the advent of a new era.[76]

In this context a new conception of history could evolve, and in the 1890s *tōyōshi* emerged as an academic discipline.[77] The concept of *tōyō*, the Orient that Japan constructed for itself, enabled Japan to perceive itself as both separate from and equal to the West, rather than as part of a Western past; it made Japan part of world history and gave it a leading role in Asia. As an academic discipline *tōyōshi* was part of *akademizumu*; Shiratori Kurakuchi, who played a central role in defining the field, had studied under Rieß. *Tōyōshi* appeared to solve Japan's dilemma: how to define itself in the relationship between past and present and East and

West. But as a field of study it had the same methodology and thus the same 'objective' trappings as *kokushi*, the history of Japan. *Tōyōshi*, therefore, may have provided a new basis for interpreting Japan's history, but not necessarily a new form for writing it.

The failure to formulate a new conception of history that matched the new era may account in part for the failure of Shigeno and his colleagues to complete the narrative history of Japan they envisaged. However, ultimately their greatest problem was the dilemma of Mori Ōgai's Hidemaro: how could they write a history that clearly distinguished between myth and fact and yet preserve the myths that gave meaning to the nation? How could they reconcile their view that historians must be free from political and moral bias with their belief that history had a vital part to play in fostering a sense of nation and providing orientation? The *Kokushigan* (Chapter 3.4), the only overview of Japan's entire history that they did complete and publish, represented national history as imperial and as divine history.[78] Such an interpretation of Japanese history was in line with that of Japan's earliest chronicles, which provided the model for the Office of Historiography. However, it is hardly what the compilers believed to be historical truth.

The issue is not only one of 'objectivity' versus bias; 'objectivity' is unattainable, because any representation of history, including the annalistic form, involves choices that are not 'given' by the material itself. The controversy about the imperial schism in the fourteenth century is a prime example. As the 'Answer to the inquiry concerning the revision of the representation of the period of Northern and Southern courts in *Dainihon shiryō*' (Chapter 6.6) shows, it was impossible for the scholars at the Historiographical Institute to choose a wording that described the events without implying a certain interpretation. The problem of the *akademizumu* school is not only that it is weak on ideas and theory, as the conventional criticism has it, but that it is not 'objective' either; Tanaka has shown this for the discipline of *tōyōshi*.

The failures of *akademizumu* are often blamed for the emergence of the ultranationalist interpretation of Japanese history that emerged in the 1930s, known as *kōkoku shikan*; it describes the unbroken line of emperors as the essence of the Japanese national polity and treats the myths of the deities as history.[79] Hiraizumi Kiyoshi (1895–1984), its foremost representative, was a student of Kuroita Katsumi, who succeeded Mikami Sanji as director of the Historiographical Institute. Hiraizumi's early work on medieval Japan is still respected, but in the mid-1920s he expressly distanced himself from the over-emphasis on facts and evidence. He solved the dilemma that had plagued his Meiji predecessors by force; in his article '*Rekishi ni okeru jitsu to ma*' ('Factual and Genuine Truth in History'), he criticized the *kōshō* school for over-emphasizing facts and analysis and contrasts it with a 'synthesizing' approach, which seeks genuine truth and is an art (*geijutsu*) rather than a science (*kagaku*). Hiraizumi criticized the historians at the Historiographical Institute for collecting materials while ignoring the spirit pervading the history of Japan from its foundation (*daiseishin*).[80] *Kōkoku shikan* was the official interpretation of history when the Japanese colonial empire was at its height and provided legitimation for it at the cost of the 'objectivity' Shigeno and his colleagues prized so highly. Hiraizumi was isolated among his colleagues; he resigned at the end of the war, and most of his work is now thoroughly discredited. However, the fact that *akademizumu* could bring forth a leading proponent of myth-history is a result of its neglecting to question the idea of objectivity and to address the relationship between the search for historical truth and the representation of history.

The dilemma remains unresolved and largely unaddressed. In postwar Japan historical objectivity re-emerged and became dominant; issues of theory and understanding were neglected. Positivist studies still dominate in the field of history in Japan.[81] Narrowly focused articles offering a wealth of facts and extensive quotations from the sources (*shiryō*) and minimal interpretation appear in innumerable scholarly journals. On the other hand, historical novels, some based on thorough research, are extremely popular and (unlike in Germany) far more influential than the works of professional historians.[82] The Ministry of Education still upholds the distinction between 'pure' and 'applied' history to defend the treatment of Japanese history in school textbooks, and its alleged attempts to revive an emperor-centred ideology are criticized by many historians, including members of the Historiographical Institute (Chapter 7.1).

When Yamaji Aizan criticized the historians of his day in 1909, he emphasized both the continuity from the Edo period and the similarities between Japan and the West. In the end, the tensions experienced by Shigeno and his colleagues attempting to write a history for their nation – between truth and myth, fact and interpretation, disinterestedness and partisanship, science and art, research and writing – have to be confronted by historians in every time and place.

Notes

1 Introduction

1. Author's translation from the text quoted in Ōkubo Toshiaki, *Nihon kindai shigaku no seiritsu* (Yoshikawa kōbunkan, 1988): 42. For a brief discussion of it see Francine Hérail, 'Regards sur l'historiographie de l'époque Meiji', *Storia della Storiografia/ Histoire de l'Historiographie* 5 (1984): 92–114.
2. E.g. Paul Akamatsu, *Meiji 1868: Revolution and Counter-Revolution in Japan* (London: Allen & Unwin, 1972).
3. Margaret Mehl, 'Tradition as Justification for Change: History in the Service of the Japanese Government', in *War, Revolution & Japan*, ed. Ian Neary (Sandgate, Folkestone, Kent: Japan Library, 1993): 39–49.
4. Carol Gluck, *Japan's Modern Myths: Ideology in the Late Meiji Period* (Princeton, N.J.: Princeton University Press, 1985): 37–9.
5. For the following summary see Arthur Marwick, *The Nature of History* (London: Macmillan, 3rd edn, 1989): 38–43; Friedrich Jaeger and Jörn Rüsen, *Geschichte des Historismus* (Munich: C.H. Beck, 1992): 21–4.
6. Jaeger/Rüsen 1992: 1, 7.
7. Jaeger/Rüsen 1992: 69–70.
8. E.g. Benedict Anderson, *Imagined Communities* (London: Verso, 1991, rev. edn): 194, 197; Wolfgang Hardtwig, *Geschichtskultur und Wissenschaft* (Munich: dtv, 1990) *passim*; Jaeger/Rüsen 1992: 9–10; Marwick 1989: 41–2.
9. Hardtwig 1990: 224.
10. Eric Hobsbawm and Terence Ranger (eds), *The Invention of Tradition* (Cambridge: CUP, 1983, 1984): 14.
11. Christian Meier, 'Was ist nationale Identität?' in *Die Last der Geschichte: Kontroversen zur deutschen Identität*, ed. Thomas M. Gauly (Cologne: Verlag Wissenschaft und Politik, 1988): 55–67.
12. Hobsbawm/Ranger 1984: 9.
13. The following summary is limited to developments immediately relevant to this book. The standard work on the history of historiography in Japan is Sakamoto Tarō, *Nihon no shūshi to shigaku* (Shibundō, 1966). Most useful, especially for the period after 1868, is the work of Ōkubo Toshiaki; most of his essays on historiography are now accessible in volume 7 of his collected works: *Nihon kindai shigaku no seiritsu* (Yoshikawa kōbunkan, 1988). On major individual projects, see relevant articles in Shigakukai (ed.), *Honpō shigakushi ronsō*, 2 vols (Fuzanbō, 1939). See also W.G. Beasley and E.G. Pulleyblank (eds), *Historians of China and Japan* (London: OUP, 1961); John S. Brownlee, *Political Thought in Japanese Historical Writing: From*

Kojiki (712) to Tokushi Yoron (1712) (Waterloo, Ontario: Wilfried Laurier, UP, 1991); Ulrich Goch, *Abriß der japanischen Geschichtsschreibung* (Munich: iudicium, 1992); Goch has an alphabetical list of the works he discusses, with information about editions and translations into European languages.

14. On the early chronicles: Bitō Masahide, 'Nihon ni okeru rekishi ishiki no hattatsu', in *Iwanami kōza Nihon rekishi*, 22, (Iwanami, 1968): 5–20; Sakamoto Tarō, *Rikkokushi* (Yoshikawa kōbunkan, 1970, repr. 1986; Engl. *The Six National Histories of Japan* by J.S. Brownlee (University of British Columbia Press, 1991); G.W. Robinson, 'Early Japanese Chronicles: The Six National Histories', in Beasley/Pulleyblank 1961: 213–28.

15. Ōkubo 1988: 13; Goch 1992: 53.

16. Paul Varley, *Warriors of Japan as Portrayed in the War Tales* (Honolulu: University of Hawaii Press, 1994).

17. Goch 1992: 53.

18. On historiography of the Tokugawa period in general: W.G. Beasley, Carmen Blacker, 'Japanese Historical Writing in the Tokugawa Period (1603–1868)', in Beasley/Pulleyblank 1961: 245–67; Kate Wildman Nakai, 'Tokugawa Confucian Historiography: The Hayashi, Early Mito School and Arai Hakuseki', in *Confucianism and Tokugawa Culture*, ed. Peter Nosco (Princeton: UP, 1987): 62–91.

19. Goch 1992: 31–4.

20. Goch 1992: 44–5.

21. Goch 1992: 14, 37.

22. The Mito school of study is usually divided into the early Mito school, at the time of Mitsukuni, and the late Mito school, from the end of the eighteenth century. The later Mito school was characterized by a more nationalistic, mythical view of history and its engagement in the political affairs of the time.

23. On the *Dainihonshi* and the Mito school: Bitō Masahide, 'Mitogaku no tokushitsu', in *Mitogaku*, eds. Imai Jisaburō, Seya Yoshihiko and Bitō Masahide (*Nihon shisō taikei* 53; Iwanami, 1973, repr. 1976): 562–70. Miura Hiroyuki, 'Tokugawa Mitsukuni no shūshi jigyō', *Nihonshi no kenkyū dai ni shū*, vol. 1, (Iwanami shoten, 1930): 515–34. Herschel Webb, 'What is the Dai Nihon Shi?' *Journal of Asian Studies*, 19.2 (1960): 135–49.

24. Ōta Yoshimaro, *Hanawa Hokiichi* (Yoshikawa kōbunkan, 1966). Onko gakkai (ed.), *Hanawa Hokiichi kinen ronbunshū* (Onko gakkai, 1971). Onko gakkai (ed.), *Hanawa Hokiichi ronsan*, 2 vols (Kinseisha, 1986); Sakamoto Tarō, 'Wagaku kōdansho ni okeru henshū shuppan jigyō', in *Koten to rekishi* (Yoshikawa kōbunkan, 1972): 367–85. Yamazaki Tōkichi, 'Wagaku kōdansho ni okeru *Shiryō* hensan jigyō', *Shigaku zasshi*, 12 (1910): 864–81.

25. Goch 1992: 48–50.

26. On *kōshōgaku* and historiography: Ōkubo 1988: 33–5.

27. On National Learning and historiography: Sakamoto 1966: 218–32; Itō Tasaburō, 'Edo jidai kōki no rekishi shisō – omo to shite kokugaku o chūshin ni', in *Nihon ni okeru rekishi shisō no hatten*, ed. Nihon shisōshi kenkyūkai (Yoshikawa kōbunkan, 1965): 215, 242 (first published by Tōhoku shuppan 1961).

28. Robert Bellah, *Tokugawa Religion: The Cultural Roots of Modern Japan* (New York: The Free Press, 1957, 1985): 98–106.

29. On historiography in the Meiji period in general: Ōkubo 1988; Hérail 1984.
30. Ōkubo 1988: 69–70, 398 and *passim*.
31. Among these were François Guizot (1787–1874), Histoire générale de la civilisation en Europe (translated 1874–7); Thomas Henry Buckle (1821–62), *History of Civilisation in England* (translated 1875) and Herbert Spencer (1820–1903), *The Principles of Sociology* (translated 1882).
32. On Yamaji Aizan: Sakamoto Takao, *Yamaji Aizan* (Yoshikawa kōbunkan, 1988). On the Min'yūsha historians: Peter Duus, 'Whig History, Japanese Style: The Min'yūsha Historians and the Meiji Restoration', *Journal of Asian Studies*, 33 (1974): 415–36.
33. Ienaga Saburō, *Nihon no kindai shigaku* (Nihon hyōronsha, 1957): 75–8.
34. Ōkubo 1988: 59–60.
35. Hardtwig 1990; Friedrich Nietzsche, *Vom Nutzen und Nachteil der Historie für das Leben* (1874), translated by Peter Preuss as *On the Advantage and Disadvantage of History for Life* (Indianapolis/Cambridge: Hackett Publishing, 1980).
36. Herbert Butterfield, *The Whig Interpretation of History, 1931* (New York/London: W.W. Norton & Company, 1965): 97.
37. Jaeger/Rüsen 1992: 65–6.
38. John Clive, *Not by Fact Alone: Essays on the Writing and Reading of History* (London: Collins Harvill, 1990): ix.
39. For example, Kadowaki Teiji, 'Kangaku akademizumu no seiritsu', in *Nihon rekishi kōza*, ed. Rekishigaku kenkyūkai/Nihonshi kenkyūkai, vol. 8, (Tōkyō daigaku shuppankai, 1957): 163–86 (183–4). The same point is made for German historicism in Jaeger/Rüsen 1992: 66.

2 Historiography in the Service of the Meiji Government

1. *Dajō ruiten 1130* Book 45: 88–9; 1/19 Book 29: 39–40 (the numbers refer to the photographed edition, *shashinban*, which can be found among other places in the *Shiryō hensanjo*). *Hōki bunrui taizen* 1/14 *Kanshokumon kansei monbushō* 6–9; 1/1–6; *Kanshokumon kansei dajōkan naikaku* 1: 139; 2: 339–51. For an explanation of the Executive Council and Cabinet documents see Takayuki Ishiwata, 'Dajōkan, naikaku monjo', in *Nihon komonjogaku kōza* (Yūzankaku, 1979): 33–47.
2. For this and the following information see Asakura Haruhiko, *Meiji kansei jiten* (Tōkyō bijutsu, 1969): 314/15. Kyōikushi hensankai (ed.), *Meiji ikō kyōiku seido hattatsushi* (Ryūginsha, 1938),1: 87–160.
3. Ōkubo Toshiaki, *Meiji ishin to kyōiku* (*Ōkubo Toshiaki rekishi chosakushū* 4) (Yoshikawa kōbunkan, 1987): 190.
4. Ōkubo 1984: 236–7; 254–5. Rivalries between the Scholars of National Learning and of Chinese Learning: Ōkubo 1987: 257–315.
5. *Dajō ruiten* 1/19.
6. *Dajō ruiten* 1/30; Meiji 1.12.10; Ōkubo 1987: 184–6.
7. Ōkubo 1987: 4: 261–3.
8. Sakamoto Tarō, *Nihon no shūshi to shigaku* (Shibundō, 1966; repr. 1983): 29/30.
9. Fukui Tamotsu, 'Wagaku kōdansho to naikaku bunko', in *Hanawa Hokiichi ronsan*, ed. *Onko gakukai* (Kinseisha, 1986): 1: 219–40 (221).
10. Numata Jirō, 'Shigeno Yasutsugu and the Modern Tokyo Tradition of Historical Writing', in *Historians of China and Japan*, eds W.G. Beasley and E.G. Pulleyblank

(London: Oxford University Press, 1961): 264–87 (265). Francine Hérail, 'Regards sur l'historiographie de l'époque Meiji', *Storia della Storiografia/Histoire de l' Historiographie*, 5 (1984): 92–114.

11. Kuwabara Nobusuke, 'Kindai seiji shiryō shūshū no ayumi', in *Sankō shoshi kenkyū*,17, 18, 21 (1979–81); 1979: 2.

12. W.G. Beasley, *The Modern History of Japan* (Tuttle, 1982; 3rd rev. edn): 108–10.

13. *Dajōkan* (ed.), *Fukkoki* (Naigai shoseki; Tōkyō teikoku daigaku zōhan, 1930): 2.

14. Like the *Rekishika*, the *Chishika* had predecessors; see Asakura 1969: 413.

15. Asakura 1969: 205.

16. Miyachi Masato, 'Seiji to rekishigaku. Meijiki no ishinshi kenkyū o tegakari to shite', in *Gendai shigaku nyūmon*, ed. Nishikawa Masao and Kotani Hiroyuki (Tōkyō daigaku shuppankai, 1987): 92–123 (p. 94). Ōkubo Toshiaki, *Nihon kindai shigaku no seiritsu* (*Ōkubo Toshiaki rekishi chosakushū* 7) (Yoshikawa kōbunkan, 1988): 249. Kuwabara 1979: 2: 2.

17. On the general historical situation, see Beasley (1982).

18. Miyachi 1987: 95.

19. Meiji 8; *Shiryō hensan shimatsu* in the Historiographical Institute (23 vols; 0171.19), vol 3 (hereafter quoted as *Shimatsu*).

20. *Hōki bunrui taizen, Dai 1 hen, Kanshokumon 3 (Kansei, Dajōkan/Naikaku 2)*, p. 341; as a commentary, part of *Shūshi jigi* is quoted.

21. *Shimatsu* 4; *Shimatsu* 5: Meiji 10.1.19 and Meiji 12.4.24.

22. Letters 21 October 1877, 28 June 1877, memorandum 29 January 1877; archives of the Imperial Household (*Shoryōbu*), *Sankō shiryō zatsusan* 111, 114; 112. Ijichi Masaharu also suggested possible candidates for appointment to the College. The problems of the College are also illustrated in comments enclosed with one of the regular reports in 1879 (*Henshū kōkahyō fukei*, Meiji 12.7, papers of Shigeno Yasutsugu in the Historiographical Institute).

23. Letters from Ogō to Iwakura 12 May 1875, 31 May 1875; printed in Ōtsuka Takematsu, *Iwakura Tomomi monjo* (Nihon shiseki kyōkai, 1931) 6: 325–27; 4 May (year not given; between 1875 and 1877) in the archives of the Imperial Household (Mei 426 *Sankō shiryō zatsusan* 105); in this letter Ogō mentions that Shigeno often turned to Ōkubo Toshimichi for support, and Nagamatsu to Kido Kōin.

24. Albert M. Craig, 'The Central Government', in *Japan in Transition: From Tokugawa to Meiji*, eds Marius B. Jansen and Gilbert Rozman (Princeton, N.J.: Princeton University Press, 1986): 37–67. Carol Gluck, *Japan's Modern Myths: Ideology in the Late Meiji Period* (Princeton, N.J.: Princeton University Press, 1985): 52–3; 239.

25. Richard Rubinger, 'Education: From One Room to One System', in *Japan in Transition*, eds Marius B. Jansen and Gilbert Rozman (Princeton: Princeton University Press 1986): 195–230; George B. Sansom, *The Western World and Japan: A Study in the Interaction of European and Asiatic Cultures* (Tuttle, 1977; first published in 1950): 449–50.

26. *Bo gakushi shiseki henshū ron: Shūshikan kaikaku no gi*, Papers of Sanjō Sanetomi in the National Diet Library (shorui 55/21). For a detailed discussion of the memorandum see Chapter 4.3.

27. *Hōki bunrui taizen, Dai 1 hen, Kanshokumon 3 (Kansei, Dajōkan/Naikaku 2)*, p. 350.

28. *Shigaku kyōkai zasshi* 1: 1–8. Ōkubo 1988: 51-2; 203. See also Chapter 4.3.

29. On Iwakura's attempt to publish a history of Japan: Akimoto Nobuhide, 'Taisei kiyō no kenkyū', in *Shintōgaku* 64: 32–51; 65: 39–58; 66: 43–51; 67: 41–61; 68: 37–43.1970/1. See also Ōkubo 1988: 291–329.

30. The transcriptions of Stein's lectures (in Japanese) are published in: Shimizu Shin, *Meiji kenpō seiteishi 1: Doku-Ō ni okeru Itō Hirobumi no kenpō chōsa* (*Meiji hyakunenshi sōsho 165*) (Hara shobō, 1971), 1: 353–445. See also Inada Masatsugu, *Meiji kenpō seiritsu shi*, 2 vols (Yūhaikaku, 1960–2; repr. 1987). On Lorenz von Stein see Dirk Blasius, 'Lorenz von Stein', in *Deutsche Historiker I*, ed. Hans-Ulrich Wehler (Göttingen: Vandenhoeck & Ruprecht, 1971): 25–38. Excerpts from Itō's letters to Iwakura about von Stein in Inada 1987: 1: 583–97) and Shimizu 1971.

31. Shimizu 1971: 388; 440–1. Japanese translation of Stein's letter to Itō in: *Shunpokō tsuishōkai* (ed.), *Itō Hirobumi den*, 3 vols. (*Meiji hyakunenshi sōsho 144*) (Hara shobō, 1970; first printed 1940): 323–31.

32. Inada 1987: 2: 948–56.

33. Memorandum addressed to Sanjō Sanetomi dated Meiji 13.12 in the Papers of Iwakura Tomomi (National Diet Library), Dai 6 rui 24; Microfilm reel 7 (also in the Imperial Household Archives: *Sankō shiryō zatsusan* Mei 426; 116). Memorandum addressed to Itō Hirobumi dated Meiji 15.3.4 in the papers of Motoda Eifu (National Diet Library), *Itō sangikō hōchoku no Ōshū e okuru tsuide* 109–15.

34. On Fukuba' s memorandum on history, see Ōkubo 1988: 307.

35. That is, not in *kanbun*. See Ōkubo 1988: 309–10; see Chapter 4.3.

36. Miyachi 1987: 101–2.

37. Ōkubo 1987: 316–18; Miyachi 1987: 101–2. Tanaka Akira, *Meiji ishinkan no kenkyū* (Sapporo: Hokkaidō daigaku tosho kankōkai, 1987): 79–80.

38. Haraguchi Kiyoshi, 'Meiji kenpō taisei no seiritsu', *Iwanami kōza Nihon rekishi* (Iwanami shoten, 1976): 15: 135–75 (153); Asakura 1969: 498.

39. Tōkyō daigaku hyakunenshi henshū iinkai (ed.), *Tōkyō daigaku hyakunenshi, Shiryō 1* (Tōkyō daigaku, 1984): 157–9.

40. The memorandum is quoted in Tōkyō teikoku daigaku (ed.), *Tōkyō teikoku daigaku gojū nenshi*, 2 vols (Tōkyō teikoku daigaku, 1932): 1: 1296–9. Also (including the cabinet order and the attachments concerning the budget) in *Tōkyō daigaku, Shiryō 1*, 1984: 157–8.

41. Gluck 1985: 25.

42. The lecture and most of Shigeno's other publications are reprinted in Satsumashi kenkyūkai/Ōkubo Toshiaki (eds), *Zōtei Shigeno hakushi shigaku ronbunshū*, 4 vols (Meicho fukyūkai, 1989; vols 1–3 first published 1938–9), 1989: 1: 186–292.

43. *Bun* 2.6 (1889): 337–43; Shigeno also gave a lecture with almost the same content at the Academy of Science (*Tōkyō gakushi kaiin*); Satsumashi kenkyūkai/Ōkubo Toshiaki 1989: 1: 479–92.

44. Ishikawa Shōtarō (ed.), 'Mikami Sanji sensei dankyūkai sokkiroku', *Nihon rekishi* Nos 390–6, 398–402, 404, 406–11 (1980–2); 401: 86–7.

45. *Shimatsu* 10.

3 The Activities of the Office of Historiography

1. Kuwabara Nobusuke, 'Kindai seiji shiryō shūshū no ayumi', Sankō shoshi kenkyū 17 (1979): 1: 3; Tōkyō daigaku hyakunenshi henshū iinkai (ed.), *Tōkyō daigaku hyakunenshi, Bukyokushi* 4 (Tōkyō daigaku, 1987): 546.
2. *Dajō ruiten* 2/14; 405: 145.
3. Biographical information from *Meiji ishin jinmei jiten* (Yoshikawa kōbunkan, 1981); *Konsaisu jinmei jiten* (Sanseidō, 1976); *Nihon jinmei daijiten* (Heibonsha, 1937) (Yotsuya); *Meiji kakochō* (Tōkyō bijutsu, 1935, 1971) (Hirose).
4. See map in Kodama Kōta, *Hyōjun Nihonshi chizu. Shinshūhan* (Yoshikawa kōbunkan, 1984): 44.
5. Kuwabara 1979: 1: 5.
6. Iwai Tadakuma, 'Shigeno Yasutsugu', Nagahara Keiji/Kano Masanao (ed.), *Nihon no Rekishika* (Nihon hyōronsha, 1976): 3–10.
7. Harada Fumio, 'Shigeno Yasutsugu hakushi no shikan ni tsuite', *Shigaku zasshi* 53 (1942): 801; Ōkubo Toshiaki *Nihon kindai shigaku no seiritsu* (*Ōkubo Toshiaki rekishi chosakushū* 7; Yoshikawa kōbunkan, 1988): 221–33.
8. Yoda Gakkai (ed. Gakkai nichiroku kenkyūkai), *Gakkai nichiroku*, 12 vols (Iwanami, 1991–3): 4: 7–9; 191; 274–5; 304; 309–10; 5: 86–90; 101–3; 143–4. See also Sakaguchi Chikubo, 'Yoda Bikyōko no 'Shigeno seisai ni kansuru jikō' (Gakkai nichiroku yori shōshutsu)', *Gakkai nichiroku: Geppō* 2: 1–4 (Iwanami, 1991).
9. *Kokuji ōshō* 1: 280. Fujino wrote an autobiography in *kanbun*, edited by Shigeno together with other papers; *Kainan shuki* (Fujino Susumu, 1891).
10. Obituary by Shigeno, quoted in Uno Tetsujin (ed.), *Kangakusha denki shūsei* (Seki shoin, 1928): 1230.
11. Meiji 8; *Hōki bunrui taizen, Dai 1 hen, Kanshokumon 3* (*Kansei, Dajōkan/Naikaku* 2), p.341–2 (Tokyo: Naikaku kiroku kyoku, 1891–94).
12. *Shimatsu* 8. Some letters by Ijichi Masaharu concerning personnel for the Office are preserved in the Imperial Household Archives (*Shoryōbu*). See also the diary of Miyajima Seiichirō, Meiji 11.5.13 (see following note 14).
13. Both *shūsen* and *henshūkan* mean 'editor'; the expressions originated in Ming China, where *henshūkan* was one rank below *shūsen*.
14. Biographical information on Miyajima from the introduction by Kajita Akihiro to the catalogue of his papers in the possession of his descendants (MS 1985). The catalogue was compiled by a group of students and researchers from Tokyo University. Nishikawa Makoto kindly lent me a copy of the diary transcribed in part by members of the group. On the diary: Ōkubo Toshiaki, 'Miyajima Seiichirō to sono nikki (1)' (the article was not continued), *Nihon rekishi* 300 (1973): 190–4. Some of Miyajima's papers are in the archives in the National Diet Library. Miyajima's dissertation on the beginnings of compilation of the Meiji Constitution (*Kokken hensan kigen*) is printed in *Meiji bunka zenshū* (vol. 4), ed. Yoshino Sakuzō *et al.* (Nihon hyōronsha, 1928): 343–60. See also Ōkubo Toshiaki, 'Naimushō kikō kettei no keii', in Daikakai naikakushi hensan iinkai (ed.), *Naimushō shi*. (Daikakai, 1971): 3: 897–996.
15. *Meiji kakochō* 1193; *Ehime kenshi jinbutsu* 589. Mirura's relationship with Shigeno and Fujino and his role in the Office of Historiography: Kume Kunitake, 'Yo ga mitaru Shigeno hakushi', *Rekishi chiri* 17.3 (1912): 274–306 (280, 283).

16. *Nihon jinmei daijiten* 1: 399.
17. *Shūshikan kōkahyō* in the National Archives: Meiji 9 (1876) to Meiji 18 (1885), 2A 35-3 ki 922; Meiji 19 (1886) to Meiji 21 (1888), 2A 35-3 ki 923. Also in *Shimatsu* in the Historiographical Institute. The reports include the names and ranks of the officials.
18. Kume 1912: 485.
19. *Gakkai nichiroku*; comment on the reorganization, 25 May 1882 (5: 143–4).
20. Akimoto Nobuhide, 'Kawada Takeshi no shūshi jigyō to shiron', *Kokugakuin joshi tanki daigaku kiyō* 2 (1984): 95.
21. Warren Smith, *Confucianism in Modern Japan: A Study of Conservatism in Japanese Intellectual History* (The Hokuseido Press, 1959): 54.
22. Akimoto 1984: 45-6.
23. *Seijika shitsu no gakusha*, p.304; 294. *shikan*; Ōkubo 1988: 243–4.
24. Kume 1912: 281, 286, 288; 290.
25. The copyists are named in the reports. In *Shimatsu* 6 an examination of candidates is mentioned (Meiji 10.12). One copyist was Suzumura Yuzuru (1854–1930), a Confucian scholar from Uwajima, who was employed from 1885 to 1886. Documents concerning his employment and correspondence with Shigeno Yasutsugu are in the papers of the Suzumura family in Uwajima City Library. The local historian Miyoshi Masafumi kindly drew my attention to these papers. Another copyist was Tanaka Yoshinari, who later became editor and professor at the Imperial University. On his employment as a copyist see Akimoto Nobuhide, 'Tanaka Yoshinari hakushi no shajisei nin'yō', *Nihon rekishi* 437 (1984): 45–6.
26. *Shimatsu* 9, Meiji 14.12.26.
27. On Hoshino: *Shigaku zasshi* 28: 86; *Rekishi chiri* 30/4: 52–4; Ichijima Shunjo, 'Hōjō Hoshino Hisashi sensei', *Kōshiro* 3/9 (1937).
28. Ichijima 1937: 5.
29. Iwai Tadakuma, 'Kume Kunitake', in *Nihon no rekishika*, eds Nagahara Keiji/Kano Masanao (Nihon hyōronsha, 1976): 11–18; Ōkubo Toshiaki, *Kume Kunitake no kenkyū* (Yoshikawa kōbunkan, 1991); see also Chapter 6.4.
30. On Ijichi Sadaka: Shidankai (ed.), *Shidankai sokkiroku,dai* 187 *shū* 1906: 86.
31. The principality became Okinawa prefecture in 1879; the conflict with China over the possession of the islands was not resolved.
32. The papers of Date Munenari are in the archives in the House of Date in Uwajima administered by the *Date bunka hozon kai*. Some of them have been investigated by the Historiographical Institute and photographs of some of the material (e.g. the journal he kept as vice president, *Shūshikan bibō*) are kept there. Part of the collections is described in: Fukuji Jin, 'Shiryō Shōkai: Date Munenari nikki oyobi shiki "gijin tansho yori hitsugi tome"', *Nenpō kindai Nihon kenkyū 3: Bakumatsu ishin no Nihon* (Yamakawa, 1981): 301–9. On the appointments held by Munenari: *Hyakkan rireki* 2: 459–65. The last entry given is for 1881, and his appointment as vice president to the College of Historiography is not mentioned.
33. *Shimatsu* 12; Meiji 17.
34. *Kokuji ōshō* 2: 100–1.
35. The memorandum is in *Shimatsu* 12, the two letters are preserved in the archives of the House of Date in Uwajima. For a discussion of the letter from Iwaya and Shigeno

to Sanjō and the two letters to Date, see Margaret Mehl, 'Shūshikan fukusōsai Date Munenari ate fukuchō Shigeno Yasutsugu shokan nitsū', *Nihon rekishi* 507 (1990): 88–92.

36. *Shimatsu* 14; Meiji 19.
37. Ludwig Rieß uses the term Historiographical Institute in his articles on Japanese history (Chapter 5.3) and it is still the official English name for the Institute today, although not only the Japanese name has changed but also the function of the Institute: see Chapter 6.5.
38. *Shimatsu* 16; see Chapters 6.5 and 7.1.
39. 'Shigaku ni tsuite', *Shigaku zasshi* 5/1 (1894); Saitō Takashi, *Shōwa shigakushi nōto: rekishigaku no hassō* (Shōgakukan, 1984): 19–20.
40. 'Rekishigaku no katsugan', *Shigaku zasshi* 6 (1895): 535–727; 623–34.
41. Miyachi, Masato, 'Seiji to rekishigaku. Meijiki no ishinshi kenkyū o tegakari to shite', *Gendai shigaku nyūmon*, eds Nishikawa Masao and Kotani Hiroyuki (Tōkyō daigaku shuppankai, 1987): 92–123 (93).
42. Miyachi 1987: 93–6.
43. Nitta Yūji (ed.), *Maikurofuirumu han Fuken shiryō. Kaisetsu. Saimoku* (Yūshōdō fuirumu shuppan yūgen kaisha, 1962): 7.
44. Miyachi 1987: 94; *Shimatsu* 1, Meiji 5.11.19.
45. *Shimatsu* 1, Meiji 6.8; see Chapter 4.2.
46. *Shimatsu* 2, Meiji 7.2.
47. *Shimatsu* 4.
48. *Shimatsu* 7, Meiji 11.6.
49. Seven: Satsuma, Chōshū, Tosa, Aki, Owari, Echizen, Uwajima. Eight: Satsuma, Chōshū, Tosa, Aki, Owari, Echizen, Tottori, Bitchū. Documents in *Shimatsu* 7. Whereas most discussions in the Office seem to have been about facts, this one was a question of judgement. According to the reports submitted twice a year, work on the histories of the domains was carried out between 1876 and 1878.
50. A printed catalogue of books in the Cabinet Library was published in 1961.
51. Nitta 1962.
52. Nitta 1962: 8.
53. *Shimatsu* 1, Meiji 6.9.10 and Meiji 6.9.19; letter from the Ministry of Education and answering letter from the Department of History. The details of the correspondence between the Council of State and the Ministry of Education are not entirely clear: apparently not all the relevant documents are preserved in *Shimatsu*. The Council of State, to which the Department of History belonged, apparently acted as intermediary.
54. *Shūshi jigi* (Chapter 4.2). On *Kinsei shiryaku*: Ōkubo 1988: 283–7; 290. The translation was published as *Kinsé shiriaku: A history of Japan from the first visit of Commodore Perry in 1853 to the capture of Hakodate by the Mikado's forces in 1869.* Translation from the Japanese by E.M. Satow. Yokohama: Printed at Japan Mail Office, 1873. (Data from the online catalogue of the National Diet Library).
55. *Shimatsu* 1, Meiji 6.6.23.
56. *Shimatsu* 1, Meiji 6.6.23. Ironically Iida Tadahiko was imprisoned for his criticism of bakufu politics in 1834, and in 1860 was arrested in connection with the assassination of Ii Naosuke; see Yamamoto Takeo in *Kokushi daijiten* 1: 414–15. The

Dainihon yashi was printed in 30 volumes in 1905–6. See Hans Dettmer, *Einführung in das Studium der japanischen Geschichte* (Darmstadt: Wissenschaftliche Buchgesellschaft, 1987): 41.

57. *Shimatsu* 2 (Meiji.7.4.10); 10 (Meiji 14). See Chapter 5.1.
58. *Shimatsu* 4; Meiji 10.1.16.
59. *Shimatsu* 8, Meiji 12.3.19.
60. For the significance of the fourteenth century and the schism of the imperial house see Chapters 6.3, 6.6.
61. *Shimatsu* 12; answer from the Office of Historiography 22 February 1884.
62. *Shimatsu* 11.
63. *Shimatsu* 12. The conflicts in question are treated in detail in the history of Ehime prefecture: Ehime kenshi hensan iinkai (ed.), *Ehime kenshi*, vol. 2 (Matsuyama: Ehime-ken, 1984).
64. Papers of Sanjō Sanetomi, *Shorui* 54/6 and *Shimatsu* 10; on Kojima Takanori see Chapter 6.3.
65. *Shimatsu* 6; 7; 9.
66. *Shimatsu* 9; Meiji 14.7.28; see Akimoto Nobuhide 'Kume Kunitake *Tōkai tōsan junkō nikki* no jinja wo meguru shohō', *Nihon kindai shisō taikei 13, Rekishi ninshiki*, eds Miyachi Masato and Tanaka Akira (Iwanami, 1991): Furoku (geppō 21).
67. *Nihon chishi teiyō; Nihon zenchizu; Shimatsu* 4.
68. *Shimatsu* 6.
69. On history education in the Tokugawa period: Ōkubo 1988: 376–405.
70. Richard Rubinger, 'Education: From One Room to One System', in *Japan in Transition*, eds Marius B. Jansen and Gilbert Rozman (Princeton: Princeton University Press 1986). On textbooks: Kokuritsu kyōiku kenkyūjo (ed.), *Nihon kindai kyōiku hyakunenshi* (Bunshōdō, 1974): 4: 877–905.
71. Kaigo Tokiomi, *Nihon kyōkasho taikei. Kindaihen*, vols 18–20 (Kōdansha, 1963): 18: 722–3.
72. *Shimatsu* 2; Meiji 7.4.10.
73. *Shimatsu* 17; Meiji 24; Kaigo 1963: 504.
74. *Shimatsu* 15; on Suematsu, see Chapter 4.4.
75. 'Kyōiku rekishi', 1888; 'Rekishi to kyōiku', 1890; in Satsumashi kenkyūkai/Ōkubo Toshiaki, eds. *Zōtei Shigeno hakushi shigaku ronbunshū* (Meicho fukyūkai, 1989): 1: 61-5); 49–61.
76. Kaigo 1963: 582.
77. Horio Teruhisa (ed. and transl. Steven Platzer), *Educational Thought and Ideology in Modern Japan: State Authority and Intellectual Freedom* (Tokyo University Press, 1988): 100–1.
78. Ishikawa Shōtarō (ed.), 'Mikami Sanji sensei dankyūkai sokukiroku', *Nihon rekishi* 390–6, 398–402, 404, 406–11 (1980-2): 400: 82 (hereafter cited as Mikami).
79. The two cannot always be distinguished, because the collections of sources usually arranged their material in chronological order with comments, and the histories were often not much more than chronicles with extensive quotations from the sources. Useful hints on such compilations can be found in: Dettmer (1987) and John Whitney Hall, *Japanese History: A Guide to Japanese Reference and Research Materials* (Ann

Arbor: University of Michigan Press, 1954; repr. Greenwood Press, 1976). See also Sakamoto Tarō, *Nihon no shūshi to shigaku* (Shibundō, 1966): 147–244.

80. Tanaka Masahiro, *'Tsūshin zenran* hensan no keii – gaikokukata kara gaimushō e', *Kokugakuin daigaku Tochigi tanki daigaku kiyō* 211 (1987): 1–32 and 'Tokugawa bakufu gaikokukata to gaikō monjo seibi mondai – Nihon gaikō monjo hensan no keifu', *Tochigi shigaku* 1 (1987): 111–47.

81. Ishiwata Takayuki, 'Dajōkan, naikaku monjo', *Nihon komomjogaku kōza*,11 vols (Yūzankaku, 1980): 10: 33–47.

82. A list of these publications can be found in Sakamoto 1966: 243.

83. Akimoto Nobuhide: 'Chūkō jitsuroku henshūkyoku no kōsō', *Kokugakuin daigaku Nihon bunka kenkyūjohō* 13.4 (1976): 11–13.

84. Ōkubo 1988: 354–65

85. Ōkubo 1988: 365–75.

86. Sakamoto 1966: 244; Hall 1954: 52.

87. On the *Bōchō kaitenshi:* Tanaka Akira, *Meiji ishinkan no kenkyū* (Sapporo: Hokkaidō daigaku tosho kankōkai, 1987): 196–219. Tanaka also edited and introduced the revised version in one volume, *Shūtei Bōchō kaitenshi* (Kashiwa shobō, 1980).

88. No. 33, February 1893; for compilations of literature see Michael C. Brownstein, 'From Kokugaku to Kokubungaku: Canon-Formation in the Meiji-Period', *Harvard Journal of Asiatic Studies* 47/2 (1987): 435–60.

89. Carol Gluck, *Japan's Modern Myths* (Princeton: Princeton University Press, 1985): 24.

4 The Form of Official Historiography

1. *Shūshi jigi*, papers of Shigeno Yasutsugu in the Historiographical Institute.

2. *Dajōkan* (ed.) *Fukkoki* (Naigai shoseki; Tōkyō teikoku daigaku zōhan, 1830). Nagamatsu's memorandum is quoted in the preface (3–5).

3. On the *Fukkoki:* Ōkubo Toshiaki, *Nihon kindai shigaku no seiritsu* (Yoshikawa kōbunkan, 1988): 278, 289. Based on the original sources: Miyachi Masato, *'Fukkoki* genshiryō no kisoteki kenkyū', *Tōkyō daigaku shiryō hensanjo kenkyū kiyō* 1 (1990): 66–139.

4. Miyachi Masato, 'Seiji to rekishigaku. Meijiki no ishinshi kenkyū o tegakari to shite', in *Gendai shigaku nyūmon*, eds Nishikawa Masao and Kotani Hiroyuki (Tōkyō daigaku shuppankai, 1987): 92–123 (93); Tanaka Akira, *Meiji ishinkan no kenkyū* (Sapporo: Hokkaidō daigaku tosho kankōkai, 1987): 73.

5. Ōkubo 1988: 278; 351–2.

6. Ōkubo 1988: 278–9; 328–9; Tōkyō daigaku hyakunenshi iinkai, ed. *Tōkyō daigaku hyakunenshi. Bukyokushi* 4 (Tōkyō daigaku, 1987): 611.

7. *Shimatsu* 4, Meiji 10.1.

8. *Shimatsu* 6; Meiji 10.

9. *Shimatsu* 7; the rules were confirmed by the government on 4 April 1878.

10. The translation by the Translation Office in 1879 has been published with comments by the editor: Yasuoka Akio (ed.), *Satsuma hanranki* (*Tōyō bunko* 350; Heibonsha, 1979).

11. *Hōki bunrui taizen, Dai 1 hen, Kanshokumon 3 (Kansei, Dajōkan/Naikaku* 2) (Tōkyō naikaku kiroku kyoku, 1891): 359 (1873).
12. *Shimatsu* 1: *Rekishi henshū reisoku; Dajōkan* order no. 147 in *Hōrei zensho* (Ōkurasho insatsu kyoku, (1889): 7/1: 363–66.
13. *Shimatsu* 3.
14. Ulrich Goch, *Abriß der japanischen Geschichtsschreibung* (Munich: iudicium, 1992): 47–9, 116.
15. Summary; *Shimatsu* 3. According to the accompanying letter the document was submitted to Sanjō Sanetomi on 13 September 1875 together with details of the division of tasks. The content was accepted and passed as a decree: *Dajō ruiten* 2/14/54; Book 405: 145; excerpt in *Hōki bunrui taizen, Dai 1 hen, Kanshokumon 3 (Kansei, Dajōkan/Naikaku* 2): 342-3.
16. Papers of Sanjō Sanetomi, *shorui* 55/21.
17. That is, *hennentai* or *kidentai*; see Chapter 1.
18. Richard Bowring, 'Language', *Cambridge Encyclopedia of Japan* (Cambridge: CUP, 1993): 116–21.
19. Nanette Twine, *Language and the Modern State: The Reform of Written Japanese* (London, New York: Routledge, 1991).
20. Yaeko Sato Habein, *The History of the Japanese Written Language* (Tokyo University Press, 1984): 77–9. Donald Keene, *Dawn to the West: Japanese Literature of the Modern Era* (New York: Henry Holt and Company, 1987): 40. Robert N. Bellah, *Tokugawa Religion: The Values of Pre-Industrial Japan* (Glencoe, Illinois: The Tree Press, 1957): 122–3.
21. *Shūshi buntai ron*, papers of Sanjō Sanetomi, *shorui* 55/23 or in the Historiographical Institute (4170.68). There is another copy in the Kume papers at the Kume Art Museum.
22. Twine 1991: 36.
23. Biography of Suematsu with list of his works and reference materials in Shōwa joshi daigaku kindai bungaku kenkyūshitsu (ed.) *Kindai bungaku kenkyū sōsho* 20 (Shōwa joshi daigaku, 1963); Tamae Hikotarō, *Seibyō Suematsu Kenchō no shōgai* (Fukuoka: Ishobō yūgenkai, 1985); Kaneko Atsuo, *Suematsu Kenchō to 'Bōchō kaitenshi'* (Kumamoto: Shinchō shakan, 1980).
24. 7 February 1878 (Meiji 11); *Shimatsu* 7.
25. *Ōkubo Toshimichi monjo* (Nihon shiseki kyōkai, 1929): 9: 13–14; Nakai's letter from the papers of Shigeno Yasutsugu has recently been published in Miyachi Masato, Tanaka Akira (ed.), *Rekishi ninshiki* (Iwanami shoten, 1991): 307–8.
26. *Shimatsu* 7.
27. Tamae Hikotarō, *Seibyō Suematsu Kenchō no shōgai* (Fukuoka: Ishobō yūgenkai, 1985); *Wakaki hi no Suematsu Kenchō* (Fukuoka: Kaichōsha, 1992). The latter quotes long passages from Suematsu's letters to his family, which are now in the National Diet Library. Suematsu's letters to Itō are printed in Itō Hirobumi kankei monjo kenkyūkai (ed.), *Itō Hirobumi kankei monjo* (9 vols, Hanawa shobō 1973–7), vol. 5. Details of Suematsu's years in England in Margaret Mehl, 'Suematsu Kenchō in Britain, 1878–1886', *Japan Forum* 5.2 (1993): 173–93.

28. *Shimatsu* 7; especially the *Shūshikan*'s report dated 25 May 1879 and Suematsu's letters to Shigeno and Miura, January 1880. The English original of *Shiyō monmoku* is not among the documents preserved in *Shimatsu*.

29. On Zerffi, *Dictionary of National Biography* 21: 1323–4; obituary in *The Times* 30 January 1892 (p.7/3); Frank Tibor, 'Zerffi Gusztáv György a történetíró', *Századok* 117 (1978): 497–592, Japanese translation by Nishizawa Ryūsei in *Rekishi jinrui* 8 (1980): 33–83. Frank Tibor has also published a detailed biography: *Egy emigráns alakváltásai: Zerffi Gusztáv pályaképe 1820–1892* (Budapest: Akadémiai Kiadó, 1985) (*The Metamorphoses of an Emigrant: The Career of G.G. Zerffi*; table of contents in English).

30. *Dictionary of National Biography* 1909: 21: 1323–4. Zerffi's popularity as a lecturer is mentioned in the obituary in *The Times*, and in *Transactions of the Royal Historical Society* 9 (1881) a series of lectures by Zerffi is mentioned, which was well attended with about 190 visitors per lecture.

31. *Transactions of the Royal Historical Society* 7 (1878): 334.

32. Carr, Edward Hallett, *What Is History?* (2nd edn by R.W. Davies; London: Penguin 1987, repr. 1988): 61.

33. Zerffi, George Gustav, *The Science of History* (London: W.H. and L. Collingridge, 1879): 4.

34. *Transactions of the Royal Historical Society* 3 (1875).

35. 'Seiyō shigaku no honpō shigaku ni ataeta eikyō', Shigakkai (ed.) *Honpō shigakushi ronsō*, vol. 1 (Fuzanbō, 1939): 1439–69. See also Kanai Madoka, 'Rekishigaku – Rūtouihi Riisu o megutte -', in *Oyatoi gaikokujin* 17, *Jinbun kagaku* (Kashima shuppan, 1976): 108–201.

36. *Itō Hirobumi kankei monjo* 5: 374; the date, Meiji 15 (1882), added by the editors is not correct. This is not only evident from the mention of Zerffi's book; the Zulu War, the death of Napoleon III's son (Eugene Louis died in South Africa) and of Suematsu's own father point to 1879.

37. *Transactions of the Royal Historical Society*, vols 3 and 6–8.

38. Zerffi's Eurocentrism is pointed out by Arnaldo Momigliano: 'Da G.G. Zerffi a Ssuma Ch'ien', *Rivista Storica Italiana* 67 (1964): 1058–69; his statement that Japanese scholars had hardly attempted a critical analysis of Zerffi's book still holds.

39. The translation was never published; the manuscript is in the Historiographical Institute (4140.0/1). Another copy of the translation by Nakamura is in the papers of Iwakura Tomomi (No. 435, materials of the *Shidankai*) in the National Diet Library; see Ōkubo 1988: 322–9 on this copy.

40. *Shimatsu* 7; *Itō Hirobumi kankei monjo* 5: 352–71; 10 June 1879; 27 November 1879; May 1882.

41. Ōkubo 1988: 328–9.

42. Numata Jirō, 'Meiji shōki ni okeru seiyō shigaku no yunyū ni tsuite – Shigeno Yasutsugu to G.G. Zerffi', in *Kokumin seikatsushi kenkyū*, vol. 3, ed. Itō Tasaburō (Yoshikawa kōbunkan, 1958): 401–29 (419-20). The final version was produced in 1888.

43. Ōkubo 1988: 322–9.

44. Ozawa Eiichi, *Kindai Nihon shigakushi no kenkyū. Meiji hen* (Yoshikawa kōbunkan, 1968): 380–91.

45. On his historical writings while in England: Mehl 1993.
46. Kaneko Atsuo, *Suematsu Kenchō to 'Bōchō kaitenshi'* (Kumamoto, Shinchō shakan, 1980); Tanaka Akira 1987: 196–219; see also Tanaka's introduction to the one-volume edition of the *Bōchō kaitenshi* (Kashiwa shobō, 1980).
47. Kume Kunitake, 'Yo ga mitaru Shigeno Hakushi', *Rekishi chiri* 17.3 (1912): 274–306 (290).
48. There are two versions of an untitled document concerning the compilation of sources, one in Shigeno's papers and one in *Shiryō hensan shimatsu*. Both are dated 28 December 1881. They differ in the period to be covered. The one in Shigeno's papers reads: from the year 1392 (Meitoku 3) in the reign of Emperor Gokomatsu, to the year 1867 (Keio 3.10) in the reign of the present emperor. The other version has: from the accession of Godaigo to the throne in 1318 (Gennō 1) to the Meiji Restoration, 1867 (Keiō 3.10). See Kume 1912: 290. The earliest manuscript of the *Dainihon hennenshi* (4140.1/20) shows how Kume constantly referred to the *Dainihonshi*; sections that represented corrections or additions to the *Dainihonshi* are written in red ink.
49. Papers of Shigeno, dated Meiji 12.7 (1879) and in *Shimatsu* 9 (Meiji 14/1881).
50. Papers of Shigeno Yasutsugu; *Shimatsu* 9, undated, and *Shimatsu* 8, dated Meiji 12.7. (1879).
51. Papers of Shigeno on paper of the Office of Historiography, dated Meiji 14 (1881).12.28, and *Shimatsu* 9 with some alterations.
52. Papers of Shigeno (without title) and *Shimatsu* 9 (1881).
53. Papers of Shigeno, Meiji 15 (1882).1 and *Shimatsu* 9, with the same date, but in Sino-Japanese.
54. *Shimatsu* 9; this paragraph is not in the version from Shigeno's papers.
55. *Shimatsu* 9; the kings of the Ryukyu Islands are not mentioned in Shigeno's version.
56. *Shimatsu* 9; papers of Shigeno.
57. Examples in Nakayama Jiichi, *Shigaku gairon* (Gakuyō, 1974): 20.
58. Naitō Torajirō, *Shina shigakushi* (Kōbundō, 1949): 642.
59. *Tenmonshi, chirishi, shajishi, shokukanshi, reigakushi, heishi, keihoshi, shokukashi, geibunshi, fūzokushi, kōgeishi, gaikōshi, shizokushi*. Document in Shigeno's papers about the work in the sub-departments; it includes guidelines for the contents of the treatises; *Shimatsu* 8.
60. Ōkubo 1988: 73.
61. Herschel Webb, 'What Is the Dai Nihon Shi?' *Journal of Asian Studies* 19 (1960): 142.
62. *Meiji ishin jinmei jiten*, 318.
63. Ōkubo 1988: 75–6.
64. This is mentioned in the document beginning *Kaku bu shiryō saishū no mokuhyō* mentioned above.

5 History as an Academic Discipine

1. 'Gakumon wa tsui ni kōshō ni ki su', reprinted in Satsumashi kenkyūkai/Ōkubo Toshiaki, eds. *Zōtei Shigeno hakushi shigaku ronbunshū,* 4 vols (Meicho fukyūkai, 1989): 1: 35–47.
2. Ōkubo Toshiaki, *Nihon kindai shigaku no seiritsu* (Yoshikawa kōbunkan, 1988): 75–80.

3. *Shimatsu* 2, Meiji 7.4.10 and *Shimatsu* 4.
4. Copies of Ogō's letters to Iwakura in *Shimatsu* 4; the originals are in the papers of Iwakura Tomomi in the National Diet Library: *Iwakura Monjo* 6: 276, *Ogō Kazutoshi kōtō iken*. Another memorandum by Ogō is in the papers of Sanjō Sanetomi: *Sanjōke Monjo. Shorui* 56/1. The papers of Ogō himself in the National Diet Library indude a memorandum on the two imperial courts in the fourteenth century: *Ogō Kazutoshi Monjo* 83/63. Some memoranda are printed in the biography of Ogō by Ogō Tadao (Osaka: Ōitaken Naoirigun kyōikukai, 1915).
5. For the discussion about Iitoyo-ao-no-himemiko see Akimoto Nobuhide, 'Meiji zenki no shūshi jigyō to Iitoyo-ao-no-himemiko sokui setsu', *Nihon rekishi* 420 (1983): 46–63.
6. Correspondence with the Office of Historiography in *Shimatsu* 10; see Akimoto 1983: 51–8.
7. Akimoto 1983: 59–61.
8. Ōkubo 1988: 74.
9. Ōkubo 1988: 76; 79.
10. *Kotei shiwa* (Historical talks in the restaurant by the lake); 5 fascicles, Meiji 15.1 to 17.3 and *Seikō shiwa* (Historical talks in the restaurant 'Seikō'); 3 fascicles, Meiji 17.4 to 18.6; Historiographical Institute 4140.1/40.
11. January and May 1882 (Meiji 15); April 1882; February 1884 (Meiji 17).
12. May 1882; April 1884.
13. *Seikō shiwa* 2.
14. "Rekishigaku no susumi", *Seikō shiwa* 3; printed in Miyachi Masato, Tanaka Akira (ed.), *Rekishi ninshiki* (Iwanami, 1991): 222–7. Kume later published an article with the same title and content in *Shigaku zasshi* 9.7 (1898).
15. 'Taiheiki wa shigaku ni eki nashi', *Shigaku zasshi* 2 (1891): 230–40, 279–92, 487–501, 562–78.
16. *Shimatsu* 4; the application for permission to travel to Yamato and Yamashiro was passed on to the Council of State by Vice President Ijichi Masaharu on 27 June 1876. Another copy of it is in the National Archives (2 A/33-5/tankōbon 235).
17. *Komonjo sōhō ikensho, Shimatsu* 12, 1884.
18. Shigeno 1989: 3: 522–40; Akimoto Nobuhide, 'Meiji jūhachinen jūichigatsu no Shūshikan sōsai Sanjō Sanetomi ate no shūshi ikensho', *Kokugakuin zasshi* 71.10 (1970): 57–62.
19. Printed in *Kume Kunitake rekishi chosakushū* 4 (Yoshikawa kōbunkan, 1989): 551–79.
20. Ulrich Goch, *Abriß der japanischen Geschichtsschreibung* (Munich: iudicium, 1992): 48–50.
21. On the history of the University of Tokyo: *Tōkyō teikoku daigaku gojūnenshi*, 2 vols, 1932; *Tōkyō teikoku daigaku gakujutsu taikan*, 2 vols, 1942; *Tōkyō daigaku hyakunenshi*, 10 vols, 1984–7 (all edited by the University).
22. The University was established in 1877 as Tokyo University; it became Tokyo Imperial University in 1897 when Kyoto Imperial University was established.
23. On what was taught: Ōkubo 1988: 117–20.
24. *Erwin Bälz: Das Leben eines deutschen Arztes im erwachenden Japan Tagebücher, Briefe, Berichte*, ed. Toku Bälz (Stuttgart: J. Engelhorns Nachf. Adolf Spemann, 1930).

25. The memorandum is printed in Tōkyō teikoku daigaku 1932: 1299–1302.
26. Ozawa Eiichi, *Kindai Nihon shigakushi no kenkyū. Meiji hen* (Yoshikawa kōbunkan, 1968): 331–4; 430–7.
27. *Shigakkai shōshi. Sōritsu gojūnen kinen* (Fuzanbō, 1939). See also *Shigakkai hyakunen shōshi 1889–1989*, ed. Shigakkai (Yamakawa shuppansha, 1989).
28. 'Shigaku ni jūji suru mono wa sono kokoro shikō shihei narazaru bekarazu', *Shigaku zasshi* 1 (1889): 1–4; reprinted in Satsumashi kenkyūkai/Ōkubo Toshiaki 1989: 1: 30–2.
29. Shigakkai 1939: 19.
30. Shigakkai 1939: 19-21; List of the principal members in Shigakkai 1989.
31. List of names in *Shigaku zasshi* 1: 70–1.
32. For literature on Rieß, see Takeuchi Hiroshi, *Rainichi seiyō jinmei jiten* (Dainihon insatsu, 1983): 486–7. The most detailed biography is Kanai Madoka, 'Rekishigaku – Rūtoihi Riisu o megutte – ', *Oyatoi gaikokujin 17, Jinbun kagaku* (Kashima shuppan, 1976): 108–201. Kanai Madoka, together with Yoshimi Kaneko, also edited the memoirs of Rieß's daughter Katō Seiko, together with Rieß's letters to her (in Japanese translation from the English originals): *Waga chichi wa oyatoi gaikokujin* (Gōdō shuppan, 1978). In English: *Encyclopedia Judaica* (14: 166; Hyman Kublin). Most of Rieß's publications are in the main library of Tokyo University, which purchased them in 1957 from the papers of Felix Liebermann (1851–1925), historian and editor of English legal sources, who was a friend of Rieß.
33. *A Short Survey of Universal History: Being Notes of a Course of Lectures Delivered in the Literature College of the Imperial University of Tokyo*, 2 vols (Fuzanbō, 1899): 1: 6; article about Ranke in *Shigaku zasshi* 10.1 (1899).
34. Leipzig, 1885; translated by Kathleen Louise Wood-Legh as *The History of the English Electoral Law in the Middle Ages* (Cambridge, 1940).
35. Bernd Martin, 'Deutsche Geschichtswissenschaft als Instrument nationaler Selbstfindung in Japan', in *Universalgeschichte und Nationalgeschichten*, ed. Gangolf Hübinger, Jürgen Osterhammel and Erich Pelzer (Rombach Verlag 1994): 216.
36. Kanai 1976: 133, 134.
37. Martin 1994: 215–16.
38. On the history department in Berlin, see Christian Simon, *Staat und Geschichtswissenschaft in Deutschland und Frankreich 1871–1914: Situation und Werk von Geschichtsprofessoren an den Universitäten Berlin, München, Paris,* 2 vols (Bern, Frankfurt, New York, Paris: Verlag Peter Lang, 1988). Simon gives examples of historians whose careers were hindered because they were Jews.
39. Mori's letter to Inoue is in the archives of the Japanese Foreign Ministry (Meiji 16–22: *Zaigai teikoku kōshikan keiyū gaikoku jinkankō zakken* 3, 9.3.19: *Gaku* 381). Koike Seiichi from the archives kindly made the document available to me. Tōkyō teikoku daigaku 1942: 1: 314.
40. Kanai 1976: 151.
41. *Mitteilungen der Gesellschaft für Natur- und Völkerkunde Ostasiens* 9: 395. Details about the Japanese translations of his articles: Kanai Madoka, 'Rūtoihi Riisu to Nihon kankei kaigai shiryō', *Shigaku zasshi* 87.10 (1978): 43–53.

42. *Rekishi kyōiku* 15/16, 1960 (hereafter quoted as Segawa 1960). Mikami Sanji in *Nihon rekishi* No. 390–411.

43. Segawa 1960: 30; 31; 32.

44. OAG *Mitteilungen* 5 (1989–92): 213.

45. Rieß's other lectures were on the following subjects:
'History of the Island of Formosa' (1895).
'The Causes of the Expulsion of the Portuguese from Japan (1614–1639)' (1898)
'William Adams and his "Grave" in Hemimura' (1900).
At the Asiatic Society Rieß lectured on the 'History of the English Factory at Hirado (1613–22). With an introductory chapter on the Origin of English Enterprise in the Far East': OAG *Mitteilungen* 5 (1897): 405–47; 7 (1898–9): 1–52; 8 (1899–1902): 237. TASJ 36 (1898): 1–218.

46. On Shiratori, Hara, Uchida, Miura, Kuroita, Kita, Tsuji and Kōda see Kano Masanao and Nagahara Keiji (eds), *Nihon no rekishika* (Nihon hyōronsha, 1976).

47. Stefan Tanaka, *Japan's Orient* (Berkeley: University of California Press, 1993).

48. These reasons are given by Kanai 1976: 182–3.

49. Kanai 1976: 191–2.

50. *Shigaku zasshi* 30.

51. See also the criticism by Erwin Bälz of the treatment of foreign teachers (1930: 120–1). Bälz deplored the lack of courtesy towards Rieß at his farewell ceremony on 3 July 1902 (1930: 128–9).

52. Chapter 5.2; Ōkubo 1988: 56–8.

53. Rieß acknowledges Mikami's help in his article on the expulsion of the Portuguese (1898–9), where he mentions research done by 'my colleague Mikami' (31) and thanks him for his friendly advice (27).

54. Chapter 5.4; Mikami 401: 79.

55. On *akademizumu*,see Ōkubo 1988: 52–5; 62–93; Ozawa 1968: 331–48. See also Iwai Tadakuma. 'Nihon kindai shigaku no keisei', *Iwanami kōza Nihon rekishi*, vol. 22 (Iwanami shoten, 1968): 61–102; Kadowaki Teiji, 'Kangaku akademizumu no seiritsu', in Rekishigaku kenkyūkai/Nihonshi kenkyūkai (eds), *Nihon rekishi kōza*, vol. 8, (Tōkyō daigaku shuppankai, 1957): 163–86; Sakai Tadao, *Nihon shigakushi nōto* (Osaka: Ueda insatsu, 1962); Saitō Takashi, *Shōwa shigakushi nōto: rekishigaku no hassō* (Shōgakukan, 1984).

56. Quoted from Nagai Michio (tr. Jerry Dusenburry), *Higher Education in Japan: Its Take-off and Crash* (University of Tokyo Press, 1971): 21.

57. Tanaka 1993: 40–5.

58. 'Shigaku ni jūji suru mono wa sono kokoro shikō shihei narazaru bekarazu'; quoted from Satsumashi kenkyūkai/Ōkubo Toshiaki 1989: 1: 30–2.

59. 'Shigaku kōkyō rekishi hensan wa zairyō o seitaku subeki setsu', 1: 10–15.

60. 'Rekishi no ōyō', 14 (1991): 1–24.

61. 'Shigaku ni taisuru sehyō ni tsukite', *Shigaku zasshi* 38, 4 (1893): 97–116.

62. 'Rekishi tetsugaku no taiyō', 2: 6–9.

63. 'Nihon rekishi kyōjujō no iken', 4: 10–17.

64. 'Hakubutsugaku to rekishigaku', 4: 1–9.

65. *Shigakkai* 1939: 33–4 therefore rightly states that the Japanese scholars had already realized what Rieß was telling them.
66. Chapter 5.5; on Kume's lectures, see also Ōkubo 1988: 80–81; 86–8.
67. See also Ozawa 1968: 442–3.
68. See *Shimatsu* 16 and the following volumes.
69. See Carol Gluck, *Japan's Modern Myths* (Princeton: Princeton UP, 1985): 24.
70. News about the *Kyūji shimon kai* in *Shigaku zasshi*. The minutes are published in two volumes as Iwanami paperbacks (it seems that they still hold some attraction for a wide audience); Shinji Yoshimoto (ed.), *Kyūuji shimonkai* (Iwanami, 1986). In his introduction the programme of the committee is quoted in full.
71. Shinji 1986: 20.
72. On Rieß and the foreign sources relating to Japan, see Numata, 'Zaigai mikan Nihon kankei shiryō shūshi jigyō no enkaku ni tsuite', *Nihon rekishi* 186 (1963): 49–56 and Kanai 1978: 43–53. Part of the correspondence between the University, the Ministry of Foreign Affairs and the archive in Leiden (1888–9) is in the archives of Tokyo University: *Shokanchō ōfuku* Meiji 21/22, B7.
73. 7/6: 435–60.
74. On these and other histories, see Sakamoto Tarō, *Nihon no shūshi to shigaku* (Shibundō, 1966).
75. Helen Craig McCullough (transl.), *The Taiheiki: A Chronicle of Medieval Japan* (Tuttle, 1979; repr. 1987): xix.
76. 1993: 42.
77. Kadowaki 1957: 174.
78. Friedrich Jaeger and Jörn Rüsen (eds), *Geschichte des Historismus* (Munich: C.H. Beck, 1992): 66.
79. No 1.20 (October 1891): 12–13.
80. No. 35 (3 October 1893; bunkai genshō): 89–92.
81. Yamaji's article appeared in *Taiyō* in 1909.
82. Ōkubo 1988: 251–3; Akimoto 1984: 251.
83. 'Shigaku kōshō no hei', *Shigaku zasshi* 12 (1901): 905–32.
84. In *Shigaku zasshi* 23 (1912): 1030–49.
85. 'Genkon shigaku no konnan', No 192 (3 June 1893): 827–30.
86. 2.29 (1 March 1897; ihō): 109.
87. 'Shikai', 3.6 (April 1897): 93–5.
88. 'Kokushi ni okeru kagakuteki kenkyū', 3.7 (May 1893): 103–5. He also alleged that Kume's article on Shinto had not been sufficiently researched.
89. Ōkubo 1988: 58.

6 History and Ideology in Conflict
1. Carol Gluck, *Japan's Modern Myths* (Princeton: Princeton UP, 1985): 18, 25.
2. Kenneth Pyle, *The New Generation in Meiji Japan: Problems of Cultural Identity, 1885–1895* (Stanford: Stanford UP, 1969): 189.
3. Pyle 1969: 3–21; Gluck 1985: 17–26.
4. Yoshino Kosaku, *Cultural Nationalism in Contemporary Japan* (London: Routledge, 1992): 85.
5. Gluck 1985: 23.

6. Gluck 1985: 120–8.

7. *Kokumin no tomo* 100 (1890): 42–3; Gluck 1985: 125.

8. Yoshino 1992: 44–5.

9. *Rekishi no ryūkōnetsu* or *rekishinetsu*; 36 (January 1893): 11–14. See also, Margaret Mehl, 'The Mid-Meiji History Boom: Professionalization of Historical Scholarship and Growing Pains of an Emerging Academic Discipline', *Japan Forum*, 10.1 (1998): 67–83.

10. *Sekibaku no sugata*; 'Shikai no genjō', 49 (10 October 1893, bunkai genshō): 1–2.

11. 'Shiheki wa kaheki', *Shigaku zasshi* 2.

12. For a brief discussion of the articles in the first few issues of *Shigaku zasshi* see Margaret Mehl, *Eine Vergangenheit für die japanische Nation* (Frankfurt: Peter Lang, 1992): 171–4.

13. Ōkubo Toshiaki, 'Teiken Taguchi Ukichi to Shikai', in *Shikai goshū* (Meicho fukyūkai,1988): 30–1.

14. The *Tōkyō nichinichi shinbun* reported the establishment of the Office on 16 April 1875 and its replacement by the College of Historiography on 27 January 1877 giving details about the ranks and salaries of its officials: newspaper articles quoted from *Shinbun shūsei Meiji hennenshi*, 15 vols, ed. Meiji hennenshi hensankai (Zaisei keizai gakkai 1936).

15. *Tōkyō nichinichi shinbun*. Doctorates: Shigeno Yasutsugu and Konakamura Kiyonori on 7 May 1888, Kawada Takeshi and Kurokawa Mayori on 7 June 1888, Hoshino Hisashi and Tsuboi Kumezō on 24 August 1891 (*Shinbun shūsei Meiji hennenshi* 7: 66; 81; 8: 127). House of Peers: Miura Yasushi, Shigeno Yasutsugu, Konakamura Kiyonori, Kawada Takeshi on 1 October 1890 (*Shinbun shūsei Meiji hennenshi* 7: 23).

16. *Tōkyō nichinichi shinbun*, 13 March 1880; 23 January 1883. *Tōkyō akebono shinbun,* 7 June 1883.

17. *Tōkyō nichinichi shinbun* 10 March 1891.

18. A chronological list of the published lectures included in the collection of his works can be found in vol. 3 (pp.1–20 at the end of the volume).

19. 'Shiron'; quoted from *Meiji shisōshū*, ed. Matumoto Sannosuke (Chikuma shobō 1976): 282–4.

20. Quoted in Takao Tsurumaki (ed.), *Meiji kenpakusho shūsei*, vol. 6 (Chikuma shobō, 1987): 888–92. The original is in the papers of Sanjō Sanetomi. There is no addressee.

21. Akimoto Nobuhide, 'Okamatsu Ōkoku no seishi kan'yaku iken', *Kokugakuin zasshi* 71.5 (1970): 58–63. The original is in the papers of Iwakuara Tomomi (Iwakurakō kyūseki hozonkai) and Sanjō Sanetomi (55/19).

22. Akimoto 1970: 62.

23. Akimoto Nobuhide, 'Yano Gendō, Inoue Yorikuni no shūshi iken', *Kokugakuin daigaku Nihon bunka kenkyū johō* 17.5 (1988): 11–12. The original is in the papers of Sanjō Sanetomi.

24. *Bun* 3.2 (1890): 101–3.

25. *Bun* 4.10 (1891): 617–18.

26. *Bun* 4.12 (1891): 710–13; see Chapter 6.3.

27. For the discussion about the *Taiheiki*, see Chapter 6.3.

28. Byron K. Marshall, *Academic Freedom and the Japanese Imperial University, 1868–1939* (Berkeley: University of Califomia Press, 1992): 48–9.
29. Shigeno Yasutsugu. 1891. 'Gaijin naijū ron', in Satsumashi kenkyūkai/Ōkubo Toshiaki, eds., *'Zōtei Shigeno hakushi rekishi ronbunshū*, vol. l, (Meicho fukyūkai, 1989): 221–32. Preface to the first issue of *Kokugakuin zasshi*; Taguchi Ukichi, 'Sakanoue Tamuramaro', *Shikai 11: 1–25*. Hōsō Inshi, comment on Taguchi's article on Kanmu *tennō*, *Shikai 14: hihyō* 69. Konakamura Kiyonori, *Kokushi no shiori*, (Yoshikawa Hanshichi, 1895): 7. See also Gluck 1985: 36–137.
30. Taguchi Ukichi, *Iryūchi seido to naichi zakkyo* (Keizai zasshisha, 1892). Reprinted in: *Naichi zakkyōron shiryō shūsei* 3, ed. Inō Tentarō (Hara shobō, 1993; *Meiji hyakunenshi sōsho*): 15–55.
31. Gluck 1985: 132; see also Ide Magoroku, *Meiji minshūshi o aruku* (Shin jinbutsu ōraisha, 1980): 163 on Uchimura Kanzō.
32. Ōkubo Toshiaki speaks of 'Meijiteki riberarizumu' (Meiji liberalism); the state hardly intervened in intellectual discussions; *Nihon no rekishi no rekishi* (Shinchōsha, 1959): 48.
33. Marshall 1992.
34. 'Kyōiku to rekishi' (1890); Satsumashi kenkyūkai/Ōkubo Toshiaki 1989: 1: 53.
35. Biographies of Konakamura Kiyonori, Inoue Yorikuni, Kurita Hiroshi and Iida Takesato in *Kōten kōkyūjo sōritsuki no hitobito*, ed. Kokugakuin daigaku (Kokugakuin daigaku, 1982). On Kurita Hiroshi see also Teranuma Yoshibumi, *Kurita Hiroshi no kenkyū – sono shōgai to rekishigaku* (Kinseisha, 1974).
36. *Meiji ishin jinmei jiten* 1981: 5.
37. Tōkyō teikoku daigaku (ed.) *Gojūnenshi*, 2 vols. (Tōkyō teikoku daigaku, 1932) 1: 317–320. On Naito: Akimoto Nobuhide, 'Naitō Chisō no bakumatsu shiron', *Ishin zenki ni okeru kokugaku no shomondai*, ed. Kokugakuin daigaku Nihon bunka kenkyūjo (Kokugakuin daigaku, 1983): Bessatsu: 185–232 and 'Bakumatsu, Meiji shoki no Naitō Chisō', *Kokugakuin joshi tanki daigaku kiyō* 3 (1985): 29–80. Also in Kokugakuin daigaku 1982.
38. *Kokushi no shiori* (Yoshikawa Hanshichi, 1895): 2.
39. *Kokushi no shiori* (1895): 7; for the ideological discussion about the new freedom of residence for foreigners (*naichi zakkyo*) after the revision of the unequal treaties from 1894 onward, see Gluck 1985: 136–7.
40. Ōkubo Toshiaki, *Nihon kindai shigaku no seiritsu* (Yoshikawa kōbunkan, 1988): 51, 52.
41. Paul H. Varley, *Imperial Restoration in Medieval Japan* (New York, London: Columbia UP, 1971); Murata Masashi, *Zokuzoku Nanbokuchō shiron* (Shibunkaku, 1983).
42. Shigeno: 'Yojō ryūfu no shiden oku jijitsu o ayamaru no setsu' (On the statement that many of the commonly known historical accounts contain factual errors), lecture at the learned society *Tōkyō gakushi kaiin* 1884 (1989: 1: 9–19). Kan Masatomo: 'Taiheiki no byūbō irō ōki koto o benzu' (On the numerous errors and omissions in the *Taiheiki*), see *Shigaku zasshi* 1 (Nos 3, 4), 1890 and (slightly altered) *Kan Masatomo zenshū* (Kokusho kankōkai, 1908): 632–39. Hoshino: '*Taiheiki* wa hatashite shōsetsuka no saku ni arazaru ka' (Is not the *Taiheiki* really the work of a Romancer?), *Bun* 1.24 (1888). Kume: '*Taiheiki* wa shigaku ni eki nashi' (The *Taiheiki*

is useless for historical scholarship), *Shigaku zasshi* 2 (1891): 230–40; 279–92; 487–501; 562–78.

43. Kume Kunitake, 'Yo ga mitaru Shigeno hakushi', *Rekishi chiri* 17.3 (1912): 274–306; (290). In his lecture on the causes of the Meiji Restoration in 1889 (1989: 2: 479–92), Shigeno clearly distinguished between the Kemmu Restoration as a series of power struggles of individuals and the Meiji Restoration as an act of patriotism; but by comparing the events in the first place Shigeno also drew a connection.

44. Murata 1983: 209 provides a list of these heroes.

45. Ōkubo 1988: 138–42.

46. *Shimatsu* 10.

47. Ōkubo 1988: 139; Kume 1912: 3–4. Kan Masatomo, *Kan Masatomo zenshū* (Kokusho kankōkai, 1908): 587–91.

48. Kume 1912: 189.

49. 'Massatsu hakase no shōtai', *Yomiuri shinbun*, 1 October 1909; quoted from *Shinbun shūsei Meiji hennenshi* 14: 152.

50. 'Yojō ryūfu no shiden ōku jijitsu ayamaru setsu' (Satsumashi kenkyūkai/Ōkubo Toshiaki 1989: 1: 9–19). *'Dainihonshi* o ronji rekishi no teisai ni oyobu' (ibid. 1: 20–9).

51. 'Kojima Takanori kō (Satsumashi kenkyūkai/Ōkubo Toshiaki 1889: 2: 577–90).

52. The court noble Tōin Kinsada (1340–99) recorded the death of the monk Kojima under the date Ōan 7 (1374).5.3., noting that he was the author of the *Taiheiki*.

53. Examples: *Nihon* shinbun, 18 October 1882, on Musashi Benkei; 7 November 1893, on Yamamoto Kansuke. *Yūbin hōchi shinbun*, 7 September 1892, on Shigeno's opinion that the memorial stone for Kusunoki Masashige at the Minato River was not erected by the lord of Mito. *Yomiuri shinbun*, 14 September 1895: the *massatsu* treatises extended to China. (All quoted from *Shinbun shūsei Meiji hennenshi* 8, 9).

54. 5 March 1892: 1; although I translated *benjo* as 'privy' for the 1998 edition of this book, it escaped my notice that the copy editor had corrected this to 'privacy.' For the translated poem, see Kojima Hōshi, Helen Craig McCullogh (transl.), *The Taiheiki: A Chronicle of Medieval Japan* (New York: Columbia University Press, 1959): 107-8.

55. *Shinbun shūsei Meiji hennenshi* 14: 141.

56. Sidney Devere Brown, Akiko Hirata (transl.), *The Dairies of Kido Kōin*, 3 vols (University of Tokyo Press, 1983–6): vol. 1: 15, 207, 669; vol. 3: 123, 483.

57. 'Sakurai no ketsubetsu', Kindaiichi Haruhiko, Anzei Aiko (ed.), *Nihon no shōka*, vol. 1 (Kōdansha, 1977): 112–14.

58. Peter Wetzler, 'Kriegspremier Tōjō Hideki und das kaiserliche System: Zur Ideenwelt eines japanischen Militars und Politikers im pazifischen Krieg', *Beiträge zur Japanologie* 29, ed. Eva Bachmayer, Wolfgang Herbert and Sepp Linhart (Universitat Wien, 1991): 328–43. For an account of Kusunoki Masashige's life and his importance to later generations see Ivan Morris, *The Nobility of Failure: Tragic Heroes in the History of Japan* (Tuttle, 1982; first published 1975).

59. Newspaper article in *Tōkyō nichinichi shinbun Meiji* 19.10.19 (*Shinbun shūsei Meiji hennenshi* 9: 342/3). On Yoda and the Japanese theatre, see articles 'Yoda Gakkai' and 'Katsureki geki' by Yamamoto Jirō in *Engeki hyakka daijiten*, ed. Waseda daigaku engeki hakubutsukan (Heibonsha, 1961): 2: 63; 5: 526.

60. Ōkubo 1988: 239.
61. 'Kyōiku rekishi', Satsumashi kenkyūkai/Ōkubo Toshiaki 1989: 1: 61–5.
62. Ibid. 1989: 2: 364–72.
63. 'Rikoku shinshi ni saisuru Sōbōsei no setsu ni kotau', *Shigaku zasshi* 1 (1890): 39–42.
64. The content of this chapter is treated in more detail in Margaret Mehl, *Eine Vergangenheit fur die japanische Nation* (Frankfurt: Peter Lang, 1992) and 'Scholarship and Ideology in Conflict: The Kume Affair, 1892', *Monumenta Nipponica* 48.3 (1993): 337–57. The best article on the Kume Affair is still Ōkubo Toshiaki, 'Yugamerareta rekishi' (first published in 1952) in Ōkubo 1988: 7: 142–53. Focusing on the problems of the Imperial system (*tennōsei*): Miyachi Masato, 'Kindai tennōsei ideorogii to rekishigaku – Kume jiken no seijishiteki kōsatsu' in *Tennōsei no seijishiteki kenkyū*, ed. Miyachi Masato (Kōsō shobō, 1981): 150–84. In relation to other clashes between scholarship and ideology: Ishida Takeshi, *Meiji seiji shisōshi kenkyū* (Miraisha, 1954, reprinted 1971): 219–91; Ide Magoroku, *Meiji minshūshi o aruku* (Shin jinbutsu ōraisha, 1980): 155–78. From the viewpoint of the Shintoists: *Meiji ishin Shintō hyakunenshi*, ed. Shintō bunkakai (Shintō bunkakai, 1967): 83–94. Summary of research: Imai Osamu, Kano Masanao, 'Nihon kindai shisōshi no naka no Kume jiken', in *Kume Kunitake no kenkyū*, ed. Ōkubo Toshiaki (Yoshikawa kōbunkan, 1991): 201–316.
65. *Shikai* No. 8 (25 January 1892). *Shigaku zasshi* Nos 23–5 (October to December 1891). The article has been reprinted several times; here reference is made to Matsushima Eiichi, ed. *Meiji shiron shū*, vol. 2 (*Meiji bungaku zenshū* 78; Chikuma shobō 1956, reprinted 1989): 86–98.
66. Ōkubo 1988: 86. The treatise is now available in volume four of Kume's collected works, together with the notes of his lectures at *Tōkyō senmon gakko; Kume Kunitake rekishi chosakushū* 4, *Komonjo no kenkyū*, ed. Ōkubo Toshiaki et al. (Yoshikawa kōbunkan, 1989): 1–82.
67. Few authors take more than a passing interest in what Kume actually said in his article. Exceptions: Shintō bunkakai 1967 includes a summary of the article and a discussion of its main points (83–94); Akimoto Nobuhide quotes from 'Shintō wa saiten no kozoku' in 'Kume Kunitake to Takegoshi Yosaburō no renzokusei', *Kokugakuin joshi tanki daigaku kiyō* 5 (1987): 51–88; Detailed summary in Mehl 1992: 212–14. See also Imai/ Kano 1991: 205–11.
68. Helen Hardacre, *Shintō and the State 1868–1988* (Princeton: Princeton UP, 1989, 1991): 129.
69. Imai/Kano1991: 209–11. A commentator in the literary review *Waseda bungaku* speculated that this may have been why Kume's colleagues were not ready to defend him. *Waseda bungaku* 12 (March 1892). A commentator in *Kokugakuin zasshi* also criticized the article for not having been sufficiently researched; Vol. 3.7 (May 1893): 103–5.
70. Shintō bunkakai 1967: 94. Influence of the Enlightenment on Kume: Iwai (in Nagahara/Kano, 1976): 15–16.
71. Yasumaru Yoshio, Miyachi Masato (ed.) *Shūkyō to kokka,* (Iwanami shoten, 1988; *Nihon kindai shisō taikei* 5): 544; 551–9.
72. 'Rakugosei' expressed his suprise at the long silence in *Shikai*. According to Ōkubo,

'Rakugosei' was Yoshida Tōgo. See the 'hihyō' sections in *Shikai* 9, 10. Also Imai/Kano 1991: 237–42.

73. *Tōkyō nichinichi shinbun; Hōchi shinbun; Suntetsu; Nihon no seinen; Aizu, Hokuriku shinpō* and *Fusō shinbun*. For details see Imai/Kano 1991: 220–2.

74. *Tōkyō nichinichi shinbun*. Quoted in *Shikai* and in Imai/Kano1991: 231.

75. Ōmori Kingorō, 'Ko Kume Kunitake sensei o omou', *Rekishi chiri* 57 (1931): 563–7 (564). Also quoted in Imai/Kano 1991: 216–17.

76. *Dōseikan*, founded at the end of the Edo period by Watanabe Ikarimaro, scholar of National Learning and Shinto.

77. The account was published in a collection entitled *Saiten kozoku benmei* (Explanation concerning the article '*Shintō wa saiten no kozoku*') on 25 May 1892; reprinted in *Meiji bungaku zenshū* 78: 102–5. According to Ōmori (1931: 562), Kume thought the account misleading.

78. Editors' remarks at the end of Kume's memoirs *Kume hakushi kyūjūnen kaikoroku*. It seems that Taguchi soon distanced himself from the church, and in *Shintōsha shoshi ni tsugu* (see below) he denied being a believer; See Yamazaki Minako, 'Kume Kunitake to kirisutokyō, in Ōkubo 1991: 159–200 (177).

79. Quoted in *Meiji bungaku zenshū* 78: 105.

80. Imai/Kano 1991: 227–8 point out that the retraction was worded more strongly than Kume's own letter.

81. Ōkubo 1988: 147. See also *Waseda bungaku* (11 March 1892): 5.

82. Later he even claimed that losing his official position was a relief to him; Kume 1912: 296; Ōmori 1931: 561–4. The commentator in *Waseda bungaku* reported that Kume had resigned: No. 22 (August.1892): 12–13, 'Shigaku no fūchō'. On Kume's reaction (of which the sources tell us very little), see also Imai/Kano 1991: 256; 260–1.

83. Both articles quoted from *Meiji bungaku zenshū* 78: 99–102. On Taguchi's Proclamation and the ensuing dispute: Imai/Kano1991: 242–6.

84. Shintō bunkakai 1967: 91–3. Kuramochi's article 'Taguchi Ukichi shi ni kotau' appeared in *Keikoku* (No. 3) on 1 April. Taguchi published a response in *Tōkyō keizai zasshi* and the two exchanged views several times; Imai/Kano 1991: 219–31.

85. Shintō bunkakai 1967: 90–5, especially p.94.

86. 'Kume Kunitake shi ni shissu', *Kokkō* 3.9 (February 1892). Quoted from Shintō bunkakai 1967: 89–90.

87. Ōkubo 1988: 150–3. Miyachi (1981: 171–9) also treats the arguments of the Shintoists in some detail; Imai/Kano (1991: 219–31) list all the known articles published in connection with the Affair and summarize some of the reactions (232–54).

88. Anon., 'Kokka no daiji o bakurō suru mono no fukei fugi o ronzu' *Kokkō* 3.9 (1892); Iwashita Masahira, 'Hennenshi hensan iin o ikani sen', *Kokkō* 4.2 (May 1892); Okajima Yasuhira, 'Jōfūken hōtenkyō', *Kokkō* 4.2 (May 1892); in *Rekishi ninshiki*, ed. Miyachi Masato, Tanaka Akira (Iwanami, 1991; *Nihon kindai shiso taikei* 13): 466–9; 474–5; 475–8.

89. Newspaper article in *Nihon* (27 March 1892); Taguchi Shin, in his foreword to the reprint of *Shikai* quotes Kume's speech in memory of Taguchi in 1911 (Ōkubo, ed.1988: 34–5).

90. Ōmori 1931: 561–565. See also Akimoto Nobuhide, 'Kume Kunitake jiken sandai', *Nihon rekishi* 475 (1987): 92–6.

91. Akimoto 1987: 95.
92. Akimoto 1987: 95; Tsuji Zennosuke, 'Omoiizuru mama', *Kokumin no rekishi* 1.10 (1938).
93. Quoted from *Waseda bungaku* No. 11 (March 1892): 6. See also *Waseda bungaku* 12 (March 1892): 6–7 and 37 (April 1893): 136.
94. 'Shigaku no fūchō', *Waseda bungaku* 22 (August 1892): 12–14.
95. The Tomizu Affair and the Kume Affair are sometimes compared: Byron K. Marshall, 'Professors and Politics: The Meiji Academic Elite', *Journal of Japanese Studies* 3.1 (1977): 71–97 (85–6); Saitō Takashi, *Shōwa shigakushi nōto. Rekishigaku no hassō* (Shōgakkan, 1984): 11–12. See also Marshall 1992: 7–17; 61–7.
96. Marshall 1992: 212.
97. Marshall 1992: 66; 76; 189.
98. Marshall 1977: 95.
99. 'Genkon no shiron', *Waseda bungaku* 32 (January 1893): 51–6 and 33 (February 1893): 34–7.
100. Author's translation from Ludwig Rieß, *Allerlei aus Japan*, 2 vols (Berlin: Deutsche Bücherei, 3rd edn n.d.): 117–18; the chapter was written around the time of the Russo-Japanese War. Katō's diaries are preserved in the archives of Tokyo University, but Kume is not mentioned, at least not during the period in question (Spring 1892).
101. *Waseda bungaku* published several articles on the different schools of thought in historiography in the years 1892–3, e.g. 'Shigaku no fūchō', No. 1 (20 October 1891): 12–13, No. 7 (15 January 1892): 6–8, No. 32 (30 August 1892): 12–14; 'Shiron yonha', No. 35 (3 October 1893): 89–92. See also 'Kokushi ni okeru kagakuteki kenkyū', *Kokugakuin zasshi* Vol. 3.7 (May 1897): 103–5.
102. *Waseda bungaku* 12 (March 1892): 6–7. Also between Shinto and Christianity and between officials and the people. Presumably the conservative historians were the National Scholars and the progressive ones were Kume and his colleagues and Rieß and his students. Quoted also in Imai/Kano1991: 248.
103. It is, however, doubtful what academic freedom meant to the professors; their privileges as an academic elite seem to have been more important than freedom of opinion in general: Akimoto 1987: 95; Horio Teruhisa (ed. and transl. Steven Platzer), *Educational Thought and Ideology in Modern Japan: State Authority and Intellectual Freedom* (Tokyo UP, 1988): 103–5. Richard Mitchell, *Censorship in Imperial Japan* (Princeton UP, 1983): 110. Marshall (1992: 180) points out that in the controversies from 1928 onward the freedom of individuals was sacrificed to institutional autonomy.
104. Quoted in Saitō 1984: 12.
105. Kaigo Tokiomi, *Inoue Kowashi no kyōiku seisaku* (Tōkyō daigaku shuppankai, 1968). On Inoue's views on history: Kino Kazue, 'Inoue Kowashi no rekishikan', *Shintōgaku* 62 (1969): 17–29. See also Mikami 394: 81.
106. Quoted in Kaigo 1968: 1021–2.
107. *Itō Hirobumi kankei monjo*, 9 vols, ed. Itō Hirobumi kankei monjo kenkyūkai (Hanawa shobō, 1973–7): 1: 488; undated, but probably Meiji 26=1893, as suggested by the editors.

108. Miyachi 1981: 180–4 (183, 184). Miyachi cites as his source for Inoue's letter, *Inoue Kowashiden shiryō hen* (vol. 2 p. 605). I have translated *kenryoku* as "state authority", although it is not entirely clear to me who exactly Miyachi is referring to.

109. Among Inoue's papers is a memorandum by the Historiographical Institute, dated January 1889, in which the Institute defended itself against the accusation that it was producing no results (B-3130; no addressee is named). Inoue and the *Taisei kiyō:* Kino Kazue, 'Inoue Kowashi no rekishikan', *Shintōgaku* 62 (1969): 17–29 (23–6); see Chapter 2.5.

110. Mikami 401: 81; 394: 86. Ōkubo 1988: 51.

111. Akimoto Nobuhide, 'Meiji nijūroku nen shigatsu ni okeru shin shikyoku no teishitsu setchi an', *Kokushigaku* 99 (1976): 26–44.

112. Quoted from *Shinbun shūsei Meiji hennenshi* 8: 406.

113. Letter to Itō Hirobumi, 29 March 1893 (Meiji 26) in *Itō Hirobumi kankei monjo* 1: 448–9 and in Inoue Kowashi denki hensan iinkai (ed.), *Inoue Kowashi den, Shiryōhen* 4 (Kokugakuin daigaku toshokan, 1977): 335. The following proposals are preserved in the papers of Inoue Kowashi at *Kokugakuin* University: Kurita Hiroshi, 27 March 1893 (Meiji 26; B-3112) and 7 July 1893 (B-3113). Hoshino's letter to Toyama Masakazu, 12 April 1893 (B-3124), enclosed with the proposal by Toyama, 14 April (B-3122). Letter from Aoyama Isamu, 19 April (B-3114) to Inoue Kowashi, in which he alludes to a letter from Kan Masatomo to himself; two letters from Kan Masatomo to Aoyama, dated 17 and 21 April (B-3115, 3116), enclosed with the letter from Aoyama. Takatsu Shūsaburō, 29 April (B-3119). Ikeda Kōen, April 1893 (B-3123). Kawada Higuma, April 1893 (B-3118). N.N., not dated, 1893 (B-1321). Some of these proposals have been printed in *Inoue Kowashi den, Shiryōhen* 5: Kurita (120–3), Aoyama and Kan (1–5), Kawada (106–12). Excerpts in Kaigo 1968: 1026–7. The main library of Tokyo University holds microfilms of some of the Inoue papers and kindly copied the relevant documents for me (B-3104 to B-3130).

114. Proposal by Toyama (B-3122).

115. They are analysed in detail in Kaigo 1968: 1020–1137. The two versions of an undated memo, one written by Inoue himself, are in the papers of Inoue Kowashi (B-3111); printed in *Inoue Kowashi den Shiryōhen* 5 (758); the year given there is 1894. One of the four drafts is dated 20 June 1894 (B-3110). In the volume quoted above, the fourth draft is published (684–88) and the order of the four drafts given as B-3109, B-3110, B-3104, B-3117. However, the authors are probably right in assuming that B-3110 was drafted before B-3109. It is unclear why they think Toyama's memorandum was decisive, since Inoue's first draft is dated over a year after the proposals were submitted.

116. Inoue's papers include the memorandum by the College of Historiography submitted in 1885 (B-3127; Chapter 5.1) and a memorandum by the Historiograpical Institue about the *Dainihon hennenshi* (it was planned to extend the period it covered) drawn up in 1889 (B-3130).

117. Mikami (394: 87); according to Mikami, it was planned from the start to extend the period to 15 years.

118. Drafts for the rescript in Inoue's papers enclosed with B-3109.

119. At the same time there was a debate on the question of financial support for the

Shidankai (Chapter 3.5) to collect sources on the Meiji Restoration; Dainihon teikoku gikaishi kankōkai (ed.), *Dainihon teikoku gikai shi* 3 (Sanseidō, 1927): 464–6; 611–13.

120. Mikami 396: 86–7.
121. Mikami 396: 87.
122. *Tōkyō daigaku hyakunenshi, bukyokushi* 4 1987: 562. The names of the newly appointed members can be found in *Shimatsu* 18.
123. On Tanaka: Akimoto Nobuhide, 'Tanaka Yoshinari hakushi no shajisei nin'yō', *Nihon rekishi* 437 (1984): 45–6; Mikami Sanji in Tanaka Yoshinari, *Nanbokuchō jidaishi* (Kodansha, 1979; first published 1922, reprinted 1986); Satō Kazuhiko in Kano Masanao/Nagahara Keiji (ed.), *Nihon no rekishika* (Nihon hyōronsha, 1976): 70–7. Tsuji Zennosuke, 'Omoiizuru mama', *Kokumin no rekishi* 1.10 (1947): 38–41.
124. Mikami's own reminiscences, which have already been quoted, are the best biographical source. See also Nakamura Takanari (narrator), 'Shiriizu kindai shigaku o tsukutta hitobito: Mikami Sanji', *Kikan rekishi kyōiku kenkyū* (pub. *Rekishi kyōiku kenkyūjo*) 1959: 16–28; Tsuji Zennosuke in *Kokumin no rekishi* 1.7 (1946): 54–5.
125. Mikami 400: 86.
126. *Shimatsu* 18 (summary).
127. Mikami 316: 87.
128. Ishida Takeshi, *Meiji seiji shisōshi kenkyū* (Miraisha 1954, repr. 1977): 277.
129. The best account of the controversy in English is in Varley 1971. Less comprehensive, without citing Japanese scholarship on the subject: Uyenaka, Shuzo, 'The Textbook Controversy of 1911: National Needs and Historical Truth', in John Brownlee (ed.), *History in the Service of the Japanese Nation* (Toronto: University of Toronto–York University Joint Centre on Modern East Asia, 1983): 94–120. A good description of the events based on the sources can be found in Matsumoto Seichō, *Shōsetsu Tōkyō teikoku daigaku* (Shinchōsha, 1975). The best scholarly article on the subject is still Ōkubo 1988: 153–66 (first published in 1952). Murata (1983; first pub. 1949) discusses the controversy about the two imperial courts through the ages. Ishida (1954) treats it as part of the history of political ideas. Sakata Yoshio, *Tennō shinsei. Meijiki no tennōkan* (Shibunkaku, 1984) is not much more than a few quotations from the sources strung together.
130. Yūseikai (ed.), *Seijun dan'an. Kokutai no yōgo* (Tōkyōdō, 1911; reprinted by Misuzu shobō, Misuzu Reprints 19, 1989); on the *Taisei kiyō*, from which extracts are published at the end of the volume, see the article by Mishio (265).
131. The 'three great innovations' of the *Dainihonshi* (*san dai tokuhitsu*) are as follows. (1) Jingū (201–69) is not counted as an empress but as a regent for Emperor Ōjin. (2) Temmu (673–686) is described as usurper to the throne of his nephew Ōtomo. (3) The Southern court is called the Yoshino court and treated as the only imperial court; H. Webb, 'What is the Dai Nihon Shi?', *Journal of Asian Studies* 19 (1960): 135–49 (141); Sakamoto Tarō, *Nihon no shūshi to shigaku* (Shibundō 1966): 183–7. Shigeno gave the lecture to the Academy (1989: 1: 168–84). Kikuchi Kenjirō contradicted Shigeno's views in *Shigaku zasshi* 1.12 (1900).
132. In Tanaka Yoshinari, *Nanbokuchō jidaishi* (Kōdansha, 1979): 14–15; Mikami 401: 82–3.

133. Kita's role in the textbook controversy is treated in detail in his biography by Narusawa Eiju in Nagahara/Kano 1976: 137–44.
134. *Shigaku zasshi* 22.4 (1911): 489–98.
135. It is of course possible that many teachers simply ignored the account and taught the version they were accustomed to from previous textbooks, such as the *Kokushigan*, as Mishio suggests (Yūseikai 1911: 265).
136. Gluck 1985: 93.
137. Ōkubo 1988: 156.
138. Newspaper articles concerning the textbook controversy are reprinted in Shigaku kyōkai (ed), *Nanbokuchō seijunron* (Shūbunkaku, 1911); also in *Shinbun shūsei Meiji hennenshi* 14.
139. Fujisawa's speech and the brief debate following it are printed in *Dainihon teikoku gikai shi* 8: 381–4 and in Abe lsoo, *Teikoku gikai. Kyōiku giji sōran*, 3 (Kōseikaku, 1932–3): 78–91. Newspaper articles (including two cartoons of Fujisawa) in *Shinbun shūsei Meiji hennenshi* 14: 375–7.
140. The political problems of the Katsura government in February 1911 are the subject of several entries in the diary of his political opponent Hara Kei (1856–1921); *Hara Kei Nikki* 3 (ed. Hara Keiichirō; Kangensha, 1950–1): 192–203; 206–7; 223.
141. Yūseikai (successor to the *Dainihon kokutai yōgodan*) 1911 (repr. 1989): 365–93. See also the reminiscenses of one of its members, Uchida Shūhei, *Nanbokuchō seijun mondai no kaiko* (Kokumon seisha, 1938).
142. On Yamagata's role in the affair: Ōkubo 1988: 160–1. Excerpts from his correspondence with Katsura, Terauchi and Katō Hiroyuki as well as reminiscences of Inoue Michiyasu (1866–1941), who conducted negotiations with the court for him: Tokutomi Iichirō, *Kōshaku Yamagata Aritomo den* (Yamagaka Aritomo ko kinen jigyō kai, 1938): 767–76. The originals of the letters are in the Yamagata papers in the National Diet Library. Minutes of the debate in the Privy Council on 1 March 1911 in *Sūmitsuin kaigi gijiroku* 13: 5–7.
143. Examples: *Shigaku zasshi* 22.3; 22.4; see also Tanaka Yoshinari, 'Rekishi no katsuyō', 23.10: 1013–49 (1040–1). *Rekishi chiri* 17.4; 17.5; 18.4. *Kyōiku jiron* 927–36 (Jan. to Mar.). *Nihon oyobi Nihonjin* 553–8; 561. The most important articles can be found in the collections published at the time: *Shigaku kyōkai* 1911; *Yūseikai* 1911; Yamazaki Tōkichi and Horie Yoshio (eds) *Nanbokuchō seijun ronsan* (Kōten kōkyūjo, 1911). All three collections were edited by advocates of the Southern court; *Yūseikai* only includes articles by its members, but the others also include articles in favour of the Northern court or undecided.
144. Satō Kazuhiko in Nagahara/Kano 1976: 74.
145. *Shigaku kyōkai* 1911: 150–1; 159.
146. Yūseikai 1911: 260–6.
147. Mikami in Tanaka 1979: 15.
148. Quoted in *Tōkyō daigaku hakunenshi, Tsūshi 1*, 1984: 1047–51.
149. *Tōkyō daigaku hyakunenshi, Tsūshi 1*, 1984: 1051.
150. Inoue's story can be found in Saitō 1984: 21, Ōkubo's in Nakamura 1959: 25–6; see also Mikami 410: 90–1.
151. Ishida 1954: 278.

152. In *Shigaku zasshi* 23 (1912): 1030–49.

153. English translation by G.M. Sinclair and Suita Kazo in Sinclair/Suita (ed.), *Tōkyō People: Three Stories from the Japanese* (Tokyo: Keibunkan, 1925). On the connection between the story and the textbook controversy, see Saitō 1984: 6–8 and Ishida Takeshi, 'Meijimatsu no sensōron to kokutairon – tayō na giron no tenkai', in *Seijun dan'an: Kokutai no yōgo*, ed. Yūseikai, (1911; Mizusu shobō, 1989): *Furoku* 1.

7 Conclusion

1. For details see Mikami Sanji's reminiscences 'Mikami Sanji sensei dankyūkai sokukiroku', ed. Ishikawa Shōtarō, *Nihon rekishi* 390–6, 398–402, 404, 406–11 (1980–2): 407: 85–6

2. *Shiryō hensan kakari jigyō no keijōhi jigyō to subeki riyū* (Reasons why the task of the Department for Compilation should be made permanent), 1905, in *Shimatsu* 20.

3. *Chokurei* No. 95, in *Shimatsu* 20.

4. Details of organization and staff: Tōkyō daigaku hyakunenshi iinkai, ed. *Tōkyō daigaku hyakunenshi Bukyokushi* 4 (Tōkyō daigaku, 1987): 567–73; Mikami mentions arguments with the members of the older generation, namely Hoshino (401: 86–7).

5. There are eleven sub-departments; see the prospectus of the Institute, *Tōkyō daigaku Shiryō hensanjo yōran*, 1995.

6. *Kokan shūei*, 1923-32; also one volume, *Komonjo jidaikan*, 1925–7.

7. Tōkyō daigaku 1987: 563, 570–1; 573; 592–3. See also Mikami's reminiscences about the first building (400: 88–9). Information on the present Institute from the prospectus, 1995.

8. *Shimatsu* 18 and the following volumes. Also Mikami Sanji's reminiscences. Hoshino's report of a field trip to Kyoto and Wakayama from June to September 1901 is printed in his collected works: *Shigaku sōsetsu*, 2 vols (Fuzanbō, 1909): 2: 688–774.

9. Mikami 408: 71; *Shidankai sokukiroku* 88 (1900): 62–3; *Shimatsu* 18.

10. Information given by Hōya Tōru, research assistant, letter dated 4 February 1991.

11. Numata Jirō, interview on 13 November 1989. Numata became a member of the Institute after graduating from the department of Japanese history at Tokyo University in 1935 and became its director in 1971. He retired in 1973.

12. Details in the 1995 prospectus of the Institute (18–19).

13. *Shimatsu* 19–21; Mikami 399: 81–3.

14. *Shimatsu* 19.

15. Mikami 408: 77; 410: 87; for Kusunoki and Kojima see Chapter 6.3.

16. *Shimatsu* 20.

17. *Nihon no ayumi*, 1946 and *E de miru Nihonshi*, 1949: Tōkyō daigaku 1987: 598.

18. Mikami 410: 88–9; Ii Naosuke was the regent who in 1858 had the Bakufu conclude the Treaty of Amity and Commerce with the US without imperial sanction. Shimada's book, *Kaikoku shimatsu*, was published in 1888.

19. Mikami 410: 90.

20. Numata, interview on 13 November 1989.

21. Numata, 13 November 1989.

22. Murata Masashi, *Zokuzoku Nanbokuchō shiron* (Shibunkaku, 1983): 153–4; *Rikugun*

jikan Hashimoto Toranosuke jogyōmu yōkō oboe (written after 1935), in *Gendai shiryō* 23, *Kokkashugi undō* 1974: 392–95; Tōkyō daigaku 1987: 576.

23. 'Minshū shihai no seitō to takoku e no yūetsu o utau ka'i shisō no keifu', *Asahi jānaru*, 25 January 1989, 126–31.

24. Takano and Kondō in Rekishigaku kenkyūkai (ed.), *'Sokui no rei' to dajōsai. Rekishika wa dō kangaeru* (Aoki shoten, 1990).

25. R.C. Van Caenegem and F.L. Ganshof, *Kurze Quellenkunde des Westeuropäischen Mittelalters* (Göttingen: Vandenhoeck & Ruprecht, 1962): 180–1.

26. Thomas Nipperdey, 'Auf der Suche nach der Identität: Romantischer Nationalismus', in *Nachdenken über die deutsche Geschichte* (Munich: dtv, 1990): 132–50; Engl. in *Romantic Nationalism in Europe*, ed. J.C. Eade (Humanities Research Centre, Australian National University, 1983); Yoshino Kosaku, *Cultural Nationalism in Contemporary Japan: A Sociological Enquiry* (London, New York: Routledge, 1992): 44–5.

27. Friedrich Jaeger and Jörn Rüsen, *Geschichte des Historismus* (Munich: C.H. Beck, 1992).

28. Wolfgang Hardtwig, 'Geschichtsstudium, Geschichtswissenschaft und Geschichtstheorie in Deutschland von der Aufklärung bis zur Gegenwart', in *Geschichtskultur und Wissenschaft* (Munich: dtv, 1990): 13–57.

29. Hellmut Seier, 'Heinrich von Sybel', in *Deutsche Historiker*, vol 2, ed. H.-U. Wehler (Göttingen: Vandenhoeck & Ruprecht, 1971): 24–38.

30. Franz Schnabel, 'Die Idee und ihre Erscheinung', in *Die Historische Kommission bei der Bayrischen Akademie der Wissenschaften 1858–1958* (Göttingen: Vandenhoeck & Ruprecht, 1958): 7–69.

31. Schnabel 1958: 37; 38.

32. Schnabel 1958: 50.

33. Seier 1971: 32–3.

34. Reinhard Elze/Arnold Esch (eds), *Das Deutsche Historische Institut in Rom 1888–1988* (Tübingen: Max Niermeyer, 1990).

35. Wolfgang Mommsen, *Nation und Geschichte: Über die Deutschen und die Deutsche Frage* (Munich/Zürich: Piper, 1990): 12–13.

36. Hardtwig 1990: 232–3.

37. Seier 1971: 32.

38. Hardtwig 1990: 104, 225, 230, 233–4.

39. Hardtwig 1990: 112; Arthur Marwick, *The Nature of History* (London: Macmillan, 1989): 44.

40. Hardtwig 1990: 103–60; 107; 112.

41. Hardtwig 1990: 154.

42. Hardtwig 1990: 236

43. Details on this in Bernd Martin, 'Fatal Affinities: The German Role in the Modernisation of Japan in the Early Meiji Period (1868–1895) and Its Aftermath', in *Japan and Germany in the Modern World* (Providence/Oxford: Berghahn Books, 1995): 17–76.

44. Yoshino 1992: 84–5.

45. See the memoranda by Miura Yasushi, discussed in Chapter 2.5. These metaphors were very similar to European ones, facilitating the adoption of European

constitutional thought; Reinhard Zöllner, 'Lorenz von Stein und *kokutai*', *Oriens Extremus* 33 (1990): 65–76.

46. Atsuko Hirai, 'The State and Ideology in Meiji Japan – A Review Article', *Journal of Asian Studies* 46 (1987): 89–103 (91–2).

47. Klaus Antoni, 'Inoue Tetsujirō und die Ideologie der späten Meiji-Zeit', *Oriens Extremus* 33 (1990): 99–115. See also Ōgai's portrayal of Adolf Harnack (1851–1930) in 'As If' (see Chapter 6.6). Lorenz von Stein, 'Studien zur Reichs- und Rechtsgeschichte Japans', *Österreichische Monatsschrift für den Orient* 13 (1887): 1–9 (5); he also mentions historical scholarship at the Imperial University and expresses the hope that it will soon free itself from annalistic history in the Chinese tradition.

48. Ōtsuki Minao, *Meiji ishin to doitsu shisō* (Nagasaki shuppan, 1977): 10–11.

49. Bernd Martin, 'Deutsche Geschichtswissenschaft als Instrument nationaler Selbstfindung in Japan', in *Universalgeschichte und Nationalgeschichten*, ed. Gangolf Hübinger/Jürgen Osterhammel/Erich Pelzer (Rombach Verlag, 1994): 209–29 (211–12).

50. Peter Novick, *That Noble Dream* (Cambridge: Cambridge Univeristy Press, 1988): 66.

51. Ernst Breisach, *Historiography: Ancient Medieval & Modern* (Chicago: The University of Chicago Press, 1983, 1994): 233; 236.

52. Jaeger/Rüsen 1992: 65.

53. Helmut Berding, 'Theodor Mommsen. Das Problem der Geschichtsschreibung', in *Geschichte und politisches Handeln* (1985): 243–60; Ernst Breisach, *Historiography, Ancient Medieval & Modern* (Chicago/London: University of Chicago Press, 1983, 1994): 237. Jaeger/Rüsen 1992: 50.

54. Jaeger/Rüsen 1992: 63.

55. Martin 1994: 219. In addition to lectures on methodology, Rieß published *Historik – Ein Organon geschichtlichen Denkens und Forschens* (Berlin 1912).

56. Nakayama makes much of the difference between Rieß and Tsuboi, pointing out that Bernheim's book appeared after Rieß had gone to Japan, but Bernheim's book did not present anything fundamentally new. Rieß cites Bernheim in his *Methodology*, and it seems clear that Rieß's emphasis was on methodology. Tanaka 1993: 25–6, citing Tsuda Sōkichi, makes the same point. Nakayama Jiichi, 'Doitsu shigaku no juyū to Shiratori hakushi', *Shiratori Kurakichi zenshū daikyūkai hai geppō* 9 (1971): 5–7.

57. Breisach 1994: 233–4; on the selective reception and misunderstanding of Ranke in America, see Novic 1988: 26–31; Joyce Appleby, Lynn Hunt, Margaret Jacob, *Telling the Truth About History* (New York/London: Norton, 1994): 73–4.

58. Jaeger/Rüsen 1992: 53–66.

59. Quoted by Numata Jirō, 'Shigeno Yasutsugu and the Modern Tokyo Tradition of Historical Writing', in *Historians of China and Japan*, eds W.G. Beasley and E.G. Pulleyblank (London: Oxford University Press, 1961) 264–87.

60. Fernand Braudel, quoted in Tanaka 1993: 29.

61. Wolfgang Küttler, Jörn Rüsen, Ernst Schulin (ed.), *Geschichtsdiskurs*, vol. I, *Grundlagen und Methoden der Historiographiegeschichte* (Frankfurt a.M.: Fischer, 1993).

62. 'Geschichtsschreibung als Theorieproblem der Geschichtswissenschaft. Skizze zum historischen Hintergrund der gegenwartigen Diskussion', *Formen der Geschichtsschreibung*, eds Reinhart Koselleck, Heinrich Lutz und Jörn Rüsen (Munich: dtv 1982): 14–35.
63. Jaeger/Rüsen 1992: 49–50.
64. See for example Wilhelm Giesebrecht, 'Die Entwicklung der modernen deutschen Geschichtswissenschaft', *Historische Zeitschrift* 1 (1859): 1–17 (8).
65. Hermann Oncken, 'Wandlungen des Geschichtsbildes in revolutionären Epochen', *Historische Zeitschrift* 189 (1959): 124–38 (135).
66. Attributed to Shiratori Kurakichi, quoted in Tanaka 1993: 28.
67. *Kokugakuin zasshi* 3.3 (January 1997): 89–93.
68. 2.1 (January 1896): 23–8 (27).
69. 'Nihon gendai no shigaku oyobi shika', *Taiyō* 15.12 (1909): 30–40.
70. Kenneth B. Pyle, The New Generation in Meiji Japan: Problems of Cultural Identity, 1885–1895 (Stanford: Stanford University Press, 1969): 98.
71. Tanaka 1993: 266.
72. Pyle, 1969: 203.
73. 'Yo ga mitaru Shigeno hakushi', *Rekishi chiri* 17.3 (1912): 305–6.
74. Tanaka 1993: 36–40.
75. Tanaka 1993: 45.
76. Marius B. Jansen (ed.), *Changing Japanese Attitudes toward Modernization* (Princeton: Princeton UP, 1964): 43–97.
77. Tanaka 1993.
78. James Edward Ketelaar, *Of Heretics and Martyrs in Meiji Japan: Buddhism and its Persecution* (Princeton: Princeton University Press, 1990): 192.
79. Nagahara Keiji, *Kōkoku shikan* (Iwanami, 1983). On Hiraizumi: Saitō Takashi, *Shōwa shigakushi nōto: rekishigaku no hassō* (Shōgakkan, 1984): 88–110.
80. Saitō 1984: 95; 99; 103. Hiraizumi equated *daiseishin* with Heraklit's *logos*.
81. Tanaka 1993: 283. See George Akita, 'Trends in Modern Japanese Political History. The "Positivist Studies,"' *Monumenta Nipponica* 1982: 497–521.
82. An example of a historical novel that stays close to historical facts and even includes summaries of primary documents is Matsumoto Seichō, *Shōsetsu Tōkyō teikoku daigaku* (Shinchōsha, 1975).

Select Bibliography

Unprinted Materials

CHISHIKAMEI O HAISHI SHŪSHIKYOKU E GAPPEI NO GI, National Archives 2A 35-5(tan) 234.

DAINIHON HENNENSHI, Manuscript in the Historiographical Institute, 4140.1/19–24; 4140.1/44.

DAJŌ RUITEN, Photographed copy in the Historiographical Institute.

DATE MUNENARI; DATE BUNKA HOZONKAI, Uwajima.
  Copies of Date Munenari's correspondence vol. 23 Shigeno to Date, Meiji 18.6.3, Meiji 18.6.6.

DATE MUNENARI, photographed documents of the *Date bunka hozonkai* in the Historiographical Institute.
  Uwajima Date ke shiryō vol. 41, Shūshikan bibō (Meiji 16: 2–19).

GOIN BUNKO (Papers of Inoue Kowashi). *Kokugakuin daigaku*. Historiography (*shūshi ken*), B-3104 to B-3130.

  B-3104, Meiji 27 (1894).

  B-3105 *Shiryō hensan iin kiteian*, Meiji 27 (1894).

  B-3106 *Shishi hensan kakari kaku nendo yosan chō*, Meiji 21-8 (1888–95).

  B-3107 *Shiryō shūshū yosan ni kansuru ikensho* (Kurita Hiroshi), Meiji 27 (1894).

  B-3108 *Shiryō hensan hiyō saigaku gaisan oboegaki*, Meiji 18 (1895).

  B-3109 *Teikoku daigaku shūshi jigyō keizoku ni kansuru seigian*, Meiji 27 (1894).

  B-3110 *Teikoku daigaku shūshi jigyō ni kansuru seigian*, Meiji 27 (1894).

  B-3111 *Shūshi jigyō ni kansuru oboegaki* (Inoue Kowashi), Meiji 27 (1894).

  B-3112 *Shūshi jigyō ni kansuru Kurita Hiroshi shokan*, Meiji 26.3.27 (1893).

  B-3113 *Shūshi jigyō ni kansuru Kurita Hiroshi shokan*, Meiji 26.7.7.

  B-3114 *Shūshi jigyō ni kansuru Aoyama Isamu shokan*, Meiji 26.4.19.

  B-3115 *Shūshi jigyō ni kansuru Kan Masatomo shokan*, Meiji 26.4.17.

  B-3116 *Shūshi jigyō ni kansuru Kan Masatomo shokan*, Meiji 26.4.21.

  B-3117 *Teikoku daigaku shūshi jigyō keizoku ni kansuru seigi*, Meiji 27 (1894).

  B-3118 *Chishi hensan hōhō ni kansuru Kawada Higuma (hishoku bunka daigaku shoki) ikensho*, Meiji 26.4.

  B-3119 *Kokushi hensan jigyō ni tsukite no iken*, Meiji 26.

  B-3120 *Tokugawa shi hensan no hitsuyō*, Meiji 26.4.

  B-3121 *Shishi hensan ni tsukite no iken* [n.d.; 1893].

  B-3122 *Shūshi oyobi shiryō jigyō ni kansuru iken* (Toyama Masakazu), Meiji 26.4.24.

  B-3123 *Shūshi jigyō ni tsuki iken* (Ikeda Kōen), Meiji 26.4.

  B-3124 *Shiryō hensan jigyō ni kansuru Hoshino Hisashi (bunka daigaku kyōju) ikensho*, Meiji 26.4.12.

B-3125 *Shiryō shūshū yosan*, Meiji 27.6.

B-3126 *Hensei shishi mokuroku.*

B-3127 *Shūshi ikensho (Shūshikan)*, Meiji 18.11 (1885).

B-3128 *Hennenshi oyobi shiryō. Hensei saido yosansho*, Meiji 18.12.

B-3129 *Naikaku rinji Shūshikyoku haishi no chokurei*, Meiji 21.10.29 (1888).

B-3130 *Hennenshi hensan ni kansuru jōshinsho*, Meiji 22.1 (1889).

IWAKURA TOMOMI MONJO (Papers of Iwakura Tomomi), National Diet Library (*Kensei shiryō shitsu*).

Dai 6 rui 124 *Shūshikan kanji Miura Yasushi jōsho sōan* (Microfilm).

276 *Ogō Kazutoshi kōtō iken.*

435 *Shidankai; Nakamura Masanao yaku Shigaku.*

IWAKURA TOMOMI MONJO, National Archives.

Naikaku bunko 122, *Iwakura monjo* 107, *Shoken zasshū*, Meiji 8 (1875).

KŌBUN RUISHŪ (Classified documents), Photographed copies in the Historiographical Institute.

KOTEI SHIWA (Historical Talks in the Restaurant by the Lake), 5 fascicles, Meiji 15.1– 17.3; continued as *Seikō shiwa*, 3 fascicles, Meiji 17.4–18.6; Historiographical Institute 4140.1/40.

KUNAICHŌ SHORYŌBU, Sources for the *Meiji tennō ki* Nr.426, *Sankō shiryō zatsusan*.

105 (Meiji 10?).5.4 From Ogō to Iwakura.

111 Meiji 10.10.21 From Ijichi to Iwakura.

112 Meiji 10.11.29 *Ijichi shinritsu sho.*

114 Meiji ll.6.28 From Ijichi to Yoshie.

KYŪ RINJI SHŪSHIKYOKU YORI HIKITSUGU SHORUI NO GI NI TSUKI TEIKOKU DAIGAKU WA DŌJŌ, National Archives 2A 35-7(chō) 87.

MIYAJIMA SEIICHIRŌ, Papers in the National Diet Library and in private possession of the Miyajima family; diary.

MONBUSHŌ ŌFUKU Archives of the University of Tokyo (*Daigakushi shiryō shitsu*).

MOTODA EIFU MONJO (Papers of Motoda Eifu), National Diet Library (*Kensei shiryō shitsu*).

109-15 *Sō Itō sangikō hōchoku no ōshō yo (Shūshikan kanji* Miura Yasushi)

OGŌ KAZUTOSHI (ICHIBIN) MONJO (Papers of Ogō Kazutoshi), National Diet Library (*Kensei shiryō shitsu*).

83 *Ikensho sōan. Nanbokuchō seijun mondai.*

SANJŌ SANETOMI MONJO (Papers of Sanjō Sanetomi), National Diet Library (*Kensei shiryō shitsu*).

54/6 *Kitabatake Chikafusa kyaku sūshi no gi ni tsuki jōshin.*

55/7 *Narishima Ryūhoku, Kodama Shōsuke ikensho.*

55/19 *Okamatsu Ōkoku shohaku. Seiyōshi kan'yaku no ken.*

55/20 *Jinnō shōtōkihoshu santei no gi.* (Maruyama Sakura)

5/21 *Shūshikan kaikaku o kou no gi.*

55/22 *Ōshū gakujutsu chōsa haken shogen.*

55/23 *Shūshi buntai ron.*

56/1 *Ogō Kazutoshi kenpakusho. Kōtō torishirabe rekishi hensan hōshin.*

71/27 *Kokushi hensan, Dainihonshi rōi teisei no ken hoka.*

75/18 *Ikensho*.
SANTŌ SHŪSEN OGŌ KAZUTOSHI HOKA ICHIMEI YAMASHIRO, YAMATO HAKEN, National Archives 2A 35-5(tan) 235.
SEIKŌ SHIWA, see KOTEI SHIWA.
SHIGENO YASUTSUGU (Papers in the Historiographical Institute).
Shūshi jigi, Henshū chakushu no hōhō (undated; 1875).
Shiryō henshū reisoku.
Shiryō hanrei.
Saihō monjo mokuroku daigen.
Kokushi sōran kō.
Shiryō shikō satsusū gaisan hyō.
Henshū reisoku.
Henshū kōkahyō fukei (Meiji 12.7).
'Rekishi wa kuni no keireki ...' (*Kume hakushi kō*)
Letter from Nakai Hiroshi to Shigeno Yasutsugu, Meiji 11.2.6 (1878).
SHIRYŌ HENSAN SHIMATSU *Shiryō hensanjo*, 23 vols, 2 vols *kōbun*, Showa 3 (1928) 0171.19.
SHOKANCHŌ ŌFUKU, Meiji 21-2 (B7), Archives of the University of Tokyo (*Daigakushi shiryō shitsu*).
SHŪSHI BUNTAI RON, *Shiryō hensanjo* 4170-68.
SHŪSHIKAN, BUNKYOKU OYOBI HENSHŪ CHAKUSHU NO HŌHŌ, National Archives 2A 35-5(tan) 236.
SHŪSHIKAN KŌKAHYŌ, National Archives.
Meiji 9–18; 2A 35-3(ki) 922.
Meiji 19–21; 2A 3J-3(ki) 923.
SUEMATSU KENCHŌ (11 letters, one incomplete letter and one note were given to the National Diet Library by the family in 1992).
SUZUMURA KE MONJO (Papers of the Suzumura Family) in the City Library of Uwajima.
ZAIGAI TEIKOKU KŌSHIKAN KEIYŪ GAIJINKANKŌ ZAKKEN (Meiji 16–22), Archives of the Foreign Ministry 3.9.3.19.
ZERFFI, *Shigaku* (Japanese translation of *The Science of History*), Historiographical Institute.

Printed Materials
If no place of publication is given, the publisher is in Tokyo.
Asakura, Haruhiko. *Meiji kansei jiten*. Tōkyō bijutsu, 1969.
Beasley, W.G. and E.G. Pulleyblank, eds. *Historians of China and Japan*. London: Oxford UP, 1961.
Bitō, Masahide. 'Nihon ni okeru rekishi ishiki no hattatsu'. In *Iwanami kōza Nihon rekishi*, 22: 2–58. Iwanami shoten, 1968.
———. 'Mitogaku no tokushitsu'. In *Mitogaku*, ed. Imai Jisaburō, Seya Yoshihiko, Bitō Masahide (*Nihon shisō taikei* 53): 562–70. Iwanami, 1973, repr.1976.
Blussé, Leonard. 'Japanese Historiography and European Sources'. In *Reappraisals in Overseas History*, eds P.C. Emmer, H.L. Wesseling, 193–222. Leiden: University Press, 1979.

Brownlee, John. *Political Thought in Japanese Historical Writing: From Kojiki (712) to Tokushi Yoron (1712),* Waterloo, Ontario: Wilfrid Laurier University Press, 1991.

——. ed. *History in the Service of the Japanese Nation.* Toronto: University of Toronto–York University Joint Centre on Modern East Asia, 1983.

Dajōkan, ed. *Fukkoki.* Naigai shoseki; Tōkyō teikoku daigaku zōhan, 1930.

Dettmer, Hans. *Einführung in das Studium der japanischen Geschichte.* Darmstadt: Wissenschaftliche Buchgesellschaft, 1987.

Duus, Peter. 'Whig History, Japanese Style: The Min'yūsha Historians and the Meiji Restoration', *Journal of Asian Studies,* 33 (1974): 415–36.

Gluck, Carol. *Japan's Modern Myths: Ideology in the Late Meiji Period.* Princeton, New Jersey: Princeton University Press, 1985.

Goch (Kemper), Ulrich. 'Die Entstehung einer modernen Geschichtswissenschaft in Japan'. *Bochumer Jahrbuch für Ostasienforschung* 1 (1978): 238–71.

——. *Abriß der japanischen Geschichtsschreibung.* Munich: iudicium, 1992.

Haga Noboru. *Hihan Kindai Nihon shigaku shisōshi.* Kashiwa shobō, 1974.

Harada Fumio. 'Shigeno Yasutsugu hakushi no shikan ni tsuite', *Shigaku zasshi* 53 (1942): 775–826.

Hardtwig, Wolfgang. *Geschichtskultur und Wissenschaft.* Munich: dtv, 1990.

——. 'Geschichtsreligion – Wissenschaft als Arbeit – Objektivität. Der Historismus in neuer Sicht'. *Historische Zeitschrift* 252 (1991): 1–32.

Hérail, Francine.'Regards sur l'historiographie de l'époque Meiji' *Storia della Storiografia/Histoire de l'Historiographie* 5 (1984): 92–114.

Hiraga Noboru. 'Historiography'. In *Kodansha Encyclopedia of Japan,* 3: 152–8. Kōdansha, 1983.

Hōki bunrui taizen, 24 vols. Tōkyō naikaku kiroku kyoku, 1891–94.

Hōrei zensho. Ōkurasho insatsukyoku, 1885–.

Hoshino Hisashi. *Shigaku sōsetsu,* 2 vols, Fuzanbō, 1909.

Ienaga Saburō. *Nihon no kindai shigaku.* Nihon hyōronsha, 1957.

——. 'Keimō shigaku'. In *Nihon rekishi kōza,* ed. Rekishigaku kenkyūkai/Nihonshi kenkyūkai, 8: 147–61. Tōkyō daigaku shuppankai, 1957.

Imai Hiroshi. 'British Influence on Modern Japanese Historiography'. *Saeculum* 38 (1987): 99–112.

Imai Osamu, Kano Masanao, 'Nihon kindai shisōshi no naka no Kume jiken', in *Kume Kunitake no kenkyū,* ed. Ōkubo Toshiaki (Yoshikawa kōbunkan, 1991): 201–316.

Ishikawa Shōtarō (ed.), 'Mikami Sanji sensei dankyūkai sokukiroku', *Nihon rekishi* 390: 42–59; 391: 73–87; 392: 112–123; 393: 77–85; 394: 80–87; 395: 77–86; 396: 78–88; 398: 77–85; 399: 78–90; 400: 82–92; 401: 77–87; 402: 74–88; 404: 113–120; 406: 77–87; 407: 81–89; 408: 71–83; 409: 78–89; 410: 81–91; 411: 76–89 (1980–2). Mikami's reminiscences have now been published in book form: *Meiji jidai no rekishi gaku kai: Mikami Sanji kaikyūdan.* Yoshikawa kōbunkan, 1991.

Iwai Tadakuma. 'Nihon kindai shigaku no keisei'. In *Iwanami kōza Nihon rekishi* 22 (*Bekkan* 1): 59–103. Iwanami shoten, 1963.

Izu Kimio. *Shinhan Nihon shigakushi.* Kōsō shobō, 1972.

Jaeger, Friedrich and Jörn Rüsen. *Geschichte des Historismus.* Munich: C.H. Beck, 1992.

Jansen, Marius B. and Gilbert Rozman, eds. *Japan in Transition: From Tokugawa to Meiji.* Princeton, New Jersey: Princeton University Press, 1986.

Kadowaki Teiji. 'Kangaku akademizumu no seiritsu'. In *Nihon rekishi kōza*, ed. Rekishigaku kenkyūkai/Nihonshi kenkyūkai 8: 163–86. Tōkyō daigaku shuppankai, 1957.

Kaji Ryūichi. *Rekishi o sōzuru hitobito*. Ōyashima shuppan, 1948.

Kan Masatomo. *Kan Masatomo zenshū*. Kokusho kankōkai, 1908.

Kanai Madoka. 'Rekishigaku – Rūtouihi Riisu o megutte'. In *Oyatoi gaikokujin 17, Jinbun kagaku*, 108–201. Kashima shuppan, 1976.

Kaneko Atsuo. *Suematsu Kenchō to 'Bōchō kaitenshi'*. Kumamoto: Shichō shakan, 1980.

Kangakusha denki shūsei, ed. Uno Tetsujin. Seki shoin, 1928.

Kano Masanao and Nagahara Keiji, eds. *Nihon no rekishika*. Nihon hyōronsha, 1976.

Kimura Takeyasu. *Tōdai: arashi no naka no Yonjūnen*. Shunjūsha, 1970.

Kitayama Shigeo. 'Nihon kindai shigaku no hatten'. In *Iwanami kōza Nihon rekishi*, 22: 107–63. Iwanami shoten, 1968.

Kokugakuin daigaku, ed. *Kōten kōkyūjo sōritsuki no hitobito*. Kokugakuin daigaku, 1982.

Kokushi daijiten henshū iinkai, ed. *Kokushi daijiten*, 15 vols. Yoshikawa kōbunkan, 1979–97.

Kōhon Kokushigan (Foreword by Shigeno Yasutsugu). Taiseikan: Teikoku daigaku zōhan, 1890.

Konakamura Kiyonori. 'Shigaku no hanashi'. *Shigaku zasshi* l (1889): 5–10.

———. *Kokushi no shiori*. Yoshikawa Hanshichi, 1895.

Kume Kunitake, 'Yo ga mitaru Shigeno Hakushi', *Rekishi chiri* 17.3 (1912): 274–306 (reprinted in *Zōtei Shigeno hakushi rekishi ronbunshū*, vol. 4).

———. *Kyūjūnen Kaikoroku*, 2 vols. Waseda daigaku shuppanbu, 1934.

———. *Tokumei zenken taishi Bei-Ō kairan jikki*, 5 vols, ed. Tanaka Akira. Iwanami shoten, 1977–82 (reprinted 1987–8).

———. *Kume Kunitake chosakushū*, 5 vols. Yoshikawa kōbunkan, 1988–91.

Küttler, Wolfgang, Jörn Rüsen, Ernst Schulin, eds. *Geschichtsdiskurs Band 1: Grundlagen und Methoden der Historiographiegeschichte*. Frankfurt am Main: Fischer, 1993.

Kuwabara Nobusuke, 'Kindai seiji shiryō shūshū no ayumi', *Sankō shoshi kenkyū* 17, 18, 21 (1979–81).

Kyūji shimon kai, ed. *Kyūji shimon roku*, 2 vols (revised with an introduction by Shinji Yoshimoto) Iwanami shoten, 1987 (first published 1891).

Marshall, Byron K. *Academic Freedom and the Japanese Imperial University, 1868–1939*. Berkeley: University of California Press, 1992.

Martin, Bernd. 'Fatal Affinities: The German Role in the Modernisation of Japan in the Early Meiji Period (1868–1895) and its Aftermath'. In *Japan and Germany in the Modern World*. Providence/Oxford: Berghahn Books, 1995: 17–76.

———. 'Deutsche Geschichtswissenschaft als Instrument nationaler Selbstfindung in Japan'. In *Universalgeschichte und Nationalgeschichten*, eds Gangolf Hübinger, Jürgen Osterhammel, Erich Pelzer: 209–29. Rombach Verlag, 1994.

Marwick, Arthur. *The Nature of History*. London: Macmillan, 3rd edn, 1989.

Matsumoto Seichō. *Shōsetsu Tōkyō teikoku daigaku*. Shinchōsha, 1975.

Matsumoto Yoshio. *Nihon shigakushi*. Keiō tsūshin, 1968.

Matsushima Eiichi, ed. *Meiji shiron shū*, 2 vols (*Meiji bungaku zenshū* 77, 78). Chikuma shobō, 1956, reprinted 1989.

Mayo, Marlene. 'The Western Education of Kume Kunitake', *Monumenta Nipponica* 28.1 (1973): 3–67.

Mehl, Margaret. 'Shūshikan fukusōsai Date Munenari ate fukuchō Shigeno Yasutsugu shokan nitsū', *Nihon rekishi* 507 (1990): 88–92.

———. *Eine Vergangenheit für die japanische Nation: Die Entstehung des historischen Forschungsinstituts Tōkyō daigaku Shiryō hensanjo (1869–1895).* Frankfurt am Main: Peter Lang, 1992.

———. 'Tradition as justification for change: History in the service of the Japanese government'. In *War, Revolution & Japan*, ed. Ian Neary, 39–49. Sandgate, Folkestone, Kent: Japan Library, 1993.

———. 'Scholarship and Ideology in Conflict: The Kume Affair, 1892', *Monumenta Nipponica* 48.3 (1993): 337–57.

———. 'Suematsu Kenchō in Britain, 1878–1886', *Japan Forum*, 5.2 (1993): 173–93.

———. 'The Mid-Meiji History Boom: Professionalization of Historical Scholarship and Growing Pains of an Emerging Academic Discipline', *Japan Forum*, 10.1 (1998): 67–83.

Meiji ishin jinmei jiten, ed. Nihon rekishi gakkai. Yoshikawa kōbunkan, 1981.

Mikami Sanji (see Ishikawa Shōtarō, ed.).

Mikami Sanji. *Kokushi gaisetsu.* Fuzanbō, 1944.

Miura Hiroyuki. 'Nihon shigaku gaisetsu'. In *Nihonshi no kenkyū dai nishū*, 2 vols, 1: 404–515. Iwanami shoten, 1930.

Miyachi, Masato. 'Kindai tennōsei ideorogii to rekishigaku – Kume jiken no seijishiteki kōsatsu'. In *Tennōsei no seijishiteki kenkyū*, 150–84. Kōsō shobō, 1981.

———. 'Seiji to rekishigaku. Meijiki no ishinshi kenkyū o tegakari to shite'. In *Gendai shigaku nyūmon*, ed. Nishikawa Masao, Kotani Hiroyuki, 92–123. Tōkyō daigaku shuppankai, 1987.

———. 'Fukkoki genshiryō no kisoteki kenkyū'. *Tōkyō daigaku Shiryō hensanjo kenkyū kiyō* 1 (1990): 66–139.

Miyachi Masato, Tanaka Akira, ed. *Rekishi ninshiki (Nihon kindai shisō taikei 13).* Iwanami shoten, 1991.

Mochida Yukio. *Hikaku kindaishi no ronri: Nihon to Doitsu.* Kyoto: Minerva shobō, 1970.

———. *Futatsu no kindai: Doitsu to Nihon wa dō chigau ka.* Asahi shinbunsha, 1988.

Nagahara Keiji. *Kōkoku shikan.* Iwanami shoten, 1983 (reprinted 1988).

Naitō Torajirō (Konan). *Shina shigakushi.* Kōbundō kankō, 1949.

Nakayama Jiichi. *Shigaku gairon.* Gakuyō, 1974.

Nishimura Tokihiko. 'Seisai sensei gyōjō shiryō'. *Shigaku zasshi* 22.5 (1911): 515–87. Reprinted in Satsumashi kenkyūkai/Ōkubo Toshiaki, eds. *Zōtei Shigeno hakushi shigaku ronbunshū* 1: 1–51.

Numata, Jirō. 'Shigeno Yasutsugu and the Modern Tokyo Tradition of Historical Writing'. In *Historians of China and Japan*, eds W.G. Beasley and E.G. Pulleyblank, 264–87. London: Oxford University Press, 1961.

Ōkubo Toshiaki. *Nihon no rekishi no rekishi.* Shinchōsha, 1959.

———. *Meiji ishin to kyōiku (Ōkubo Toshiaki rekishi chosakushū 4).* Yoshikawa kōbunkan, 1987.

———. *Nihon kindai shigaku no seiritsu (Ōkubo Toshiaki rekishi chosakushū 7).* Yoshikawa kōbunkan, 1988.

Ōkubo Toshiaki, ed. *Shikai* (Reprint of Taguchi Ukichi's journal *Shikai*). Meicho fukyūkai, 1988.

Ōkubo Toshiaki, ed. *Kume Kunitake no kenkyū*. Yoshikawa kōbunkan, 1991.

Ōkubo Toshiaki/Satsumashi kenkyūkai, eds; *see* Satsumashi kenkyūkai/Ōkubo Toshiaki, eds.

Ōtsuki Minao. *Meiji ishin to doitsu shisō* (ed. posthumously by Yamashita Takashi; English summary transl. Ōtsuka Ryūtarō). Nagasaki shuppan, 1977.

Ozawa Eiichi. *Kindai Nihon shigakushi no kenkyū. Meiji hen*. Yoshikawa kōbunkan, 1968.

Saitō Takashi. *Shōwa shigakushi nōto: rekishigaku no hassō*. Shōgakukan, 1984.

Sakamoto Takao. *Yamaji Aizan*. Yoshikawa kōbunkan, 1988.

Sakamoto Tarō. *Nihon no shūshi to shigaku*. Shibundō, 1966 (reprint 1983).

———. *Rikkokushi*. Yoshikawa kōbunkan, 1970 (repr. 1986); Engl. *The Six National Histories of Japan* by J.S. Brownlee. University of British Columbia Press, 1991.

———. 'Wagaku kōdansho ni okeru henshū shuppan jigyō'. In *Koten to rekishi*, 367–85. Yoshikawa kōbunkan, 1972.

Sakai Tadao. *Nihon shigakushi nōto*. Osaka: Ueda insatsu, 1962.

Sakizaka Itsurō, ed. *Arashi no naka no hyakunen: gakumon dan'atsu shōshi*. Keisō shobō, 1952.

Satsumashi kenkyūkai/Ōkubo Toshiaki, eds, *Zōtei Shigeno hakushi shigaku ronbunshū*, 4 vols. Meicho fukyūkai, 1989 (Vols 1–3 first published 1938–9).

Shidankai, ed. *Shidankai sokukiroku*, 86–94; 167, 1906 (reprint Hara shobō, 1972).

Shigakukai, ed. *Honpō shigakushi ronsō*, 2 vols. Fuzanbō, 1939.

Shigeno, Yasutsugu; *see* Satsumashi kenkyūkai/Ōkubo Toshiaki, eds.

Shinbun shūsei Meiji hennenshi, 15 vols, ed. Meiji hennenshi hensankai. Zaisei keizai gakukai, 1936.

Shiveley, Donald H. 'The Japanization of the Middle Meiji'. In *Tradition and Modernization in Japanese Culture*, 77–119. Princeton, New Jersey: Princeton University Press, 1971.

Shūshikan, ed. *Meiji shiyō*. Shūshikan, 1876.

Simon, Christian. *Staat und Geschichtswissenschaft in Deutschland und Frankreich 1871–1914: Situation und Werk von Geschichtsprofessoren and den Universitäten Berlin, München, Paris*, 2 vols. Bern etc.: Peter Lang, 1988.

Suematsu Kenchō. 'Rekishi kenkyūhō ni tsukite'. *Shigaku zasshi* 17.8 (1906): 1–18.

———. (ed. Tanaka Akira). *Shūtei Bōchō kaiten shi*. Kashiwa shobō, 1980.

Takeuchi Hiroshi. *Rainichi seiyō jinmei jiten*. Nichigai Associates, 1983.

Tanaka, Akira. *Meiji ishinkan no kenkyū*. Sapporo: Hokkaidō daigaku tosho kankōkai, 1987.

Tanaka, Stefan. *Japan's Orient: Rendering Past into History*. Berkeley: University of California Press, 1993.

Taranczewski, Detlev. 'Einige Aspekte der Rezeption deutscher Geschichtswissenschaft in Japan'. In *Deutschland–Japan in der Zwischenkriegszeit*, eds Josef Kreiner and Regine Mathias, 385–402. Bonn: Bouvier, 1990.

Tōkyō daigaku hyakunenshi iinkai, ed. *Tōkyō daigaku hyakunenshi: Tsūshi 1–3; Bukyokushi 1–4; Shiryō 1–3*. Tōkyō daigaku, 1984–7.

Tōkyō teikoku daigaku, ed. *Tōkyō teikoku daigaku gojūnenshi*, 2 vols. Tōkyō teikoku daigaku, 1932.

————. *Tōkyō teikoku daigaku gakujutsu taikan,* 2 vols. Monbushō, 1942.

Wildman Nakai, Kate. 'Tokugawa Confucian Historiography: The Hayashi, Early Mito School and Arai Hakuseki'. In *Confucianism and Tokugawa Culture,* ed. Peter Nosco, 62–91. Princeton: Princeton University Press, 1987.

Yamazaki Tōkichi.'Wagaku kōdansho ni okeru *Shiryō* hensan jigyō', *Shigaku zasshi,* 12 (1910): 864–81.

Yoda Gakkai (ed. Gakkai nichiroku kenkyūkai), *Gakkai nichiroku,* 12 vols. Iwanami, 1991–3.

Yoshino Kosaku. *Cultural Nationalism in Contemporary Japan: A Sociological Enquiry.* London, New York: Routledge, 1992.

Zerffi, George Gustav. *The Science of History.* London: W.H. and L. Collingridge, 1879.

Index

f=figure; n=footnote or endnote; **bold**=extended discussion

Abe (Shinzō) government xl
Abe Hideo 116, 118
Abe Hidesuke 118
Academy of Sciences (*Tōkyō gakushi kaiin*)
     67
Acts of Imperial Diet (Germany) 180
administration 74–5, 107
Aichi prefecture 145
Aizu domain 67
akademizumu school xxi–ii, xxii(n), xxxvi,
     xlvii, 108, **119–31**, 189, 191–3, **210–11**
Akamon ('Red Gate') 173
Akasaka 143
Akı 67, 116, 202(n49)
Akizuki Tanetatsu (1833–1904) 19, 20, 21
Allerlei Japanisches (*Various Things
     Japanese*, Rieß) 115, 217(n100)
Ancient Greece and Rome 33, 86, 89, 91
Ansei purges 54
anthologies (literary) 70, 204(n88)
Aoyama Nobuhisa (1820–1906) 20, 139
Aoyama Nobumitsu (1808–70) 20
Aoyama Nobuyuki (1776–1843) 13
applied history xli, xlii, 16, **56–66**, 128, 129,
     169, 193
Arai Hakuseki 14, 101
archives xvii, xxviii, xxxix, xlvii, 6, 26, 58,
     125, 217(n100)
     see also National Archives
archivists 53, 139
ari no mama (historical facts 'as they were')
     xxiii, **15–16**, 127, 188
Arisugawa no Miya (family of court nobles)
     60
Asahi shinbun 153
Ashikaga period 48, 126, 162
Ashikaga Takauji 62, 142
Asia 91, 92, 191
Asiatic Society of Japan 115
Assembly for Protection of National Polity of
     Great Japan 167
Atarashii Rekishi Kyōkasho (2001) xxxix,
     xl(n)
Atarashii Rekishi Kyōkasho o Tsukurukai

xxxviii–ix, xli
Austria 33, 125
Austrian Historical Institute (1881–) 181
available modernities xxvi, xxix

Baishōron (historical tale) 126, 211(n74)
     see also Taiheiki
bakufu 2, 3, 19–21, 25, 38, 45, 54, 57, 141,
     142, 202(n56), 221(n18)
Bälz, Erwin 108, 208(n24), 210(n51)
Ban Nobutomo 101
bankoku no chijoku o ukuru xxv
bankoku to gotaiji xxv
Barraclough, Geoffrey (1908–84) xx, 4
Bavarian Academy: Historical Commission 6,
     180–1
Bayly, Christopher Alan xxiv
Bei-Ō kairan jikki xxix(n)
Berlin xiii, 109, 114, 118, 162
Bernheim, Ernst (1850–1942) 186–7,
     223(n56)
big history xli–ii
biography xlvii, 10, 14, 47, 54, 58, 64, 67, 69,
     72, 78, 80, 88, 105, 113, 162, 209(n32),
     213(n35)
Bismarck, Otto von 184
Bitchū domain 202(n49)
blended modernities (Gluck) xxviii
Bo gakushi shiseki henshū ron (*A Certain
     Scholar's Discussion of Compiling
     Histories*) 79
Bōchō kaitenshi (*History of Great
     Achievements of Chōshū and Suō*)
     (Suematsu) 14, 69, 94, 204(n87),
     205(n23), 207(n46), 229
Bod, Rens **xxxiii–iv**
Boshin war (1868) 18, 57
Breisach, Ernst 187, 223(n51, n57)
Buckle, Thomas Henry (1821–62) 87, 123,
     197(n31)
Buddhism 8, 12, 57
Bun (journal) 38, 136
bungakuteki shiha (literary faction) 128
bunmei ha (enlightenment faction) 127

bunmei kaika (civilization and enlightenment) xxix

Bunmeiron no gairyaku (*Theory of Civilization*, Fukuzawa, 1875) 13

bunmeishi (civilization) **13**, 122, 133

bunsai (literary talent) 54

bureaucracy 20, 22, 30, 82, 120, 179

Butterfield, (Sir) Herbert (1900–79) **15**

Buzen (Fukuoka prefecture) 83

cabinet system (*naikaku seido*, 1885–) 30, 94, 166–8

Cabinet: College of Historiography (1886) 36

Cabinet: Temporary Office of Historiography (*Rinji shūshikyoku*, 1886–8) **36–9**, 199(n40)

   transferred to Imperial University (1888) 2, 3, 48, 49, 54, 56, 93, **109–10**, 112, 139, 141

   see also Historiographical Institute

Caesar 87

Cambridge University xxxii(n), 94

censorship 90, 137, 217(n103)

central government 27, 59

centralization 7, 18, **24–6**, 107, 132, 183

Chamberlain, Basil Hall (1850–1935) 112, 122

Chiba Isao xi , xlvi

Chiba prefecture 107

Chihaya fortress 146

China **xxvii**, 7, 11, 26, 30, 52, 96, **97**, 102, 129, 138, 164, 191, 201(n31), 214(n53)

   history 63, 111, 117, 184

Chinese histories 7, 10, 71, 72, 78, 85, 95, 188, 223(n47)

Chinese Learning (*kangaku*) **xxxiv–v**, 19–20, 22, 32, 41–3, 45–6, 51, 56, 79, 83, 91, 106, 120–2, 135, 150, 154, 158, 191, 197(n4)

   versus National Learning **138–41**, **213**

Chinese literature 149, 184

Chō Hikaru 25, 43, 46, 49

Chō Jukichi 116

Chōkei Emperor 103

Chōno Tōkage (1831–1916) **55–6**

Chōshū domain 2, 14, 18, 47, 67, 69, 202(n49)

Chōya Kyūbun hōkō (draft collection of documents) 76, 101, 108

Chōya shinbunsha (newspaper company) 135

Christianity 90, 92, **137**, 150, 151, 154, 156, 187, 216(n78), 217(n102)

chronicles xvii, xxxiv, **7**, **9–10**, 41, 62, **103**, 175, 192, **196(n14)**, 203(n79)

   'annals' xxii, xxiii, **8**, 14, 69, 76, 78–9, 95,

97, 98, 126, 181, 188, 205(n17), 223(n47)

   see also Fukkoki

Chronicles of German Towns 180–1

Chronological History of Great Japan see Dainihon hennenshi

citizenship **xli**

Clarendon: Edward Hyde, Earl of (1609–74) 87

clerks (*shoki*) 41, 56, 77, 161

co-editor (*kyōshū*) 41

College of Historiography (*Shūshikan*, 1877–86) 20, **28–9**, 59, 198(n22), 212(n14), 218(n116)

   budget 28, 32

   central task (compilation of official history) 50, 94

   failure to produce short-term results 36

   goal 'clearly defined' (1881) 36

   from government office to University Institute **32–9**

   internal problems (1881) **31–2**

   officials (criticism) **36**

   progress reports (1876–1888) **49–50**, 201(n17)

   reorganization (1881) **29–32**, 47–8, **50–6**, 71, 94, **201–2**

   see also 'Cabinet: Temporary Office of Historiography'

College of Historiography: activities **40–70**, **200–4**

   'applied history' **56–66**

   organization and staff (from 1881) **50–6**

   organization and staff (to 1881) **40–50**, **200–1**

   rivals **66–70**

College of Historiography: Department of Topography 28, 49, 50

   see also topography

Commander for Subjugation of East (*tōsei taisōtoku*) 72

Comprehensive Mirror for Aid in Government (*Shiji zukan*) 97

Confucianism **11–12**, 16, 19, 22, 31, 34, 42, 43, 52, 63, **97**, 100, 105, 133, 138, 167

constitutional government **26–7**, 34

constitutional history 114, 115

constitutional monarchy 3, 184

'Constitutions of Our Country' (Shigeno lecture, 1889) 38

contemporary history (Barraclough) 4

'Control of Customs during Spring Festivities' xxv

copyists 51, 153, **201(n25)**

Council of State (*Dajōkan*) 18, 47, 49, 55, 75, 93, 174, 208(n16), 228

abolition (1885) 36
headquarters destroyed by fire (1873) 19,
    57, 71
reorganization (1875) 27
reorganized around Central Chamber (*Seiin*)
    24
Council of State: Central Chamber (abolished,
    1877) 8, 24, 28
Council of State: Department of Imperial
    Genealogies 25
Council of State: Department of History
    (*Rekishika*, 1872–5) 23–8, 40–1, 43–6,
    57–8, **59–61**, 63–4, 67, 71, 74, 102,
    198(n14), 202(n53)
    centralization of government **24–6**
    definition of tasks (1873) 25
    officials **25**
    see also Office of Historiography
Council of State: Department of Topography
    (*Chishika*, 1872–) **24–5**, 28, 58,
    198(n14)
    see also topography
cultural borrowing (Gibb) **xxviii**
culture xiv, 183, 191

Daigakkō or University **19–20**
Dainihon hennenshi (*Chronological History of
    Japan*) xviii, xxiii, xxvii, xlvii, **3–4**, **32**,
    35–7, 53–4, 56, 70, **94–100**, 102, 104,
    107, 123, 141–3, 148, 161, 181,
    207(n48), 218(n116), 225
    abandoned (1893) 100
    close connection with *Dainihonshi* 98–9
    commencement of research (1882) 3, 32
    discontent (broader) 36
    editors **52–3**
    essays **97–9**
    guidelines **95–7**
    Iwakura's discontent 35
    'not fundamental departure from traditional
        historiography' 94, 99
    work 'did not progress satisfactorily' 32
Dainihon ishin shiryō (documents of Meiji
    Restoration) 175
Dainihon ishin shiryō kōyō (essential
    materials of Meiji Restoration) 175
Dainihon kinsei shiryō (1953–) 175
Dainihon kokiroku (old journals, 1952–) 175
Dainihon kokutai yōgodan 167
Dainihon komonjo (official documents,
    published 1901–) 172, **174–5**, 176
Dainihon shiryō (historical materials,
    published 1901–) 97, 125, 164, 168–9,
    172, **174**, 175, 176, 178, 192
    'inspired by MGH' 179

Dainihon yashi (*Private History of Japan*,
    Iida) **60**, 202–3(n56)
Dainihonshi (*History of Great Japan*) **9–11**,
    20, 38, 47, 63, 66, 75–6, 80–1, 94–5, 99,
    101, **104**, 106, 136, 139, 142, 144, 161,
    164, 168, 190, 207(n48)
    essays **97–8**
    final version (1906) 10
    imperial imprimatur (1809) 10
    main section (*honki*) 10
    'most remarkable feature' 10
    preface (1897) 98
daiseishin (foundation of Japan) 193
Dajō ruiten (imperial decrees) 19, 66,
    197(n1), 225
Dajōkan see Council of State
Date, house of 175
Date Munenari (1817–92) 48, **54–5**, 67, **201–
    2(n32–5)**, 225, 230
    'relieved of office' (1886) 54
Delbrück, Ernst 114
Delbrück, Hans (1848–1939) **113–14**
democracy **xli**
Department for Examination of Imperial
    Genealogies (1870–) 23
Department of History *see* 'Council of State:
    Department of History'
Department of Rites (*Jingikan*) 18, 22, 23, 40,
    45, 55, 61
Department of Shrines (*Jingū shichō*) 67
Department of Topography 62, 73
Derrida, Jacques xxxii(n)
diaries 175, 176, 200(n12, n14), 217(n100),
    220(n140), 226
digital revolution xi, xi(n)
'Discussing the Methods for Compiling
    National History' (Shigeno lecture, 1879)
    78
discovery versus representation **15–16**
Dixon, James Main (1856–1933) 108
Doi Michimasu (?–1336) 61–2
Doitsugaku kyōkai (Association for German
    Sciences, 1881) 184
domains 26, **57–9**, **67–8**, 72, **202(n49)**
    abolition (1871) 18, 24
Dōseikan (private school) 149, 216(n76)
dōtoku (morals) 122
'Dr Obliterator' (Shigeno Yasutsugu) 15,
    141–7, 174, **213–15**
Droysen, Johann Gustav (1808–86)
    xxx(n71), 115, 180, 182, 189
    lectures on *Historik* 186

earthquake (1923) 173
East Asia xxxvi, xl(n)

Echigo (Niigata prefecture) 52
Echizen domain 202(n49)
editors 31–2, 41, 46, 48–9, **52–3**, 56, 77, 94,
  161–2, 200(n13)
editorial 'Datsu-A ron' (Escape from Asia,
  1885) xxvi
Edo *see* Tokyo
Edo period *see* Tokugawa shogunate
Edo Society (1889–) 124
education xxvi–vii, xxxix(n), xl, **xli**, xliii, 1,
  2, 16, **19**, 23, **30–1**, 45, 54, 66, 79, 81, 83,
  134, 147, **184**, 185, 188
  versus scholarship **163–71, 219–21**
Education Law (*gakusei*, 1872) 63
Education Office 25, 32
Ehime prefecture 47, 49, 54, 203(n63)
Eine Vergangenheit für die japanische Nation
  (Mehl, 1992) xii, 230
elites xxi, 81, 153, 154, 170, 186, 217(n95,
  n103)
emperor-centred view xviii, xxi–ii, 178, 192,
  193
emperors xxxvi, 10, 63, 96, 174, 178, 179,
  192
  'imperial rule'/'imperial rulers' 10, 11, 20,
  21, 22, 55
  unbroken line 34
Encyclopedia Judaica 114
England 34, 64, **113–14**, 176, 210(n45)
English Constitutional History (Rieß, 1897–8)
  115
English Historical Review (1886–) 111–12
Enlightenment 5, 35, 63, 100, 120, 133, 149,
  185, 187, 191, 215(n70)
Etō Shinpei 23, **26**
Etsuko Kang xxxvii
Europe xxii, xxvi, xxviii, xxxiii–iv, xl, 23, 26,
  33–4, 108, 115, 117–18, 120, 125, 135–7,
  162, 179, 184, 222–3(n45)
  state of historical studies (late C19) **5–7**

facts xxii–iii, xxx, 9, 14, 16, 27, 76–8, 88, 96,
  99–102, 105, 120, 122, 124, 127, **128**,
  130, 135, 166, 171, 186, 188, 192–3,
  202(n49), 224(n82)
Faust (Goethe) 87
feudal domains (abolition, 1871) 2
feudal lords 57–8, 174
Florenz, Karl 118
foreign affairs 66, 84, **125–6**, 132, **153–4**,
  175, **176**, 179, 211(n72)
foreigners 140, 213(n39)
Formosa (Taiwan) 53
France xxix, xxxi, 4, 33, 34, 90, 111, 126,
  161, 180

Franco-Prussian War (1870–1) xiii(n), 184
Frederick the Great (1712–86) 87
freedom of speech/academic freedom xl,
  129–30, 134, 137, **153–5**, 170, 177, **178**,
  186, 217(n103)
French Revolution 136
Fudoki (provincial topographies) 25
Fujikawa Shōgen (1818–91) 44, 46
Fujino Masahira (1826–88) 20, 22, 23, 46,
  47–8, 49, 52, 94, 99
Fujino Tatsuji 149
Fujioka Nobukatsu xxxviii, xxxix, xxxix(n)
Fujisawa Genzō **166–7**, 220(n139)
Fujisawa Nangaku 167
Fujishima shrine 61
Fujita Yūkoku 105
Fujiyama Bun (or Yutaka) 136
Fuken shiryō (Historical Materials of
  Prefectures) 25, **58–9**
fukenshi (histories of prefectures) 58
fukko (return to imperial rule; restoration) 72
Fukko gaiki 71
Fukko kōjin 57
Fukko ran'yō (Brief Account of Meiji
  Restoration, Nagamatsu) **23–4**, 71
Fukkoki (*Chronicle of Meiji Restoration*) 26–
  7, 29, 36, 40–1, 49–50, 51, 54, 58, 67–8,
  71–2, 75–6, 135, 175, 204(n3)
  'almost abandoned' (1882) 73
  motivation **72–3**
  preface 24
fukoku kyōhei (rich country, strong army)
  xxix, 3
fuku kanji (deputy inspector) 49
fuku kyokuchō 42
Fukuba Bisei (1831–1907) 34–5, 199(n34)
Fukuchi Gen'ichirō (Ōchi; 1841–1906) **135**
Fukui prefecture 59
Fukushima prefecture 123
Fukuzawa Yukichi (1835–1901) xxvi, xxxi,
  13, 37, 149
fukyō (strengthening and enriching) 79
Futatsu no kindai (Mochida Yukio, 1988) xvi

Gaikan ishinshi (*Outline of Meiji Restoration*;
  1940) 68
Gakkō see Shōheikō
gakuryoku (scholarly abilities) 54
Gakushūin (Peers' School) 117
Gamō Keitei 20, 42, 45
geijutsu (art) 190, 193
genealogies 9, 58, 61
  see also imperial genealogies
general public **132–7**, 162, 174, 217(n102)
genrō (elder statesmen) 68

German Asiatic Society (OAG) xv(n)
German Historical Institute (1888–) 181
German History in 19th Century (Treitschke, 1871) 182
Germany xvii, xx, xxi, xxiv, **xxx**, 90–1, 111–12, **113–14**, 115, 118, 122–3, 154, 193
historical scholarship 180
historical scholarship (exemplar for Europe) 16
history and memory **xv–xvi**
history and nation **16–17**, **179–94**, **222–4**
national unification (1871) 16–17, 181–2
Germany: Wars of Liberation (1813–15) 179
Geschichtskultur (historical culture) 14
Gesellschaft für Natur- und Völkerkunde Ostasiens (OAG) 115, 116
Gibb, Sir Hamilton **xxviii**
globalism (global history) **xxiv–v**
Gluck, Carol ix, xxviii, xxx, 4, 228
Godaigo Emperor (1318–39) **61**, 95, 104, **142–3**, 144–7, 167, 207(n48)
Goethe, Johann Wolfgang von (1749–1832) 87
Goethe Institute xiv
Gojō Hidemaro (fictional) **171**, 192
Gokeizu torishirabe kakari (1870–) 23
Gokomatsu Emperor 25, 40, 76, 142, 207(n48)
Gokyū Hisabumi (1823–86) 43, 45
Gomizunoo Emperor 76
Gōmoku Chōhō 43
Gomurakami Emperor 143
Goslar: Imperial Palace 183
Gotō Shōjirō 26, 27
government historiography project (*shūshi jigyō*) xvii
goyō kakari (commissioners) 21, 22, 25, 41, 43–4, 47, 49, 138
Goyōzei Emperor 9, 76
Groot, Adolf (1854–1934) 108
Guizot, François (1787–1874) 87, 197(n31)
Gukanshō (*Outline of Foolish View of History*, Jien, 1220) 8
gundan senki (war tales) 82
gunki monogatari (war tales) 8
gunki senki monogatari (military and war tales) 106
Gyōseikan (Executive Council) 19

Hachisuka Mochiaki 67
Hagi domain 23
Hagino Yoshiyuki (1860–1924) 119, 141, 158, 165
Hagiwara Seichū (1830–98) 42, 46
Hagyūda Morio 149

haihan chiken (establishment of prefectures) order (1871) xxv(n)
Hamao Arata (1849–1925) 158, 160–3, 169, 177
Hanawa Hokiichi (1746–1821) 9, **11**, xxvii, 21, 41, 66, **76**, 101, 138, 174, 179
Hanawa Tadatsugu (1832–1918) 21, 22, **23**, 138
hanbatsu government **68**
hanshi henshū 58
Hanshi kō (history of domains, 1876) 50
Hara Kei (1856–1921), 220(n140)
Harbin 68
Harnack, Adolf (1851–1930) 223(n47)
Hardtwig, Wolfgang 14, 195(n8), 228
Hayashi Gahō (1618–80) 9, 19
Hayashi Jussai (1768–1841) 76
Hayashi Razan (1583–1657) 9, 19
Heian period (794–1185) 2, 80, 175
Hennen komonjo ('Primary Documents in Chronological Order') (Tanaka, 1884) 105
Hennenshi hensan kakari see Historiographical Institute
hennenshi o sen su ('compilation of chronological history') 51
hennentai (annals) 10, 78, 95, 205(n17)
hensan (compilation) 172
hensan iin (editors) 56, 161–2
hensan iinchō (chief editor) 56
hensan joshu (assistant) 56
Henshū chakushu no hōhō (*Methods of Beginning Compilation*) 75, 77
henshū chōkan, henshū fukuchōkan (chief editors) 31–2, 51
Henshū reisoku (guidelines for compilation) **95–8**, 207(n98), 227
henshūkan (editors) 31–2, 48, 49, 94, 200(n13)
Herbart, Johann Friedrich (1776–1841) 123
heroes (debunked) 122, 126, 137
High Treason Incident (1911) **166–7**, 170
higher education 138, 210(n56)
'Hints for Using Historiographical Institute' (omission) xlv
Hiraizumi Kiyoshi (1895–1984) 178, **193**, 224(n79–80)
Hirano Shigehisa (1814–83) 44, 45
Hirata Kanetane (1799–1880) 22, 23, 139
Hirose Shin'ichi (1819–84) 25, 43, 46
historians **89–91**, 160, 169, 171, 189–90, 194
academic ~ (*kokkaha, kōshōha, risōha*) 128
professional ~ **xl–xlii**, 3, 4, 6, 15, 186, 193
qualities required **89**
see also historical scholarship

historians' dispute (*Historikerstreit*, 1986–7)
  xv–xvi, 17
'Historical Development of Realism' (Zerffi
  lectures, 1876–80) **87–8**, 92
historical interpretation 16, 188
historical meaning xix, xx, xxi
historical novels 5, 193, 224(n82)
historical research xii–xiii, xix, **xxi–xxiii** ,
  xxxi, xliv, **6**, 131, 193, 194
  core principles xlii
historical revisionism xiv, xxxix(n)
historical scholarship 4, 14, 16, **65**, **101–2**,
  105, **126**, 142, **163–71**, 189–90,
  208(n15), 215(n64), **219–21**
  external demands **131**
  taken into service of politics 188
  see also scientific historiography
Historical Society (*Shigakkai*, 1889–) xiii,
  111–12, 123, **124**, 125, 144
  Shigeno's inaugural lecture 147
historical success **182**
historical terminology **64**
historical writing xix, **xxi–xxiii** , xliv, 16, 47,
  74–80, **89–90**, 131, 134, 140, 189, 194
  versus 'recording current affairs' 26
historicism **5–7**, 127, 197(n39), 180, 182,
  185, 187, 189
Historiographical Institute (Tokyo, 1888–) ii,
  ix, xii, xxxvi, **xlv**, xlvi, xlix, 2–3, 13, 16,
  57–8, **65–6**, 68–9, 72, 97, 99, 104, 107,
  110–13, 116–17, **119**, 120–2, 128–9, 134,
  136, 139–40, 147, 154, 164, 168, 170–1,
  185, 187, 192–3
  annual report (*Tōkyō daigaku Shiryō
    hensanjo hō*, 1967–) 178
  budget 161, 172
  closure (1893–5) xxxv, 4, 52, 123, 125,
    137, 141, 148, **156–63**, **217–18**
  compilation (1907–) of documents on
    foreign relations 66
  core questions **xxi–iii**
  databases (1984–) 176
  development (since 1895) **172–9**, **221–2**
  field trips 173–4
  functions 202(n37), **159–63**
  headquarters (1911–) 173, 221(n7)
  Japanese title 56, 202(n37)
  known informally as 'History Office'
    (*Shikyoku*) 39, 176
  main task **159–60**, 173
  members (own research) 162, 177, 178
  official authority on past 177
  organization and staff **172–3**, 221(n4–5)
  origins 176
  permanence (1905–) 163
  present name, *Shiryō hensanjo* (1929) 172
  publication of documents (1901–) 163
  regulations (1895) **162–3**
  representation abroad **177**
  self-defence (1889 memorandum)
    218(n109)
  textbook compilation 177
  see also 'Council of State: Department of
    History'
Historiographical Institute: Library 175
Historiographical Institute: Topographical
  Department 159
historiography xi, **xvii–xxiii**, xxvii(n), xxviii,
  185, 189
  aim 88
  conservative v progressive (*hoshu shigaku* v
    kaishin shigaku) 155, 217(n102)
  European 117
  factions **127–8**
  imperial rescript (1869) **1**
  institutional xxx
  Japanese tradition **7–8**, **195–6(n13–14)**
  Japanese tradition (summary) **12**
  lessons **xxxvii–xliii**
  public expectations **15**
  Rankean **xxxiii–iv**
  schools of thought (1892–3), 217(n101)
  in service of Meiji Government **18–39**,
    197–9
  terminology **xliv**
  Tokugawa period **196(n18)**
  traditional 94, 104, 188
  trends **127–8**
  Western 79, 81–2, **83–6**, 99, 100, **113–19**,
    121, 151–2, 188, **209–10**
  see also official historiography
Historische Zeitschrift (1859–) 111, 180
Historisches Jahrbuch (1880–) 111
history
  as academic discipline 3, **4–7**, **101–31**, 132,
    134, **207–11**
  conflict with ideology xvii, **132–71**, **211–
    21**
  in courtroom **xxxviii**
  decided by imperial edict 16, 64
  definition **75**, 205(n12)
  meaning of ~ 185
  modern academic discipline xxx, 3, 13, 14
  national identity (definition) 180
  official distortion (failure of academic
    history to resist, 1930s) 16
  philosophy of ~ 5, 122, **186–7**
  pragmatic view 5
  public debates **xl–xliii**, xlvii, **132–7**
  purpose **1–2**

role 3, 131, 154
scholarly traditions **101–8**
scientific xix, xxi, xxx, xxxi
see also national history
history education xxi, **62–6**, 170, 203(n69–70)
versus history scholarship **65**
history fever xxxv, 133, 134, 189
history office (*shikyoku*) 39, 79, 106, 139, 141, 176
branches in Mito and Tokyo (1702–) **10**
History of Prussian Politics (Droysen) 182
History Society (*Shigaku kyōkai*, 1883–) **32–3**, 36, 82, 139–40
History and the State in Nineteenth-Century Japan
bigger picture **xxiv–xxxvii**
book purpose **12**
conclusion **172–94**, **221–4**
contribution xi
English version (1998) xxii, xxxii(n), **xliv–v**, **xlvii–viii**
first edition (1998) **ix–x**
first edition (circumstances in which written) **xii–xvi**
first edition (reception) **xvii–xxiii**
further research xvii, 183
German version (1992) xxxv, **xlvii**
idea for book **17**
importance and relevance **xlii**
introduction xxxvii, **1–17**, **195–7**
jacket illustration xlv
Japanese edition xi, xvii, **xliv**, xlvi
nation and modern world **xxiv–xxxi**
national history and scientific history **xxxi–vii**
new preface (purpose) x
notes on new edition **xliv–v**
reason for second edition ix
Hizen (domain) 2, 18
Hizen (Saga prefecture) 53
hōken jidai (time of feudalism) 27
Hōki bunrui taizen (collection of government decrees) 19, 66, 197(n1), 228
Hokkaidō Colonization Assets Scandal 29
Hoko hirohi Sasaki Takayuki nikki (1970–7) 176
Honchō seiki 126, 211(n74)
Honchō tsugan (official annals) 9, 76, 97, 98
Hongō Sadao 149
Honshu 45
Hōrei zensho (imperial decrees) 66, 228
Horiguchi Shōkai 42
Hoshino Hisashi (Tsune, Hōjō; 1839–1917) 38, 43, **52–3**, 54, 56, 94, 99, 105, 109,

111–12, 124, 126, 134, 136, 139–40, 144–5, 147, 152, 156, **159–61**, 173, 177, 179, 212(n15), 213(n42), 218(n113), 221(n4, n8), 225, 228
abandonment of Kume (1892) 153
on application of history **122**
'few original ideas' **123**
on selection of sources **122**
Hosokawa, house of 69
Hōya Tōru xlvi, xlvii, 52, 221(n10)
humanities xxxii, **xxxiii–iv**, 5
hyō (tables) 10
hyōronka (publicists) 189

Ibaraki prefecture 107, 123
Ichimura Sanjirō 117
ideology xvii, xx, xxxv, 4, 7, 17, 65, 127, 178–9, 181
conflict with history **132–71**, **211–21**
versus scholarship 215(n64)
Iemochi (shogun) 124
Ieyasu (shogun) 9, 14
Igakusho (school of medicine) 19
Igirisu shōkanchō nikki 176
Ii family 175
Ii Naosuke 177, 202(n56), 221(n18)
Iida Tadahiko (1799–1861) **60**, 202–3(n56)
Iida Takesato (1827–1902) 109, 139
Iitoyo-ao-no-himemiko 61, **103**, 208(n5)
Ijichi Masaharu (1828–86) **28–9**, **41**, 46, 48, 53, 54, 198(n22), 200(n12), 208(n16)
Ijichi Sadaka (1826–87) 52, **53**, 94, 99
Ikeda Kōen 159, 161, 218(n113), 225
imperial edict (1905) 172
see also Dajō ruiten
imperial genealogies 23, 25, 29, 40–1, 44, 48, 50, 61, **64**, **102–4**, 106
imperial house 8, 61, 130, 140, 150, 152, 154, 156, 163, 168, 171, 176, 178, 183, 190, 203(n60)
discussion 'severely restricted' 186
financial position 30
Imperial Household Archives (*Shoryōbu*) 200(n12)
Imperial Household Ministry 22, **28–9**, 36, 41, 44–5, 48, 51, 55, 61, **67**, 73, 103, 138–40, 151, 158, 160, 164–5
Imperial Household Ministry: Office of Compilation (*Henshūkyoku*, 1883) 23, **34–5**, 63
Imperial Household Office 69
Imperial Oath (1868) xxv, 18
Imperial Rescript on Education (1890) **132–3**, 137, 156
Imperial Rescript on Historiography (*Shūshi*

no choku; 1869) ii, **xlv, 1–2**, 3, 20, **21–2**, 32, 48, 62, 71, 74, 83, 94–5, 97, 100, 134, 158, 185
Meiji Tennō shinkan gosatasho, Meiji ninen shigatsu yokka ii
Shūshi no choku 22
Imperial University, Tokyo (1886–97; 'Tokyo Imperial University' from 1897) 12, 14, 23, 35, 41, 48–9, 51, 52–3, **65–6**, 70, 101, **108–12**, 113–18, 131, 137, 150, **152–4**, 155, 160, 170, 184, 201(n25), **208(n22)**, 211(n72), 223(n47)
graduation ceremonies 176
library destroyed by fire (1923) 58
literature department 161
promulgation of Meiji Constitution (celebrations, 1889) 38
songen (dignity) 153
see also University of Tokyo
Imperial University: Department of Chinese History (1904–10; subsequently Department of Oriental History) 117
Imperial University: Department of Chinese Literature 139
Imperial University: Department of Classics (*Koten kōshūka*) 109, 111–12, 120, 139–41, 162, 173
Imperial University: Department for Historical and Topographical Compilation 110
Imperial University: Department of History (*Shigakka*, 1887–) 38, **108–9**, 110, 112, 119–20, 125, 187
Imperial University: Department of Japanese History (*Kokushika*, 1889–) xvi, 3, 34, 37–9, 62, 109, **110–11**, 112, 119–20, 141, 165, 173, 178
Imperial University: Department of Japanese Literature 139
Imperial University: Department of Oriental History (1910–) 117
Imperial University: Department of Western History (1904–) 117
Imperial University: Faculty of Law 140
Imperial University: Historiographical Institute (1888–) **37–9**, 116
Imperial University: 'Temporary Department for Compilation of Chronological History' (1888–91) 109
Indians 156
industrialization xxiv, 4, 7
Inoue Kaoru (1835–1915) 68, 69, 114
Inoue Kiyoshi (historian) 169, 220(n150)
Inoue Kowashi (1843–95) 29, 35, **156–61**, 177, **217–18**
papers 218(n113–16), **225-6**

Inoue Michiyasu (1866–1941), 220(n142)
Inoue Tetsujirō (1856–1944) 126, 137, **154**, 183–4, 223(n47)
Inoue Yorikuni (1839–1914) 136, 139, 212(n23), 213(n35)
'Insight in History' (Kume) 56
Institute for Japanese Literature (*Kōten kōkyūjo*, 1882–) 31, 51, 67, 139, 140, 162
later Kokugakuin University 31
institutions xxxiii, 189
internet **xliv–v**
Inukai Tsuyoshi (1855–1932) 167
Isawa Shūji (1851–1917) 64
Ise Sadatake 101
ishin ('renewal') 2
Ishin shiryō hensankai (Association for Compilation of History of Meiji Restoration) **68**, 69, 175
Ishin shiryō hikitsugibon 68
Ishin shiryō kōyō 176
Ishinshi (*History of Meiji Restoration*; 1936–41) **68**
Isoda, M. 116–17, 124
Itagaki Taisuke (1837–1919) **26–7**
Itō Hirobumi (1841–1909) 26, 29–30, **33–4**, 35–6, 69, 83–5, 91–2, 94, 146, **156**, 166–7, 184, 199(n30–1), 205(n27), 217(n107), 218(n113)
assassination (1909) 68
Itō Myōji (1857–1934) 33–4
Itō Sukeo 42
Itō Takashi xiii–xiv, **xxxix**, xlvi, xlvii–viii
ittō kyōshū 42
ittō shoki 42, 44, 45
ittō shūsen 41, 42, 43
Iwagaki Matsunae 13
Iwakura Embassy (1871–3) xxv, xxix, xxxv, 23, 26–7, 37, 53, 71, 135, 148, 184, 191
Iwakura kō jikki (1906) 69
Iwakura Tomomi (1825–83) 18–19, 26, 28–9, **33–6**, 51, 57, 61, 64, 67–8, 94, 103, 157, 164, 199(n29–30), 208(n4), **226**
Iwate prefecture 123
Iwaya Osamu (1834–1905) 49, **54–5**, 201–2(n35)
Iyo (Ehime prefecture) 49

Jahrbücher zur deutschen Geschichte 181
Japan
borrowings from West 5, 7
colonial empire 193
contemporaneous with West **4–5**
cultural achievements 177
cultural imports (confirmation of existing

tendencies) 185
cultural imports (selectivity) xx, 185
cultural uniqueness 35, 133, 137, 149, 190
Germany 'prime model' (late C19) 183,
   222(n43)
history and nation **179–94, 222–4**
'land of gods' 183
medieval xxxvi
names and terms **xlix**
road to empire **xxxv–vii**, xlii
second-largest economy in world xv
special characteristics 34, 183
watershed (1890) 132
Japan-British Exhibition (1910) 177
Japanese Bride (Tamura) 137
*Japanese Historians and the National Myths,
   1600–1945* (Brownlee, 1997) xxxvi
Japanese history 63, 111, 115, 117, 119, 121,
   129, 156, 184, 192
Japanese language 58, 111, 135, 136, 156
spoken versus written **80–2**, 205(n20)
Japanese Learning (*kokugaku*) xxxiv, 79, 122
Japanese literature 156, 158, 184
'classical texts' 31, 149
Japanese Society for History Textbook Reform
   (Tsukurukai) xxxviii–ix
Japan's Modern Myths (Gluck, 1985) 4
Japan's Orient (Tanaka, 1993) xxii
Jefferson, Thomas (1743–1826) 116
Jews 114, 209(n38)
Jien (Buddhist historian) 8
Jimmu Emperor 169
Jingikan see Department of Rites
Jingū Empress (201–69) 219(n131)
Jinjō shōgaku Nihon rekishi (textbook) 165
Jinnō shōtōki (*Right Succession of Emperors*)
   (Kitabatake, 1339) **8**, 62, 81, 164, 190
jitsuroku
   'government records' 73
   'reliable historical account' 136
jōi tōgō 166
join (assistants) 161
journals 72, 133, 134, 178–9, 193
Juge Shigekuni (1822–84) 45, 46, **55**
junshō shigaku ('pure history') 16, 56, 169

ka'i naigai ('the alien and the proper') 1, **2**
Kaei era (1848–53) 46
Kaga residence 173
Kagahan shiryō 69
kagaku (science) 193
kagakuteki kenkyū (scientific research) 130
Kagoshima 29
Kaifu Toshiki **xxxvii–viii**
Kaikoku shimatsu (Shimada, 1888) 221(n18)

Kaiseijo (Western studies) 19
Kaitei Higohan kokuji shiryō 69
Kajiyama Yoshikado 45
Kamakura period (1185–1333) 1, 38, 146
Kamunagara (journal) 151
kan (officials) xxi, 186
Kan Masatomo (1824–97) 56, 99, 105, 126,
   143–4, 159–60, 168, 213(n42),
   218(n113), 225, 229
Kanagawa prefecture 107
kanbun (Sino-Japanese writing) 33, 58, 95,
   134, 156–8, 199(n35)
   'pure' Chinese **80–3**
Kaneko Kentarō 34
kangae (thought) 158
kangaku (Chinese Learning) 52, 101
kangaku akademizumu xvi(n), xxx
   'tautology' 119
kangakusha (Scholars of Chinese Learning)
   45, 150, 229
kanji (inspector) 49, 51
Kano yō ni (*As If*) 171, 223(n47)
Kant, Immanuel (1724–1804) 90
Kaō kagami (signatures) 176
Kariya Ekisai 101
Kasagi 143
Kashiwazaki prefecture xxv
Katō Hiroyuki (1836–1916) 109, **123, 152–3,
   155**, 158, 220(n142)
Katsura Tarō 166, **167–8**, 220(n140, n142)
katsureki mono (history plays) 146
Kawada Higuma 49, 159, 218(n113), 225
Kawada Takeshi (Ōkō; 1830–96) xlvii, **25–6**,
   40–1, 45, **47**, 49, 62, 104, 106, **128**, 144,
   158, 212(n15)
   achievements 'virtually unknown today' 51
   national history **50–1**
kazoku rei (peerage) 61
Kazoku ruibetsu roku (register of nobles) 61,
   203(n61)
Kazunomiya (sister to emperor) 124
Keene, Donald xiv
Kei-En-jidai 166
Keikoku 216(n84)
Keiō University 115, 118
Keizai zasshi sha 70
Kemmu Restoration 95, 143, 167, 214(n43)
   six hundredth anniversary (1934) 178
kenkyū (research) 172
Kenzō Emperor 103
kiden (biographies) 78
kidentai **10**, 205(n17)
Kido Kōin 26–7, 43, 62, 146, 198(n23),
   214(n56)
Kihara Genrei 43

kiji honmatsu (treatises) 78
Kikuchi Dairoku 118
Kimura Masakoto (1827–1913) 21, **22–3**, 32, **63**, 141
kinnō (loyalty to emperor) 122
kinō (induction) 102
Kinoshita Masatomo 105
Kinsei Nihon kokumin shi (*Modern History of Japanese People*, Tokutomi) 13
Kinsei shiryaku (*Outline of Modern History*, Yamaguchi) xxv, 60, 202(n54)
Kita Sadakichi (1871–1939) **xxxvi–vii**, 65, **165–6**, 168, 170, 200(n15), 220(n133)
Kitabatake Chikafusa 8, 62, 164
kō (chronological outline) 72
Kobayashi Yoshinori xxxix, xxxix(n)
kōbun (annalistic sections) 175
Kōbun ruishū (imperial decrees) 66
Kōbunroku 66
Kōchi domain 55
Kōchō seikan (chronological history of Japan) 47
Kōchō shiryaku (*Historical Outline of Japan*, Aoyama, 1826) 13
Kodama Shōsuke (1836–1905) **135**, 226
kodō ('ancient way') 12
Koeber, Raphael von (1848–1922) 116
Koji ruien (collection of sources) 65, **66–7**, 139
Kojiki (*Records of Ancient Matters*, 712) 7, 103
Kojima (monk) 144, 214(n52)
Kojima Takanori 62, 122, 136, 140, **143–5**, 146–7, 177
kokiroku (documents) 173
kokka (nation state) 132
kokkaha (historians, academic) 128
Kokkō (journal) 151–2, 216(n86)
Kōkoku chishi (Topographies of Empire) 25, 58
kōkoku no seishi (official histories of empire) 75
kōkoku shikan (emperor-centred history) 178, 192, 193
kokubun
  'national language' 81
  'national literature' 141
Kokubungaku (*National Literature*) xxxiv, 141
kokufū (national customs) 135
kokugaku (National Learning) **11–12**, 101, **196(n27)**
Kokugakuin University 218(n113)
Kokugakuin zasshi (journal) **130**, 140, 215(n69)

kokugakuteki kenkyū (nationalistic research) 130
Kokuji kinrō 57
Kokuji ōshō kōkō shishi jinmeiroku (1907) 67
kokumin (people) 132
Kokumin no tomo (journal) 130
Kokumintō party 167
Kokura domain 69
kokushi see national history
Kokushi gan (*View of Our National History*) 62
Kokushi hensan no hōhō o ronzu (Shigeno lecture, 1879) **78**
kokushi henshū (historiography) 74
kokushi henshū goyō kakari (officials for compilation of National History) 22
Kokushi henshū kyoku ('Office for Compilation of National History', 1869) 22, 23
kokushi kōetsu goyō kakari (revision of National History) 22
kokushi no henshū (compilation of history of Japan) 25
Kokushi no shiori (*Introduction to National History*) **140**
Kokushi taikei (*Compendium of Japanese History*, Taguchi) 70
kokushigaku 111
Kokushigan (Shigeno) xxii(n), 128, 152, 164, 192, 220(n135), 229
Kokushika xvi
Kokushiryaku (*Outline of Our National History*, Iwagaki, 1826) 13
kokutai (national polity) 68, 149, 150
Kōmei Emperor 76
Kōmei tennō ki (1906) 69
Komiyama Yasusuke 141
kōmoku format **11**, 72, 79
komonjo (documents) xxvii, 173
Kōmyō Emperor (r. 1336–48) 142
Konakamura Kiyonori (1821–95) 21, **23**, 32, 35, 109, 111, 124, 138, **139–41**, 154, **157**, 212(n15), 213(n35), 229
Konakamura Yorikata (1861–1923) **157–8**, 161
konkyō (fundamental evidence) 106
Kōno Bukichirō 61
Kōno Michimori or Michiharu (?–1364) **61–2**
Konsaisu jinmei jiten (biographical dictionary) 54
Korea xviii, **xxxvi–vii**, 8, 26, 96, 152, 156
kōshō (textual criticism) **101–4**, 122, 124–6, 128, 148, 193
kōshōgaku ('school of verifications and proofs') **11–12**, 101, 108, 121, 126, 191

kōshōha (textual criticism faction) 128
Kōtoku Shūsui 166
koyū no gokokushitsu (special qualities of Japan) 34
kōzasei (professorships) 111
Kreiner, Josef xlvii
Kumamoto 23, 29
Kume Affair (1892) xlvii, 4, 130, 137, 147, **148–56**, 157, 163, 170, 186, **215–17**
literature 215(n64)
Kume Art Museum 205(n21)
Kume hakushi kyūjūnen kaikoroku (memoirs) 216(n78)
Kume Kunitake (1839–1931) xvii, xxvii–xxxi, **xxxv**, 38, **50–1**, **53**, 54, 56, 62, 82, 94–5, 99, **105**, 107, 109, 112, 119, 124, **126**, 134, 136, 139, 168, 189, 191, 207(n48), 211(n66, n88), 214(n43), 229, 230
abandoned by colleagues (1892) 152, 153, 155, 215(n69)
'Abuse of *kōshō*' (lecture, 1901) 111
dismissal (1892) 52–3, **151**, 153, 179, 216(n82)
'real Dr Obliterator' 144
as historian xxxv(n), **51**
influence (failure to exercise) **185–6**
later career 151
'most original scholar' 123, 148
Shiryō sanshū ni tsuki seikyū no ken 105
'some demands concerning the compilation of sources' 105
speech in memory of Taguchi (1911) 216(n89)
'stuck in tradition of Chinese Learning' 155
on *Taiheiki* 213–14(n42)
on textual criticism **128**, 130, 211(n83)
unpopularity **154**
kundoku (Chinese read as Japanese) 80
Kuramochi Jikyū 149, 151, 216(n84)
Kurita Hiroshi (1835–99) 99, 109, 139, 141, **158–9**, 161, 213(n35), 218(n113), 225
Kuroita Katsumi (1874–1946) **xxxvi**, 70, **117–18**, 119, 134, 173, 193, 200(n15)
Kurokawa Harumura 101
Kurokawa Mayori)1829–1906) 109, 141, 212(n15)
Kusaka Hiroshi (1852–1926) 56, 99, 105
Kusunoki Masashige (d 1336) 143, **145–7**, 177, 183, 214(n53, n58)
Kuwana domain 67
kyōiku rekishi ('education history') 169
kyokuchō 43
kyōshū (co-editors) 77

Kyoto 19, 22, 23, 45, 55, 59, 106, 142, 221(n8)
Kyoto: Imperial University (1897) 117, 170, 208(n22)
Kyoto: Nichibunken (1987) **xiv–xv**
kyūha (traditional faction) 127
Kyūji shimon kai (Committee for Inquiring into Ancient Matters, 1890) **124**, 211(n70), 229
Kyushu 45, 107

land ownership **24**
language **80–3**
law 66, 140, 141, 153
League for Establishment of Diet (*Kokkai kisei dōmei*) 29
legitimacy **1–2**, 22, 35, 38, 71, 102–3, **142**, 156, 163
two imperial courts (C14) **163–71**, **219–21**
legitimation xxxvi, 4, 7, **9–10**, 12, **70**, 72, 73, 131, 182, 184, 187–8, 190, 193
Lehrbuch der historischen Methode (Bernheim, 1889) 187, 223(n56)
Leiden (archives) 211(n72)
Leo XIII, Pope (1810–1903) 181
Lévi-Strauss, Claude (1908–2009) xiv
Liberal Democratic Party (LDP) 17
Liebermann, Felix (1851–1925) 209(n32)
Locke, John (1632–1704) 116
loyalists (*sonnōka* or *kinnōka*) 46
Lu (Chinese province) 97

Macaulay, Lord (1800–59) 87, 190
MacMillan, Margaret **xl–xliii**
Maeda, house of 69
Maeda Toshichika 55
Makino Kenjirō 166, 167
Marumaru chinbun 158, 159f
Maruyama Sakura **32–3**
mass society 4, 7
massatsu ron (obliteration theories) **126–7**, 128, 143, 147
Matsudaira Noritsugu 55
Matsudaira Yasukuni 166, 167
Matsumoto Seichō 219(n129), 224(n82), 229
Matsuoka Tokitoshi (1814–77) 19
Matsuura Chōnen 45
Matsuyama (Takahashi) domain 47
Matsuzawa Yūsaku xi, **xvii–xix**, xxvii(n), xxx, xlvi
Maximilian II, King 6, 180
Mazlish, Bruce ix
Mehl, Margaret xxvii(n), xxxv(n), xxxvi(n), xl(n), 195(n3), 202(n35), 205(n27), 207(n45), 212(n9, n12), 215(n64, n67)

doctoral thesis (1991) x, **xii–xiii**, xvi,
xvi(n), xix, xxi
doctoral thesis (1998 edition) xix
personal library **xiv(n)**
publications **230**
meibun (subjects) 121
Meido no tayori (*Mail from Other World*)
144–5
Meiji chūkōshi (*History of Meiji Restoration*)
67
Meiji Constitution (1889) xiii, 3, 7, 16, 29,
30, **32–9**, 114, 132, 183–4, 200(n14),
222–3(n45)
first draft (April 1888) 36–7
Meiji Emperor 30, 64–6, 164–5, 167, 169–70,
176
biography 162
personal rule 24
supremacy to be upheld versus parliament
33
Meiji government xi, xviii, xxv, xxvii
historiography in service of ~ **18–39**, **197–9**
Meiji historiography **xii–xvi**, **14**, 197(n29)
Meiji ishin jinmei jiten (biographical
dictionary) 54
Meiji ishin shiryō senshū (two volumes) 176
Meiji Japan xix, xxviii, xxix, xxxiv, 4
global context xxxi
Meiji liberalism 137, 213(n32)
Meiji no Sandai bunsō ('Three Literary
Masters of Meiji Era') 51
Meiji parliament 3, 7, 16, **29–30**, 31–3, 36,
79, 132, 161, 166–7
see also National Parliament
Meiji parliament: Upper House 30, 143,
212(n15)
Meiji Restoration (1868) xxiii, xlv, **1–3**, 10,
13, 35, 44, 46–8, 70
causes (Shigeno, 1889) **38**
centenary **176**
fulfilment of Kemmu Restoration 167
historiographical revival **18–24**
ideology 142
intellectual foundations 12
ōsei fukko (restoration of imperial rule) 68,
72
pace of change **7**
record of fallen (*Junnan jinmeishi*, 1877–8)
50
recorded **71–4**
successful conclusion of Kemmu
Restoration 142–3
tombs of deceased (inscriptions) 62
Meiji shiyō (*Outline of Meiji Restoration*) 50,
62, 73, 135, 175

Meiji tennō ki (1932) 69
Mervart, David xxvi–vii
methodological nationalism xi, xxxvii
methodology 186, 187, 223(n55)
Methodology of History (Rieß, 1896) 115
Mie prefecture 59
Mikami Sanji (1865–1939) xxxvi, xl, 56, **65**,
69, 116, **119**, 124–5, **141**, **157**, 160, **161–
2**, 163–5, 168, **169–70**, 172, 174, 176,
177, 186, 193, 210(n42, n53), **218–21**,
230
reminiscences 219(n124), 221(n8), 228
military power 2, 18, 24
min (people) xxi, 186
Min'yūsha historians 13, 128, 130
Minamoto military house 13
Minamoto Yoritomo (shogun) 38, 174
Minato River 146, 214(n53)
Minatogawa Shrine 146
Ming China 200(n13)
ministers 27, 30
minister of left 24
minister of right 24, 36, 64
ministries 18, 57
Ministry of Education (*Monbushō*, 1871–) xii,
xiv, xlvii, 19, 25, 42, 47, **59–66**, 68, 109,
140, 151, 156–7, 161, 164–5, 167–8, 170,
173, 175, 177, 193, 202(n53)
origins 62
Ministry of Education: Department of Rites
22, 23, 40
Ministry of Education: Office for Compilation
63, 64
Ministry of Finance 41
Ministry of Foreign Affairs 66, 84, 175,
211(n72)
Ministry of Home Affairs 28, 64, 151
Ministry of Home Affairs: Department of
Topography (*Chishi hensan kakari*,
1890–1) 110
Ministry of Home Affairs: Office of
Ceremonies (*Shikiburyō*) 61
Ministry of Interior 25
Ministry of Justice 22
Ministry of Religious Affairs (*Kyōbushō*) 23
minkan shigaku (private historical scholarship)
14
Minobe Tatsukichi 126
minshūshi (history of the common people)
174, 221(n11)
Mishio Kumata 168, 220(n135)
Mito 139, 141
Mito: *Shōkōkan* academy 159
Mito domain 9, 20, 38, 67, 106, 214(n53)
Mito school (of historiography) **10**, 12, 13,

47, 94, 98, 105, 139, 142, 168, **196(n22–3)**

Mito Tokugawa 69

Mitohan shiryō 69

Mitsukuri Genpachi (1862–1919) 112, **118**

Mitsukuru Rinshō (1846–97) 37

Miura Hiroyuki (1871–1931) 117, 230

Miura Yasushi (1829–1910) **34**, 38, 46, 49, 53, 84, 190, 200(n15), 206(n28), 210(n46), 212(n15), 222(n45), 226

Miyagi prefecture 123

Miyajima Seiichirō (1838–1911) **49, 200(n14)**, 226

Miyake (supposed heir to Kojima Takanori) 145

Miyazaki Michizaburō (1855–1928) 124

Mizumoto Seibi 20

Mochida Yukio xvi, xvi(n)

modernity xlii
  global nature **xxiv–vi**
  means to achieving xxix
  rise of science 'common characteristic' xxxiii

modernization xix, xxvii, 1, 7, 13
  difficult to separate from 'Westernization' xxviii

Mommsen, Theodor (1817–1903) 182, **187**, 189, 222(n35), 223(n53)

monjo (primary sources) **122**

Montesquieu, Baron de (1689–1755) 123

Monumenta Germaniae Historica (MGH) 179, 180

monumental history 14

monuments 61, 75, 182–3

moral principles 63, 78, 121–2, 128, 141, 148–9, 152, 157, 166

Mōri (ruling house, Chōshū) 67, **69**, 94

Mori Arinori (1847–89) **30–1**, 93, 114, 156, 184

Mōri Motonori (d 1896) 69

Mori Ōgai (1862–1922) xxx, xxxi, 171, 192, 223(n47)

Motoori Norinaga (1730–1801) 82, 101

Mounsey, Augustus Henry 74

Movement for Democratic Rights 35, 135

Mozume Takami (1847–1928) 65

Murakami Naojirō (1868–1966) **125–6**

Muromachi period (1338–1573) 82

Musashi Benkei 214(n53)

myth xxi, xxxix–xl, **15**, 131, 171, 192–4

Nagamatsu Miki (1834–1903) **23–4**, 25–6, 28, 40, **43**, 46–7, 49, **64, 71, 75**, 103, 105, 164, 198(n23), 204(n2), 205(n15)
  higher in rank than Shigeno 51

only worked on *Fukkoki* 51
  prevented abandonment of *Fukkoki* (1882) 54

Nagasaki xxv, 59

Nagato 116

naichi zakkyō 137

Naitō Chisō (1826–1902) 109, 111, 139, 158, 213(n37)

Nakai Hiroshi **84**, 205(n25)

Nakamura Masanao (1832–91) **92–3**, 226

Nakamura Teigo (1822–97) 25, 44, 46

Namamugi Incident (1862) 53

Nanbokuchō period (Northern versus Southern Courts, C14) xvii, xviii, xxxvi, 50, 60–1, **64**, 75, 95, 99, 103–4, **141–2**, 156, 162, **163–71**, 178, 192, 203(n60), **219–21**
  Southern court declared legitimate one (edict, 1911) 167–8

Nanbu Moroyuki (?–1338) 61

Nanbu Toshichika 61

Nanki Tokugawa shi 69

Napoleon 87

Nara 106, 142

Nara period (704 84) 2, 18, 20–1, 25, 129

Narishima Ryūhoku (1837–84) 135, 226

narrative xxi, **xxiii**, xxx–i, **8**, 13, 14, 16, 73–4, 76, 78, 127–8, 169, 186–90

nation xxx(n), xxxv, 133, 194
  and modern world **xxiv–xxxi**

nation-building xi, xii, xxiv, xxix

nation state ix, xix, xxix, xlii, 4, 5, **6**, 12, 180–1, 183–5, 189–90
  close relationship with historical discipline xi, 16
  link with historical scholarship 4
  see also state

National Archives (1971–) xxviii(n), 201(n17), 208(n16), 225–7

National Archives: *Naikaku bunko* (library of Cabinet) 59, 202(n50)

National Diet xxxviii, 172
  see also Meiji Parliament

national history (*kokushi*) xxii, xxiv, xxx, **xxxi–vii**, xliii, 3, 13, 17, 22, 26, 28–9, 31, 34, 40, 48, **50–1**, 62, 74, 78, 83, 92, 111, 134, 136, 138, **140**, 185, 189–90, 192
  see also official history

National History and World of Nations (Hill, 2008) **xxx–i**

national identity xi, xxiii, xxxvii, 3, 6, 7, 14, 17, 70, 131–2, 137, 180–2

national ideology xx, xxxv, 7

National Learning (*kokugaku*) **11–12**, 19–22, 31–2, 34, 43, 46, 48, 55–6, 109, 112, 120,

136–7, 150, 154–5, 157–8, 183, 197(n4), 216(n76), 217(n102)
versus Chinese Learning **138–41, 213**
National Socialism **xv–xvi**
national unity 4, 136–7
nationalism xv, xxii, xxx, xxxiv–v, xxxviii–xl, 4, 8, 12, 17, 68, 81–2, 130, 132, 137, 147, 163, **179–80**, 189, 192, 196(n22), 222(n26)
source (culture) **183–4**
'Natural History and History' (Katō Hiroyuki) 123
Netherlands 34, 125, 126, 176
newspapers/media xxxviii, xl, 115, 134, 137–8, 144–5, 147, 149–50, 152–3, **157–8**, 166–7, 178, 220(n138–9)
Nietzsche, F.W. (1844–1900) 14
Nihon (newspaper) 157, 216(n89)
Nihon bungaku (*Japanese Literature*) 141
Nihon bungaku zensho (*Complete Works of Japanese Literature*, 1890) 70
Nihon gaishi (*Extra History of Japan*, Rai San'yō, 1827) 13, 81, 104, 128, 144
Nihon kaika shōshi (*Short History of Enlightenment in Japan*, Taguchi, 1877–82) 13
Nihon kyōikushi shiryō (*Materials on History of Education in Japan,* 1883) 66
Nihon ryakushi (*Short History of Japan*) (1875 textbook) 63
Nihon shiryaku (*Outline of Japanese History*, 1879) 50, 62, 64
Nihon shoki (720) 129, 139
Nihongi (*Chronicles of Ancient Japan*, 720) 7, **103**
Niigata prefecture xxv
nikki monjo (journals and primary documents) 106
Ninken Emperor (488–99) 103
Ninkō Emperor (1817–45) 25
Nisen gohyaku nenshi (*History of Two Thousand Five Hundred Years,* Takegoshi) 13–14
Nishi Amane (1829–97) 34–5
nitō kyōshū 43, 44, 45
nitō shoki 42, 44
nitō shūsen 41
Nitta no Yoshisada 61
nobility/aristocracy 130, 132, 174, 177
'court nobility' 2, 57, 60, 72, 214(n52)
Nōgensei (anonymous author) 136
Nonomura Kaizō 116
North America 6, 16, 26, 108, 120
Numata Jirō (1912–94) 21, 197(n10), 211(n72), 221(n11, n20), 223(n59), 230

Ō-Bei shokoku (countries of Europe and America) xxix
objectivity xxii, xxii(n), xxiii, xxxiv, 9, 10, 78, **127**, 131, 151–2, 160, 186, 188, 192–3
Ochiai Naobumi (1861–1903) 141, 146, 158
Oda Nobunaga 160, 162
Office of Compilation (*Henshūkyoku*) see Imperial Household Ministry
office of historiography (1869 manifestation) 21, 22, 32, 40
Office of Historiography (*Shūshikyoku,* 1875–7) xvii, xx, xxv, xxxii, xlvii, xlix, 3, 4, 9, 15–16, 20, 22, 25, **26–9**, 36, 57, 69, 73, 75–80, 82–5, 89–93, 99–104, **106–7**, 113, 119, 121, 128, 134–6, 139, 142–3, 146–7, 153, 164, 168, 176, 190, 192, 212(n14)
abolition (1877) 28, 48
budget 28, 79, 93, 136
Department of Topography (1875–) 28
four departments 28, **40–5**, 46
'much larger than previous Department of History' 28
replaced (1875) Department of History (*Rekishika*) 27
representation of Japan abroad **62**
'slow progress' 50
succeeded by College of Historiography 28
'tasks clearly defined' 28
see also College of Historiography
official historiography 2, 12–13, 106, 135, 138
abandonment (1893) 47
continuity (Edo into Meiji periods) 66, 204(n80)
development **14–15**
failure **14–15**
form **71–100, 204–7**
language **80–3**
'little importance' 56
nature 57
need for overseer (whose opinion must be decisive) 78
see also historiography
official history **xxi**, xxvii, 10–11 14, 18, 134, 188
end **156–63, 217–19**
failure to progress (as at 1881) 50
see also seishi
Ogawa Ginjirō 124
Ogawa (Ogō) Kazutoshi (Ichibin; 1813–86) 29, 44, 49, 103, 106, 164, 198(n23), **208(n4)**, 226
Ōjin Emperor 219(n131)
Ogyū Sorai 14

Oka Senjin (1833–1914) 42, 46
Oka Shigezane (1835–1919) 105
Okamatsu Ōkoku (1820–95) 20, 22, 23, **135–6**, 212(n21), 226
Okamoto Yasutaka 101
Okayama prefecture 47, 143
Okinawa prefecture (1879) 201(n31)
Okinawa shi 53
Ōkubo Toshiaki (1900–95) v, xlv, xlviii, 20, 25, 98, 104, 157, 169, 195(n1, n13), 200(n14), 204(n3), 210(n55), 213(n32), 215(n64), 216(n72), 219(n129), 220(n142, n150), 228, **230–1**
Ōkubo Toshimichi (1830–78) **26–7**, 65, **84**, 198(n23)
Ōkuma Shigenobu (1838–1922) 26, 29, 30, 151
Okuyama Tomoyasu 146
oligarchs 26, 30, 68
Ōmori Kingorō 152, 216(n75, n77, n82, n90)
'On History' (Tsuboi) 56
'On Possibility of Scientific Treatment of History' (Zerffi) 88, 91–2
'Open Letter in Support of Historians in Japan' **xl**
Oranda shōkanchō nikki 176
Osaka Conference (1875) **26–9**
Osaka prefecture 146
ōsei fukko (restoration of imperial rule) 2
Osterhammel, Jürgen xxiv, xxvi, xxx(n), xxxiii, xli(n)
Ōtani Hidezane 45
Owari domain 67, 202(n49)
ōyō shigaku see applied history
ōyō shiha (applied history faction) 128
ōyōsha (those who apply historical knowledge)
  versus *senshūsha* (specialists) 56

Paris exhibition (1878) 62
Park Yu-ha xxxviii
patriotism 79, 147, 151, 154, 214(n43)
pedantry 91, 136
peerage 30, 117, 143, 171, 212(n15)
  law regulating ranks (1884) 61
People's Rights Movement (*Jiyū minken undō*) 26, 27, 29
Perry, Commodore (1794-1858) 60, 202(n54)
Pertz, Georg Heinrich 180
Pfizmaier, August Philipp (1808–87) xiii(n)
Philadelphia world exhibition (1876) 62, 73, 103
philology **xxxiv**, 6, 12, 187
philosophy 154, 184
Pinyin system xlix

political crises
  (1875) **26–7**, 29
  (1881) **29–32**
political influence 54, 68, 141, 182, 185–6
  see also ideology
positivism xvi, xxi, xxiii, 11, 103, 128, 130–1, 149, 187, 193
Praise of a Celebrated Poem Found in Yoshino (Yoda, 1886) **146–7**
preexisting conditions xxvi, xxviii
prefectures (1871–) xxv(n), 2, 24–6, 55, **57–9**, 63, **74–5**, 102, 106–7
  assemblies (1878–) 30
  assembly of governors (1875) 27
primary schools **165–6**, 220(n135)
primary sources xii, xiii(n), xiv, xx–xxii, xxvii–xxxix, xxxvii, xlii, xlii(n), 3, **4**, **6**, **8–9**, 12, 16, 19, 26, 31–2, 37, 41, 52, 55, 58, **59**, **66**, 68, 71–2, 91, 95–6, **102**, 104–5, **106–8**, 110, 116, 121–8, 135, 140–2, 144, 146–7, 157, **159–60**, 161, **163**, 165, 168–9, 171, **173–7**, 179–81, **203–4(n79)**, 221(n6), 224(n82)
  collection **74–80**
  collection 'more to do with administration than with historiography' 57
  foreign (relating to Japan) **125–6**, **176**, 211(n72)
  see also *shiryō*
Private Academies of Chinese Learning in Meiji Japan (Mehl, 2003) x
Privy Council 220(n142)
'Proclamation to All Shintoists' (Taguchi, 1892) 151
progress 5, 129, 130, 191
Prussia 33, 34, 120
Prussian Academy of Science 181
Prussian Archives (Berlin) 181, 182
Prussian School (of historiography) xxx, 17, 182
psychology xxix–xxx
public opinion 122, 153, 169
Public Party of Patriots (*Aikoku kōtō*) 26
Pyle, Kenneth B. **190**, 211(n2), 224(n70, n72)

Qing Dynasty (1644–1912) 11

Rai Matajirō (1823–89) 20, 22, 23
Rai San'yō (1780–1832) 13, 22, 144
Ranke, Leopold von (1795–1886) xxi, **xxx**, **xxxiii–iv**, **6**, **113–14**, 127, 186, **187–8**, 223(n57)
  history and nation **180–1**
ranks (*ittō*, *nitō*, *santō*/first, second, third) 41
'Regulations for Office of Historiography'

(1875) **40–1**
rekishi monogatari (historical tale) 8
Rekishi chiri (journal) 177
Rekishi kyōiku (*History Education,* magazine)
    116
'*Rekishi ni okeru jitsu to ma*' ('Genuine Truth
    in History') (Hiraizumi) 193
rekishi no ryūkōnetsu ('history fashion fever')
    133
Rekishigaku to rekishi kenkyū (2003) xlvi
Rekishika see 'Council of State: Department
    of History'
rekishinetsu ('historical fever') 133, 134
retsuden (biographies) 10
Revue Historique (1876–) 111
Richardson, Charles 53
Rieß, Ludwig (1861–1928) xviii, 16, 93, 109,
    110–23, 128, 162, 176, 184, 186, **187**,
    191, 202(n37), 209(n25, **n32**), 211(n65),
    217(n102), **223(n55–6)**
    biography **113**
    doctoral thesis 113
    foreign documents relating to Japan **125**,
        211(n72)
    Kume Affair (1892) **155**, 217(n100)
    lecture notes 115
    lectures 210(n45)
    lessons and seminars 116, 119
    low status **118–19**
    publications **115**
    teaching methods **116–17**
Rikken seitai no shōchoku (imperial edict,
    1875) 27
rinji (temporary) 36, 39
risōha (historians, academic) 128
ritsu ryō (imperial bureaucratic state) 21
Rokumeikan (Western-style hall) 183
Roman History (Mommsen, 1854–6) 187
Rome 125, 181
Rousseau, Jean Jacques (1712–78) 90
Royal Historical Society (UK) **87–8**
Rüsen, Jörn **xxii–iii**, 189, 195(n8), 228
Russia (Tsarist) xxiv
Russo-Japanese War (1905) 165, 177,
    217(n100)
ryōshi (good history) 79
Ryukyu Islands **53**, 96, 201(n31)

Saeki Ariyoshi 152, 216(n86)
Saga Shōsaku (1853–90) 92, 94
Saigō Takamori (1828–77) 26, 29, **73**
Saionji Cabinet 168
Saionji Kinmochi (1849–1940) 161, 166
Saitama prefecture 107
Sakura domain 44

Sakurai (post station) 146, 147
samurai 2, 19, **26**, 29, 51, 55, 68, 177
San'in district 45
San'yō district 45, 91
Sand, Jordan xl
Sanjō Sanetomi (1837–91) 18, 21, 27–8, 31,
    34, 48, 50, **54–5**, 57, 67, 71, 75, 78–9,
    107, 201–2(n35), 205(n15–16), 208(n4),
    212(n20, n23), **226–7**
Sanjō Sanetomi kō nenpu (1901) 69
sankō (reference) 106
santō kyōshū 43, 44, 45
santō shoki 42, 43
santō shūsen 42, 44
Sasaki Takayuki (1830–1910) 176
Satō Jōjitsu (1839–1908) 65
Satow, Sir Ernest 60, 202(n54)
Satsuma domain 2, 18, 41, 47, 48, 53, 67, 84,
    104, 202(n49)
Satsuma rebellion 28, 30, 78
Satsuma Rebellion (Mounsey) 74, 204(n10)
Satsuma war (1877) 73, 134
Sawato Kōkō 44
science(s) xxii, xxiv, xxxiv, 120, 194
    versus '*Wissenschaft*' **xxxi–iii**
science-versus-authority narrative xxi–ii
Science of History (Zerffi, 1879) xxvii(n),
    87–94, 114, 135, 188, 227, 232
    influence on Japanese historiography 94
    Japanese translation (unpublished, 1887)
        92, 206(n39)
scientific historiography **xxxi–vii**, **xli**, xlii, 69,
    74, 77, 91, 101, 115
scientific history 127, 148, 157, 187, 188
    see also historians
scribes 77, 161
secondary sources
    fallibility **xxi–ii**
Seeley, Sir John 128
Segawa Hideo **116–17**
seiji (politics) 122
Seisei shimatsu (*Account of Pacification of
    West*) 29, 54, **73–4**
seishi xxx–i, 11, 27, **78**, 108, 131, 147
    'Japanese dynastic histories' 7
    'national history' 74
    'official history' **75–6**, 79, 83
    'standard history' 95, **100**
    see also Six National Histories
seishi kōshaku (expounding history) 147
Self-Help (Smiles) 92
seminars 180, 181
Senate (*Genrōin*, 1875–) 27, 43, 44, 61
Senbō junnan shishi jinmeiroku (1907) 67
Senchō kiryaku (Shigeno and Fujino) 48, 50

senmonka (specialists) 189
setai fūzoku (customs) 140
'seven doctors' 153
Seventeen Articles (604) 38
shajisei (copyists) 51, **201(n25)**
Shakespeare, William (1564–1616) 90
shi (essays) 10
Shidankai (Society for Historical Narration)
    67–8, 69–70, 174, 219(n119), 231
Shidankai sokkiroku (shorthand notes) 67
Shigakkai zasshi (Journal of Historical
    Society, 1889–92) 111
shigaku ('historical science') xxx, 111
Shigaku kenkyūhō (*Research Methods of
    Historical Science*, Tsuboi, 1893) 187
Shigaku kyōkai (History Society, 1883–) **32–
    3**, 36, 82, 112, 139–40
Shigaku kyōkai zasshi (journal) 32, 33
Shigaku zasshi (Journal of History, 1892)
    xlvii, 111, 113, 115, 121, 123–6, 133,
    148, 151–2, 154, 208(n14), 209(n33),
    211(n70), 212(n12), 213–14(n42),
    215(n65), 219(n131), 220(n143), 228–32
Shigakukai (Historical Society) xiii, xvi(n),
    xxii, 195(n13), 231
Shigeno Yasutsugu (1827–1910) xiv(n), xvii,
    xxi–ii, xxiii, xxvii, **xxvii(n)**, xxviii, xxx–
    i, xxxv, xxxvii, xlvii, 20, **42**, 46–9, 53,
    54–5, 62, 74, **75**, **79**, 84, 94–5, **100**, 104–
    5, 107, 109, 116, 119, **123–4**, 126, 133–4,
    136–41, 146, 152, 163, 168–9, 179, **188**,
    189, 192, 194, 198(n23), 201–2(n35),
    205(n15), 207(n48), 212(n15), 213(n42),
    223(n59), 231
    abandonment of Kume (1892) 153
    'All Scholarship is *kōshō* Textual Criticism'
        (lecture, 1890) **101–2**
    attempts to reconcile old and new 191
    biography **47**
    chief editor (*hensan iinchō*) (1888) 56
    dismissal (1893) 42, 52, 156
    'Dr Obliterator' (*massatsu hakase*) 15, 144,
        174
    errors in traditional histories (lecture, 1884)
        144
    'failure to distinguish sufficiently between
        research and writing' 127
    field trip (1885) 161
    first travelled abroad (1907) 191
    history and education (lecture) 138
    influence (failure to exercise) **185–6**
    influence on national ideology (limited) 17
    influence on school textbooks **64–5**
    lectures **38**, 64–5, 75, 77–8, 81, 111, **121–2**,
        127, 147, 164, 188, 214(n43), 219(n131)

methodology **15–16**
narrative history (failure to complete) 192
national history **50–1**
papers **227**
personal agenda 15
president of Historical Society (1889–1910)
    112
spoof letter from Kojima Takanori **145**
and Zerffi, *Science of History* **92–3**
shihanbon (trade edition) xxxix
shijō (history, annals) 79
Shikai (journal, 1891–6) **133–4**, 136, 148–9,
    151, 154, 215(n65), 215–16(n72),
    216(n89), 231
shikan ('history official') 51
Shikan kaikau o kou no gi (memorandum)
    81–3
Shikyoku (history office) 1, 176
Shimabara uprising (1637–38) 116
Shimada Saburō 177, 221(n18)
Shimatsu see Shiryō hensan shimatsu
Shimazu, house of 67, 174
Shimazu Hisamitsu (1817–87) 47, 67
Shin kigen magazine 156
shin kōshōgaku (New School of Textual
    Criticism) 104
Shin Nihonshi (*New History of Japan*,
    Takegoshi) 13
shin shigaku ka (new historians) 130
Shinagawa Yajirō (1843–1900) 114
shinkoku ('land of gods') 8, 190
Shinto 8, 12, 57, 140, 157, 170, 179,
    211(n88), 217(n102)
'Shinto Outdated Custom' (Kume, 1892)
    148–56, 215–17
'Shintō wa saiten no kozoku' (Kume, 1892)
    148–56, 215–17
'Shintōsha shoshi ni tsugu' (Taguchi, 1892)
    151
Shioda Ekisui 45, 106
Shionoya Tōin (1809–67) 52
Shiratori Kurakichi (1865–1942) 117, 124,
    191, 210(n46), 224(n66)
shiron (theoretical discussions of history,
    historical treatise) **xliv**, 8
Shiryaku (*Outline of History*, 1872 textbook)
    63
shiryō (historical documents) xxxix, 9, 11,
    172, 193
    see also primary sources
Shiryō (Hanawa Hokiichi) xxvii, 21, 41, 66,
    76, 101, 108, 138, 174, 179
Shiryō hensan shimatsu (document collection)
    xlv, 59, 95, **198(n19)**, **199–208**, 211, 214,
    219, **221**, 227

Shiryō hensanjo 175
Shiryō henshū kokushi kōsei kyoku (Office for Collection of Historical Materials, 1869) 21, 22, 32, 40
s*hiryō henshū Rikkokushi kōsei goyō kakari* 21
Shiryō henshū Rikkokushi kōsei kenshū 21
shiryō kōhon 49
Shiryō sōran (*Overview of Historical Materials*) 175
Shiyō monmoku (*Catalogue of Historical Topics*) 85, 87
Shizuoka domain 57
shoguns xxxiv, 7, 10, 22, 61, 71, 96, 142, 174
Shōheikō (academy of Hayashi in Edo) 22, 44–5, 47–9, 53
  renamed *Shōhei gakkō* or *Gakkō* (1869) **19–20**
  renamed again: *Daigakkō* or University (summer, 1869) 19
  as school (closed, 1870) 19, 138
  as Schools Administration Office 19, **21**, 62, 74
  'status of ministry of education' (1869–71) 18, 23
Shōheizaka gakumonjo 9
shōki
  'archivists' 51, 161
  'clerks' 41, 56, 77, 161
Shōkōkan (history office of Mito domain) 106
Shōmeikai society 68, 175
Shōwa Emperor xiii, xiv, 17, 178
shuppan (publication) 172
shuppan jōrei (publishing regulations, 1869, 1872) 59
shūsen (editors) 41, 46, 77, 200(n13)
shūshi (historiography) **xliv**, 27, 74
Shūshi buntai ron 100, 205(n21), 226, 227
Shūshi jigi (*Proper Historiography*) **27–8**, 48, **75–7**, 81, 83, 95, 188
Shūshikan see College of Historiography
Shūshikan bibō (journal of Date Munenari) 54, 201(n32)
Shūshikan kaikaku no gi (On Reform of College of Historiography, 1881) 31, 198(n26)
Shūshikyoku see Office of Historiography
Shūshikyoku shokusei oyobi henshū chakushu no hōhō o sadamu (1875) **40–1**
Shūshikyoku sōsai 41
shūshinka (moral education) 63
Sima Guang (1019–89) 97
Sino-Japanese War (1895) xxxv–vi, 81, 132, 191
Six National Histories (*Rikkokushi*) 1, 2, 4, 7,

11, **20–1**, 71, 74–6, 80, 95, 97, 100, 126, 129, 136, 139, 140, 190, **196(n14)**, 211(n74)
  first attempt at resumption 'failed' (1869) 22
  see also history
Smiles, Samuel (1812–1904) 92
social sciences xxxii–iv
socialist groups 165–6
Society for the Study of Early German History (1819) 179
Soejima Taneomi 26, 32
sōetsu (chief inspector) 77
Sonderweg debate **xvi**
sonnō aikoku (love for nation) 64
Sonnō jiseki (Achievements of Reverence for Emperor) 23
sōsai (president) 77
specialists 15, 56, 83,129, 154, 159, 189
Spencer, Herbert (1820–1903) 123, 197(n31)
Spring and Autumn Annals **97**
state xlii, 30–1, 130–1, 150, 152, 155, 157, 160, 218(n108)
  see also nation state
state control xxx(n), 184
Stein, Lorenz von (1815–90) **33–4**, 37, **184**, **199(n30–1)**, 223(n47)
  on constitutions as part of society as whole 33
students 178, 183–4
Subrahmanyam, Sanjay xxvi
Suehiro Tetchō xxxi
Suematsu Kenchō (1855–1920) 64, **69**, 74, **83–94**, 146, 205(n23), 205–6(n27–8), 227, 231
Sugawara no Fumitoki (899–981) 129
Suō 43, 69, 94, 116
Supreme Court (1875) 27
Suzuki Jun xxii
Suzuki Shigeaya 136
Suzumura family 201(n25), 227
Suzumura Yuzuru (1854–1930) 201(n25)
Sybel, Heinrich von (1817–95) xxx(n71), **180–3**, 189, 222(n29)
  projects to publish documents **181**

Taguchi Shin 216(n89)
Taguchi Ukichi (1855–1905) xxxi, 13, 70, 133, 137, 148–50, **151**, 152, 154, 212(n13), 213(n29–30), 216(n78, n83–4, n89), 231
taigi meibun (relationship between ruler and subject) 60
Taiheiki 126, 142–6, 211(n74–5), **213(n42)**, 214(n52)

'no use for historical scholarship' (Kume)
105, 126, 142, 208(n15)
'reliable historical account' (Suzuki
Shigeaya) 136
Taihō Code (701) 38
Taira military house 13
Taisei kiyō (Outline of Imperial Rule) **35–6**,
51, 67–8, 94, 140, 157, 164, 219(n130)
agenda (revelation of Japan's unique
political culture) 35
written in Japanese rather than *kanbun* 35
Taishō period (1912–25) 14, 176
taiten (state ritual; norm-giving work) 1, 74
Taiwan (Japanese colony) xxxvi
Taiyō (Sun; journal) xxxv, 191
Takagi Shōsaku 178–9
Takatsu Shūsaburō 124, 141, 159, 218(n113)
Takegoshi Yosaburō 13–14
Takezoe Shin'ichirō (1841–1917) 41, 46
Tale of Genji 8, 88
Tamura Naoomi (1858–1935) 137
Tanabe Ta'ichi (1831–1915) 66
Tanaka Fujimaro (1845–1909) **64**
Tanaka Yoshinari (1860–1919) 56, 65, 105,
112, 116, **129–30, 153**, 156, 160, 164–5,
168, 171–3, 177, 192, 201(n25),
211(n84), 219(n123, n132), 220(n143,
n147)
career **161–2, 219(n123)**, 219(n132)
lecture on application of history 170,
221(n152)
lecture on Northern and Southern Courts
(change of title, 1911) 168
Tanaka, Stefan xix(n), xxii, xxii(n), 127,
223(n56), 224(n66, n74), 231
Tanimori Yoshiomi (1817–1911) 22, 23, 44,
45, 47, 55, 106
taxation **24**, 74–5, 96
Teikoku daigaku see Imperial University
teitoku (commander) 79
Temmu Emperor (673–686) 219(n131)
tennōsei kokka (authoritarian emperor state)
157
Terauchi Masatake, General 167, 220(n142)
textbook (1903; revised 1908) **65**
textbook controversy (1911) xxxv, xxxvi, 16,
65, 130, **163–71**, 186, **219–21**
best account **219(n129)**
textbook controversy (1982) xiv
textbooks **xxxviii–xl**, 13, 22, 60, **62–5**, 108,
140, 152, 162, 177, 189, 193, 203(n70)
nationalization of publication (1902) 65
textual criticism xxxiv, 8, **11–12**, 14, 32, 51,
101, 105–6, 113, 116, 123, 126, **128–30**,
148, 152, 162, 171, 186, 189

The Hague 110, 125
theatre 146, 214(n59)
Thiers, Adolphe (1797-1877) 87
Thucydides 87
Tientsin 41
Tochigi prefecture 107
Tōichi Makoto 136
Tōin Kinsada (1340–99) 214(n52)
Tōjō Hideki 146, 214(n58)
Tōkai tōsan junkō nikki (imperial journey to
Pacific coast) 62
Tokugawa (ruling house, Mito) 67
Tokugawa jikki 98
Tokugawa: Mito branch 69
Tokugawa Mitsukuni **9–11**, 196(n22–3)
Tokugawa period (1600–1868) 48, 55, 60, 65,
69–70, 72–3, 76, 100–1, 108, 119, 125,
139, 161, 183
Tokugawa shogunate (1600–1868) xxiv, xxvi,
1, 8, 10, 11, 13, 47
Edo period xxvii, xxxiv, 14, 21, 26, 49–51,
63, 66, 99, 104, **124**, 162, 169, 175, 194,
203(n69), 216(n76)
Tokugawa: Kii branch 69
Tokunō Michitsuna (?–1337) 62
Tokushi yoron 81
Tokushima 61, 67
tokushu shiryō (special materials) **175–6**
Tokutomi Sohō xxxi, 13, 220(n142)
Tokyo x, 19, 45, 69
Tokyo: *Asakusa bunko* public library 102
Tokyo: *Doitsu gaku kyōkai* 114
Tokyo: *Dokkyō daigaku* (Dokkyo University)
114
Tokyo: Edo 45, 52, 139
see also Shōheikō
Tokyo: German Institute for Japanese Studies
(1988) **xv**
Tokyo: Institute of Japanese Learning
(*Wagaku kōdansho*) 102
Tokyo: *Momijiyama bunko* (library of
shogunate) 102
Tokyo: Russian Orthodox Nikolai Church 134
Tokyo: School of German Studies Society
114
Tokyo: Ueno Park 104
Tokyo Academy 77, 134
Tōkyō akebono shinbun (newspaper) 134
Tōkyō Daigaku Shiryō Hensanjo
(Historiographical Institute [*qv*]) ix, 3
Tōkyō nichinichi shinbun (newspaper) 83,
135, 150, 144–5, 212(n14–15)
Tōkyō senmon gakkō (1882–; later Waseda
University) 30, 148, 151
Tokyo University (1877–) xii, xxii, xxxviii,

xxxix, xlviii, 117, 178, 200(n14),
208(n22), 211(n72), 217(n100), 226
became 'Imperial University' [*qv*] (1886)
30
Tokyo University: Department of Classics
(*Koten kōshūka*, 1882–7) 31
Tokyo University: Department of Japanese
History 221(n11)
Tomizu Affair **153–4**, 156, 170, **217**
Tomizu Hirondo (1861–1935) **153–4**
topography **24–5**, 28, 49, 50, 58, 62, 73, 110,
159, 198(n14)
Tosa (domain) 2, 18, 67, 202(n49)
Tosh, John xxxii(n), xxxviii(n), **xl–xliii**
Tottori domain 202(n49)
Toyama Masakazu (1848–1900) 64, 124, 158,
159–60, 161, 218(n113, n115), 225
tōyō 191
Toyooka Hanrei 166
tōyōshi (Oriental history) xxii, xxxiv, 117,
191–2
Toyotomi Hideyoshi 160, 162
tōzai nanboku 165
tradition 5, **6**, 195(n10)
translation xxv, 13, 84–5, 87–8, 91–4, 108,
115, 116, 176, **197(n31)**, 206(n29)
Treaty of Amity and Commerce (Japan–USA)
221(n18)
Treitschke, Heinrich von (1834–98) xxx(n71),
182
truth **15**, 89, 104, 129, 171, 192–4
Tsuboi Kumezō (1858–1930) 56, 108–9, 112,
117, 121, 160, 169, 186–7, 212(n15),
223(n56)
Tsubouchi Shōyō xxxv
Tsuda Sōkichi (1873–1961) 170, 223(n56)
Tsuji Zennosuke (1877–1955) xxxvi, 115, **118**,
119, 173, 178, 200(n15), 219(n123–4)
Tsukamoto Akitake (1833–85) 25, 49
Tsukurukai *see* Atarashii Rekishi Kyōkasho
o Tsukurukai
Tsushima shrine 145
Tsūshin zenran (*Complete Overview of
Correspondence*) 66

Uchimura Kanzō (1861–1930) 137, 213(n31)
Uda Emperor (887–97) 11
Ueda Kazutoshi (Mannen; 1867–1937) **122–
3**, 168, 169
Ueno Keihan 84
Umehara Takeshi xiv
unequal treaties 132, 137, 191, 213(n39)
United Kingdom xxix, 30, 33, 83–7, 90, 91
United States xxiv, xxxi, xxxix, xl, 23, 30,
115, 116, 223(n57)

universal history xxiv, 13, 63, 86, 88, 90, **91–2**,
108, 113, **115**, 187–8, 191, 209, 223, 229
Universal History (Rieß, 1893) 115
universities 6, 12, 38, 109, 118, 120, 181
university graduates **56**
University of Berlin 6, 113, 117, 180,
209(n38)
University of Bonn xii, xvi, xvi(n), xlvii
University of Breslau 180
University of Cambridge 94
University of London 87, 88
University of Marburg 180
University of Munich 180
University of Tokyo *see* Tokyo University
Urai, T. 116
Uses and Abuses of History (MacMillan,
2008) **xl–xliii**
Uwajima (Ehime prefecture) 54
Uwajima domain 67, 202(n49)

vassals 41, 45, 47, 48, 49, 53, 60, 68
Vatican 125, 126, 181
Vienna 33, 34, 109

wabun ('pure' Japanese) 58, 80
Wagaku kōdansho (Institute of Japanese
Studies, 1793) **11, 21**
*Wagakuni korai no kenpō oyobi daigaku no
keikyō* (Shigeno, 1889) 38
Waitz, Georg 181
Wakabayashi, Bob Tadashi xvii
wakangaku 122
Wakayama 221(n8)
Waseda bungaku (literary review) 70, 127,
130, 133, 155, 189, 215(n69), 216(n81–
2), 217(n93, n101–2)
Waseda University x, 30, 151, 162, 166, 170
Watanabe Akira 42
Watanabe Ikarimaro 216(n76)
Watanabe Kōki (1848–1911) **37–8, 109**, 110,
111, 121, 123, 125, 199(n40)
Wattenbach, Wilhelm 181
Weizsäcker, Julius von 181
Weltgeschichte (Ranke) 115
Western countries **xx**, xxvi–viii, xxxiv, xlii, 3,
12, 33, 34, 37, 63, 82, 172, 191, 194
Western Learning 19, 154–5
Western methods **83–94**
Westernization 1, 13, 30, 138
height (1880s) 183
White, Hayden 15–16
Why History Matters (Tosh, 2008) **xl–xliii**
Wilhelm, Emperor 182
Wissenschaft
versus 'science' **xxxi–iii**

women **xxxvii–viii**, xl, 173
Women's High School 162
World War II xiii, xiv, xxxviii, xxxix(n), xl,
17, 59, 68, 146, 170, 173, 177, 178

Yamagata Aritomo (1838–1922) 35, 57, 85,
146, 166–7, 171, 177, 220(n142)
Yamagata prefecture 49
Yamagata Shōzō 122, 210(n62)
Yamaguchi Ken (author of Kinsei shiryaku)
xxv, 60, 202(n54)
Yamaji Aizan (1864–1917) **14**, 128, 189–90,
193–4, **197(n32)**, 211(n81)
Yamanashi (prefectual archives) 59
Yamanouchi (ruling house, Tosa) 67
Yamanouchi Toyoshige (1827–72) 19
Yamashiro 106, 164, 208(n16)
Yamato 106, 164, 208(n16)
Yamato damashii 140, 141
Yamato imperial court xxxiv(n)
Yano Gendō 136, 212(n23)
Yasui Sokken (1799–1876) 105
Yoda Hyakusen (Gakukai; 1833–1909) 42,
46, 47, 49, 51, **146–7**, 214(n59)

Yokoyama Yoshikiyo (1826–79) 21, **23**
Yomiuri shinbun 144, 157, 166
Yonezawa 49
Yoshikawa, Lisa xxxvi, xxxvii
Yoshimi Yoshiaki **xxxviii**
Yoshino 142, 168, 219(n131)
Yoshino jūmeika no homare (Yoda, 1886)
146–7
Yotsuya Suihō (Tsune; 1831–1906) 25, 43, 46
Yushima 21, 23

zenshasei (copyists) 51, **201(n25)**
Zerffi, George Gustav (Gusztáv György;
1820–92) xxvii(n), xxxii, **83–94**, 114,
135, 188, **206**, 227, 232
Eurocentrism 92, 206(n38)
zheng shi (Chinese dynastic histories) 7
*Zoku hankanpu (Sequel to Daimyō Family
Trees)* 57
*Zoku kokushi taikei (Continuation of
Compendium of Japanese History,*
Taguchi) 70
Zoku Tsūshin zenran 66
Zuo Qiuming (Sakyūmei) 97